Studies in Emotion and Social Interaction

Paul Ekman
University of California, San Francisco

Klaus R. Scherer
Université de Genève

General Editors

The Individual, Communication and Society:
Essays in Memory of Gregory Bateson

Studies in Emotion and Social Interaction

This series is jointly published by the Cambridge University Press and the Editions de la Maison des Sciences de l'Homme, as part of the joint publishing agreement established in 1977 between the Fondation de la Maison des Sciences de l'Homme and the Syndics of the Cambridge University Press.

Cette collection est publiée co-édition par Cambridge University Press et les Editions de la Maison des Sciences de l'Homme. Elle s'intègre dans le programme de co-édition établi en 1977 par la Fondation de la Maison des Sciences de l'Homme et les Syndics de Cambridge University Press.

The individual, communication, and society

Essays in memory of Gregory Bateson

Edited by
Robert W. Rieber
John Jay College of Criminal Justice
City University of New York
New York City

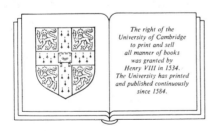

The right of the
University of Cambridge
to print and sell
all manner of books
was granted by
Henry VIII in 1534.
The University has printed
and published continuously
since 1584.

Cambridge University Press

Cambridge
New York   Port Chester
Melbourne   Sydney

Editions de la Maison des Science de l'Homme

Paris

Published by the Press Syndicate of the University of Cambridge
The Pitt Building, Trumpington Street, Cambridge CB2 1RP
40 West 20th Street, New York, NY 10011, USA
10 Stamford Road, Oakleigh, Melbourne 3166, Australia
and
Editions de la Maison des Sciences de l'Homme
54 Boulevard Raspail, 75270 Paris, Cedex 06

First published 1989

Printed in the United States of America

Library of Congress Cataloging-in-Publication Data

The Individual, communication, and society : essays in memory of
  Gregory Bateson / edited by Robert W. Rieber.
    p.   cm. – (Studies in emotion and social interaction)
    Contents: In search of the impertinent question : an overview of
Bateson's theory of communication / Robert W. Rieber – A reflection on Bateson's view of
moral and national character / David Bakan – The
psychopathy of everyday life : anti-social behavior and social
distress / Robert W. Rieber and Maurice Green – Bateson's
concept of mental illness / Theodore Skolnik – Language,
languages, and song : the experience of systems / Mary Catherine
Bateson – Affective and communicative problems in young, developmentally
deviant language users / Theodore Shapiro and Elena Goldstein Lister – A
cross-cultural study of language universals : the emotional meaning
of iconic and graphic stimuli / Robert W. Rieber, Oliver C. S. Tzeng, and
Carl Wiedmann – Machine dreams : computers in the fantasies of young
adults / John M. Broughton – In search of coronary-prone behavior /
Aron W. Siegman – Two principles of communicative functioning /
Norbert Freedman – Gregory Bateson (1904-1980) and Oscar Wilde (1854-1900) : a heavenly
discourse / Peter Ostwald – Body and mind : a dialogue / Gregory
Bateson and Robert W. Rieber.
    ISBN 0-521-26741-2
1. Communication – Psychological aspects.   2. Social interaction.
3. Mental health.   4. Bateson, Gregory.   I. Bateson, Gregory.
II. Rieber, R. W. (Robert W.)   III. Series.
BF637.C45I52   1989
301–dc20   89-33206
                                                                              CIP

British Library Cataloguing in Publication Data

The individual, communication and society: essays in
  memory of Gregory Bateson. – (Studies in emotion and
  social interaction)
    1. Man. Communication – Sociological perspectives
    I. Rieber, Robert W.   II. Bateson, Gregory, 1904–1980
    III. Series
    302.2

ISBN 0-521-26741-2 hard covers

ISBN 2 7351 0312 9 France only

How is a leaf on a tree similar to a noun in a sentence?

Both grammar and biological structure are products of communicational and organizational processes.

Gregory Bateson, *Steps Towards an Ecology of Mind*

To the memory of Gregory Bateson

Contents

Contributors

David Bakan
York University

Mary Catherine Bateson
George Mason University

John M. Broughton
Columbia University

Paul Ekman
University of California
San Francisco

Norbert Freedman
Downstate Medical Center
Columbia University

Elena Goldstein Lister
Payne Whitney
Psychiatric Clinic
Cornell Medical Center

Maurice Green
Columbia University

Peter Ostwald
University of California
San Francisco

Robert W. Rieber
John Jay College
of Criminal Justice

Klaus R. Scherer
Universite de Geneve

Theodore Shapiro
Payne Whitney
Psychiatric Clinic
Cornell Medical Center

Aron W. Siegman
University of Maryland
Baltimore

Theodore Skolnik
Manhattan Psychiatric
Center

Oliver C. S. Tzeng
Purdue University

Carl Wiedmann
John Jay College
of Criminal Justice

Preface

Gregory Bateson devoted most of his life to developing a global theory of epistemology that would give, in cybernetic terms, an integrated account of the capabilities of all living things to assimilate, organize, and communicate information. To inform his theory, Bateson drew on a wide range of intellectual fields including mechanics, electronics, mathematics, cybernetics and information theory, biology and genetics, psychology, anthropology, philosophy, and religion. Within Bateson's framework, the integrity of explanation uniting disparate phenomena (for example: learning in animals, learning in humans, or the structure of plants, the structure of grammar) is accomplished through the identification of homologies and analogies. Through this integration, composite structures such as human societies came, for Bateson, to be viewed as similar to individual organisms, and evolutionary change as analogous to individual learning.

Given the wide angle of Bateson's persepctive, it may seem almost a violation of his vision to use it as a means of focusing solely upon human communication. Yet for all its mechanics, its electronics, its contextualism, its formal logic, and comparative biology, the underlying agenda of Batesons' universal epistemology is, in the end, to explain the human mind and thereby to understand human behavior. Bateson's theory is particularly useful for any understanding of interactions between human beings or between humans and their non-living environment, much of which occurs as communication.

Within this frame of reference the chapters of this book are all written in the spirit of the Batesonian tradition. A detailed description of each is given in Chapter One. The book is not intended as any kind of *festeschrift*, but rather as an appreciation and clarification of the tradition that Bateson did so much to foster during his liftime.

Acknowledgments: To all of the authors for their patience and cooperation and to John Kerr for his invaluable assistance in the preparation of the manuscript.

Robert W. Rieber
New York, New York

1. In search of the impertinent question: an overview of Bateson's theory of communication

ROBERT W. RIEBER

Jacob Bronowski once remarked about Joseph Priestly that if you ask an impertinent question you will open the doors to a pertinent answer. This paradoxical yet pregnant remark captures the essence of Gregory Bateson's unique career as a scientist. For Bateson grasped almost from the outset of his career that pertinent answers could *not* be had if theory continued to go about draped in the hand-me-down Cartesian epistemology that nineteenth-century materialism had bequeathed to twentieth-century social science. What was needed was a new set of questions, impertinent questions, that would open the door to new ways of conceptualizing phenomena. What Bateson wanted was an epistemology worthy of the term, an epistemology that would make sense, not nonsense, an epistemology that could serve as a worldview, or *Weltanschauung*, and yet be serviceable as a vehicle for scientific inquiry.

If we want to state the matter formally, we can describe Bateson's career thus: For most of his life, Gregory Bateson strove to develop a universal epistemology that would, in an essentially systems-theory frame of reference, give an integrated account of the capabilities of all living things to integrate information, organize and reorganize it, and communicate it outward from themselves. Bateson drew on a wide range of intellectual fields to inform and illustrate his approach, among them mechanics, electronics, mathematics, cybernetics, and information theory, as well as biology, psychology, genetics, anthropology, philosophy, and religion. Within Bateson's framework, the integrity of explanation across widely differing phenomena is accomplished through the identification of analogies and homologies. Thus, for example, to the putative question, How is a leaf on a tree similar to a noun in a sentence?, Bateson (1972) would argue, "Both grammar and biological structure are products of communicational and organizational processes" (p. 154).

But if we want to capture the essence of Bateson's career, we might say more simply that he was perennially in search of the impertinent question. The reason for going into so many different areas was not to acquire the diversity of a polymath, even less to make a display of erudition, but to find new ways of conceptualizing basic epistemic phenomena. He was obsessed by the thought that our traditional categories of thought had grown stale and, worse, that our current search for practical solutions has become utterly bogged down in this backwash of stale ideas. What was needed first and foremost were new ways of looking at the human mind and its relation to nature in the context of a universal ecological system that would include both organism and ideas.

It may be jumping the gun here to bring in Bateson's later theory, but perhaps the reader should be apprised at the outset that according to the theory in its totality it is no simple matter to find new conceptual approaches. As mind is part of a larger system that includes the environment, and as that larger system is characterized by redundancy *and* stability, it is all too easy to fall into a thinking-as-usual approach. To be sure, it is possible to break out of thinking as usual through creativity, or exposure to novelty, or a combination of the two. But this is the exception, not the rule. The trick is to be constantly on the lookout, as Bateson was, for possible intellectual spurs to thinking in new ways – the difference that makes a difference – but neither creativity nor fresh experience can be planned, and they do not readily lend themselves to budget proposals and the like. Nor does a career based on trying out new things readily lend itself to academic tenure or research grants.

To search for the impertinent question thus is itself impertinent; it is a tricky, even hard, road to follow. Bateson's was a career of an intellectual nomad, traveling from place to place, and from one field to another, without ever settling into the safety of a secure niche. Too often, he was offered positions not entirely appropriate to his gifts or else he was offered posts that for reasons of intellectual conscience he could not accept. He collaborated with many – some misused him – but he was continually moving on. As a consequence, this gentle, sincere, warm – and warming – man enjoyed neither the reputation he deserved nor the real security appropriate to his achievements until very nearly the last decade of his life.

None of this was evident in Bateson's attitude toward life, and none of it comes through in his own account of his career. Bateson seems to have been blessed from the beginning by a deeply felt intuition that it was *important* to be constantly trying new things and that he was lucky to have the chance. To be sure, the search for novelty was in the context of a consistency of endeavor. In a certain sense, Bateson was always plowing the same field. Certain topics he comes back to again and again. But each time he returns, he has added something new. It is as if while plowing his one field, he was forever experimenting with different seeds and different regimens and thereby coming up with new produce.

Bateson's writing conveys this sense or openness to novelty, this sense that one might learn something new and enjoy it at the same time. Reading a Bateson essay, one has the feeling of getting ready to play rather than to work. The feeling is altogether surprising, given the great difficulty of some of the concepts that Bateson is continually "playing" with. The pleasing quality of a Bateson essay is one of the marvels of our time. Most readers will jump here to remember their favorite of the "metalogues," those playful/serious conversations between Bateson and his daughter on such topics as "Why Do Frenchmen?" and "What Is an Instinct?" Yet, at least some of these imaginative forays are marvels of intellectual construction; the very process of the dialogue reflects the thing being talked about. Both process and content have to constantly keep up with one another. Conceptually, these double tightrope acts are quite difficult – one has only to try writing one to see how easy it is to fall – and yet none of the difficulty comes through.

1.1. The epistemology that makes a difference

Part of Bateson's secret is a wry humor; part of it, too, is that he is never in too much of a hurry to stop and notice something a little to the side of his main argument that is nonetheless interesting. Often enough, this leads to a detour, sometimes two. And even in the course of a detour, he might suddenly pause to take in yet something else again. His overall argument is growing in complexity at each juncture, but the effect is pleasant, refreshing, as though in the middle of a hike one has paused to take in a wildflower or two or three. Which, after all, is part of what hiking ought to be about. Bateson's originality lies in this: He has the knack for picking the right wildflowers to bring back in his bouquet and then he has the further knack for arranging his selections in the right patterns.

Hiking with Bateson is never dull. Consider for example the following item from "Style, Grace and Information in Primitive Art" (Bateson, 1972). It comes amidst a discussion of the "unconscious," which is itself part of a discussion of art, which in its turn is a prelude to an analysis of a Balinese painting. In his discussion of the unconscious Bateson becomes concerned to make it clear that unconscious mental processes necessarily have a great deal of cognitive structure built into them. This leads to a new emphasis within an old maxim: The heart has *reasons* that reason does not at all perceive. Furthermore, it is *important* that these "reasons" stay unconscious; they can do their work better and faster that way. (All this is relevant, for art in Bateson's view communicates in terms of a balance it strikes between conscious and unconscious reasons, both of which are present by virtue of the skill of the artist. He quotes Isadora Duncan to good effect: "If I could tell you what it meant, there would be no point in dancing it.") But this discussion leads Bateson to a Freudian counterthought: The unconscious can also be a cupboard or closet for emotional skeletons, and insofar as this is the case, we would reverse the general rule and wish, with Freud, to make the unconscious conscious. And just here Bateson stops yet again – remember, we are discussing a Balinese painting – because something new has just occured to him: "But there may still be advantages to keeping the skeleton off the dining room table." No more is said about this, nor does any more have to be said; Bateson just noticed it, he thought it was interesting, and he thought you might find it so, too.

This business of noticing things is important. It gets one to thinking. And thinking, *real* thinking, is good for the soul. It recharges one's batteries: Suddenly one is coming up with answers; suddenly one is up to the tasks of the day. We can put this in terms of Bateson's overall theory. We start by noticing something different or, in Bateson's terms, with simply a "difference." *That* wasn't there yesterday, we say to ourselves, or perhaps something like, Now why did I think about *her* all of a sudden? The difference has provoked our mind to activity. But, notice, please, that the difference has not *caused* our activity, at least not in any materialistic sense. It would be more precise to say that the difference has *provoked* our mind to activity. The energy for our mind's activity comes not from the object of contemplation but from within, ultimately from our physiology. The cat's reaction to a kick is quite different from a football's; it comes from inside the cat, not from our shoe. Notice, too, that what we now find ourselves thinking about is not the same thing as what provoked it. It is a mirror image of it, perhaps, but not the thing. The map, as Bateson so often quoted Korzybski as saying, is not the territory it represents. The girl I am now thinking of is, sad to say, not the actual girl herself. Or maybe it is better this way.

This is the beginning of a sound epistemology. It reflects the way minds actually work; it makes sense. Bateson's next step is to point out that these various differences begin to generate classes in our mind, and reflections about these classes, or differences between the differences. Thus we begin to consider cats, footballs, girls, and thoughts about girls. These, in turn, initiate various actions that in turn yield new differences in the form of feedback. Some of these feedback loops involve direct interaction with the environment; others are internal and reflect various summations and reclassifications of previous experience. Thus we also begin to consider kicking, kicking cats, flirting, regretting, forgetting. Which in turn may generate further interchanges with the environment of an even more complex nature. Chasing, retrieving, chasing, longing hopelessly. In all this, the organism is actively involved or, as we should say, thoughtfully involved. Consider Bateson's "boot," which is described in my dialogue with him at the end of this volume. To some it is a boot, to others the letter "J," and to still others a rectangle with something like a hexagon attached. All of these interpretations of the figure involve mental activity; something is being done to the figure mentally to make it intelligible. But one can go even further in this activity. All at once, new geometric relations become apparent, and a more systematic examination of the figure becomes possible. And juxtaposed against all this activity stands the boot offering feedback, feedback that varies according to the activity that is brought to bear on it. (If you start with the hexagon idea, the lower left-hand portion of the boot is initially maddening. "No, I am not a hexagon," it seems to be saying, "nor am I anything else you know about." But when one hits on completing the hexagon figure by adding an inner diagonal, then all of a sudden the boot turns friendly and seems to say, "Now you're onto something.")

With the mention of feedback, however, we should hasten to add that contrary to what some encounter group leaders seem to believe, not all feedback is benign. Some of Bateson's earliest work was concerned with identifying patterns of interchange between self and others that lead to a rapid escalation of behavior and a concomitant breakdown of social integration. In his collaboration with Margaret Mead doing anthropological fieldwork, he originated the concept of "schismogenesis" to describe situations, such as mutual threat, in which the behavior of one individual serves as a signal to another to initiate more drastic behavior which in turn serves as a signal to the first to do the same, and so on. In such a system, only a slight initial difference, a threatening gesture from one individual, causes the system to run rapidly out of control. Bateson identified two classes of schismogenic systems. These he designated as "symmetrical" and "complementary." Conditions of mutual threat, whether between animals, individual humans, nations, or races, constitute a symmetrical system: A given behavior in one entity causes the same behavior in the other. In complementary systems, a given behavior induces the reciprocal behavior in another. Dominance induces submission; sadism, masochism; haughty indifference, hopeless longing.

What distinguishes both kinds of system is that they rapidly get "stuck" and further learning does not occur. Though internally they show a hair-trigger dynamic, they are relatively static in comparison to the larger environment of which they are a subsystem. It took some time, however, for Bateson to realize that though schismogenic systems certainly can and do exist, their very nature militates against their indefinite survival. The adaptive value of such runaway systems is nil. Nature abhors schismogenesis. What tends to happen is that the two kinds of different systems, symmetrical and complementary, come alternately into play, with the one operating as a negative feedback with regard to the other. Thus, between mammals of the same species, a situation of threat leads rapidly to more threat, but before the interchange gets out of hand, and real injury occurs, one or the other typically makes a submissive display. The two possible ways of responding to threat – symmetrical or complementary, threatening or submissive – balance each other out. The resulting system is more flexible, more adaptable, and more likely to exist.

Schismogenic systems can be distinguished from more normal systems of interaction in yet another way. In these latter systems, there is a progressive gain in organization. This gain, moreover, is on more than one level. Kicking a football is not the same thing as shooting baskets. But if one practices kicking a football, one is learning more than just how to split the uprights. One is also learning what it is to practice, how much time is involved, how much discipline and concentration are needed, and so on. And these metaskills may indeed be transferred to another sport. Recognition of this phenomenon – it has been observed in laboratory mice – and its classification and elucidation as "deutero-learning" (learning to learn) was one of Bateson's many contributions.

But, we must be careful not to get caught in enumerating Bateson's "contributions," most especially in a volume dedicated to his memory. For essential to Bateson's outlook was a sense that even fresh ideas rapidly tend to become stale, especially when they become shibboleths. It was necessary to keep playing with ideas, to keep juxtaposing them in new combinations, if one wanted to continue to make sense. In this regard, in the combination of intellectual openness and theoretical playfulness, Bateson most resembles William James; he had as well some of that same geniality and essential gentleness of spirit.

Thus we come to another feature of Bateson's epistemology – the constant integration of concepts derived from one branch of research with problems and concepts derived from another. Through this integration, composite organisms, such as human societies, came to be viewed as similar to individual organisms, and evolutionary change as of a kind with individual learning. This multilayer integration of concepts is both method and result for Bateson. It exemplifies the power of mind to operate across different logical categories in search of ever more relevant patterns of metaknowledge. It is also the means by which that power comes into being. Put another way, the search for the impertinent question is as endless as life. For no sooner has it generated a pertinent solution, than it becomes time to push ahead and find a new impertinent question. And it is perhaps best if this new impertinent question can be put to the solution that has just been found.

1.2. Patterns of abnormality

This is not merely words. Consider Bateson's own seminal contribution to schizophrenia research, his theory of the double bind. The first step in this theory lay in the recognition that certain interaction systems could be dysfunctional. Bateson had realized this as early as his articulation of the idea of schismogenesis. But, before he could go any further (we are assuming a direction) a detour was necessary. Thus, he took up an invitation from the director of the Fleishhacker Zoo in California to observe a very strange rarity: two otters that would not play with one another. Otters are the most playful creatures on earth; a pair of otters that would not play was indeed worth investigating. Bateson tried various initial approaches, most centered around a tentative hypothesis that something was missing from their environment that was ordinarily present in nature, but to no avail. Next, for want of a better alternative, he undertook to see if the otters *could* play. This was simple enough to test – he rigged up a string device hardly more sophisticated than what children use to get the household cat to chase a paper ball – and before long he found that both otters could in fact play, at least with him. The next step was to create situations in which the two otters played together with him. Now it came time to withdraw as the intermediary and see if they would continue to play with each other. This they did, but only for a time.

The experience profoundly impressed Bateson with the possibility that two organisms could exist side by side yet fail to communicate in meaningful ways. The autism of his otters made him reflect anew on the mental disturbances of schizophrenic children and schizophrenic adults. But something else was at work, too. For as Bateson contemplated what he had actually *taught* the otters, he realized that it was a message on more than one level. He had taught them not only that a paper ball on the end of the string could be made to make eccentric, somewhat unpredictable movements, but also that it might be fun to engage it in this way. The message, more properly the metamessage, was "play."

But where exactly had the metamessage been embedded in the concrete actions of jerking the string? The problem is general: When one considers the play of various different mammal species one sees that many of the elements of play are composed of the very same gestures that in another context constitute threats. How is it that an animal can come to grasp that this bite is not only not real, but is a signal that a real bite will not be forthcoming in this exchange? (The process can go awry, too. Bateson noted with interest the observation of Edmund Leach of certain tribal peace-making rituals involving threat gestures that, when not done quite right, led instead to renewed combat.)

What is involved here is the kind of paradox that Russell (1925–1927) had already analyzed with the principle of logical types. According to Russell, a statement about a class could not simultaneously be a member of the class to which it referred. Violation of this rule generated a form of logically invalid paradox, of which the simplest form is: This statement is false. But here it was that all sorts of mammalian species regularly violated Russell's law in their play behavior – and made it work. And with reflection, it readily became apparent that much human behavior, from poetry to painting to religious metaphor, involved similar violations of Russell's law, which, nonetheless, did not render them meaningless.

The next step was Jay Haley's suggestion that the symptoms of schizophrenia were suggestive of an inability to discriminate logical types. With this, Bateson finally had enough impertinent questions to generate a fresh perspective on the etiology of schizophrenia – the double bind. Three elements were needed to constitute a double bind: a primary injunction; a secondary injunction that distorted the communicational context of the primary injunction and thus effectively contradicted it; and a situation structured in such a way that the victim could not leave the field. The point of it all is that the victim has no satisfactory response: The victim can respond to neither the primary nor the secondary injunction. In such a communicational context, accordingly, the victim learns to distort responses in such a way as to neutralize the implicit threat. Specifically, the victim will hit on a perceptual–communicational tactic in which levels of logical meaning are blurred. And once this tactic has become deeply enough ingrained, it will tend to perpetuate itself by bringing forth responses from the environment that foster a continued sense of threat.

We are moving briskly through a complicated theory here. Let us point out only that a double bind is neither a conflict nor a trauma in any usual sense. It is a situation in which no response is possible without the threat of catastrophe. At a conference (Berger, 1978) devoted to his theory, Bateson was moved by confusion over this issue to take up the example of Lewis Carroll's "bread-and-butter flies." The wings of the bread-and-butter fly are made of bread and butter; its body is made of pure sugar. The bread-and-butter fly can only eat, or rather drink, lukewarm tea; if it does not do this, it will, of course, die. But if it does, the tea will dissolved the sugar and that will not work out so well either. That, Bateson told his audience, is a double bind: Either way you lose.

Stepping back from the specifics of this elegant theory, not adequately captured in our short summary, we should note some of the different elements that went into making it. Bateson has taken concepts from ethnology (schismogenesis), logic (logical types), ethology (those otters and the play of mammals generally), and used them to generate a psychiatric hypothesis about specific, etiologically important, modes of interpersonal communication that could be empirically verified. And the theory was finally exemplified, once the ensuing discussion became confused, with a fantasy creature from *Through the Looking-Glass*.[1]

This is what is meant by integrating schemas from different areas of inquiry, and at different levels of abstraction, into an overall pattern that establishes an intelligible examination of a puzzling phenomena. And notice how many times impertinence has gotten into it, beginning with those very unotterish otters and ending with Bateson's realization that certain logical fallacies are no obstacle to meaningful communication. Notice, too, that to arrive at this theory Bateson has had to be impertinent with Bateson; had he stuck with his original view of schismogenesis he would never have seen the multilayered negative feedback that constitutes the double bind.

As a matter of fact, Bateson was continually impertinent with Bateson. No theory was safe for long and his later work is characterized by unabashed admissions that certain early theories have now hit the junk heap. But there was progress. His brilliant analysis of the psychology of alcoholics (1972) could probably never have been penned earlier in his career, for it depends upon the realization that alcoholics with their determined willpower and their conviction that they can beat this thing are in a symmetrical and escalating struggle with a phantom. The more alcoholics resist drink, the more their fine display of willpower becomes meaningless, since they now lack their diabolical opponent. They have destroyed the system that makes their mastery meaningful. Getting drunk, on the other hand, represents a complementary system that acts as a corrective. Not only do alcoholics have their symmetrical demon back on the premises to fight with again, but while they have the demon there they can relax those very systems of pride and self-control that are the starting point for this predicament. Getting drunk is the necessary complementary system that acts as the negative feedback loop to keep the whole system in balance. We have come far from the simple run-away system of the early theory of schismogenesis. Not that we have lost track of its essential epistemological point (the pathological rupture of an integrated system). The telltale non-sense-making rupture is still there to be found, but it is to be found in an altogether different level in the system, in the relations between conscious self-control and the wider ecological circles of mind and environment. This, Bateson is quick to point out, is what Alcoholics Anonymous has known all along. The first step to recovering is to admit that one has no control over alcohol. The second is to place one's reliance not on the false promise of increased willpower but on an agency outside the self, namely, one's "Higher Power."

1.3. Creative processes

As we noted at the outset, the constant search for the impertinent question is a tricky path. It gave Bateson's thought its perennial playfulness, but it also made it hard for his students to come to grips with it whole. As he himself remarked in good-natured self-deprecation, when he taught a seminar for psychiatric residents, he was invariably asked sometime about the third or fourth lecture what the course was *really* about. As he later recalled it, every year the same rumor went around, alleging that "Bateson knows something that he does not tell you" or that "there's something behind what Bateson says, but he never says what it is." In person, Bateson had a quiet demeanor and twinkling eyes; asked a question, he would often pause a long time, as he thought it over, and then reply with gnomic brevity. The search for impertinence went on.

When I first met Gregory Bateson, he was coming to the end of his career. Facing the last of many operations for cancer, he was pressed for time: What projects needed finishing needed to be finished now. But, he never allowed time pressure to become mental pressure – premature closure was as alien to him at the end of his career as it has been at the beginning. A thought that was incomplete was allowed to stay incomplete until a favorable gust of imagination or chance might blow a fresh angle on it his way. One could play at finding the answer and while play can be serious – indeed, it must be serious if it is to be truly play – it can never be rushed. It would be like trying to hurry history.

I remember when he first visited me at my home. Perusing my bookshelves, he was arrested by a single volume, *Natural Theology*, by the Rev. William Paley. This early nineteenth-century tract had argued for the existence of God on the basis of the manifest planfulness of nature; with such elegant design everywhere before us, in Paley's view, we must a priori concede the existence of a single all-knowing Creator. *Natural Theology* had inspired that series of tracts about design in nature known as the Bridgewater treatises. Paley's approach had been roundly trounced by the areligious perspective opened up by Darwin. Historical curiosity had largely been behind my purchase of it, that and the prospect of owning an unusually beautiful early edition. Now, however, to my complete surprise, Bateson told me that this was one of his favorite volumes and he added, to my somewhat stunned satisfaction, that I must be a smart man to own it and even smarter one if I had read it.

Why would a twentieth-century social scientist, one who particularly interested himself in teasing out evolution's puzzles, also interest himself in the Reverend Paley's arguments for the existence of God? It was a typical Batesonian paradox. As he had written in *Mind and Nature* (1979), "adaptation" in the language of the evolutionists is approximately synonymous with "design" in the language of the theologians. Consider the following example: If one looks at a piece of wood, one is initially struck by its sturdiness, a sturdiness that is nonetheless neither brittle nor totally inflexible; it is remarkably good material to build with, as the tree already knows. But if one examines it under the microscope, one discovers that this same piece of wood is a miraculously intricate set of pipes; plumbing, not building, seems to be its essence. It is this economy of form and function, and their simultaneous integration at both microscopic and macroscopic levels, that constitutes adaptive design. The economy is such that finally form and function collapse into an essential unity – the pipes hold the building up. Such economy could never arise in a purely random, and thus chaotic, context; there must be successive negative feedback loops from the environment inhibiting and eventually eliminating less economic structures within the tree. These negative feedback loops – the concept is expressly borrowed from cybernetics – operate together with the tree's ability to preserve what it has "learnt" to generate the tree's miraculous economy of design.

Elsewhere, in his lecture "Conscious Purpose and Nature," Bateson (1972, pp. 426–439) observed with satisfaction that Darwin's contemporary and collaborator Russell Wallace had specifically compared the action of natural selection with the governor on a steam engine "which checks and corrects any irregularities almost before they can become evident." Wallace, Bateson observed, had actually proposed the first cybernetic model. And when we take the next step up, to viewing whole systems of organisms circularly interacting with one another, we are confronted with a set of forces of daunting complexity and daunting exactitude. "Call the systemic forces 'God' if you will," added Bateson in his lecture. He wanted his audience to be aware of humans' increasingly precarious ecological position in this very complicated, and ultimately self-correcting, world. He was at pains to make clear that this system does not readily reveal itself to human beings, who as creatures are altogether too accustomed to thinking in the linear fashion of conscious purpose.

Here we come to another aspect of Bateson's thought – his insistence on retaining a normative vision within his overall framework. To separate values out from the twin enterprises of description and explanation was thought to be just exactly the kind of endeavor that necessarily generates an artificially segmented view of mind and the world. In short, such an endeavor makes non-sense. Thus, no sooner did Margaret Mead report on their joint work in New Guinea than Bateson supplemented it with his essay "Culture Contact and Schismogenesis" (1972), which criticized a committee of the Social Science Research

Council for seeking utilitarian answers to questions of colonial administration under the guise of doing anthropological research. This was bad science; it was also bad policy. The contact of two cultures needed to be understood as its own separate metasystem and studied as such. When this had been done, Bateson observed with some irony, the colonial administrator might then decide which of several possible intercultural systems, including a schismogenic one, to participate in.

The epistemology that makes sense, not non-sense, must perforce be an epistemology that does not banish normative questions, but that assigns them their necessary place in the overall network of mind conceived as a multilayered interaction between organism and environment. As an epistemologist, Bateson was most sensitive to and worried most about the innate reliance of evil upon ignorance. If you break the connections between terms in an epistemic system, he believed, you prepare yourself to do violence to the living systems that comprise them. In many ways, his view parallels that of Robert Jay Lifton (1979) in *The Broken Connection*. But whereas Lifton focuses on the catastrophic rupture of one set of complementarities – life and death and the struggle for immortality – Bateson saw the threat of such breaks in a full gamut of connections. Thus, the connections between mind and body, between nature and nurture, between organism and environment, between self and society, between a statement and its frame – in these and other connections, Bateson saw the potential for rupture and ruin.

1.4. Mending the connections

It may be pertinent here to state for the record that this belief in maintaining the connections between different parts of any complex system, and in mending the connections when they had been broken, was quite deeply felt by this singular man. At the end of the present volume is a dialogue I had with Bateson titled "Mind and Body." As a dialogue it has its limitations, though it does illustrate how ideas interact with one another in a true ecology of mind. Specifically, we could not work through to a mutual understanding of one set of ideas (Bateson's view of the mind–body problem) before we had surmounted a separate problem (time and space), itself brought into play by Bateson's concept of difference. But what I would point out to the reader here is the real passion that becomes palpably present in Bateson's final remarks on the subject of why we should struggle so hard to clarify our understanding of mind – "because it's bloody dangerous if you don't."

If there is one thing that unites the essays in this volume it is that they share Bateson's sense of reverence for the multileveled pattern of connections entailed in healthy human communication. The patterns of connections may range in specificity from the microscopic to the macroscopic levels of existence. At the most abstract level of discourse one may deal with all the possible connections, say, within the universal human experience of the body–mind interaction or of the life–death continuum; but, moving down the ladder, one must also be prepared to see connections with the most microscopic constituents of those continua as they take shape in cultural products.

Perhaps here we should go back and have another look at that Balinese painting. In his discussion, Bateson observes that what we have before us, once we accustom ourselves to a different system of iconography, is readily decodable as a funeral procession. And, almost as easily detectable to the psychoanalytic eye, we also have an evident sexual pun: From a certain angle, and with a certain frame of mind, one sees that the cremation tower stands between two round elephant heads and appears nervously ready to penetrate through a narrow entrance into a serene courtyard. But Bateson is in no hurry to bring his interpretation to a psychoanalytic fare-thee-well. Thus, he also notes that the painting could be taken as a comment on Balinese social structure, with the graceful postures of the figures contrasting with the powerful emotions lying just below the scene's surface. And even this thought does not exhaust his interpretive energies. By far the bulk of his analysis is concerned with the minutiae of composition and texture. Tiny details of the painter's craft are taken up – we learn that to paint leaves typically requires seven separate color washes while this particular painting has only four – as well as certain oddities of composition. Thus, in contrast to the expectations of the Western eye, the top of the painting is serene, the bottom turbulent and dark. As well, the painting is crammed with detail – Bateson draws an analogy to the style of a crank letter where all the available space is filled in with writing – which creates an effect of nervous tension that is then offset by the artist's sense of balance and composition. And this level of analysis figures prominently in Bateson's summary interpretation. For finally, in his view, the picture is concerned with striking a balance between turbulence and serenity and thus with depicting their necessary interconnection. What the painter is telling us, Bateson concludes, is that to choose either serenity or turbulence to the exclusion of the other is a "vulgar error": "The unity and integration of the picture assert that neither of these contrasting poles can be chosen to the exclusion of the other, because the poles are mutually dependent. This profound and general truth is simultaneously asserted for the fields of sex, social organization, and death" (Bateson, 1972, p. 152).

In this example, in order to arrive at meaning we had to see the connections in the pattern between the macroscopic and the microscopic, and both in relation to a continuum defined by the two poles, turbulence and serenity. But the Batesonian approach is scarcely restricted to the semiotics of iconography. As well one can apply it to other patterns of communication. Thus the same tension that Bateson espies in the painting can be found in other aspects of Balinese social life, in which correct behavior typically involves a delicate tension between anxiety and graceful self-control.

A further Batesonian insight is that the meaning of a given continuum between two poles will be shaped by the set of behavioral contexts appropriate to that continuum as they are defined in any given culture. Thus while the same behavioral continuum, exhibitionism and spectatorship say, can be found across cultures, its meaning varies considerably according to the context assigned to it by any specific culture. For example, in England, as Bateson (1972) pointed out in a war-time essay, "Morale and National Character," verbal exhibitionism is typically an adult prerogative and spectatorship is the filial reciprocal. Children are to be seen and not heard; more precisely, they are to listen. Thus, when one takes the floor to state one's own opinion, whether at the typewriter or at the House of Commons, one is implicitly taking on the mantle of superiority and authority. But, in America, the typical pattern is almost exactly the reverse: In America it is the children who speak of their deeds, this to show their growing independence, and it is the parents who take the role of admiring spectators, this by way of acknowledging that the child has done what they want. Thus when Americans boast, they are contextually taking a junior role; they invite approval, not submission. And they are liable to offend their English allies just at the moment when they are trying to please them.

1.5. Communication among humans

Given Bateson's wide-ranging perspective, it seems almost to do violence to his outlook to focus in on human communication by means of it. Yet this is not really the case on several counts. To begin with, the underlying agenda beneath Bateson's theory is, in the end, to explain the human mind and thereby to gain an understanding of human behavior, including the interaction of one human with another, or with others, or with the nonliving environment. All these interactions involve communication.

To be sure, as with his conceptions of mind, organism, thought, knowledge, and learning, Bateson's notion of communication is a great deal more comprehensive than the usual sense of the term. In keeping with his general theory, communication for Bateson included all the interrelated phenomena that, because of their formal properties, can be communicated in some sense:

> A priori it can be argued that all perception and all response, all behavior and all classes of behavior, all learning and all genetics, all neurophysiology and endocrinology, all organization and all evolution – one entire subject matter – must be regarded as communicational in nature, and therefore subject to the great generalizations or "laws" which apply to communicative phenomena. We therefore are warned to expect to find in our data those principles of order which fundamental communication theory would propose. (Bateson, 1972, pp. 282–283)

This means that communication, in the Batesonian sense, starts with such basic phenomena as irritability and adaptive action, ranges through the various processes of codifying and internally representing knowledge engaged in by all higher organisms, and goes on to include, ultimately, human communication (and metacommunication) in all its modes, verbal and nonverbal.

Then, too, Bateson considered it no violation of his overall scheme to focus on distinctively human communicational acts. He did so himself, many times, and within this realm produced some of his most widely known and gifted work. (See, for example, Bateson, 1936, and Mead & Bateson, 1942.) No, what would constitute a violation of Bateson's approach is not so much to focus on human communication per se as to focus on only one of its elements or modes in isolation. What characterized Bateson's approach, even when focused on human communicative events, was an insistence that all potentially communicative modes be included in the description – verbal and nonverbal – as well as all participants, and the context itself. It is a fool's errand to attempt to find much in Bateson's writings about any one communication mode, such as language, because there will be little there that is isolable and that, when isolated, makes sense. That is because Bateson considered it a waste of time to focus in on an isolated communication mode that itself conveyed only a part of what was communicated in normal interactions. In general, he preferred to include more, rather than less, in his definition of the communicative act. And anyone who resists the pressure to narrow the definition of communication is carrying on his legacy.

Ultimately, for Bateson, the patterns of human communication are related to the patterns that connect life at all levels and in some manner account for the reciprocal relationships that exist between genetically inherited characteristics and learned behavior on the one hand and mind–body interaction on the other. Ultimately, communication is grounded in biology, grounded but not determined. That is to say, from another perspective, that communication is related to health. The breakup of the human mind into cognitive, emotional, and volitional processes has no status in Bateson's approach. He understood them as constituting an essentially indivisible gestalt. Better than perhaps anyone, he recognized that to focus, say, on emotion, to the detriment of cognition and volition, generated results that were likely to be wrong. Wrong, and also unhealthy. What matters is the integrity of the patterns of connection linking these categories of behavior in the organism. If you break the pattern that connects the learning that takes place between the cognitive, emotional, and volitional processes of the mind, you destroy the healthy quality of the organism's life-style. Healthy communication, needless to say, is communication that proceeds simultaneously on all these levels.

The same is true of the individual in relation to society. Although we have a conscious sense of our own identity, of our own existence as separate people, we always "live" our lives in a contextual sense within a social interaction network. To be sure, at times this contextual living in an interaction network may be psychodynamically incorporated into our personal thoughts, feelings, and dreams. But we run a terrible risk when we mistake the relative privacy of reflection and fantasy for a real separateness of the self. The self is but one pole of our life: It cannot exist alone and be meaningful. This is epistemologically sound. It is also experientially valid.

It is here that Bateson's approach to human communication links up with the study of human psychopathology. The mental life of the human organism has a powerful capacity to consciously as well as unconsciously associate or dissociate life experiences, to concentrate upon and to then declare that this or that is either "me" or "not me." Both processes are necessary; both need to be balanced against the other. In the dissociation in particular lies the potential for both creative and destructive aspects of life and mind. When mental dissociative processes are out of conscious control, they are more prone to realize destructive ends. On the other hand, when under conscious control they may be utilized for the higher creative accomplishments of the human organism. But granting dissociation a role in human mental life is not the same thing as negating the significance of social context. For each dissociative act needs to be understood in relation to the life experience that is declared "not me."

1.6. Bateson and contemporary thought

If one were to select a contemporary figure who can most readily be contrasted with Bateson, one might well begin with the seminal linguist Noam Chomsky. Where Bateson is concerned with language as part of a cultural system, Chomsky has largely dispensed with the contextual influences shaping language and language use, this on the basis that language functioning is, in the abstract terms described by the rules of transformation within his basic grammar, virtually the same across all cultures. Accordingly, Chomsky assumes that the capacity for language is inborn; cultural influences and social interaction constitute little more than the "priming" or "triggering" necessary to inaugurate this essentially instinctive behavior. The marvel of Chomsky's system is that with a few basic rules, he can generate a discrete but nonetheless infinite universe of grammatic possibilities. And he demonstrates that the logic of these rules of transformation is in fact followed by beginning language users in all cultures to the detriment of their assimilating culturally specific irregular grammatical forms. The small boy says "runned" instead of "ran" and – the decisive point – we can be sure "runned" is a word he has never ever heard.

To be sure, the astonishing beauty of Chomsky's putative language system was scarcely lost on the appreciative Bateson. For intuitively he felt in it reminiscences of the marvels of natural design. Indeed it probably made more sense to him than to anyone, for Bateson could simultaneously appreciate how this species-specific acquisition was grounded in the larger systems of mammalian communication generally. But Chomsky's approach was to consider language one of the faculties of cognition – he straightforwardly called for a revived "neofaculty psychology" – and its functioning within the overall system was depicted in terms of its discrete status as a specific function. The analogy was explicitly made to the various organs of the body (liver, spleen, lungs, etc.) with each making its separate and distinct contribution to physiology. And in the analogy, one can see trouble brewing for the theory: Modern physiology stumbles daily on surprising patterns of chemical communication linking the various separate organs into an overall whole. With regard to language, Bateson's view was always that the various subsystems serving cognition, language included, would, if one teased them out, show far more interconnectedness than was first apparent. Bateson could accept the thought that perhaps a noun was like a leaf and depended on various stem and branch structures to make sense; but he knew well that those stem and branch structures were themselves intricate, multipurpose marvels of design.

Accordingly, Bateson saw Chomsky's theory as a threat both for its hyperrationalism and for its devaluation of environmental interaction. In this respect, Bateson shares common ground with Piaget. Like Piaget, he concerned himself with the behavioral ground of cognition and communication. Like Piaget, he believed that both developed in a spiral of interaction between organism and environment. And like Piaget, he believed that language reflected the level of cognitive adaptation to the environment as much as, or more than, it determined it. (For Chomsky, language develops according to its own laws; its interactions are essentially with its own prior products.) But, even more than Piaget's, Bateson's views resemble those of the great Russian psychologist L. S. Vygotsky.

The resemblance between Bateson's and Vygotsky's views is both striking and puzzling. Essentially, both men understood, almost from the outset of their work, that language was part of a cultural context and that the progressive development of language functioning could not be discussed apart from the child's experience of culture. Likewise, both understood, again almost from the outset, that the developing pattern of language usage in the growing organism would interact with cognitive, emotional, and volitional systems that were themselves undergoing their own development.

The shared emphasis on cultural context between Bateson and Vygotsky is to be differently explained. In this respect, Bateson was plainly the disciple of Edward Sapir, Franz Boas's brilliant student and the originator of the modern perspective in American anthropology. It was Sapir's genius to recognize that culture, language, and personality form an interacting system and that this system in turn interacts with the biological givens of perception to generate cognition. Even before Whorf's splendid demonstrations to the point, Sapir intuitively recognized that a Navaho's perception of a sunny day was distinctively shaped by the Navaho language, which renders the perception only in a series of connected statements all taken from the point of view of the speaker: There is sunshine before me – there is sunshine behind me – there is sunshine on either side of me – I walk in sunshine. Vygotsky, on the other hand, got his emphasis on cultural context from his devotion to Marxist–Leninist philosophy. Indeed, if there is a central difference between the two thinkers, it is derived from this difference in their own cultural context. For Vygotsky, history, and its materialist result in technology, are causative principles; in large measure they create the conditions of culture the child is born into and then adapts to. Bateson, by contrast, adopts toward history the attitude of an explorer. The linear development of the present out of the past over time does not concern him. Rather, for Bateson's purposes, history constitutes a track that runs parallel to the present. One can jump in and out of it, make forays back and forth, and thereby gain a clearer idea of the meaning of where one is now.

But if the shared emphasis on cultural context is to be differently explained, the shared sense of multiple interactive systems is not to be explained at all. Both men sought to go beyond the limitations of the received paradigms in the social sciences and both elected to go in the *same* utterly new direction. Perhaps we should consider here that we are dealing with the compass needle of genius pointing in the same direction in two entirely different men and let it go at that. To be sure, their talents were different. Vygotsky was a brilliant experimentalist, constantly coming up with new methods and new areas where those methods might be applied. Bateson, though no less original, experimented principally with ideas while taking his stimulus from fieldwork; his laboratory was a triangular one, involving fieldwork, his own mind and the written word. But once we get past this difference in the manner of working, there is a striking convergence.

Consider for example, Vygotsky's notion of the Zone of Proximal Development. It arises out of a consideration of a weakness in the usual methods of experimental verification of cognitive development. If you test a child on a given level of tasks—this is true even if you use a Piagetian task – you are only measuring what the child does or does not yet know. But, you have learnt nothing of what the child is *about* to know, that is, what he is prepared to learn forthwith provided he is given some sensitive instruction. And yet, given that in Vygotsky's view development proceeds intermittently through a series of crises, with the transition periods as frequent as the periods of stable assimilation, then it is terribly important to find out whether the child is in fact in one of these transitional periods, whether, in other words, he is just about to get to the next level. This is the Zone of the Proximal Development. (John Dewey had previously sketched out the general idea in broad brushstrokes, giving it the term "readiness.") But to find out about it, you must do more than just test the child; you must interact with him, give him clues, teach him, and then see if he has caught on. This is the reverse of the clinical method used so brilliantly by Piaget. (Piaget quizzed the child on his errors; Vygotsky, in effect, is quizzing the child on the answer he has just given him. One wonders, incidentally, what the Miss Grundys of this world would have made of first giving the answer, then the exam; I think they would have considered it impertinent.) Accordingly Vygotsky's sense of a true assessment calls for the experimenter to interact with the child so as to find out what he might be able to learn. But this is precisely the sort of approach that Bateson utilized right along. Those otters, remember, had to be taught to play to see if they *could* play. And "deutero-learning" in general can be seen as complementary to Vygotsky's sense of how transitional stages work: something is being grasped in the usual way, but something else is also being learnt, something that in short order will bootstrap cognition up to the next level.

The parallel between Bateson and Vygotsky can be seen in other areas as well. Take for example Vygotsky's incisive criticism of Piaget's concept of the child's egocentric speech. For Piaget, the verbalized monologue that often accompanies the child's action is "egocentric" in the sense that is not directed to an other nor does it express logical, analytic thought. Such egocentric monologues are, in a manner of speaking, a continuation of the autism of the infant and for Piaget they indicate, chiefly, that the wholly interior and abstract thought of the adolescent stage has not yet been reached. Vygotsky elegantly demolished this view by showing that such "egocentric" speech *increased* as soon as an obstacle to the child's activity was introduced. Moreover, the content of the monologue could be shown to be clearly related to the nature of the obstacle. What was happening, in Vygotsky's view, was quite other than merely a continued assimilation to oneself. In effect, the child's monologue constitutes an attempt to adapt to the outer world by using language as a means of generating various helpful hints and partial solutions to practical problems. What happens in adolescence, further, is not that this monologue disappears, but that it has moved wholly into the interior, where it continues to exist as inner speech. To be sure, in adolescence, the growth of cognitive processes has reached the point where logical classes can be constructed. But the mode of operation of inner speech need not be identical with this novel cognitive capacity. Indeed, inner speech often reveals itself to be the same playful muddle that is the child's spoken monologue; it may be applied to problems of greater cognitive complexity, and it will proceed until it reaches solutions of greater logical consistency, but its fundamental nature has not changed.

Bateson probably would have been comfortable with this. On the one hand, he would have strongly seconded Vygotsky's emphasis on the context in which the allegedly egocentric speech occurs. On the other, he would have been especially pleased by the further conclusion that speech does not have to be logical, or even social, to be helpful. Again and again, Bateson insisted that meaningfulness was not confined to the operations of a calculating logic. Play, poetry, art, all these activities generate meaning, and if we now add inner speech to the list, we can appreciate anew the marvelous economies of form and function that link human thought at all levels. It should not surprise us, further, to learn that fresh studies of children's monologues have recently been undertaken from a Batesonian point of departure. Furthermore, the results of these studies are strikingly in accord with Vygotsky's preliminary researches. (Again we might note the parallel with John Dewey, whose views strongly resemble Vygotsky's and Bateson's in their appreciation of cultural instrumentalities of various orders. Speech, for Dewey, was the "tool of tools." We might say of the higher orders of deuterolearning, especially as it is manifest in inner speech, that it consists diachronically in learning how to learn with the tool of tools.)

There is yet another sense in which Bateson and Vygotsky deserve comparison – their passion to get things right. Vygotsky's passion expresses itself perhaps more directly. A brilliant rhetorician, Vygotsky typically arranges his points in marching formation and then after philosophically reconnoitering the territory ahead he sends them off to annihilate a favorite adversary or two. Seldom has the polemical style of argument achieved such splendid results or such splendid clarity. Bateson's passion, by contrast, is of a gentler sort. His is the passion of a naturalist who has captured a delicate and altogether rare blossom or butterfly and is determined above all not to harm it. He is a protective fellow, this Bateson; he wants to make sure that we do not do damage to the phenomena we are studying by underestimating their complexity –

be they good, bad, or ugly. But this determination requires passion, nonetheless, and its underlying strength can be gauged from the occasional instance when, as in his report on schismogenesis to the National Research Council, his suspicions were aroused that somebody else might prefer a substantially simpler, and infinitely uglier, approach to the phenomena. Then the passion would flare up. But, in general, the passion is subsumed under Bateson's continued concentration and his continued doggedness. Insofar as he was perennially in search of impertinent questions, he sorely needed this passion to keep him going. He knew how hard it was.

1.7. Essays in memory of Gregory Bateson

With the foregoing in mind let us turn to the present volume. The contributions are diverse, which one might have expected given the diversity of Bateson's approach, but they have in common a wish to continue the Bateson legacy and apply it to the problems of human communication. In the first section, "Mending the Connection Between Mind and Society," the emphasis is on restoring a normative component to the social sciences. The point is made explicit in David Bakan's essay, "Power, Method, and Ethics: A Reflection on Bateson's 'Morale and National Character.'" Bakan takes as his point of departure Bateson's essay, referred to earlier, "Morale and National Character." In that essay, Bateson discussed various similarities and differences operating between American, English, and German value systems. His objective was clear enough: This information might be helpful in helping to prosecute the war. But, with reflection, we have opened a Pandora's box here. The same information about national character might just as well be used to manipulate public opinion, both at home and abroad. A whole new weapon has been placed at the disposal of the modern state. In his meditations on this troublesome possibility, Bakan traces our lack of preparation for it back to the traditions of Scholasticism that sought to divorce learning, and academia generally, from the intrigues of politics, this for their own protection. Unfortunately, as Bakan rightly notes, the problem will not go away and social scientists must learn to involve themselves in the political decisions as to how their discoveries are used. To be sure, this has been managed before – Bakan invokes the example of the ancient Greeks – and it is not only possible to combine the two, but it is likely to result in a more profound consideration of the data. The connection between politics and the scholarly community was broken to accord with one political and cultural reality; it needs to be mended if we are to successfully negotiate a different political and cultural reality.

In "The Psychopathy of Everyday Life. Antisocial Behavior and Social Distress," by myself and Maurice Green, the same theme of the broken connection is pursued from a different angle. It has long been part of the American tradition to suppose, with P. T. Barnum, that "a sucker is born every minute." And as a corollary, the sucker has long been considered fair game; as W. C. Fields put it, "Never give a sucker an even break." Such attitudes form, if you will, the cutting edge of the great American obsession with competition and emotional self-reliance. But once admitted into the pantheon of acceptable attitudes, this particular communicative outlook can run riot among the rapidly changing cultural circumstances of a highly technological society. The consequence is a standard of acceptable psychopathy. As a culture we have moved from seeing psychopaths as hereditary degenerates through seeing them as simply antisocial and have finally arrived at accepting them as normative. Thus, we have an Oliver North or an Ivan Boesky, routinely breaking the law and routinely expecting that no great harm will come of it, at least not to themselves. Moreover, there is a schismogenic logic causing such behavior to escalate rapidly in a culture that accepts it: When ordinary citizens discover that they are the ones who have been taken as the sucker, their own inclination to continue to play by the rules will have been substantially damaged.

In "Bateson's Concept of Mental Illness," Theodore Skolnik pursues another broken connection in the hope of mending it. Skolnik's quarry is the tendency to isolate mental illness in the people who have it, and the further tendency to isolate the people who have it into discrete diagnostic groups. The result of this double dissociation is twofold. First, there is a loss of information about how mental illness arises in a pattern of disordered interaction. And second, there is an inappropriate focus on disease entities when we would be better off studying patterns of interaction between psychological mechanisms and interpersonal systems, patterns that cut across the usual nosological classifications. In effect, Skolnik has taken Bateson's seminal work on schizophrenia and has skillfully expanded it into a revised approach to psychopathology in general. His suggestions are timely and prescient as it rapidly becomes increasingly clear that the hard lines of traditional nosology are being blurred nearly out of existence by continued research. No single symptom, for example, by itself either warrants or necessarily entails a contemporary diagnosis of schizophrenia; all the standard so-called schizophrenic symptoms can be found in other disorders. We will get further faster if we begin studying symptoms, rather than diagnoses; and we will make even faster progress still when we begin to understand symptoms in terms of specific psychological mechanisms that arise in specific environmental contexts.

The four essays that go to make up the second portion of this volume, "Language and Communication in Context," hail from Bateson's work in a different way. Here the emphasis is on relating language to the wider contexts involved in effective human communication. This note is hit at the outset by Mary Catherine Bateson's wide-ranging reflections "Language, Languages, and Song: The Experience of System." The initial concern here is one we have seen before (the effect of conscious purposefulness on human adaptation), but several new considerations – should we say new impertinences – have entered in. To begin with, M. C. Bateson takes up the relation of certain inherent linguistic biases to human purposefulness. Language as a code is beautifully designed to handle purposive statements of a linear kind; further it works wonderfully well as a many-faceted crystal that can break the stream of perceptual experience up into a thousand useful fragments. But it is poorly designed for apprehending circular systems of reciprocal interaction in which all elements come simultaneously into play. Formal propositional language, however, is but one mode of communication. There are also the languages of poetry and religious ritual and song. In these languages human beings catch a glimpse into the circularity of nature; here they can have, in M. C. Bateson's phrase, the "experience of system" that is otherwise so hard for them to apprehend. Thus, if we cannot always talk sense, we can sometimes sing it.

The following paper, "Affective and Communicative Problems in Young Developmentally Deviant Language Users," by Theodore Shapiro and Elena Goldstein Lister, takes the Batesonian approach and applies it to a specific set of clinical phenomena. Taking six children with severely impaired language use, Shapiro and Lister describe a variety of faults and arrests (the use of jargon, echolalia) that can occur. These faults reflect different final pathways of deviant language organization; in turn, they are reflective of basic faults in ego functioning, and ultimately of central nervous system integration, that are also to be found in these children. What makes the two authors' contribution exciting is the recognition of the interaction between language and cognition on the one hand and between language and interpersonal integration on the other. Disturbances in language usage thus make a useful barometer of disturbances in both cognitive and affective areas. Thus, as the authors contend, there is a good reason to hope that it will eventually prove possible to employ language usage as a predictor of subsequent emotional development and of breakdown.

The third paper in this section, by myself, Oliver C. S. Tzeng, and Carl Wiedmann, entitled "A Cross-Cultural Study of Language Universals: The Emotional Meaning of Iconic and Graphic Stimuli," hails directly from Bateson's own work. Bateson posed the idea that primitive art can be cross-culturally appreciated on the basis that it communicates a sense of what he called "grace." In our study, we sought to begin to tease out how this communication about grace was contained within the image. Using pre-Columbian icons, and graphic line drawings derived from them, we asked subjects from a variety of cultures to rate them using scales derived from Osgood's work with the semantic differential. This gave us the opportunity both to compare effective reactions to nonverbal stimuli with what has already been discovered about cross-culturally valid structures of affective responses to verbal stimuli and to make comparisons across cultures. Of great interest, in line with Bateson's own conclusions about primitive art, was the discovery of "dynamisms" in the subject responses; these dynamisms, moreover, varied across cultures.

The section on language concludes with John Broughton's stimulating paper "Machine Dreams: Computers in the Fantasies of Young Adults." Broughton begins with a paradox worthy of Bateson, namely, that part of the meaning of computers in the modern age is that we are not sure what their meaning is. We have yet to decide if they are truly helpful or truly harmful. To get at this ambiguity, hard to capture through ordinary methods of interrogation, Broughton employs a novel technique for group generation of fantasies in which each subject contributes a single sentence to a narrative on the basis of knowing only the sentence before. The resulting stories are surprising and frequently delightful; they also serve to capture well the full range of the continuum of ambiguity associated with the computer. Here, in lieu of further summary, let us offer just one of them: "Norman sat down at the computer. He placed his apple on top of the terminal. He thought of taking a byte of his apple and laughed. But maybe the fruit is forbidden, he thought. Second thoughts flooded his mind."

The pair of essays that make up the third section of this volume, "Mind and Paralinguistic Communication," are both concerned with the nonverbal accompaniments of spoken speech. Both follow Bateson's lead in supposing that much of the meaning in verbal interaction is carried by parallel channels operating in tandem with language such as vocal tone and gesturing. Moreover, in both papers, the level of analysis shifts from the macroscopic to the microscopic and back again in an attempt to relate the two levels in the meaningful description of the overall pattern. Thus, Aron Siegman's contribution, "In Search of Coronary-Prone Behavior," seeks to examine such minutiae of verbal interaction as turn-taking behavior, latency of response, explosiveness of speech. For one unaware of the connectedness of component systems in a living organism, this might not sound like a promising approach, but Siegman gets surprising results. Coronary-prone individuals exhibit a distinctive pattern all their own: They are quick to speak, quicker to interrupt, and everything they say seems to carry an equal urgency to judge by the constant pressure of their vocal tone. What we see here is a hard-driving organismic pattern that is in a constant hurry to get nowhere in particular. The same pattern, needless to say, can be detected in other aspects of such persons' behavior; and it extracts its final, brutal price at the level of inducing pathological functioning in a single vulnerable organ system. A heart attack at a young age is, indeed, getting nowhere in particular in a hurry.

In "Two Principles of Communicative Functioning," Norbert Freedman reports on over a decade of research into kinetics, that is into the gestural accompaniments to spoken speech. Again the emphasis is on the integration of various different levels of behavior and their combination into a single overall whole. In one of his metalogues with his daughter, Bateson wondered why the French wave their arms when they speak. He would be pleased with the delicate conclusions Freedman has arrived at, conclusions that are difficult to summarize briefly. Freedman identifies his two principles as first, rhythmic motor movement, and second, repetitive tactile self-stimulation. The first he sees as an essential building block to the development of representational thought. By regulating the basic mode of approach–withdrawal, such movements provide a stable relation between the self and the object; as well they provide a motivational force that lends cohesiveness to the cognitive structures subsumed under language functioning. Repetitive tactile self-stimulation, by contrast, serves a different set of functions; it is essentially an attention-filtering device that, by producing optimal innervation, makes it possible to maintain optimal attentional freedom. Both systems regulate the diverse attitudinal and motivational structures needed for successful language processing, and both are shown to be profoundly disturbed by severe stress or severe psychopathology.

The volume ends with the section "Dialogues and Dialectics." Peter Ostwald's paper, "Gregory Bateson (1904–1980) and Oscar Wilde (1854–1900): A Heavenly Discourse," is, simply, a tour de force. Taking his material from the extant writings of the two men, Ostwald ingeniously constructs an imagined dialogue in heaven on the subject of paradox and ambiguity. Then, backtracking, he shows how this dialogue takes on the structure of a mutual psychotherapy in which each man contributes what the other needs – namely, a partner who recognizes that in the search for truth the goal constantly recedes with each new definite step toward it.

It seems fitting that in a volume dedicated to his memory, Bateson should have the final word. Accordingly I have placed "Body and Mind: A Dialogue" last in the volume. Here the reader will find such things as Bateson's "boot," some sharp thoughts about Descartes, and a parable about a frog that gets boiled alive because it was not "that much alive" to begin with. But it will not do to spoil the dialogue ahead of time by giving too much of it away. Not when there is still time, in a manner of speaking, for the reader to encounter Bateson in all his impertinence just one more time. Who knows? Perhaps, the meeting will make a difference. For the contributors to this volume, Bateson has certainly made a difference. And if the disparate contributions contained here are any indication, the originality and freshness of Bateson's many-faceted approach to human communication is still alive, still opening new doors to pertinent solutions.

Notes

1. Here let me suggest that the example is a residue of design. In his writings, Lewis Carroll was attempting to work out in fantasy many of the problems arising from the Darwinian theory of evolution that would later occupy Bateson.

References

Bateson, G. (1938). *Naven.* Stanford, CA: Stanford University Press.
Bateson, G. (1972). *Steps towards an ecology of mind.* New York: Ballantine Books.
Bateson, G. (1979). *Mind and nature: A necessary unity.* New York: E. P. Dutton.
Berger, M. (1978). *Beyond the double bind.* New York: Brunner/Mazel.
Lifton, R. (1979). *The broken connection.* New York: Simon & Schuster.
Mead, M., & Bateson, G. (1942). *Balinese character: A photographic analysis.* New York: New York Academy of Science.
Russell, B., & Whitehead, A. (1925–1927) *Principia mathematica* (3 Vols.). Cambridge: Cambridge University Press.

I. Mending the connection between mind and society

2. Power, method, and ethics: a reflection on Bateson's "Morale and National Character"

DAVID BAKAN

Gregory Bateson's 1942 paper "Morale and National Character" raises a number of thoughts and concerns about the power, the methods, and the ethics of the social sciences. Although the essay was written some time ago, it can provide us with a fulcrum, if not a model, for some considerations about the place of the social sciences today. I would emphasize this distinction between fulcrum and model. For the paper is not necessarily one to which one might draw attention because it is worthy of emulation in the context of contemporary events and possibilities in the world. However, as a fulcrum, something that one might push against in order to raise oneself, the paper has more to commend it. When Bateson wrote the paper we were reaching for power for survival. Today we reach rather for the wisdom to handle power in order that we might survive.

What is of significance in this paper is the flash of the great power inherent in the social sciences that it provides. It even forces the reader to ask whether the power is proper and ordinate. It triggers a nostalgia for innocence in the reader, some desire to go back to the time before human beings had eaten of the fruit of the tree of knowledge. For the vision of knowledge in the paper is awesome enough that one might think it should not exist at all. The awesome vision makes one think to tie oneself, to ligate oneself – "ligate" and "religion" having common etymologies – to some deep antiintellectual posts planted in the ground of our common culture. On reading it, one may think that we are into Faust pacts or are playing sorcerer's apprentice, or even Dr. Strange-love.

A prior note on confidence in the human intellect. One must resist joining the ranks of those who would see antiintellectualism as being in the service of virtue. If one could ever have argued for virtue being served by any form of antiintellectualism, that time is now past. For we cannot tolerate the poverty and the suffering associated with ignorance. However awesome learning may become, we cannot oppose it. With respect to this paper by Bateson, however offensive one may find it, one has to resist the antiintellectualism that is part of the experience that is aroused in reading it. The tradition to which I would like to ally the reflections in this commentary is that which sees a convergence of the powerful, the appropriate, the valid, and the virtuous in the advancement of learning. Bateson's paper might tempt some away from that conviction. But in spite of the fact that Bateson's paper may make one nervous, one must have faith in the value of the unlimited increase of learning.

The context associated with the writing of the essay is important for our appreciation of it. The essay appeared in a collection of essays entitled *Civilian Morale* (Watson, 1942), which was published by the Society for the Psychological Study of Social Issues.

Bateson's essay has the clear and explicit purpose of raising the "war-making morale" of the English and the Americans. All the considerations and all of the analysis in the paper aim toward providing some specific suggestions whereby the English and the Americans might be persuaded to support the war effort. Bateson's article is wonderfully cogent. The cogency is particularly impressive when it is considered against the general pattern of development of the social sciences in the decades that followed. The paper by Bateson is not particularly empirical, positivistic, operationistic, or behavioral, to use some of the scientific self-congratulatory words of the social science culture of the decades following. It is nonetheless impressively cogent with respect to what it takes as its task.

The book in which the essay appeared was published in 1942. That puts the time of writing quite at the threshold of the U.S. entry into World War II. That war had begun in September 1939. France had fallen to Germany in 1940. But both Franklin Roosevelt and his opponent Wendell Willkie had campaigned in 1940 on promises to keep the United States out of the war. The isolationist sentiment in the United States was very strong. The war-making morale, addressed as the topic of Bateson's essay, was very low.

Roosevelt took steps to increase American belligerency almost immediately after he took office. The Lend–Lease Act was passed in March 1941. In August, the Atlantic Charter was proclaimed. On December 7, 1941, Pearl Harbor was bombed. There is even a widely expressed suspicion that Roosevelt, having information that the Japanese attack was to take place, since by that time the Japanese secret code had been broken, deliberately acted so as not to forestall that attack. On December 8, there was a resolution of war against Japan. On December 11, Germany and Italy declared war against the United States. In 1942 – I do not know precisely what month – the book with Bateson's article in it appeared.

Bateson, in this paper, develops a theoretical structure about "motifs of interpersonal and intergroup relationship as . . . clues to national character." With these motifs, he says, "we have been able to indicate certain orders of regular difference which we may expect to find among the peoples who share our Western civilization." This theoretical structure provides great power to influence people. "From the theoretical structure which we have built up," he says, "it is possible to extract certain formulas which may be useful to the builder of morale" (p. 103).

We cannot avoid noting that Bateson is not quite up to transcending the cynicism that his position brings him to on discovering, at least to his own persuasion, that he has inordinate powers within his hands to modify the behavior of masses of people of the world. "All of the formulas," he says, "are based upon the general assumption that people will respond most energetically when the context is structured to appeal to their habitual patterns of reaction. It is not sensible to encourage a donkey to go up hill by offering him raw meat, nor will a lion respond to grass" (p. 104).

Such remarks are certainly a ground for nervousness. In order to probe the ground of that nervousness one must make a distinction. The distinction is part of the analysis one characteristically makes of someone who is a possible threat. On the one hand, one inquires about intentions. On the other hand, one inquires about ability to carry out intention.

Let me digress to make some observations associated with behaviorism. The behaviorist, starting with the famous pronouncement made by John B. Watson, aims at the "prediction and control" of behavior. The fundamental pattern of the behaviorist has some similarities to that which is expressed by Bateson, as well as some differences. The similarity is a similarity in intention. However, for a variety of reasons, the behaviorist's ability to predict and control human behavior has rarely risen above the level of a comic-opera song of self-praise. The so-called methods of behavior modification arising out of behaviorism may be of some minor usefulness among some school teachers who otherwise have little talent for dealing with children. However, these methods of behavior modification have never even reached the level commonly possessed, say, by retail salespersons working for commissions on sales, or most candidates for public office. A behaviorist's claiming to be able to predict and control behavior is something like a child's engaging in the fantasies of superheroes in comic books: The vaulting abilities of the superheroes are compensatory for the lack of real abilities in the world for these readers of comic books.

One might be tempted to feel a kind of citizen's gratitude to John Watson and the other behaviorists for creating a "dummy" psychology to take the place of a genuine psychology, recognizing that a genuine psychology, in the wrong hands, could be a dangerous thing. The fact that behaviorist psychology dominated the academic departments of psychology of the universities for better than half a century may be regarded as a good thing, given all of the very wicked people in the world who might learn a more powerful psychology and use it for their own wicked ends. Thus, my judgment of behaviorism is that while it may be worrisome in connection with intention, it is not worrisome in connection with ability.

However, while behaviorism may be a dummy science, Bateson's approach to the modification of the attitudes and behavior of masses of people is not dummy science in any sense. Far from it. It is a powerful science. And we have some obligation to examine it carefully.

Let us reflect on the conditions associated with this particular development of Bateson's thought. For we have to look for the source of the license that it seems to possess. And it is quite from the context that the license is derived. Bateson derives a license from a deep conviction that the very existence of the civilized world depends on the entry of the United States into war.

We have to think of this conviction as being of a similar order to that of the physicists making the atom bomb. They knew that a bomb of extraordinary power could be built that was based on the release of the energy in the atom. The physicists sought to bring that possibility to the attention of the government out of a deep sense of duty and obligation. We know the story of how the physicists urged Einstein to write a letter to Roosevelt, in the belief that any letter from the famous Einstein would at least stand a chance of getting attention in the pile of mail that came to the White House; and how from that the atom bomb came into existence. The underlying dynamic is evident. In the face of what is considered an extraordinary danger, an extraordinary license arises to allow thought and to engage in action that would otherwise be quite unacceptable. When the conviction is very strong that the whole of civilization is at stake, there is hardly anything that is not licensed.

In considering this extraordinary license, we might find it valuable to consider also the place of Bateson's thought more generally in society's intellectual life of the last several decades. The fact of the matter is that Bateson's thought has received very little attention. It may be that the publication of this set of essays appreciative of Bateson may have some effect on changing that. But the very neglect of Bateson's thought in, say, the teaching and the research in the social sciences in institutions of higher education is itself something remarkable.

The fate of Bateson's thought is similar to the fate of Freudian thought in being the object of very deliberate neglect in the teaching and research in the social sciences. In the case of Freud, the phenomenon is more dramatic. For although the thought of Freud was a major presence in the intellectual culture at large, the absence of Freudian teaching and research in the departments of psychology and sociology in colleges and universities is a phenomenon whose observation cannot be avoided because of the contrast with the intellectual culture at large. Indeed, the very fact that the psychological part of Bateson's thought was itself very much under the influence of Freud might be considered as we consider the factors associated with this academic neglect.

We consider the possibility that the very power inherent in a mode of thought might be a determining factor in connection with the academic neglect of that mode of thought. We consider how the urge to conceal knowledge is benign. Thus, the argument can be made that librarians should censor books on explosives that might be useful to terrorists. However, we have always to ask whether terrorists do not already have that information; and whether the public interest demands a widespread knowledge about explosives in order that the public may be in a proper position to defend itself against terrorists. We soon conclude that every argument in favor of concealing knowledge is unacceptable. The only reasonable, reliable, and enduring protection against dangerous knowledge is the widest dissemination of that knowledge.

What is the situation with respect to the kind of knowledge represented by this essay by Bateson in the present world? Not with respect to terrorists, but what about persons with strong interests and resources? How much, for example, of the kind of knowledge that is exemplified in the paper by Bateson is available in some way to business and government agencies, on a private basis, from people who serve as employees or consultants? The kind of thought that is exemplified in this paper by Bateson, which combines an understanding of psychoanalytic dynamics with group processes, is regularly used in market research, political polling, and even labor management.

The fact of the matter is that Bateson's thought in this paper has within it two clearly identifiable sets of concepts that are quite unacceptable in the context of the prevalent academic norms for scientificity. The first is Freudian psychoanalytic thought, which we have already mentioned. The second is Bateson's being in a direct line of thought to the idea of the group mind. In 1920 William McDougall had advanced notions of national mind and character in his book *The Group Mind*. Bateson was following McDougall quite directly in bringing this type of thinking to bear on international policy as McDougall (1921, 1931) had expressed it in works such as *Is America Safe for Democracy?* and *World Chaos*. However, the notion of the group mind, which McDougall developed, and which Bateson picked up on, became the target of major opposition in the developing social psychology of the institutions of higher learning in the decades following World War II.

Our understanding of the ideological place of Bateson can be deepened further by looking at the identification of Bateson's thought with that of McDougall, especially for its course in American colleges and universities. McDougall was the major opponent to the behaviorism that had swept over the American academic institutions (see Watson & McDougall, 1929). Behaviorism, as we have indicated, came to fulfil the dummy role in America, being content that was called psychology but that was not psychology, and that served to occupy the place of psychology in teaching and research.

And Bateson was drawing quite openly and directly from Freud for his understanding of the psychological processes of character formation, "especially the processes of projection, reaction formation, compensation, and the like" (p. 91). He took from Freud the existence of conflict within the mind as quite basic. And he used the psychoanalytic notion of introjection, associated with the Oedipus complex of Freud, to characterize the educational processes relevant to his discussion (p. 96).

Group mind, psychoanalysis, nonbehavioristic social science thinking: All of these were quite opposed to the norm of scientificity of the academy. Yet, they were brought out, out of their cages, as it were, at a time of crisis, at a time when great power was needed to deal with what was regarded as a danger to the whole of Western civilization. They were licensed, as we have indicated, when their great power was seen to be a lesser risk than the power of that which they would be called upon to fight.

2.1. Observations about culture and power in the social sciences

What about Bateson's paper suggests the possibility of such power as we are ascribing? We note, to begin with, that Bateson is very aware that what he is advancing is quite different from what is ordinarily taken to be "scientific enquiry." For he begins with a section entitled "Barriers to Any Concept of 'National Character.' " He is quite aware that "scientific enquiry has been diverted from questions of this type by a number of trains of thought which lead scientists to regard all such questions as unprofitable or unsound" (p. 88).

We have to read these remarks by Bateson as a critique of the prevailing norms with respect to what constitutes science. From Bateson's point of view it is the "received view" itself with respect to what constitutes science that is deficient. If, in order to be effective, one has to modify what are claimed to be basic canons of science, claimed and acclaimed by the scientific community, then the critique is of the prevailing enterprise that calls itself scientific. The commonly accepted canons of scientific method are simply not scientific. The scientific community is itself deviant from proper norms of the scientific method.

We then have to consider whether these very canons, although not truly canons of the scientific method, might possibly be canons designed for social safety, perhaps wisely, or perhaps unwisely. A science that is more effective in a certain limited sense may be a more dangerous science, and hence an undesirable science.

Let us proceed, in this section of this reflection, to identify; paraphrase, perhaps with some interpretation; highlight; and generalize some of the observations of Bateson's text.

1. One may observe variation or commonality. The study of variation is the order of the day in the social sciences. But here the enterprise has to be the study of the commonality, rather than the differences. To this there is one great exception – namely, the differences that are particularly relevant to the particular purposes at hand. Differences among Russians, English, Germans, and Americans need to be considered. We consider the differences with respect to such relationships as enmity and alliance, and with respect to finding ways of motivating the members of the different groups toward designated behavior. We study the group mind. Yet we also study the minds of different groups. We consider grouping on the basis of enmities and alliances, as these form and differentiate group minds. We identify group minds with a view to the groups we wish to influence.

2. Differences that do exist, and that result in the appearance of general variation, are not to be thought of as independent of each other.

For sure, observations are not easily matched to the differences in the models of statistical inference, which assumes that observations are independent of each other and provide "degrees of freedom" to the analysis and the statistical inference.

3. Nor should observed variation among organisms be thought of as arising out of origins that are independent of each other, as is done in the theory of natural selection of Darwin. For in the Darwinian theory of natural selection differences come into play only after they have become actual, and not in their origin. The differences play a critical role in the theory in terms of the consequences that arise from them in the theory of natural selection, but they arise quite independently of each other. For Bateson differences exist more dialectically, more as being generated out of situations.

4. The essential subject matter is culture. And culture is learned. The simple fact that culture is learned is a major warrant for the validity of a group mind. For this learning is in and of itself a major factor in reducing variation among the members of a group, forming the members into a group. Thus because people within a culture are taught, say, how to deal with failure, they tend to vary less in the way in which they may deal with failure than in other ways. People are more like soldiers in an army where responses are predictably of low variation quite as a result of the common training that all the soldiers have been subjected to. Just as military training works to reduce variation dramatically, so are the people made common through exposure to a common culture, sharing in the common acculturation process. Thus, Bateson indicates, citing the work of Lewin, Americans respond to failure as a challenge to increase effort, while Germans respond to the same failure with discouragement. These lessons may not necessarily be deliberate or conscious. Yet they are part of the culture of Germans, Americans, and other nationalities. Bateson has little trouble accepting the Freudian idea of the unconscious. The unconscious is something quite patent for the student of culture. Most of the features of a culture are operative without the participants being conscious of it. Indeed, it is often the very contribution of culture to make culture appear as nature rather than culture. And yet, the very contribution of the student of culture is to point out how culture is culture rather than nature.

5. Differences that may exist are part of a system producing stable patterns of interaction. While they may emerge dialectically, they remain because of a dynamic stability of which they become a part. Thus, for example, the sexes differ, and "the habit system or character struc-

ture of one sex is different from that of another." But "the significant point is that the habit system of each sex cogs into the habit system of the other; that the behavior of each promotes the habits of the other" (pp. 90–91).

6. This understanding of the nature of differences applies generally to other groupings. Bateson indicates that "there is . . . no danger in applying this general conclusion to all cases of stable differentiation between groups which are living in mutual contact" (p. 91).

7. It is essential to think of traits as primarily dualistic in nature. That is, it is better to think of the learning of significant dimensions than it is to think of the identification of any individual person or group as being located on a dimension. This is a psychoanalytic notion of considerable power. It was once identified by Jung as the "law of opposites." Wherever the extreme of a trait occurs in a personality, the other extreme also exists within that personality in some sense. Bateson takes this principle from psychoanalysis directly:

> Now, all that we know of the mechanics of character formation – especially the processes of projection, reaction formation, compensation, and the like – forces us to regard these bipolar patterns as unitary within the individual. If we know that an individual is trained in overt expression of one-half of one of these patterns, e.g., in dominance behavior, we can predict with certainty that the seeds of the other half – submission – are simultaneously sown in his personality. We have to think of the individual, in fact, as trained in dominance–submission, not in either dominance or submission. (p. 91)

8. In Bateson's thought, manifest variation is itself a cultural phenomenon, an accident, and a part of the belief system of people. This goes against the general expectation of scientists in the biological and social sciences to see variation as a thing of nature, as Darwin did. He cites the seeming heterogeneity of melting pot communities, such as the great heterogeneous communities of New York City. We could, he indicates, attempt to analyze out all of the motifs of relationships in such a culture: "If we did not end up in the madhouse long before we had completed our study, we should arrive at a picture of common character that would be almost infinitely complex." Rather, he says, let us look at heterogeneity itself, sui generis, as he puts it. And we must note how the culture itself has "clear tendencies toward glorying in heterogeneity for its own sake (as in Robinson Latouche's 'Ballad for Americans') and toward regarding the world as made up of an infinity of disconnected quiz-bits

(like Ripley's 'Believe It or Not')" (p. 92). The same may also be the case with respect to manifest change: "The expectation and experience of change may, in some cases, be so important as to become a common character-determining factor *sui generis*, in the same sort of way that 'heterogeneity' may have positive effects" (p. 93).

9. Bateson makes an explicit case for the use of sharp dualisms. We have to be aware that sharp dualism, "black–white" thinking, has been a major target of criticism in connection with discussions of prejudice. Black–white thinking has been the object of attack all through history as associated with evil and error. Thus, for example, the *Talmud* deals with a rabbi, Elisha ben Abuyah, who, on reading the works of the Greek philosophers, strayed from Judaism. He, however, is credited with having promoted the classical dualistic position following on the Biblical verse from Ecclesiastes 7:14, which says "God hath made even the one as well as the other." This theme of there being an association of wickedness and error with dualism was picked up again in the modern world in the general semantics movement that arose out of the critique of Aristotelian dualism by Alfred Korzybski in his widely read book *Science and Sanity*. (It is of a certain ironic interest that Bateson, in spite of this piece of dualistic celebration, published in *ETC.*, the journal dedicated to promoting the ideas of Korzybski.)

We need to dwell on this dualism before we simply categorize Bateson as being among bigots, apostates from true religion, and promoters of madness. In the history of dualism the fundamental dualism was between good and evil. If we combine a strong ethical conviction with a strong sense of danger, a license for ignoring seemingly fine points emerges. We must again remind ourselves of the context of the writing of this paper. Adolph Hitler was the most wicked tyrant in the history of the world, as well as the most powerful. Thus, the dualism of good and evil was forced to a prominent position. Furthermore, there was a world war raging. In war, another major dualism arises, the dualism of friend and foe. The third category, the category of the neutral, was virtually impossible to maintain. And in this context of dualism, we find Bateson attempting to formulate a social science dualism to have a place among the dualism of good and evil, and friend and foe.

10. Bateson was totally aware of the fact that in the very use of his dualism, he was entering upon a cultural characteristic rather than a universal. He indicates quite clearly that the proneness for dualism is associated with being part of Western culture. It is, he says, a "pattern common in Western cultures; take, for instance, Republican–Democrat,

political Right–Left, sex differentiation, God and the devil and so on. These peoples even try to impose a binary pattern upon phenomena that are not dual in nature – youth versus age, labor versus capital, mind versus matter" (p. 95). However, the power of the dualism is all the more evident quite precisely because we are working with cultures in which such dualism is so normative.

11. The particular dualisms – motifs, he called them – that Bateson chose to consider for the purpose of generating an interest among the Americans to participate in the war were dominant/submissive, exhibitionist/spectator, and succoring/dependent.

12. And from his applications of these motifs to the national character of different nations he drew four practical suggestions:

a. "Since all Western nations tend to think and behave in bipolar terms, we shall do well, in building American morale, to think of our various enemies as a single hostile entity."
b. "Since both Americans and English respond most energetically to symmetrical stimuli, we shall be very unwise if we soft-pedal the disasters of war."
c. One must take account of the differences between Americans and English discovered by analyzing in accordance with motifs. He indicates that a "rather concentrated diet of 'blood, sweat and tears' " might be appropriate for the English, but that Americans "cannot feel their oats when fed on nothing but disaster" (p. 104). The Americans, he indicates, need to be told that they have a "man-sized job on their hands, but they will do well to insist that America is a man-sized nation" (p. 105).
d. He points out that the very vision of peace that is developed in connection with war plays a role in war-making morale. Thus it is necessary to devise a vision of a peace treaty that will make Americans and British willing to fight for it, and will "bring out the best rather than the worst characteristics of our enemies. If we approach it scientifically, such a problem is by no means beyond our skill" (p. 105).

2.2. The role of the intellectual in our society

We have reached to Bateson's considerations bearing on action. And we have a sense of the potentiality in the approach. The issue becomes sharp. If we allow our effectiveness to rise to the level of the possibility that is intimated by Bateson's considerations, there is a new imperative for the bringing to bear of ethical considerations. We try to move from the consideration of Bateson's paper and its context to our own contexts some decades later. We need especially to think about the role of the intellectual in our society.

With respect to ethics, we have to admit to the experience of some ethical vacuum, and even some dismay, as we read Bateson. Reading this today arouses the images of caricatures. Somehow the image of the social scientist is too much Dr. Strangelove, a piece of machinery in a large and comprehensive world-war-making machine; or the image of a cynical, super-Machiavellian Madison Avenue "hidden persuader," capable of influencing the public with respect to the purchases of cat food, voting, ideological conviction, let alone deciding to go to war.

One can, of course, retreat to the normative academic position, which is to insist on two things. First, one is to make a sharp distinction between knowledge and practice in the pursuit of knowledge; that is, to make the pursuit of knowledge "pure." Second, one is to insist that all truth must converge with the good of humankind. We stress these points to ourselves. We insist that the research enterprise is "value-free," and "basic." We hold that our work is immediately ethically neutral, and ultimately ethically good. We even have another argument. Because of the distance we have generated from practice, we insist that the very work itself is superior, in that it is presumably free from bias.

All of this becomes nonsensical if our research works, say, to lead the world into a nuclear conflict. If consequences are so great and unremote, then indifference is immoral. Bateson was not indifferent to the consequences of the enterprise. He, indeed, was acting in the service of his country in what he certainly must have regarded as a virtuous manner. In the modern world the action of a social scientist that in any way increased war-mindedness would be quite a different matter. Since the explosion of the atom bombs at Hiroshima and Nagasaki, many of the physicists and natural scientists have moved toward a heightened responsibility with respect to the use of knowledge. Most recently there have been strong expressions from physicists against the proposed Strategic Defense Initiative, the so-called Star Wars program, of the Reagan administration.

The Bateson paper sharpens our appreciation for the problem with respect to the social sciences. We identify three things in the contemporary world. The first is that which we have been led to appreciate by the flash in the paper by Bateson. It is the potential of the social sciences for effecting massive changes in the political, social, and economic behavior of people. The second is the potentiality for the total annihilation of all civilization, and even all life, on the planet. And the third is the potentiality for plenty that now exists on this very same planet that stands in jeopardy. The latter needs some explanation. In the middle years of the 1980s, for the first time in the history of humankind on the planet, the total world production of food became sufficient to feed all the people on the planet. This goes against all Malthusian considerations. There is now the possibility of lack of want for all human beings on the planet indefinitely into the future. And with the lack of want there should be peace.

What is needed in order to fulfill the potentiality of the third and to prevent the actualization of the potentiality indicated in the second is a giant step in connection with the first potentiality. For it is quite in the areas of social, political, and economic interactions that both the potentialities and the dangers lie. It is precisely the kind of illumination that comes from the flash of Bateson's paper that is required.

If life and civilization are to survive, then it is essential that we take two giant steps. The first has to be a giant step in cooperation on both local and world levels. Locally, there must be greater cooperation among labor, management, and government. Worldwide there must be greater cooperation among governments with a view to finding alternatives to the threat of demolition as a form of influence. The second is a giant step in intellectual activity, and in the bringing to bear of the best of the human intellect for the identification and solution of problems.

Toward achieving these goals we must hide nothing about the nature of human beings and their institutions. There should be a massive increase in social science investigations of every kind. We must be especially alert to the role of culture, even to regard all of our political, social, and economic arrangements as cultural. We must be especially alert to the instrumentality associated with various of our concepts. We must acknowledge the desirability of simplicity in the face of variation, recognizing how variation itself is the product of cultural forces, both in its generation and in its reduction. These are some of the lessons suggested in Bateson's paper.

And one of the most important things that we must see in looking to the future is that the work of the intellect cannot be harmless. Let us put together what we have mentioned already. The intellect produced the atom bomb, and the potentiality now for the total elimination of all life on the planet. The intellect produced the plan for revolutions that have variously became actual for great portions of the world. Then we look at the Bateson paper itself, at how one scholar could sit in his study and think up such considerations as to be able to move the civilian morale toward participation in a world war. We can allow that a modern Bateson might be as effective, or even more effective, in turning the minds of the people in any country capable of nuclear war into actually opening such a war. But equally he might be as effective in turning the minds of people in the direction of the elimination of war altogether, and in providing the plenty that is possible to all.

Let us consider some of the historical models of the relationship of intellect to human affairs a bit more closely. We must come to an understanding of the relationship different from that which was useful in the past.

The ambivalence of our culture about knowledge is manifested in the very existence of the most classical of all legends, that humans engaged in the greatest of sins by eating the fruit from the tree of knowledge. That theme of the wickedness of knowledge, as compared with faith, became firm in Christian history with Augustine. The power of knowledge has been well recognized. Even Augustine told of the great powers of Faust in connection with natural events, albeit he was associated with the devil. Francis Bacon proclaimed that knowledge is power. But the contrary forces have also been strong, toward suppressing and caging intellectual activity. One of the great forces in caging intellectual activity was manifested in connection with the foundation of the Royal Society, the society over which Newton presided. But let us consider some other models.

There is a model of Marx in the nineteenth century. Here we have an image of a scholar sitting for the better part of a decade in one of the great libraries of the world, the British Museum, reading, thinking, and writing and laying out the analysis of society and writing books that have become handbooks for revolutionaries, some of them very successful. We do not address the substance of Marx's work. Our interest in it is as a model of a relationship between intellectual effort and human affairs. At the very least, no one can deny the consequentiality of that intellectual activity, however much we may judge it to be good or bad. This model involves at least the following: First, it is to study the condition of human living in a way that includes the consideration of human intellection itself as a critical part of the subject matter of investigation. Second, it is to study the condition of human living by recognizing that human political existence is essential to human being. Third, it is to study the condition of human living deeply in terms of history, ends, resources, and constraints; to attempt to identify features that might lend themselves to being part of a strategy; and to design a strategy. Fourth, this particular model is associated with a most extraordinary confidence in the powers of human intellection to know the facts of the human condition, to understand the deepest ends and workings of human individuals and society, and to design and choose appropriate strategies. Sitting thus in the library did not take great courage. For us, however, the pressure that arises out of the danger in the contemporary world must bring us at least to courage in the use of human intellection, even if we lack in appropriate confidence.

We pin this Marx-in-the-British-Museum model up next to the contemporary academic model, the one in which a sharp separation between intellectual activity and human affairs is drawn. And we hold the model suggested by Bateson in our hands. The features we have identified in the Marxist model are consonant. We would have to pin Bateson closer to Marx than to the run of social science academics. Indeed, Bateson's paper is hardly of a kind that might appear in, say, any of the usual academic journals.

It will profit us to dwell on the formation in Great Britain in 1660 of the scientific society the Royal Society of London for the Improvement of Natural Knowledge, commonly referred to as the Royal Society. The important feature for our attention is that the charter establishing the Royal Society made it explicit that the members were to refrain from involving themselves in politics and religion in return for the privileges granted by the charter. As a consequence the dissociation from politics became the virtual definition of objectivity in the history of science. From the seventeeth century onward the Royal Society, and societies like it, constituted the major forums and publication sources for scientific material. The basic pattern, which we may still recognize as the academic model we have described, has its origin in this source. It is this model of intellectuality, of scientific investigation, that we have particularly to work against in the modern world.

An earlier moment in history that we identify as important to our understanding is the encounter of Augustine with Faustus, a Manichean bishop, and recorded by him in his *Confessions* in the fifth century. The conflict between the emphasis on faith in Christianity and the exercise of human intellect has to be noted. We have also to take note of the very powerful antiintellectual feature of Western civilization, especially as this was expressed by the very influential Augustine. Faust, a "great snare of the Devil," was the intellectual. Augustine describes his fame for being "most knowing in all valuable learning, and exquisitely skilled in the liberal sciences." This knowledge, Augustine explains, shows how one can predict years ahead

> eclipses of . . . the sun and the moon, – what day and hour, and how many digits, – nor did their calculation fail; and it came to pass as they foretold. . . . At these things men, that know not this art,

marvel and are astonished, and they that know it, exult, and are puffed up; and by an ungodly pride departing from Thee, and failing of Thy light, they foresee a failure of the sun's light, which shall be, so long before, but see not their own, which is. (Pusey, 1951, pp. 65–66)

The world did, however, become Faustian again after the compact made between the king and the members of the Royal Society. The traditional conflict between intellectualism and antiintellectualism was expressed again in the eighteenth century by Marlowe, and then by Goethe in his epic drama. The compact between Faust and the devil may have been purely fictional in drama. However, there was an actual compact of greater significance for the question in the charter of the Royal Society. That was the compact that the intellectual work and the freedom of expression of investigators would be protected so long as they abstained from politics. That has been the compact in effect since the foundation of the Royal Society.

Our understanding can be deepened even further by considering the historical background behind that compact struck in the seventeenth century. We consider the period in the thirteenth century when the great universities were established, the University of Paris, Oxford University, and the others. Largely through the mediation of Muslim and Jewish scholars Europe rediscovered the writings of the Greeks in the thirteenth century. Most important were the writings of "the philosopher," Aristotle. The university became an institution built around the writings of the philosopher. There is an abiding reminder of this in that even teachers in the modern university have the Doctor of Philosophy degree. They almost literally built the university around Book 10, Chapter 7, of the *Nichomachean Ethics,* which advocates contemplation as the highest activity that humans can engage in. Reason is something divine in humans. Its exercise is the highest kind of virtue. We should even strive to exercise our reason as "to make ourselves immortal, and strain every nerve to live in accordance with the best thing in us. . . . [F]or man . . . the life according to reason is best and pleasantest, since reason more than anything else is man."

However – and this is the point that must be stressed – the *Nichomachean Ethics* begins by defining human nature as political. And while it does advocate the contemplative life, it does so in combination with the idea that humans are political. Contemplation and politics are integral to one another. The contemplative life is the end of politics; and the political life is enhanced by the overflow of the contemplative life.

Then, of course, we come to the seventeenth century. Aristotle is overthrown. Newtonian cosmology replaces the Aristotelian cosmology. And instead of a great union of the contemplative life with the political life, the members of the Royal Society are given the privilege of contemplation on condition that they do not involve themselves in the political life of the community.

The point of this is to suggest that it may well be the season for a return to that vision of an integration of politics with intellectuality that characterized the thought of the ancient Greeks, and the thought of those who were able to transcend the antiintellectualism that had been carried within the church. That, of course, did not last too long, becoming "scholastic" in the sense that was quite the opposite of the sense of union of politics and intellectuality represented in Aristotle's *Nichomachean Ethics* or Plato's *Republic*. It is quite the modern academic scientists who are the scholastics. If we look at Bateson as somehow yet expressing the possibility and the value of the union of intellectuality and politics, we are not too much off the mark.

References

Bateson, G. (1942). Morale and national character. *Steps to an ecology of mind* (pp. 88–106). New York: Ballantine, 1972.

Civilian morale. (1942). In G. Watson (Ed.), Yearbook of the Society for the Psychological Study of Social Issues. Boston: Houghton Mifflin.

McDougall, W. (1920). *The group mind.* Cambridge: Cambridge University Press.

McDougall, W. (1921). *Is America safe for democracy?* New York: Scribner.

McDougall, W. (1932). *World chaos: The responsibility of science.* New York: Covici Friede.

Pusey, E. B. (Tr.). (1951). *Confessions of St. Augustine.* New York: Washington Square Press.

Watson, J. B., & McDougall, W. (1929). *The battle of behaviorism: An exposition and an exposure.* New York: Norton.

3. The psychopathy of everyday life: antisocial behavior and social distress

ROBERT W. RIEBER AND MAURICE GREEN

The psychopath may indeed be the perverted and dangerous front-runner of a new kind of personality which could become the central expression of human nature before the twentieth century is over.

> —Norman Mailer, "The White Negro," *Voices of Dissent*

Of all the recognized psychiatric syndromes, that of the antisocial personality, or psychopath, presents perhaps the greatest number of unsolved questions. Although it has long been recognized that each of us possesses an innate capacity for momentary dissociation vis-à-vis the accepted value systems of society, and thus in that degree is potentially psychopathic, true psychopaths, with their consistently antisocial behavior, present the average observer with a phenomenon so spectacularly alien that it seems almost incredible that such people can exist. And, granted that psychopaths do indeed exist, it is perplexing how they can manage to appear superficially sane, how they are able to wear, as one observer put it, the "mask of sanity." The true psychopath compels the psychiatric observer to ask the perplexing, and largely unanswered, question: "Why doesn't that person have the common decency to go crazy?"

Given the mixture of awe, horror, and perplexity that the true psychopath evokes, it is perhaps not surprising that research into the etiology, course, and psychological mechanisms specific to this syndrome has lagged far behind that of other psychiatric classifications. When we have such difficulty grasping the essentials of the presenting picture, we can only have greater difficulty in finding an overall interpretive scheme around which to organize our research questions. Indeed, we know far too little about how the psychopathic character structure comes about, how it utilizes social experience to perpetuate its fundamentally antisocial outlook, and how it often manages to secure highly stable social niches in which both accomplices and subgroup prestige can be found.

In what follows, the authors will attempt to arrive at a preliminary taxonomy of the essential psychological and interpersonal processes underlying the behavior of the true psychopath and then use that taxonomy as a point of departure for investigating patterns of antisocial behavior currently evolving in the society at large. It is the authors' contention that there has been a general trend toward a greater degree of normalized, or socially acceptable, antisocial behavior in our society generally – the psychopathy of everyday life – and that this trend in turn can be meaningfully related to an increase of what will be termed "social distress."

3.1. Historical background

The tendency to view moral failure as illness, instead of as sin or as an expression of some evil principle inherent in the universe, is scarcely new to the Western world. The ancient Greeks considered that certain kinds of behavior, either antisocial or else not in the individual's self-interest, were plainly caused by forces outside the individual. Homer, in the eighth century B.C., portrayed humans as subject to the whims of the gods; the gods acted upon humans by affecting their feeling center, or *thymos*, which was thought to reside under the sternum more or less in the area of the thymus gland. The Homeric formula for describing rash, ill-considered, or antisocial behavior typically had it that this or that god put madness in one's breast; alternatively, it was said that Zeus, or whoever, had taken away one's understanding.

Some twenty-seven hundred years later, in 1809, Pinel introduced the term "insanity *sans délire*," subsequently taken up by Morel (1857), to indicate an illness affecting the moral part of one's being. As a classificatory term, "insanity without delirium" opened the way for first "psychopathy," then "sociopathy," and more recently "antisocial personality" as means of indicating an illness of the moral part of one's being that was largely manifested by behavior injurious to fellow humans, though, as a matter of fact, Pinel applied his term to cases that today would be diagnosed as forms of bipolar affective disorder, or manic–depressive insanity. It fell to an Englishman, James Pritchard (1837), who was a disciple of Pinel's, to be the first to describe a more circumscribed kind of disorder that he termed "moral insanity": "madness, consisting in a morbid perversion of the natural feelings, affections, inclinations, temper, habit, moral disposition, and natural impulses, without any remarkable [*sic*, i.e., observable] disorder or defect of the intellect or knowing and reasoning faculties, and particularly without any insane illusions or hallucinations" (p. 16).

Walker and McCuble (1972) have been able to trace the history of the notion of moral insanity from Pritchard's term all the way to the early twentieth-century term "psychopathy." As it happened, Pritchard's (1842) case histories almost without exception ascribed the onset of the disorder to a specified illness or traumatic event. But, among Pritchard's contemporaries and his immediate successors within English psychiatry, the term "moral" was delimited by the exclusion of any kind of physical injury, organic disease, or other physical factors as contributory causes. Thus "moral" came to refer specifically to the emotional aspects of insanity and "moral insanity" to serious mental disorders *not* characterized by hallucinations, delusions, or manifest disorders of thinking.

On the continent, however, Griesinger (1882) borrowed Pritchard's term and used it to designate and describe a group of retarded patients, whom Griesinger termed "weak minded" and who were prone to mischievious, cruel, thieving, and drunken criminal behavior. Griesinger supposed these traits to be hereditary in nature. Under the influence of Henry Maudsley, this notion subsequently came to play a role in the legislation of the Royal Commission on the Care and Control of the Feeble Minded, which in 1913 described "moral imbeciles" as "persons who from an early age display some permanent mental defect coupled with strong vicious or criminal propensities and on which punishment has had little or no effect" (Walker & McCuble, 1972). In 1927, further legislation was passed in which "moral imbecility" was redefined as obtaining "In whose case there exists mental defectiveness coupled with strongly vicious or criminal propensities and who require care, supervision and control for the protection of others" (Walker & McCuble 1972). The significance of this redefinition is twofold: The ineffectiveness of punishment has been dropped as a criterion, and there is no reference to any kind of treatment as potentially effective. Nonetheless, the term was not to be applied in cases that failed to show any limitation of intelligence, even though there might otherwise be an utter lack of any kind of inhibition, restraint, or other evidence of conscience with regard to criminal behavior. The accepted nosological system had thus developed a striking lacuna with regard to nonimbecilic moral insanity.

It was in this general context that the German psychiatrist Koch (1891) introduced the term "constitutional psychopathic inferiority." Koch's term covered not only instances of criminality not covered under "moral imbecility" but also neurasthenia, compulsions, impulse disorders, and sexual perversions. For a considerable period of time thereafter, the term "psychopathic" continued to refer to a wide range of nonpsychotic disorders. Indeed, minus the implication of hereditary causation, and minus, too, the group now known as psychopaths, the term had roughly the same wide range as did the term that succeeded it and that has itself only lately been abandoned – "neurotic."

It is not altogether clear just when "psychopathic" was first used to refer exclusively to antisocial behavior, though it is clear that this usage came gradually into medical currency during the end of the nineteenth century and the early part of the twentieth. There is some evidence to suggest that in at least one American city, Boston, the gradual delimitation of the term was part and parcel of changing modes of state-sponsored mental health intervention. Specifically, as social workers came to be widely employed as agents of social control in the first decade of the new century, the term "psychopathic" became a diagnostic warrant for forcibly hospitalizing two groups of "patients" considered to be socially deviant: single working women who were promiscuous and inadequate men who shunned work. Thus did Koch's term come to be applied, at least in Boston, predominantly to social deviants.

In the United States generally, psychiatric interest in criminals received its greatest impetus from the comprehensive investigations of Bernard Glueck and his associates. Nonetheless, it is David Henderson, a Scottish disciple of Adolf Meyer, who is generally credited with establishing the modern concept of the psychopath in both European and American psychiatry. Henderson's (1939) diagnostic scheme divided psychopaths into three subgroups: (1) a predominantly aggressive type (redolent in many respects of Pinel's concept of moral insanity as well as of Koch's, and Kraepelin's, concepts of psychopathic inferiority); (2) a predominantly inadequate type, which included liars, swindlers, assorted petty criminals, and the like; and (3) a predominantly creative type. (This last group derived from the theories of Lombroso and Moebius, theories widely popularized by the writer Max Nordau, which saw genius and great artistic ability as symptoms of hereditary degeneration and thus as prima facie evidence of disordered cerebral functioning. The hallmark of genius in this scheme was the reliance on certain runaway thoughts or inclinations that were unimpeded by the ordinary inhibitions imposed by common sense, decency, and moral judgment.)

Unlike some of his predecessors, Henderson elected to make his notion of psychopathy purely behavioral; the diagnosis neither excluded nor entailed the existence of contributory organic factors. In this spirit, he described a number of electroencephalographic studies showing a high frequency of brain abnormalities in his aggressive subtype. This led to a very heated legal debate, since the possibility arose that a diagnosis of psychopathy, with or without a correlative finding of brain abnormality, might be used to establish a defense of diminished responsibility. Generally speaking, in the English courts, a diagnosis of psychopathy did gradually win status as potentially part of an acceptable defense, though the chance of winning an acquittal on this basis remained extremely low.

In the United States in this century, the term "psychopath" gradually fell into diagnostic disfavor on the basis of the opinion, held by Harry Stack Sullivan among others, that the pathology was expressed predominantly in the individual's social relations. As Sullivan (1953) saw it, such persons exhibited a massive incapacity to profit from social experience. Accordingly, beginning in the late 1920s, the term was gradually replaced by the seemingly more precise "sociopath" in the official nomenclature, though among the general public the more vivid "psychopath" still prevails as the term in general currency. "Psychopath" has entered the common language as an epithet with which to deride the moral fiber of one's enemies or people one dislikes. It is used now in legal, professional, and academic circles, as well as by the general public, to refer perjoratively to those who care only about advancing their own material interests and who are willing to do whatever they can get away with. In the most recent revamping of the standard diagnostic system, meanwhile, "sociopath" has yielded to the term "antisocial personality." In part, "sociopath" fell because of its intrinsic relation to the term that it was meant to supersede; insofar as "sociopath" was following "psychopath" into common currency to cover a wide spectrum of behavior, it was no longer suitable for the psychiatric nomenclature.

3.2. Psychopathy today

For purposes of this discussion, the term "psychopathy" is to be preferred precisely because of its wide range of meanings in ordinary parlance. For what we will presently be concerned with is a whole continuum of behavior ranging from what might be called "normal psychopathy" or "pseudopsychopathy" all the way to the horrific extreme represented by the "antisocial personality," or "true psychopath." Cleckley pointed out as early as 1941, in his *Mask of Sanity*, that each of us possesses in rudimentary degree the distinctively psychopathic capacity *not* to respond to the salient moral or social requirements of a situation. A gang of unruly 12-year-olds cutting up during a school outing to Carnegie Hall to hear Mozart are behaving psychopathically, notes Cleckley, as are we all when we momentarily break ranks with our conscience to laugh at what we otherwise hold in highest reverence. Nor is such a capacity intrinsically bad. To paraphrase a point made by Cleckley, were it not for this ability to break ranks with our conscience occasionally, we would all be in danger of turning into pompous monsters of self-righteousness.

This said, it is important that we first acquaint ourselves with the extreme pole of the continuum represented by the "true psychopath." This term indicates something more than a tendency to care about others only as means to one's own self-centered aims; it indicates a *lack of capacity* to do otherwise. The true psychopath is lost to humanity, utterly incapable of human concern and involvement with others except at the most superficial and exploitative level.

It is important to distinguish the true psychopath from the career criminal, at least as an ideal type. (There is plainly overlap.) Career criminals rely on superior strength and cunning to gain wealth; they feed their ego on the fear they evoke and on their own ability to get things "done" outside the encumbrances of the law. Nonetheless, such people are quite capable of feeling empathy and concern for their immediate family and for their partners in crime. Moreover, they rely on the support of others and are capable of erecting and adhering to quite formal procedures for inclusion within the peer group. They are concerned with winning admiration and praise from their criminal partners, and they speak in derogatory and contemptuous terms of their victims. In short, they manifest salient characteristics of group identification and group loyalty. True psychopaths, by contrast, are typically a bust even as members of an organized criminal ring; they cannot be relied on, they make unnecessary trouble, and though they may be useful for carrying out specific acts of an unusually unseemly nature, there is no question of obtaining their long-term loyalty. When trouble arises, the psychopaths are the first to go, something that career criminals understand and for which they typically plan expeditious means. (As this book goes to press, New York City police are still investigating the murder in a midtown Manhattan restaurant of one Irwin Schiff, wheeler-dealer and con man extraordinaire; the further the investigation proceeds into the incredible trail of extortion, bribery, and swindles that is this man's sole legacy, the harder it has become to fix a single motive for his death. Seemingly everybody who ever knew him, including career criminals and ordinary businessmen, had something to gain by killing this man.)

Some progress in portraying the psychopath at a phenomenological, descriptive level has been made in the third edition of the *Diagnostic and Statistical Manual of Mental Disorders* of the American Psychiatric Association. Among the diagnostic criteria needed to merit a diagnosis of antisocial personality are an inability to sustain consistent work; an inability to function as a responsible parent (evidenced by such things as not feeding children adequately and failing to obtain medical care for a seriously sick child); failure to respect the law (pimping, drug dealing, fencing); inability to maintain an enduring attachment to a sexual partner (desertion, promiscuity); failure to honor financial obligations; failure to plan ahead (impulsive traveling without prearranged job, destination, or time limit); aggressiveness (assault, wife beating, child abuse); disregard for the truth (aliases, conning); and recklessness (drunk driving). We have here a catalog of human evil; it takes the presence of at least four out of the nine criteria over a sustained period of time to merit the diagnosis, *plus* an onset before the age of 15 as manifested by a childhood history marked by such behavior as persistent lying, vandalism, theft, chronic fighting, truancy, repeated substance abuse, poor educational achievement, and so forth. (As well, a diagnostic point that need not concern us further, the behavior must not be due to mental retardation, schizophrenia, or manic episodes.)

DSM-III declares that although such antisocial individuals may present a stereotypically normal mental status, most frequently there are signs of personal distress – including complaints of tension and depression, an inability to tolerate boredom, and the conviction of the hostility of others (which to be sure is a predictable consequence of their own behavior). The interpersonal difficulties these people experience and the discordant moods that they suffer persist far into midlife and beyond, even though their more flagrantly antisocial behavior, most especially assaultiveness, typically begins to diminish by the time they pass 45 or 50 years of age. Invariably there is a markedly impaired capacity to sustain any kind of lasting, close, normal relationship with family, friends, or sexual partners. Such individuals, in fact, generally cannot become independent, self-supporting adults without persistent criminal activity and outside of the penal system. However, some who warrant this diagnosis are able to achieve some degree of political or economic success – the "adaptive psychopaths" – and to outward appearances their day-to-day functioning is not characterized by the impulsivity, hostility, and general chaos that typify the general syndrome.

The problem of the adaptive psychopath is especially elusive, since such people come to psychiatric attention late and only after they have run seriously afoul of the law. (And an indeterminate number of them, an elite subgroup, have simply never been caught; thus, they have never been examined psychiatrically.) Accordingly, it is impossible to get a clear picture of how they functioned during their period of ostensibly normal adjustment. Apparently, whether by virtue of superior endowment or because their survival was facilitated by adopting an outwardly compliant facade, their educational development was substantially less hampered than is typically the case. Theodore Bundy, the notorious serial killer who was executed in Florida in 1988, had finished law school and become active in California politics. His truly horrifying career as the nation's most prolific serial murderer was incomprehensible to many who knew him during this phase of his life, though even then his temper was considered hair-trigger. Nonetheless, it should be observed that, although the enigma of the adaptive psychopath remains largely unsolved, such people are known to show certain hallmarks of the general syndrome, most especially the characteristic search for thrill seeking through dangerous behavior, an attitude of omnipotence typically expressed in a feeling that they will never get caught, and an innate dissociative capacity that among other things enables them to demarcate periods of frankly antisocial behavior from their "normal" periods.

We might note in passing how many of the points raised in previous diagnostic schemes are echoed in the contemporary diagnostic criteria. Thus *DSM-III* subdivides the prodromal phase of a childhood "conduct disorder" into four subdivisions: unsocialized aggressive, socialized aggressive, unsocialized nonaggressive, and socialized nonaggressive. The first and third of these subgroups clearly invoke two of Henderson's subgroups, his aggressive and inadequate types. Then, too, the early onset of the syndrome – before age 15 – coupled with the typical, though not invariant, lack of educational achievement is suggestive of the hereditary taint of older systems; this observed lack of achievement would superficially appear to be linked to a general incapacity in intellectual functioning. (The elusive adaptive psychopath, meanwhile, is reminiscent of the genius–criminal of Nordau's typology.) As well, though such a finding has no status in the contemporary diagnosis per se, Henderson's observation of frequent nonspecific brain abnormalities continues to be borne out with observations on a portion of this population. And finally, the overall lack of concern with others, manifest in every facet of life, coupled with the remarkable failure to learn from experience, is indeed suggestive of an intrinsic defect for which "moral imbecility" is an altogether apt term. As for the implicit realization of the Royal Commission on the Feeble Minded that *all* treatment proved ineffective, this, too, has been confirmed by subsequent clinicians. Harry Stack Sullivan (1953a) summed up his experience thus:

> I am afraid I cannot overcome my conviction that the real psychopathic personality is a very serious miscarriage of development quite early in life, so grave that it makes a very favourable outcome possible only with an almost infinite amount of effort, which in turn, I guess no one will ever be worth. By and large, I expect to find the psychopathic personality already clearly marked off, and expect it to continue without any great change except for a slow increase in the amount of hostility that it engenders in others and the bitterness, and sometimes alcoholism, which it engenders in the person himself. (p. 360 n.)

3.3. The Mephisto syndrome

In what follows, we will attempt to identify the salient characteristics of the psychopathic syndrome with a view to establishing a taxonomy of psychopathic processes. Several points need to be made at the outset. We are far from believing that the underlying cognitive, conative, and emotional processes described below are unique to the psychopath; rather, we believe in the first place that they represent gross exaggerations of tendencies to be found in everyone and in the second place that even in their pathologically exaggerated form they are not unique to this syndrome. (For example, the kind and quality of dissociative processes exhibited by the psychopath can also be found in multiple personality.) No, what is unique to the psychopath in our view is the specific combination of these processes; it is the combination that discriminates true psychopathy from other syndromes. This said, it should also be noted that we are far from believing that ours is the last word on the subject. Much research needs to be done, particularly in the areas of potentially predisposing neuropsychological factors and etiologically significant environmental variables. It is enough for our purposes if the following discussion captures some of what is essential to psychopathy and does so in a way that allows meaningful generalization to what we term "the psychopathy of everyday life."

Let us begin at the level of discriminating characterological traits and then subsequently work our way down to the underlying processes. In our view, the following four salient characteristics – thrill seeking, pathological glibness, antisocial pursuit of power, and absence of guilt – distinguish the true psychopath.

Thrill seeking

These people habitually rush in where angels fear to tread. The more dangerous an undertaking, the more irresistible it becomes. This behavior cannot be classified as merely impulsive since it often entails planning and, in a surprisingly large number of cases, the cooperation of an accomplice. But such planning as does occur does not mitigate the element of danger. There is some evidence to suggest that psychopaths have unusually high thresholds for perceptual stimulation. Certainly, their overt behavior suggests that only in situations of threat and danger do they feel truly alive. The world of predictable cause and effect, of instrumental acts and expectable rewards, has no emotional meaning to them; they can grasp that this humdrum, predictable, and boring world exists, but they cannot relate to it. (Adaptive psychopaths have taken this to a paradoxical extreme: They can go about their routine duties successfully precisely because they have turned them into a dangerous game of charades, of passing for normal, while in their off-hours they live an entirely different life.) Much of what has been observed, by Sullivan and others, of psychopaths' inability to learn from experience needs to be related to this characteristic: Life would be less dangerous, and thus altogether less fun for psychopaths, if they really allowed themselves to "learn" and thus to "know" the altogether likely consequences of their behavior. True psychopaths prefer an open-ended world: Whether they take off in their car cross-country with no planned destination or time of arrival, or merely say something shocking and outrageous in conversation, they are looking to create situations of ambiguity and potential danger.

We might pause here to distinguish psychopathic thrill seeking from the pursuit of excitement that normal people use to offset boredom. On a continuum of thrills, one might rate tennis relatively low and ice hockey, with its sanctioned violence, relatively high. But for true psychopaths even ice hockey is boring – too many rules. Psychopathic thrill seeking consists in *breaking* the rules, whatever they might be, or else in surreptitiously making up new rules. At a poker table, psychopaths do not want to win; they want to cheat – and get away with it. That is, they want to turn the game into a new game, where they make the rules. These people invariably rush in where angels fear to tread; theirs is the "Mephisto Waltz" on the tightrope of danger.

Pathological glibness

Psychopaths invariably speak well, colorfully, persuasively, and volubly about themselves and their past (though only minimally about their future). What is said, however, has no discernible relation to facts.[1] There is a kind of "semantic dementia," as Cleckley (1976) has termed it. Cleckley's point was that the ordinary emotional demands of a situation make no impression on psychopaths; like rowdy schoolboys at a concert, they behave as if the accepted meanings of a situation simply were not there. But the same dissociation is also manifest in their speech; words have become detached from meaning and serve instead as means of placating a dangerous foe or of fleecing an unwary victim. By the same token, they do not allow themselves to be moved by words and concepts that their fellow citizens value. Consider the psychopath who was asked, out of the interviewer's exasperation, did he not have any compassion for his victims. "The only place you find compassion," the interviewer was told, "is in the dictionary – between 'shit' and 'sucker'."

It is sometimes said that pathological glibness is to be found only in intelligent psychopaths. To the contrary, what distinguishes intelligent psychopaths is their greater productivity and their greater effort at maintaining consistency. The basic trait, however, can be found at all levels of intelligence within the syndrome. Thus the experience of one of the authors with an institutionalized, borderline-retarded psychopath: Having just raped a fellow patient, this fellow promptly accosted the author at the door of the ward with a moving tale of woe of how the attendants were planning to gang up on him for no good reason.

Antisocial pursuit of power

Not only are psychopaths extremely sensitive to power relationships, and extremely interested in obtaining maximum power for themselves, but they seem hell-bent on using that power for destructive ends. Only in paranoid states and in the attitudes of career criminals can a comparable fusion of antisocial trends with the power drive be seen. It is as though, for psychopaths, power can be experienced only in the context of victimization: If they are to be strong, someone else must pay. There is no such thing, in the psychopathic universe, as the merely weak; whoever is weak is also a sucker; that is, someone who demands to be exploited. Thus, when inmates seized control of the New Mexico State Penitentiary some years ago, they engaged not only in murder but also in mutilation of selected victims. Afterward, one of the suspected ringleaders was interrogated at length: While being careful not to incriminate himself, he made it clear that the victims of the uprising "didn't understand morality". He also made it implicity clear that he and his cronies ran the prison anyway and that, apart from the freedom to leave, they enjoyed every advantage they had enjoyed on the outside. The prisoners, given room to maneuver by legal reforms designed to safeguard their rights, had in effect created a psychopathic universe in which the strong preyed on the weak in the name of "morality." To be sure, the fusion of the power drive with antisocial trends in the psychopath need not always be so bloodthirsty (violence per se is *not* a distinguishing trait of the syndrome). Consider the young man who explained that he stole cars because it was the only thing he was good at – and everyone needs to be good at something.

Absence of guilt

Psychopaths are aware that certain people at certain times will bring punitive sanctions to bear against them. Accordingly, they are skilled in evasion and rationalization. Some, gifted histrionically, can even feign remorse. But they do not feel guilt. The absence of guilt is essential to the syndrome for, as is immediately apparent upon reflection, guilt, besides being a consequence of certain acts in normal people, is also a powerful deterrent against committing those same acts in the future. Psychopaths are undeterred; indeed, just those salient characteristics that to others would portend guilt as a consequence, to psychopaths portend the excitement of danger. And when psychopaths are caught, they are in a profound sense uncomprehending. Moreover, when one investigates the absence of guilt clinically, one discovers a poverty of affective reactions generally. The young man who stole cars could distinguish only two feelings in himself, boredom and inadequacy; all other feelings were "for suckers."

If we combine these four characteristics – the absence of guilt, the antisocial pursuit of power, superficial glibness, and thrill seeking – we have what might perhaps best be called the "Mephisto Syndrome." Indeed, it is hard to resist the impression that the true psychopath is a personification of the demonic. Since time immemorial humankind has outlined in figures of the demonic an inherently human capacity to fuse despair and drive discharge in an antisocial posture; the devil has always been important to humans as a personification of what as intrinsically social creatures they cannot afford to be. But it is precisely the inhibiting sense of being *intrinsically* social – Adler's capacity for social feeling – that psychopaths lack. They are not social, only superficially gregarious; not considerate, just polite; not self-respecting, only vain; not loyal, only servile – and down deep they are really quite shallow. In a word, they are fundamentally asocial beings. Hence the observed homologies with the figures of the demonic: The psychopath is free to be what ordinary humans dare not be. For ordinary humans, the figure of the devil is always experienced as a projection, as something outside the ego. For the psychopath, the demonic is a way of life. Moreover, just as the devil has evolved through the centuries and has in the process of that evolution acquired a whole host of representations ranging from the truly bestial all the way to the suave silk-clad sophisticate of the comedy *Damn Yankees* and the philosophic troublemaker of George Burns's portrayal in *Oh God, You Devil,* so too can the presenting facade of the psychopath range from the grotesquely animallike all the way to the sweet-talking confidence man.

Indeed, since like the devil psychopaths are inherently asocial, they are difficult to comprehend within the confines of ordinary human morality. From a theological point of view, the true psychopath, like Lucifer, goes beyond the categories of evil and sin; theologically, the true psychopath is incapable of receiving the Holy Spirit and thus incapable of forming any relationship to God or humans. These are the souls who reside in Dante's *Inferno*, these the damned of Jonathan Edwards' theology. Not feeling guilt, not feeling remorse, psychopaths enter the confessional as they enter psychotherapy – only when it serves some other purpose, typically that of evading punishment.

To be sure, such visitors from another moral world are intrinsically fascinating. We can see this in our daily papers. A Bundy or a Bianchi (the "Hillside Strangler") is the stuff of tabloid headlines and made-for-television movies. But here as with other topics tabloid writers lack the psychological depth to explore their material past a few sensational details plus the inevitable body count. A detailed portrait of the psychopathic mind requires genius, and one should consult either Shakespeare's *Richard III* or George Bernard Shaw's dramatic sequence, "Don Juan in Hell." (Such are the exigencies of the material, incidentally, that both plays require great acting to come alive. Only an Olivier, or a George C. Scott, can make the audience believe that having killed a woman's father and husband, Richard now proposes to seduce her while simultaneously admitting to his crimes. Psychopaths would consider this a challenge worthy of their grandiosity; most mortals, and most actors, consider it a plain impossibility and thus an unplayable scene.)

But if we can set aside our fascination, we must ask ourselves what are the ordinary human psychological processes at work in the psychopath that generate this personification of the demonic. Let us begin with the antisocial pursuit of power, taking as our point of departure an idea of Gregory Bateson's. Bateson has proposed a distinction between symmetrical and complementary interactions. In symmetrical interactions, a given behavior leads to the same behavior in the other, which in turn becomes a signal for an increased amount of the triggering behavior in the first. Situations of mutual threat are an example of symmetrical interaction. In complementary interactions, however, the behavior of one participant evokes a reciprocal behavior in the respondent; dominance, for example, evokes submission. If we ask what exactly constitutes power in this frame of reference, it is immediately clear that power resides not in the individual but in the system of complementary interactions that identify that individual as dominant within the group. The power of the dominant individual resides in the group. Power, in short, is an abstraction pertaining to complex group processes: "It is not so much 'power' that corrupts as the myths of 'power.'. . .'Power' like 'energy,' 'tension,' and the rest of the quasi-physical metaphors are to be distrusted and among them 'power' is one of the most dangerous. He who covets a mythical abstraction must always be insatiable!" (Bateson, 1979, p. 21). To be distinguished from the power of any individual within the group is the power of the group itself, whether it be family, community, political faction, social–economic unit, or nation. The power of the group is real power; if properly organized the group can accomplish things well beyond the power of any individual. The individuals, for their part, participate in the exercise of group power through identification. And this indentification is likely to be all the stronger when the group is behaving aggressively toward another group. Every fall, stadiums fill up around the country as people root passionately for their favorite football team; it is a blatant, altogether normal occasion in which an identification with a powerful and aggressive group, be they the Los Angeles Raiders or the Duke Blue Devils, can be indulged.

Psychopaths, by contrast, appear to situate themselves altogether differently vis-à-vis the group. Rather than adopt a posture of identification, they appear to act as though they believed that their relation to the group were emulative and complementary. That is, they seem to proceed on the delusory belief that in their own person they can emulate and create the degree of power that, properly speaking, only the group has. More than a law unto themselves, psychopaths act as if they were a whole nation unto themselves. Charles de Gaulle once observed that a nation has no friends, only interests. So it is with psychopaths. And their participation in the interior network of complementary and symmetrical relationships within the group – the only route to true dominance for the individual – is correspondingly falsified by this underlying delusion. The psychopath has collapsed the two logically distinct levels of meaning. (In passing we note that we plan to investigate psychopathic individuals with the semantic differential scale developed by Charles Osgood [1975]; the prediction is that in their affective judgments, psychopaths will tend to collapse the first two dimensions of the scale, evaluation [good/bad] and potency [strong/weak] into a single overall dimension. An appropriate term for this collapsed psychopathic dimension, if it proves to be detectable, might be the inner-city slang epithet "bad," which means strong, exciting, and therefore admirable; in inner-city usage, "bad" can be applied both to friends and enemies without change of meaning.)

One can only speculate on how the psychopath's profoundly disordered orientation to issues of power and social intercourse comes about diachronically. It must be somehow characteristic of the pathogenic milieu that levels of meaning pertaining to the group – its cohesiveness, stability, continued survival – have become contaminated with levels of meaning pertaining to relations between individuals. When Bianchi, the Hillside Strangler, was seen in a child-guidance clinic at the age of 11 for school problems coupled with somatic complaints, the psychologist who examined him, Robert Dowling, noted: "It would appear from Kenneth's viewpoint that his mother has related to him in such a way that he feels his very survival depends on his being in her good graces" (cited in Fisher, 1984, p. 10).

Here we should perhaps touch on a concept derived from the study of juvenile delinquency, Sutherland's concept of "differential association." Working out of the Chicago School of Sociology, Sutherland sought out the social causes of juvenile delinquency. Sutherland proposed that membership in an antisocial group – the gang – was necessary to incubate antisocial behavior. (Clearly, the overall social structures must also tolerate this pattern or at least not interfere with it. Thus, Sutherland's thesis was supplemented by Merton's [1987] concept of social breakdown, or anomie, as a contributory variable.) By associating differentially with a gang, in other words, delinquent adolescents insulate themselves from the larger social network and from its rules. Differential association, in short, entails social disassociation. The group perception protects the individual from experiencing conflict. (Just how deeply a socially patterned delusory system can go can be seen in the Pentecostal sect described in the book *When Prophecy Fails* [Festinger, Riecken, & Schacter, 1956]. The sect in question had gathered in the desert for the end of the world; when this did not occur, the leader rechecked his calculations and told the group that a mistake had been made and the end was still fifty years off. The group went home satisfied. Thus, the self-fulfilling prophecy was readjusted and homeostasis was reestablished.)

Sutherland's delinquents were not necessarily psychopaths, but it is plain that some similar mixture of assocative and dissociative processes is relevant to the psychopath. What delinquents do by way of distancing themselves from the norms of the community, psychopaths do at a far deeper level. And here we come to the topic of dissociation as a clinical phenomenon. Dissociation is a critical cognitive process in psychopathy. It is manifest in the pathological glibness, in the inability to feel guilt, in the inability to profit from experience, and in semantic dementia generally.

We ordinarily conceive of dissociation as a hysterical trait. In this context, dissociation refers to the tendency of individuals to separate, or dissociate, their "real" selves from their "public" selves. Such people histrionically alter their public presentations to create a succession of socially acceptable images or facades. Dissociation thus serves as a mechanism for distracting others from the unpleasant realities that may constitute the real self. And it can reach the point, so spectacularly manifest in multiple personality, where it constitutes a self-distracting process so powerful that it utterly prevents the individual from experiencing and integrating painful thoughts or emotions. At a less severe level of disturbance, the charming, dramatic, or even seductive facade of histrionic personalities prevents them from dwelling on the inadequacies that they may possess, inadequacies that nonetheless are available to consciousness if histrionics are sufficiently motivated to deal with them.

With psychopaths, dissociation reaches to an even deeper level; paradoxically, it is also more readily put at the service of the pathologically inflated ego. Where the histrionic splits off the "bad me" from the "good me," to use Sullivan's terminology, the psychopath's internal split seems to take place at an even more basic level, that of the "me" and the "not me." In a double sense, in both fantasy and reality, there is nothing that is "not me" for psychopaths. There is no limit to the grandiosity of their fantasies; likewise there is no limit to what they might do. And, given that "me" and "not me" form a continuum of meaning, with each necessary as a semantic counterpole to the other, the inability of psychopaths to arrive at a "not me" self-structure results in a corresponding inability to arrive at a stable sense of "me" as well. (To avoid misunderstanding, let us make clear that though we speak of a stable self-structure, we do not conceive of the self as an entity, but rather as a system of interlocking processes that link the individual to the social milieu.)

Paradoxically, the deficit in psychopaths' self-structure or concept at this most elemental level is coupled with a greater capacity for the techniques of dissociation at the higher level of "good me" and "bad me." Whereas for the multiple personality, and for the hysteric generally, dissociation is primarily an unconscious process – this is the beauty of it, it primarily works outside of awareness – for the psychopath there is a definite ego-involvement in it, at least insofar as social judgments are concerned. Psychopaths are constantly on the lookout for ways of distracting the interviewer, of rationalizing their behavior, of deflecting the blame. They show both foresight and perceptiveness in forestalling any confrontation with the "bad me" – they know what they are doing.

We must be careful not to confuse levels here. Because at the level of the "bad me" psychopaths manifest a degree of conscious control over their self-presentation does *not* mean that they can desist from this behavior. Indeed, the contrary is true; the deeper dissociation is utterly uncontrolled and this makes it practically impossible for psychopaths to do anything else but con at the level of social valuations. Likewise, the same is true of the kind of rationalizations and trumped-up emotions psychopaths rely on. True, at this point, there is a level of conscious ego-involvement in these techniques, but this is a pathologically inflated ego we are talking about here, an ego further that has lost the ability to produce either genuine reasons or genuine feelings. Psychopaths' grandiosity may take them in, but it ought not take us in. They have lost the ability not to con people; they are slaves to this behavior. What appears to be the ultimate freedom is actually bondage.

One of the authors was recently consulted by an actor who was about to undertake a role of a psychopath in a movie. As the various constituent elements of the disorder were explained in terms of thrill seeking, grandiosity, and dissociation, the actor remarked with some justice that his own craft was being described. While on stage, he pointed out, he enjoyed the thrill of the occasion, he deliberately sought to command attention, and he called upon his own dissociative capacity in order to throw himself into his role. But actors can *control* all three elements: They can confine their thrill seeking to the hours between 7:30 and 10:00 in the evening plus two matinees during the week; they know there are times when they must yield the spotlight to their fellow actors lest they upstage them; and most important of all, they know deep down that they are not this or that English king and will soon have to catch a taxi back to a less-than-grand loft in Soho. In order to make the distinction clear to the actor, the author fell back on the well-known consultation James Joyce had with Carl Jung with regard to Joyce's schizophrenically ill daughter. Jung explained about the loosening of associations in the disease, to which Joyce replied that this precisely was what he did in his writing. To which Jung replied, "Yes, but you are swimming in it; your daughter is drowning."

The psychopath, in short, cannot turn off the dissociative tendency. This sometimes wreaks diagnostic havoc in courtroom proceedings. During the trial of Bianchi, the defense brought forth evidence suggesting that he was a multiple personality and that the crimes of the Hillside Strangler were done by a second self outside of Bianchi's control. In support of this contention, evidence derived from the use of hypnosis was also brought in. In a celebrated battle of rival experts, Martin Orne won the case for the prosecution by arguing that Bianchi had faked being a multiple personality – the police searching his home found numerous psychological texts that might have helped Bianchi do this – and that he had faked hypnosis as well. With regard to the outcome, there can be little quarrel with Orne's strategy, but in our view he could have gone much further. For Bianchi was not just a malingerer; he was also faking being normal, faking consulting with his defense attorney, and faking under cross-examination. This man could only con people; there existed no counterpole of an inwardly valid set of truths that would allow one to admit to faking one thing and not everything else.

When dissociation runs riot in this fashion, the clinician is entitled to ask why these people do not "have the common decency to go crazy." Indeed, Cleckley originally supposed that they *were* crazy; in the 1941 edition of *The Mask of Sanity*, he suggested that psychopathy constituted a subtype of schizophrenia. By the late 1970s, however, he had amended that view in favor of the more modest claim that psychopathy was closer to psychosis than to neurosis in terms of the severity of the disorder. It is interesting to speculate how and why psychopaths avoid frank psychosis. Sullivan (1953a, p. 360 n.) has made the provocative observation that certain spontaneously remitting schizophrenias result in a temporary or permanent acquisition of psychopathic traits. The implication is that psychopathic traits somehow constitute an alternative to overt schizophrenic confusion. But true psychopaths seem never to have been crazy; it as though their personality style grants them immunity in most social milieus against frankly psychotic developments.

It *is* possible to drive a psychopath crazy. Severe environmental deprivation, such as results from being put in solitary confinement within a prison, has been known to produce psychotic states both in psychopaths and in ordinary criminals. But here, too, psychopaths can be distinguished. When ordinary inmates develop a psychosis in this fashion, it acquires a momentum of its own and treatment is needed to bring them out of it. Psychopaths, by contrast, need only to be placed back into the prison milieu; once they are allowed to resume their typical pattern of acting out, their psychosis remits spontaneously. It would appear from this that schizophrenia represents a miscarriage of psychological processes that are developmentally and socially more complex than those of the psychopath. Schizophrenics have lost in their battle to establish a basic kernel of self. Psychopaths, by contrast, are not concerned with establishing a self; they are concerned only with maintaining an optimal level of stimulation coupled with an optimal opportunity for acting out. In etiological terms, our suspicion is that on a neglect–pampering continuum, the psychopath is more likely to come from a milieu loaded on the neglect end, the schizophrenic from the pampered end. But, what precisely constitutes the etiologically significant *kinds* of neglect in the case of the psychopath, we cannot say.[2]

And with the mention of etiologically significant variables, we feel obliged to pause for an observation with regard to diagnostic classifications and their relation to process taxonomies. Too frequently, clinicians are asked to make predictions about dangerousness, and when they consult the literature on topics like dangerousness and violence, they are confronted with a hodgepodge of observations derived from a mixed population. Some psychopaths are violent; so, too, are some career criminals; so, too, are some epileptics; so, too, are some drug users; so, too, are some schizophrenics; and so forth. The problem one so often encounters in the literature is that attributes of different logical types are combined willy-nilly. Violence is a behavioral unit; drug abuser is both a behavioral description and a rudimentary character portrait; psychopath is at a higher logical level still – it denotes a recognizable personality syndrome that may or may not exhibit violent or drug-taking behaviors. (In this context, our own suspicion is that the level of violence exhibited by any given psychopath will be highly correlated with the amount of overt physical abuse suffered in childhood as well as with the level of violence characteristic of the psychopath's immediate social milieu. But we would not necessarily expect these same correlations to obtain invariably for other clinical groups.)

That last example may seem straightforward but the problem is more general still. If we hope to make progress in understanding the psychopath, we must understand which psychological processes are essential to the syndrome and which peripheral. And in teasing out the etiology of the essential processes, we must be willing to cut across the walls of established diagnostic entities to observe whether or not the same or similar psychological factors obtain for any particular process regardless of diagnostic designation. Take the issue of dissociation. It is clear that a profound reliance on dissociation is an essential hallmark of the psychopathic disorder. (Indeed, we would argue that together with an abnormally high psychological threshold of stimulation – manifest in thrill seeking – and a profoundly disturbed relation to issues of power and dominance, dissociation constitutes part of the distinguishing triad of traits basic to this syndrome.) But, when we compare the degree and quality of dissociative processes in the psychopath with the degree and quality of the same processes in other syndromes, do we arrive at generally valid psychological principles? Do we learn anything about etiologically significant environmental variables? These are questions worth pursuing. There is some evidence to suggest that the dissociation typical of multiple personality originates in the context of severe physical or sexual abuse in childhood. It is also clear that some psychopaths come from comparable home situations. Nonetheless, it is likewise clear that the psychopathy syndrome, though it overlaps with multiple personality in respect to dissociation as a constituent mechanism, basically constitutes an inherently different response of the developing personality. Thus, we may well ask what other factors besides physical or sexual abuse must be present to produce the particular outcome of psychopathic dissociation. In the multiple egos of developing children who have not yet left the magical stage, and thus are readily prepared to imagine themselves as more than one person, we have the grass-roots level of dissociative capacity. Faced with traumatic physical or sexual abuse, children at this stage readily defend themselves with the thought that the abuse happened to someone else; this imagined someone else then becomes the nucleus of a second personality. Children who have a high innate dissociative capacity do this readily; children with a low innate capacity have to work at it. It seems likely, therefore, that traumatic physical or sexual abuse is instrumental in heightening the child's capacity for and reliance on the mechanism of dissociation. What has to happen in psychopathic development, however, is for this heightened capacity to attach itself to the child's own antisocial behavior; currently, it is not at all clear how this comes about. It is quite possible that the link to antisocial behavior occurs somewhat later in childhood and that differential associative networks of the sort Sutherland described play an instrumental role.

And here let us observe that psychopaths have significant social relationships, relationships that are important in the maintenance of the disorder. Fritz Redl and David Wineman (1951) discovered this to their chagrin when they set up a residential facility for antisocial youths. As they report in *Children Who Hate,* they were initially surprised and pleased to see their charges banding together into tight-knit groups – until they discovered that the group functioned as a means of perpetuating pathology and resisting the demands of the therapeutic milieu. Redl and Wineman report in vivid clinical detail how the children were masters at using the group as a means of maintaining their essential ego deficits. The same reliance on interpersonal relations can also be seen in adult psychopaths, even in the most profoundly distrubed. Thus, in a majority of cases, serial killers have been found to have employed the services of an accomplice. And, when they can be got to confess to the accomplice's existence, they invariably turn the tables on the accomplice – who not only killed, but mutilated the corpse, they say, and is really sick. In this way, they excuse their own behavior by dispersing its significance onto others. The serial killer Henry Lee Lucas, for example, decried his accomplice's alleged cannibalism. The accomplice, like the juvenile gang, protects psychopaths from a confrontation with their deficits through differential association. In this way, the innate dissociative capacity becomes more closely linked with antisocial trends.

This, then, in large overview is our portrait of the psychopath. The essential psychological mechanisms appear to be thrill seeking, dissociation, and a profound disturbance in the relationship to issues of power and dominance evident in a grandiose delusional belief in the exceptional nature of the self. Of these three traits, dissociation in all its myriad forms – psychopathic glibness, absence of guilt, semantic dementia – is the most readily observable, but all three are necessary to constitute the syndrome. (Obviously they interact. Dissociative mechanisms subserve both thrill seeking and grandiosity. By the same token grandiosity becomes a rationale for thrill seeking and an organizer of dissociative mechanisms. The techniques of rationalization rely on the dissociation of affect and the concomitant semantic dementia; so too does the absence of guilt. And so forth.) In the exercise of these psychological mechanisms, moreover, psychopaths rely on select interpersonal relations as both social insulators and preferred social instigators to further psychopathy.

3.4. The psychopathy of everyday life

The character of American social life, with its antiauthoritarian and counterdependent emphases, has traditionally fostered a certain amiable tendency to wink at evasions of community codes. In a bygone age, this was expressed in the general cultural fascination with the figure of the western outlaw. Outlaws, excepting the fact that they lived outside the law, best embodied those traits of independent initiative and emotional self-reliance that the culture valued most. And with the closing of the frontier, and the increasing urbanization of American life, the outlaw was replaced in the popular imagination by that other antisocial culture hero, depicted in countless movies, the gangster.

The peculiarly American attitude toward community norms was expressed in other phenomena as well. P. T. Barnum, for example, became a legendary national figure on the basis of a magnificent skill in conning people. Did the flow of customers through the sideshow tents get bottlenecked with people doubling back to make sure they did not miss anything? Counting on a general ignorance, Barnum simply added another attraction strategically placed the other side of a turnstile: This

Way to the Egress the sign read, and off the people went to see what exactly an egress might be.

Barnum's motto was, "A sucker is born every minute." W. C. Fields's motto was, "Never give a sucker an even break." Or as he put it on another cinematic occasion: "If it's worth having, it's worth cheating for." Sharp practice, whether at the poker table or in the boardroom, is as American as Mark Twain. And let us not forget that Twain's most memorable character, Huck Finn, should be counted, in a manner of speaking, as a juvenile delinquent. Twain's motto: "When in doubt, tell the truth."

It is worth speculating about the social and economic origins of this streak in the American character. It plainly has complex roots and is no simple offshoot of frontier mentality. For if the frontier was scouted by rugged individualists, it was settled by skilled, educated European immigrants who valued community and who excelled in the mechanics of social cooperation. And the general phenomenon of admiring certain kinds of psychopathy has increased in this century as America has become progressively more urban. Consider for example the reputation enjoyed by legendary bank robber Willie Sutton. Late in his career, as he faced his umpteenth jail term, Sutton was asked why he robbed banks. His answer constituted a classic example of semantic dementia; it is also part of the American lore. Sutton replied simply, "Because that's where the money is."

Tentatively, we would like to suggest that the origins of this attitude lie in the discontinuity between local communities and the larger society. As America became urban, it evolved into a nation of neighborhoods. It has justly been remarked that America was never a melting pot – it was a salad bowl. The urban landscape was a patchwork of different neighborhoods each with its own value systems. And it was the neighborhood that was the crucible of citizenship. It was here that one became socialized into a community of shared values, here that one acquired one's primary identifications. The larger urban landscape was just that, a landscape, a place where one could go as far as luck, talent, and drive would take one. Accordingly, Americans acquired a double attitude toward the mores of society. On the one hand, they were expected to exhibit traditional values at home and in their immediate community. On the other hand, within certain overall limits, they were expected to be as opportunistic as the situation would allow in their dealings, principally economic, outside their own social group. The split is manifest in the ubiquitous hyphen of the hyphenated American. We are Italian-

Americans, Greek-Americans, Afro-Americans, and so forth. Knowing what is entailed on the front end of that hyphen in one's dealings with other people, knowing and taking advantage where one can, has long counted as part of common sense. And when in doubt, tell the truth.

It is the hyphen of the hyphenated American, we suspect, that allows the American to pursue success so avidly. "Making it" has always been okay, even if one had to be deceitful, ruthless, and plain crooked to do so, because making it has always implicitly been understood to be at somebody else's expense, somebody from outside the neighborhood. By making it one vindicates the worthiness of one's own group in this scheme; one has in effect championed the values of the old neighborhood.

Stepping back from the latently anomic tendency of the drive for success, we ought to be aware that in the phenomenon of the hyphenated American we have a parallel to Sutherland's "selective association." What constitutes affiliation and group loyalty on one level leads to disaffiliation and potential pseudopsychopathy on another. And, indeed, hyphenated Americans, like the level of psychopathy they tolerate and even admire, are a relatively benign phenomenon. The American tolerance for disaffiliated behavior, in this vein, is the flip side of American pluralism and American tolerance generally. The implicit group rivalry that underlies the psychopathy of everyday life is still to be preferred to an explicity ruthless rivalry. Carl Jung once observed about the Swiss that they were really not a peaceful people; they had merely institutionalized their various civil wars in the form of cantonal politics. By the same token, Americans might be said to have institutionalized their own civil wars in the competition for success. Which, relatively speaking, is not such a bad solution. New York City is scarcely peaceful, but it is still not Beirut.

But there is a phenomenon on the American scene of late that in our opinion is most certainly *not* benign. We are referring to the psychopathic behavior of prominent individuals in high positions both in industry and in government. We are confronted by the spectacle of an Ivan Boesky, rich beyond the dreams of the average person, but intent on criminal strategies for beating the system. Boesky was caught and he was punished, but not before he was given the chance quietly to sell off his ill-gotten assets at current values. This, with the full cooperation of the prosecutors, was "insider trading" on a whole new level. Then, also, we are confronted by the incredible performance of an Oliver North lecturing the United States Congress about the exigencies of deniability." For this, North was very nearly canonized by the public, though what he asserted was that he had the right to lie to them and to their representatives. And few seem to mind. Corruption certainly is not new; neither is recklessness in government. What is new and noteworthy is the implicit assertion that this kind of behavior is somehow okay. It may be immoral, the attitude seems to be, but it is not *that* immoral. And if one is unlucky enough to get caught, allowances will be made to make sure that the penalities are not too severe.

In this respect, it may be that the Watergate scandal marked a turning point in American mores. From the outset, nobody doubted that Nixon and his immediate circle were behind the burglary; nor did anyone doubt that its motive and its sponsorship had been covered up. (We still do not really know what the burglars were after.) But, as the Senate hearings progressed, it also became clear that, with some pruning of the staff, the administration was going to get away with it, until it was discovered, quite accidentally, that Nixon kept tapes of all his conversations. That and that alone was his undoing. As the ensuing crisis unfolded, there were many who asserted cynically that Nixon was being unfairly hounded for doing things that others got away with, that the liberal establishment and the media had long been out to get him and now were capitalizing on the ineptness of his staff. The terms of the discussion had shifted: Nixon should have gotten away with it; only ineptness prevented him. Indeed, ineptness became a ploy for commanding sympathy among his coconspirators. To his credit, Nixon did not himself take this route; he fought to the end. But some 15 years later Oliver North pleaded ineptness repeatedly. "The old delete button" had failed him, he explained sheepishly to the committee at one point, as though a poor grasp of computer software was his only reprehensible trait.

This is something quite noteworthy. On a spectrum of psychopathic behavior, both Boesky and North were far to the normal end, and quite distant from the clinical counterpole of the true psychopath. They had homes complete with warm wives and attractive children, they were gainfully employed, they were loyal to colleagues, and so on. And yet, they were behaving psychopathically in quite profound ways. The pursuit of power, risk taking ("I still think it was a neat idea"), antisocial attitudes ("It's a dangerous world out there, Senator"), dissociation ("deniability"), and differential association ("cutouts") – all this was present in their behavior. Most importantly, they showed no grasp that they did anything wrong save get caught. They truly believed they should evade punishment – and a surprising number of their fellow citizens agree with them. The absence of guilt is remarkable – and unremarked on! Indeed, such is the climate that the suicide attempt of one of North's coconspirators, Robert McFarlane, was viewed as evidence of mental disorder and not as the altogether understandable response of a career civil servant to the drastic circumstance of having been publicly unmasked as a man who broke the law, lied to Congress, and sold guns to terrorists.

Boesky and North are exemplary, not unique. From defrocked television evangelists to Yuppie inside traders, from Wedtech to the New York City Parking Bureau scandal, the papers daily bring us fresh reports of misbehavior by respectable people in respectable places. And, to repeat, what is most surprising about all this is not the fact of it, but the attitude taken toward it, both by the principals and by the public at large. It is not *that* immoral, the public seems to be saying. We have here on a mass scale an example of the phenomenon described by Latane and Darley (1970) as "bystander intervention," which could more properly be termed "bystander nonintervention."

In trying to explicate this phenomenon – normalized psychopathy in high places we might call it – we have to be careful to distinguish it from several related phenomena.[3] First of all, there is the behavior of the average citizen when confronted by large, impersonal bureaucracies. A majority of Americans feel it is okay to cheat on their income taxes. Likewise, they feel it is okay if they can beat the phone company out of a few dollars. In both instances, moreover, they are scarcely apt to feel remorse; the only sin is getting caught. Their attitude is understandable in terms of the vast disparity between the individual and the bureaucracy. The bureaucracy interferes intimately in the life of the individual, yet is largely indifferent and unresponsive to the individual's particular needs, desires, and preferences. In such an unequal contest, anything is felt to be fair. But clearly this is quite different from the sort of normalized psychopathy we have been describing. North and Boesky had enormous power; airplanes waited for their summonses, staff members went hither and yon at their command. Their indifference to the prevailing social norms has an altogether different basis.

If we are clear that North and Boesky are not true psychopaths, and likewise clear that theirs is not the understandable situation of the underdog overmatched by a large bureaucracy, then we must look to the interaction of the group and the individual in fomenting this behavior. Which brings us to the subject of the psychopathy of the group. Since

LeBon's pioneering work on the psychology of the mob, it has long been an axiom among social scientists that a group can inculcate antisocial behavior to a disturbing degree. Partridge (1928) drew the parallel with psychopathy explicitly:

> There is another aspect of the study of the psychopathic personality . . . the problem of the psychopathy of groups. . . . Here there is scope for much progress, and a point at which psychopathology may yet introduce methods of some precision into the wider problems of sociology. It may be assumed that within any group there is a tendency towards or possibility of the production of motives, adjustments, and behavior, which are relatively pathological: a striking and perhaps sufficient illustration is the behavior of the national consciousness, particularly in its motivations in war. The thesis here is that the thorough and adequate investigation of the individual consciousness in its pathological manifestation yields us precisely the background needed for the study of the group consciousness – that is, for the development of a scientific sociopathology. (p. 92)

Quite independently, the theologian Reinhold Niebuhr arrived at a similar proposition in his work *Moral Man and Immoral Society*. According to Niebuhr, the paradox of modern society is that although individuals are constrained by the laws laid down by the groups to which they belong, the groups themselves are not similarly constrained vis-à-vis other groups. A labor union must try to get as much as it can for itself; so, too, must the company with which it deals. Neither side can afford to extend its own standards of compassion to the other. Moreover, insofar as one becomes identified with the group's status vis-à-vis other groups, one is encouraged to act egoistically. A union negotiator has to be ruthless if the occasion calls for it. So do its members on the picket line.

But, if we stay with Niebuhr's analysis a bit longer, it quickly becomes apparent that all groups must obey some set of overarching rules if society is not to fragment completely. These rules may not amount to moral codes of the profundity of the Ten Commandments, but nonetheless they offer essential restraints. Exactly here, however, the behavior of an Oliver North differs from that, say, of a labor negotiator. North was doing more than representing the interests of a group within the administration; he was breaking the rules that govern how all such group interests are to be reconciled in the formation of policy. If North's scheme for an independent, self-financing covert action agency had come to pass, we would all potentially be at its mercy. Similarly, with Boesky: He was not simply putting his firm's interests first; he was doing so in a way that if it came into general practice would result in economic chaos. Given that ours is a pluralistic society and hence one that depends on the observance of certain overarching rules, people who break them ought to merit special condemnation. Americans of all people ought to show special sensitivity on this point. Yet, just here, surprisingly, we are allowing all kinds of things to pass.

A more pertinent parallel to the current phenomenon is that described by Robert Jay Lifton in his analysis of the Nazi doctors who administered to the death camps. In chilling detail, Lifton (1986) depicts the inversion of values whereby killing became equated with social healing. But, doctors being people and true monsters like Mengele being hard to come by, the inversion of values at the ideological level was not sufficient in and of itself. Supplementing it at the individual level were techniques of "numbing" and "doubling" whereby the meaning of the process was progressively neutralized. For Lifton's "numbing" and "doubling" we would prefer the more general, if less colorful, "social dissociation." But the essential process is obviously the same. In what sense, however, can we compare the numbing Lifton describes with the indifference of a North or a Boesky? The techniques of dissociation, both individual and social, used by the Nazi doctors were necessary precisely because the conflict in values was all too palpably real. North, by contrast, seems to have been aware of no such conflict. Numbing is something that a McFarlane needed, perhaps, but then McFarlane was the exception, not the rule. North acquired his attitudes well before he put them into practice. Whether in Vietnam, or in boot camp, or someplace else, he had learned to dissociate and rationalize long before it was necessary to support the Contras.

Clearly, then, we are dealing with something that goes beyond the exigencies of intergroup competition and is qualitatively different in some respects from the special case Lifton has described. The phenomenon is quite unusual. We seem to be dealing with an apparently far-reaching if largely covert decline in values that tends to become manifest in individual behavior with the individual's ascension to a position of power. This phenomenon in the individual is mirrored in and complemented by the public perception of it as expectable and implicity acceptable. Values have lost their compelling quality in certain circumstances and everyone knows about it. This malignant phenomenon of normalized psychopathy in positions of power, like the more benign psychopathy of ordinary life that it is heir to, must derive from certain peculiarities of our ordinary social relationships. It is to these that we now turn.

3.5. Social breakdown and the social distress syndrome

In trying to observe the social relations that obtain with regard to the normalized psychopathy of powerful positions, let us begin with Sullivan's observation, shared with one of the authors, that a promising avenue toward further elucidation of the psychopathic syndrome might lie in the study of the social relations of the anthropoid apes. Anthropoid apes, Sullivan proposed (1953b) showed the same kind of organismic, and therefore blatantly instrumental, orientation toward social relations that was otherwise characteristic of the true psychopath. Sullivan's suggestion is valuable twice over in our estimation. For one thing, it captures something of the essence of psychopathic behavior: namely, its atavistic, nearly animalistic thrust. Our own view is that the same atavistic tendency is personified in the figure of the demonic that the psychopath so closely embodies. Then, also, Sullivan's suggestion is valuable because it points out how the psychopath fails to achieve truly human status.

This last point is more elusive than it might seem at first. For anthropoid apes do have social relations, often of a quite complex kind. Chimpanzees, for example, have been shown to exhibit patterns of friendship, mutual cooperation, and familial association that are quite surprisingly human. But, they have also been shown to manifest horrendously antisocial behavior, including the persecution of rivals, the elimination of the sick and elderly, and, in one recent study, systematic murder. This, too, after a fashion, is surprisingly human. Where the apes differ from ordinary humans, in our view, and resemble psychopaths, is in their failure to achieve emotional conflict with regard to these swings in behavior. Theirs is not a consistent affectivity: The murder of a vanquished rival today can follow fast upon some shared activity with that same chimp the day before. As a result, chimpanzee society is an inconstant affective affair: Judging them anthropocentrically, we see psychopathic behavior side by side with behavior that seems more sociable.

A caveat may be in order here; we mention it because it is relevant to an important point that we will be coming to in a moment. The natural habitat of the chimps is under pressure from all sides. It may be that some of the extremes of their antisocial behavior, such as systematic murder, may involve responses to environmental stresses interacting with a concomitant breakdown in social organization. Since it was first discovered that the suicidal swarming behavior of lemmings originated in a pathogenically altered endocrine system, itself a result of stress brought on by overcrowding and diminished resources, ethologists have been preoccupied with the role of stress in fomenting the breakdown of both physical health and social behavior in animals. Perhaps the most interesting work in this field is the experimental work of Calhoun (1962). Through a number of environmental manipulations, Calhoun has been able to create a variety of stressfully overcrowded situations for laboratory rats. These behavioral "sinks" have horrendous effects on the rats' physiology and on their social behavior extending over several generations. Both dominance behavior and sexual behavior, the principal forms of "instinctive" social life among rats, became rapidly disrupted in the adults.

In one of Calhoun's experiments, a struggle for control erupted over a thickly populated central enclave, with the dominant rats quickly taking over this space wherein they also became the most active sexually. But they were unable to discriminate between estrous and nonestrous females, attacking and "raping" those who were not ready as well as the submissive. Another criminal group did not participate directly in the struggle for dominance but moved in homosexual and cannibalistic gangs and often committed homosexual rape. The life of the females was disrupted most even though they had access to protected side cages. Half died of disturbances of pregnancy or from repeated sexual assault. Infant mortality reached as high as 90 percent: Infants were abandoned and eaten. Calhoun further noted among the young who survived what he termed schizoid behavior: They were frightened and withdrawn, incapable of competing in the behavioral sink and wearing all the hallmarks of great stress. In the third generation, however, Calhoun observed something more startling still: Young rats who had never seen normal adult behavior grew up sleek and fat and utterly asocial in every respect; they were simply eating machines and seemed to experience no stress at all.

The role of stress in disrupting social behavior of lower animals is potentially relevant to the study of psychopathic behavior in humans. For, of all creatures, humans are both the most adaptable and the most vulnerable to disruptions in their environment and in their development. Both traits, adaptability and vulnerability, are due to the absence of built-in regulators ("instincts"). Not being born like Athena, full-grown from the head of Zeus, human infants are shaped by their culture, their parents, and their own genetic endowments in their acquisition of coping devices and emotional responses. Many mishaps can occur during the process of maturation. Most significantly, humans are not born with a full-blown capacity for feeling. The capacity for fully socialized affective response develops only under the aegis of parental protection. Out of the child's dependent interaction with the protective parent, there arise in health the distinctively human abilities to trust, idealize, imitate, cooperate with, and have affection for another. But there is no guarantee that this will occur.

That affectivity is not inborn but must be cultivated constitutes the greatest weakness of human society. Social controls have never been perfect and variation in character has always been high, most particularly in aggressiveness and in the capacity for affection and cooperation. Further, in complex societies increased role specialization greatly complicates the maintenance of harmonious relationships and controls over aggression. Social complexity, moreover, can interact with variations in basic character formation in multiple ways. It is not true, however, that human flexibility is limitless and that therefore anything goes. Not only are there a greater or lesser number of human casualties in any given culture, but there are also situations in which shifting character styles interact pathogenically with historical circumstance to bring about widespread social dysfunction. One culture may adapt to stress with innovation and change; another may go under. There are vast cemeteries of dead cultures.

Among the more fortunate basic social antidotes to cultural dysfunction and to the potential abuses of social aggression are the institutions of marriage and of the family. Not only do they distribute sexual opportunity equitably, preventing the strong from taking all the females, but they also establish kinship structures, that basic system of social cohesion. Equally, they profit the offspring by providing stability and protection. The family also provides education with regard to accepted social patterns and in a complex society may help prepare the developing individual for an appropriate social niche. The status of the family unit thus is one of the most sensitive barometers of the success or failure of any given culture's response to changing circumstances. It constitutes, as it were, an important feedback loop with regard to social change. And when, under the impact of great stress, it becomes disrupted in its own functioning, this will tend to accelerate the social dysfunction that initiated the cycle. Occasionally, the result will be a frank and dramatic increase in true psychopathy.

An excellent illustration of such a disaster is provided by a study by Colin Turnbull (1972) of the Ik of Uganda. This tribe was originally a prosperous, religious, kindly group of hunters and gatherers who were forced from their traditional sources of food and livelihood into the mountains. Under the impact of this enforced dislocation, all social institutions deteriorated, including the family, and in only one generation the Ik were transformed into a cold people, isolated from one another socially and ruthlessly exploitative whenever the occasion presented itself. They had become, for all intents and purposes, a tribe of psychopaths. Turnbull commented, "The lack of any sense of moral responsibility toward each other, the lack of any sense of teaming up, needing or wanting each other, showed up daily" (p. 137). (The distinguished naturalist Lewis Thomas commented on Turnbull's study that the Ik acted like separate nations rather than as members of a shared society.)

Turnbull's study certainly needs to be taken into consideration with regard to any discussion of normalized psychopathy in contemporary America. Clearly, at the extreme level apparently embodied by the Ik, universally normalized psychopathy is equal to total social disintegration. And, clearly, the phenomenon of increased normalized psychopathy in our society would seem to be accompanied by a general overall increase in social fragmentation. But, we have to ask ourselves why it is that humans who occupy high positions, who sit at the pinnacle of intact organizations, would also be prone to psychopathic developments. Clearly the phenomena are more complex still. Moreover, we need to keep in mind that the impact of any given set of stresses is mediated by the value patterns of society. Not all societies respond the way the Ik did. For example, Louis Jolyon West (1967) found a parallel case that behaved quite differently. The Tarahumara tribe of Mexico were likewise forced out of fertile land into the mountains without, however, losing their humanity in the process. West discovered them still speaking their native language, Uto Aztec, and maintaining a rich cultural heritage notable for its profound affectionate bonds, its deep sense of the dignity of the individual, and an aversion to violence. The social institutions of the Tarahumara, in short, were flexible enough to accommodate themselves to an equivalent stressor without the development of normalized psychopathy. Accordingly, we must ask outselves wherein lie the peculiar vulnerabilities of the contemporary American social institutions that have fostered the startling phenomenon of nor-malized psychopathy in high places.

In many ways, a more pertinent example for our purposes is the study of Kardiner (1939) of the Tanala of Madagascar, a tribe that experienced severe stress as a result of the failure of the traditional system of rice cultivation. Under the traditional method of dry cultivation, the Tanala had simply moved on to a new area every 7 or 8 years once resources were exhausted. By the 1920s, however, they could no longer use this method without warfare, which was ruled out by the central govern-ment. Thus the old communal tribal organization had to be broken up, and there ensued a desperate scramble for the valleys, where the wet method of agriculture could be used. The old economy had been com-munally governed by a college of elders and maintained by an army of docile younger sons, the oldest being exempt from labor. In the new economy, by contrast, unbridled competition and aggression were necessary and readily rewarded.

But the majority of the population of younger sons was made up of meek, obedient creatures who had been trained simply to work in the fields and ingratiate themselves with their fathers. In a crisis they had little to draw upon. The story of a typical family constellation reflects the docility prevalent in the traditional culture. Two younger sons steal two wives from their father and run away with them. The father, learning of this, sets out to pursue them, catches up with them, reclaims his wives, forgives his sons, and all return to live happily ever after. Compare this with the Greek drama of Oedipus and note the absence of guilt, murder, or retribution in the Tanala myth. The young sons needed their father's protection and he their labor; neither could afford violence or murder; besides which, the younger sons did not possess sufficient aggressive-ness to kill the father outright.

What happens to such a people when they become caught up in a life and death struggle with starvation that demands of them that they adopt a competitive economic system? Unable to mobilize aggression against one another directly, they resort to that classic manifestation of repressed aggression, superstition. Everyone used magic against every-one else and everyone feared, logically enough, that they were them-selves victimized by the magic of others. A psychopathic universe, reminiscent of the Ik, came into being, but only in the imagination. To be sure, this imaginative hostility protected members of the community from mutual extermination through overt aggression. It did not, howev-er, protect the totally defenseless and totally dependent: Infanticide became common. These phenomena were accompanied by another, less easy to explain: a spectacular increase in male homosexuality. The incidence rose to five times what it had been before the crisis; the Tanala themselves were at a loss to explain it. Here we would observe that in many animal species, including the anthropoid apes, sexual displays frequently constitute the response of weaker individuals to situations of threat as a means of indicating submission. But to this we have to add the particularly Tanalese cultural pattern: Both before and after the crisis, homosexuals were invariably recruited from among the younger sons. In short, the culturally valued pattern of submissiveness found new expression as a means of insulating a portion of the male population from the increase in situations of threat.

The relevance of the Tanalese example lies in the relatively clear way in which cultural values continued to modulate responses to a radically altered economic reality. In particular, the taboo against overt aggression and the value placed upon submissiveness continued to exert a force in Tanalese social life, even though they were currently expressed in pathological social institutions such as magic and widespread homosexuality. Put another way, the same values that had long been the basis for social cohesiveness among the Tanala had in changed circumstances become the basis for practices that were observed with suspicion and chagrin. This is what Kardiner proposed to call the Social Distress Syndrome.

It is important to be clear at the outset that social distress as we are defining it is not identical with stress as that term is usually defined by social scientists. Stress, whether it affects an individual or a whole society, is typically defined in terms of objective misfortune. Social distress, by contrast, is defined in terms of value conflicts as these become embodied in social institutions. Among the Tanala, the enforced shift to new methods of agriculture constituted stress, but the increase in homosexuality and in magical practices, things that were distressing to the Tanala themselves, constituted social distress. Once we put the matter this way it becomes clear that although social distress may follow fast upon social stressors proper, it need not do so. Social distress may as easily follow upon ostensibly benign phenomena, such as prosperity or an increase in technical knowledge or even a shift in social expectation toward greater altruism. What is determinative is not that changed circumstances be inherently stressful, but that they occasion value shifts that then become dysfunctionally reflected in the institutions that are charged with realizing them.

If we put the matter in these terms, it is clear that the United States in the 1980s is ripe for the Social Distress Syndrome if only because there is widespread disorganization in the basic value systems of the populace. To some extent, this widespread value confusion represents an exacerbation of trends that have been longstanding in American culture. In our view, Graham Wallace (1914) deserves credit for being the first in this century to observe the close relation of political changes with changes in the individual's *Weltanschauung*. Veblen (1899) further documented the distorting influence of American economic practices on American values. Kardiner in his *Individual and Society* (1939) took this analysis a step further, as did Fromm (1956) in *The Sane Society*. Fromm's idea, that there might be a "pathology of normalcy," became tied to a specific critique of the "marketing" personality as a social type. It is a matter of curiosity why this strain of social criticism has died out among social scientists in recent years, when the need for it has only increased. Here we would like to revive Fromm's term, but free it from a specific typology. For in our view what has become pathological about normalcy is its embrace of value confusions.

Americans would seem to be confused about basic values as never before in their history. We no longer seem quite sure what we want to define as masculine and feminine. We do not seem to know whether we want to preserve the traditional family as we know it or scrap it altogether for some alternative life-style. We cannot seem to agree whether we want our democracy to evolve more along capitalistic or socialistic lines as the best way of maximizing materialistic security. We no longer are certain how to balance the claims of individual autonomy and freedom of expression against institutional prerogatives and the collective external authority of public opinion. We do not seem to know whether to value the education or the indoctrination of the mind. We do not seem to know whether to plan for war or for peace. We do not seem to be able to understand whether crime does or does not pay. We do not seem to be able to make up our minds whether God is dead or simply hiding somewhere waiting for the millennium to come. We do not seem able to decide whether we are fighting for freedom or for bondage. And so forth. Even in the social sciences we are confused as to what our basic image of humans should be, as witness the current debate over sociobiology. As Ogden Nash put it, we do not seem able to decide whether we are "ape-like, simian, or just normal men and womenian."

As our own individual culture merges into the newly dawning world culture, with the media serving as the instrument of indoctrination, there arises what can only be described as the institutionalization of stress. Seven deadly institutional stressors can be identified:

1. Private and public sector.
2. Education.
3. Religion.
4. Family, including male and female roles and relationships. We find ourselves living in a house rather than a home, somewhere between *Brave New World* and *1984*. The home has gone the way of the mental health system: Sometimes it appears to be a madhouse, sometimes a halfway house, and sometimes an outhouse.
5. Health care.
6. Criminal justice.
7. The media.

The overall uncertainty in our value orientations, institutionalized in the seven deadly institutional stressors, would appear to be at least partially the consequence of recent phenomena that were in and of themselves much heralded and ostensibly benign: Affluence, technological advance, the elimination of sexual repression, and an increase in concern with social injustice all figure in. In some respects, American public opinion has become more pluralistic, more tolerant, and more diversified than ever before. The converse side, of course, is that we are more uncertain about what ultimate course we should be steering. But in the best can-do tradition of American pragmatism, we have leapt into institutionalizing all these new values without considering the impact on existing institutions. And here, we should again make mention of the hyphenated American and the traditional discontinuity between the neighborhood and the larger political and economic landscape. The reason why the new, more diversified value systems of the contemporary scene could be translated into institutional policies so rapidly was because many citizens considered that they were still insulated from such changes by the neighborhood and by the family. These citizens were wrong, as it happens, for the family and the neighborhood were simultaneously undergoing their own assault. As a consequence, just as many Americans had begun to take their primary identification not from the neighborhood but from larger social and economic institutions, these institutions began to shift their value orientations. We have erected a world culture and the media has become the disseminator of its values.

The result, arrived at in an incredibly short period of time, has been social distress on a vast scale. We no longer seem to know what we want our institutions to do. More precisely, we have burdened our institutions with the job of realizing multiple values, values that frequently conflict with one another. One of the authors, to take an example close at hand, is employed by the City University system of New York City. The City University system was originally set up for the purpose of providing higher education at minimal cost to the city's residents. The record of City University in fulfilling this goal speaks for itself. In the past two decades, however, to this function has been added a second one: that of ameliorating the effects of racism by guaranteeing equality of opportunity in the form of open enrollment for all who seek it. While a worthwhile value in itself, equality of opportunity conflicts with an established principle of higher education that dictates that students must be ready for the education they seek. Too often the sad result of the current system is, as one colleague put it, that students who cannot learn are being taught by teachers who cannot teach them in order to guarantee them an equal opportunity to get an education. And the dropout rate citywide has reached approximately 70 percent.

Equivalent value conflicts can be found in most of our important social institutions. The criminal justice system was originally designed to punish the culpable. But, under the inpact of reforms designed to protect individual rights, the system has become a labyrinth of procedural safeguards during just that period in our social history when crime has risen dramatically. The result is clearinghouse justice that accomplishes neither goal, as prosecutors try to clear dockets through plea bargaining and seek to punish with stiff terms those who have the audacity to demand an actual trial by their peers.

The health care system is likewise a shambles. The society at large cannot decide between the values of universal health care and the principles of free enterprise. We want hospitals to take in all who need them; we also want them to pay for themselves. The result, predictably, is hospitals that take in virtually everybody but only take care of those able to afford private nurses, and sometimes not even them.

Value conflict is an abstract idea, clearly, but these are not abstract phenomena we are talking about. They are palpably real and they dominate life as it is actually lived in today's society. Consider how one would feel if one found oneself through some conjunction of misfortunes simultaneously involved in litigation and faced with hospitalization. This would constitute an incredible level of stress. Few could survive without serious damage. Yet, by rights both systems ought to provide relief, legal relief in the case of the courts, physical relief from suffering in the case of the hospital. Too often, they do not. That is the meaning of social distress.

It is the phenomenon of widespread social distress in contemporary American social life that, in our view, is to a great extent responsible for the rise of normalized psychopathy in high places. Put simply, the moral bankruptcy of individuals in positions of leadership reflects a more fundamental breakdown in the values that the principal institutions in the society are expected to embody. Often enough the connection is entirely clear-cut. The stock market, for example, is designed to serve the economy by offering a stable institutional framework for investors and entrepreneurs to find one another. But under the impact of wildly increased government spending coupled with tax decreases for the wealthy, this important institution also has also become in the 1980s a forum for adding to personal fortunes through short-term speculation in a boom market. These are quite different functions: Boesky and company ran wild by exploiting the discrepancy. Even more clear-cut is the institutional position of North and his coconspirators. The administration requested, and the Congress approved, a rider to the various Boland amendments that made it legal for private individuals and for foreign governments to do what our government wanted to do but was barred from doing – aiding the Contras. As though foreign governments and private individuals had it in them – without any tit for tat, mind you – to underwrite the specific objectives of the Reagan administration. Hence some of the sympathy for North: What else was the man supposed to do? Obey this law? When he had all but been invited to break it?

Ours is a culture that has long made allowance for a degree of discontinuity between traditional values, inculcated and embodied in the mores of the local neighborhood, and the public behavior of the hyphenated American in the larger urban landscape. The resulting tendency to wink at successful evasions of the moral code – the psychopathy of everyday life – is as American as apple pie. The experience of value conflict is painful enough for individuals as an internal affair; it is more painful still when individuals find that such conflicts have become institutionalized and confront them externally in the form of social institutions that do not work. And it becomes completely untenable when those same individuals realize that the more successful among their fellow citizens have escaped the conflict altogether in favor of frankly psychopathic institutional adjustments.

And here let us observe that we have not begun to explore the further feedback loop constituted by the loss of the family as a social insulator. The breakdown of the family is the most ominous of all the recent developments. Not only are traditional gender roles in transition, but there is a widespread abandonment of parental responsibility. Adultery, abandonment, and child abuse may be immoral, we seem to be saying, but they are not *that* immoral. This raises the interesting question, soon to be answered by the next generation, of how a child shuttled between parent and parent, between school and daycare, between one cynical social bureaucracy and another, will be able to recognize psychopathic behavior for what it is. Especially in a society that increasingly devalues sincerity and tenderness and idealizes "cool" detachment and self-gratification. (A noteworthy social symptom in this respect is the relative decline in the cohesiveness of the organized crime families; modeled so closely upon the family as a social organization, the criminal syndicates are lately finding it hard to recruit people who understand family loyalty!)

Let us close by describing a recent example of what we may call a "social dream." By social dream we mean a cultural product, such as a novel or a movie, that is distinctive in that it so closely captures something of the current impulses and conflicts of the society that its content, though typically quite fantastic, passes without reflection or comment by the general public. As does a dreamer after an ordinary dream, the audience attending a social dream comes away from it afterward undisturbed and quickly forgets all about it except perhaps a few memorable details and the general feeling tone it evoked. (The overall notion of social dreams as important indicators of social trends and unresolved social problems will be explored at greater length in a separate contribution.)

The particular social dream we have in mind is the movie *The Ruling Class*. Peter O'Toole plays the role of a well-born paranoid schizophrenic patient whose delusional system has it that he is Jesus Christ. In the asylum, he acts out the role of a benign, loving Jesus, tender and kind to all. But when he becomes heir to the family fortune, he immediately comes into conflict with his solicitous relations who would prefer to keep him institutionalized – and away from the money. Into this quarrel intrudes a helpful psychiatrist intent on curing O'Toole. The psychiatrist feels that once O'Toole accepts and identifies with his own Christian name, Jack, he will be cured. In an extraordinary experiment designed to facilitate this shift in identification, the psychiatrist confronts O'Toole with another patient who in his own delusion has elected to embody an altogether more formidable deity, the righteously persecutory Calvinistic God. In the exchange with his more severe delusional double,

O'Toole recants and is discharged as cured. Underneath, however, he has simply swapped his delusion for another, one much better adjusted to his new circumstances. Inwardly, he has become Jack the Ripper and with studied cunning he proceeds to bump off his familial rivals one by one.

The Ruling Class is an important social dream. (There are many others on the same theme.) At the upper level of society, madness gives way to psychopathy (replete with antisocial grandiosity) as a response to intolerable value conflict. But this psychopathy passes for normal, and in the end will triumph. In its appreciation of the comedy, moreover, the audience does not stumble over the improbability of it all. Because, we would submit, it recognizes implicitly, but without conscious reflection, that it is not really so improbable. It is becoming an everyday phenomenon.

3.6. Summary

Let us recall how we began. We started out with a historical overview of the diagnostic category of psychopath; our aim was to show how a variety of different clinical and social considerations gradually converged on consistently antisocial behavior as the hallmark of a specific syndrome. But no sooner did we begin to investigate this syndrome than it revealed itself to be a continuum that stretched from the horrendous extreme of the true psychopath all the way to a largely accepted psychopathy of everyday life. Further, when we began to investigate this continuum, we rapidly discovered that its description beyond a phenomenological level required multiple perspectives. We saw that dissociation, thrill seeking, and the antisocial pursuit of power were combined in a new, pathological unity. This pathological unity, in turn, needed to be understood as a particular kind of outcome resulting from breaks in the natural developmental sequence whereby man as a social entity acquires a singleness of existence in which emotional, intellectual, and conative processes blend together.

Why pay attention to these breaks in the normal order? Because, as Bateson suggested, it is dangerous if we do not. Perhaps nowhere is this more true than in the study of psychopathy. The ordinary atomistic, syndrome-bound research paradigm of contemporary social science has advanced the study of psychopathy very little in the second half of this century. At the same time, as the newspapers confirm daily, psychopathic behavior in the public at large has been rising dramatically.

And yet traditional social scientific frameworks can do nothing more with this important phenomenon than quietly ignore it. In this essay, adopting a Batesonian perspective, we have argued that the root causes for the rise in psychopathy, especially in high places, is to be found in the progressive ruptures in the links of the system linking the individual to the social group via a system of shared values. We cannot afford to ignore these ruptures: Not only will they continue to make trouble, but they will make even more trouble when they operate out of awareness. And recognizing them is not enough; we must begin repairing them. Normalized psychopathy in high places, in our view, is largely the result of social distress as it has become institutionalized in the emerging world culture. Put simply, the psychopathy of everyday life will continue to prevail until we cease to be proud of those things we should be ashamed of.

Notes

1. Charles Manson in a recent documentary program on public television commented while discussing his past criminal behavior, "I don't break the law; I make the law."
2. For a detailed discussion of this research, see Hare (1986) in Reid et al. (1986, pp. 3–25) and Doren (1987, pp. 47–74).
3. The recognition of the psychopath in terms of becoming the hero of our age has been noticed by a number of authors such as Mailer (1958) and, in a more academic version, Harrington (1974) and Smith (1978). Although the last two authors, Harrington and Smith, deserve credit for recognizing the relative adaptability of the character structure of the psychopath in its relationship to social structure, they have not accurately understood the dynamics of the process. For example, Smith argues that its prevalence in contemporary society is due to the fact that we have not adopted a Marxist social and political economy. Perhaps if Smith had read George Orwell's *Animal Farm,* he would not have needed to pursue that line of thought.

References

Bateson, G. (1972). *Mind and nature: A necessary unity.* New York: E. P. Dutton.
Calhoun, J. B. (1962). Population density and social pathology. *Scientific American, 206*(2) 139–146.
Cleckley, H. (1976). *The mask of sanity.* St. Louis: C. V. Mosby Co.
Doren, D. (1987). *Understanding and treating the psychopath.* New York: Wiley.
Festinger, L., Riecken, H. W., & Schacter, S. (1956). *When prophecy fails.* Minneapolis: University of Minnesota Press.
Fisher, (1984, April). *The A.P.A. Monitor.* Washington, DC: American Psychological Association.
Fromm, E. (1956). *The sane society.* New York: Bantam Books.
Griesinger, W. (1882). *Mental pathology and therapeutics.* New York: William Wood.

Hare, R. (1986). Twenty years of experience with the Cleckley Psychopath. In Reid, W., et al. (Eds.), *Unmasking the psychopath*. New York: W. W. Norton.

Harrington, A. (1974). *Psychopaths*. New York: Simon and Schuster.

Henderson, D. (1939). *Psychopathic states*. New York: W. W. Norton.

Kardiner, A. (1939). *The individual and his society*. New York: Columbia University Press.

Koch, J. (1891). *Die psychopraktischen Minder-wertizbetiern*. Ravensburg: Maier.

Latane, B., & Darley, J. (1970). *The unresponsive bystander and why doesn't he help?* New York: Appleton Century Crofts.

Lifton, R. (1986). *The Nazi doctors: Medical killing and the psychology of genocide*. New York: Basic Books, Inc.

Mailer, N. (1958). The white Negro. *Voices of Dissent*. New York: Grove Press.

Merton, R. (1968). *Social theory and social structure*. New York: Free Press.

Merton, R. (1987). Three fragments from a sociologist's notebooks. *The Annual Review of Sociology, 13*, 8–10.

Morel, B. (1897). *Traité des dégénérescences physiques, intellectuelles et morales de l'espece humaine*.

Niebuhr, R. (1960). *Moral man and immoral society: A study in ethics and politics*. New York: Scribners.

Orwell, G. (1946). *Animal Farm*. New York: Doubleday.

Osgood, C. E. (1975). A dinosaur caper: Psycholinguistics, past, present, and future. In D. Aaronson & R. Rieber (Eds.), *Developmental Psycholinguistics and Communicative Disorders. Annals of the N. Y. Academy of Sciences, 263*, 16–26.

Partridge, G. (1928). *Proceedings of the American psychiatric association: First colloquium on personality investigation*. New York: Privately printed.

Pritchard, J. (1837). *Treatise on insanity and other disorders affecting the mind*. Philadelphia: Caley and Hall.

Pritchard, J. (1842). *Different forms of insanity in relation to jurisprudence*. London: Hippolyte Baidliere.

Redl, F., & Wineman, D. (1951). *Children who hate*. New York: Free Press.

Smith, R. (1978). *The psychopath in society*. New York: Academic Press.

Spitzer, R., et al. (1987). *Diagnostic and statistical manual of mental disorders*, 3rd ed. rev. Washington, DC: American Psychiatric Association, 342–346.

Sullivan, H. S. (1953a). *Interpersonal theory of psychiatry*. New York: W. W. Norton.

Sullivan, H. S. (1953b). *Conceptions of modern psychiatry*. New York: W. W. Norton.

Sutherland, E. H. (1934). *Principles of criminology*. Chicago: Lippincott.

Turnbull, C. (1972). *The mountain people*. New York: Simon and Schuster.

Veblen, T. (1899). *The theory of the leisure class*. London: Macmillan.

Walker, N., & McCuble, S. (1978). From moral insanity to psychopathy. In Rieber, R. W., & Vetter, H. J. (Eds.) *The psychological foundations of criminal justice: Historical perspectives on forensic psychology*. New York: John Jay.

Wallace, G. (1914). *The great society: A psychological analysis*. New York: Macmillan.

West, L. J. (1967). The psychobiology of racial violence, *Archives of General Psychiatry. 16*(6), 645–651.

4. Bateson's concept of mental illness

THEODORE SKOLNIK

In the contemporary world when a mind deviates from some mutually agreed upon style of organization this is judged to be a case of mental illness. The choice of a particular label, such as illness, plays a particularly significant role in how mind comes to be regarded. The problem of how people organize their minds is not a new one, however. As long as there have been people with minds, I suspect some minds have been organized differently from many of the others. In different historical periods different forms of mental organization have been deemed to "require" treatment, and society has attempted to comprehend and to provide treatment for such maladies. But how a nonmaterial entity, such as a society, can communicate with and treat the nonmaterial entity we call mind is a vexing question. Society itself is also a form of organization. People structure societies for themselves. (Is that indeed true of minds?) These organizations are powered by ideas: ideas that are sometimes fashioned into various myths designed to explicate "human nature," in order to render it treatable. People have looked to various sources of inspiration in their search to comprehend what moves us; that is, the nature of being human. Indeed, this search for comprehension may be a central aspect of human nature itself. Some have attributed their inspiration to various forms of extrahuman wisdom, others to the authority of science, but all seek unshakable authority on which to base treatment. Recognizing as crucial in the response to society's disturbances (especially those we label mental) some form of indubitable proof, people have fashioned myths out of the scientific knowledge available in the societal pool. Our science allows us two major choices regarding the "truth" of human nature. We can choose to believe either that what moves us to madness is predetermined in our chemistry by heredity, or that mental disorganization has a probabilistic epigenesis communicated in the meeting of minds.

Gregory Bateson's (1979) description of mind and nature suggests a third choice. If mind is partly nature and partly nurture, a model will be needed to describe how the parts of mind communicate with each other. In the book published posthumously Bateson discussed the function of such a model.

> A model has several uses: first, to provide a language sufficiently schematic and precise so that *relations* within the subject that is being modeled can be examined by comparing them with relations within the model. Occidental languages, in general, do not lend themselves to the discussion of relations. We start by naming the parts and after that the relations between the parts appear as predicates attached usually to a single part, not to the two or more parts among which the relation existed. What is required is precise talk about relations, and a model will sometimes facilitate this. That is the first purpose of a model. (p. 37)

Epistemological models in contemporary psychology have been constructed on an outmoded paradigm derived from the British Associationists of the seventeenth century. Bateson's new model gives us a more powerful tool for the investigation of the "lost" mind.

Associationism describes a human being who takes in discontinuous, serial, state-dependent sense data from the external world. Organization has to be superimposed on the isolated states. The resulting psychoanalytic model requires intense state-dependent emotions for the organization of representations. This, in turn, yields a model of psychosis as a discontinuous state-dependent entity. That which is labeled as "diagnosable" mental illness is thought to be something so different from other kinds of consciousness that it can be explained only by reference to anomalies (in the neural substructure) caused by faulty genes.

It should be made clear at the outset that no single group within the present-day mental health delivery system is to be singled out as culpable. The epistemological model that develops in the consciousness of a society is a sincere attempt to come to terms with the problems that beset it. Some professional groups seem to champion the model more at one time; others, at another. Lately a genetic model seems to be in vogue in the clinical schools of all the professions; but another, "interactional," model is now emerging, particularly among those professionals who do research and clinical work with mothers and infants.

Reading philosophy I have always been puzzled as to how we could theorize about epistemological questions without observing the newborn infants we are supposedly theorizing about. How does an infant, in fact, take in information? Recent methods allowing infants to "tell us" the differences that matter to them (Stern 1986) have brought infant research to new levels of sophistication. It has become strikingly apparent that the mind of the newborn cannot be characterized as a tabula rasa. Nor do the classical psychoanalytic images of newborns as protected by a "stimulus barrier" (Freud, 1920) or a "normal autism" (Mahler, 1969; Mahler, Bergman, & Pine, 1975) adequately describe the newborn's avid engagement and interaction with the world. Stern argues that infants enter the world equipped, by predesign, to perceive differences in the external world in several modalities, and to transfer the information from one modality to another.

Those mental health professionals who argue a noninteractional, nature (to the exclusion of nurture), discontinuity theory, it should be emphasized, are outside the theoretical boundaries of the rest of the biological sciences. Science views life processes as continuous. Mental illness does not mean that consciousness suddenly falls off a cliff. There is highly articulated, complex organization at one end, disorganization at the other, and various forms of less articulated organization in between. The following examination of mind and epistemology will provide support for a view of mind and its possible disorganization that is consistent with a biology of continuity. The constructed model discloses how to enter the continuous process, attempt to understand how the parts communicate, and perhaps intervene to prevent disorganization. That mental–emotional systems manage, against overwhelming odds, to continue functioning is not news. The fact that the George Washington Bridge is still up generates no big splashing headlines. The significant challenge to society is the fact that mental/emotional systems break down. Instances of malfunction in the self-regulatory and self-correcting mechanisms of mind are plentiful. The challenge for us is to transpose individual instances into underlying principles. The inability to do so is a clear indictment of the simplistic inadequacies of our epistemology.

Bateson offers a list of criteria as a preliminary metatheory of mind. These criteria also structure the present investigation. There is an underlying assumption here that I would like to make explicit: The communication of adults with infants affects the development of mind. Research evidence compiled by Stern (1986) will be cited to support this.

Bateson's metatheoretical list is as follows: (1) A mind is an aggregate of interacting parts or components. (2) The interaction between parts of mind is triggered by difference, and difference is a nonsubstantial phenomenon without location in space or time; it is related to negentropy and entropy, rather than to energy. (3) Mental process requires collateral energy. (4) Mental process requires circular (or more complex) chains of determination. (5) In mental process, the effects of difference are to be regarded as transforms (i.e., coded versions) of events that preceded them. The rules of such transformation must be comparatively stable (i.e., more stable than the content) but are themselves subject to transformation. (6) The description and classification of these processes of transformation disclose a hierarchy of logical types immanent in the phenomena.

4.1. Interacting parts

As neuroanatomists have revealed, our brains are apportioned into functional areas. These sections of brain have been identified as contributing to mind. Neuroanatomists have done quite a reasonable job of mapping such areas and even some of the millions of convoluted neural pathways between areas. The mental and emotional functions of the areas have not been mapped definitively. Through interaction, the parts take on functions different from those they might perform in isolation. The debate over the functions even of the right and left halves of the brain continues (Kinsbourne, 1978; Goldberg & Costa, 1981). From the outset we can see that any theory that wants to identify mind with any one part (such as the chemistry of the transfer of a neural impulse across a synapse) will not meet this first criterion for a metatheory of mind.

Nor is mind a system closed within the brain. The interacting parts of mind must include not just the neuroanatomy, but the external world, as part of its ecosystem. How can we even imagine the human mind flourishing or malfunctioning outside of its ecosystem? The difficult task is to grasp the interaction in the same way that the developing mind perceives its environment. We tend to emphasize whatever is most important to our own conceptual scheme. Unless we can understand and adopt the organism's view of the environment, we are unlikely to discern what is really important; instead we will produce patterns that are little more than artifacts, products of our misperception of reality. The ecosystem of mind, which will determine its order and disorder, includes the body anatomy and chemistry and those parts (such as hormones) that interact with and register its synergy with other humans. Families and the values and attitudes of society have to be considered as parts of the ecosystem for mind. This is not a precise exhaustive list, but merely an impression of the extent of the mental–emotional ecosystem.

We cannot afford the illusion that the human organism can be studied apart from its ecosystem. This illusion gave human investigators the comfort that they were engaged in "pure" science, as with nineteenth century physics. But even physicists no longer labor under the illusion that they can comprehend pure elements as separate from their relations. Indeed subatomic particle physics is the study of interrelationships. That is what the human sciences need to be as well. The search for the "pure" diagnosable mental illness is illusory. No such phenomenon is to be found in nature. The human organism is a highly complex process interacting with an ecosystem also in process. Humans live in time, not as fractured fixed states.

Reviewing a large number of research studies, Sameroff (1977) reveals the complex interaction of parts in the ecosystem that go into determining the mental status of children. "Internal" physiological elements such as temperament, perinatal effects, and IQ are seen to be strongly influenced by "external" parts such as mother's psychological or socioeconomic status and family structure. For example, with well-educated mothers in stable families perinatal complications might reduce IQ scores five to seven points. Under poorer socioeconomic conditions perinatal complications resulted in IQ scores between 19 and 37 points lower. Four factors grouped together – anxiety, race, socioeconomic class, and number of children in the family – correlated positively with difficult temperament as measured at 4 months of age. Temperament in turn influenced how the children were treated: The mothers tended to stay away from them more, to look at them less, and to socialize and play with them less. Such correctional studies alert us to the interaction of physiology with society, and suggest directions for further investigation.

4.2. Triggered by difference

Mind can receive news only of difference (Bateson, 1979). Difference, being a relation, is not located in time or space. The idea that difference lacks location is hard for Western science and therefore for Western medicine (which have always wanted to locate things concretely in space) to accept. Subatomic physics, however, has demonstrated that the old laws of the material universe do not necessarily apply. Perhaps philosophy, which has been struggling since Aristotle to understand the laws of metaphysics, will be able to find superordinate laws that apply to the material universe and the universe of ideas, once subatomic particles are better understood.

Bateson gives a good illustration of the fact that difference is not located. The *difference between* a level road and the sharp bump our car drives over is not located in the road or the bump or in the space between them. But, cries the nineteenth-century physicist, my sensory organs and my mind have to be responding to something material, something "located." And here is where Bateson challenges the accepted models of mind and communication. The two stimuli that created a change relationship were material, but the change, the difference, is not.

The unchanging seems to be imperceptible to the sensory systems, probably of all creatures. And when change takes place very gradually, either because it is below detection for our senses or because it is masked or confused, the organism has difficulty noticing difference and does not take in appropriate information. Mind has difficulty distinguishing between slow change and stasis. Emotionally human beings often find this a painful distinction. It characterizes depression.

As Bateson points out, a frog sitting quietly in a saucepan of cold water will boil to death if the temperature of the water is heated up very gradually. If there is no moment that is marked for the frog to jump, it will never jump. Is our society succumbing in the same way to an epidemic of "pathology" spreading just below noticeable difference?

Mental health investigators, having trouble being aware of such gradual changes as the development of mental processes or a sense of self, isolate some static phenomenon for diagnosis. Unfortunately their descriptions of a state fool them into believing that the state, not the change process, is the reality.

When Bateson refers to information, he is referring to a world of "meaning." This information gets "represented" as relations between events in mental processes. This brings up another troublesome subject – memory. The neuroanatomical search for locating memory traces came up empty-handed, and Lashley (1951), who spent years on this research, rightly concluded that representations are not located in space, and that temporal relations must play a significant role in their storage. This is very distressing for those theoreticians who wish to reduce mind to the nineteenth-century material laws of physics. Imagine, if you will, a memory that is there, but not there. Just as with the bump in the road, the highway department can come along and level the road, but the memory of driving over the bump, the difference, does not get leveled. Perhaps this is why shock treatment, which does suspend memory for a time, fails to yield permanent results. Trying to remove an idea that is not located in time or space by altering matter that is located in space has got to have spurious results. The very logic of the undertaking is wrong. Just such faulty logic lies at the heart of the confusion about the treatment of mental illness. But just look at how much difficulty I am having in trying to convey this information, this difference, in this discussion.

4.3. Energy

A theory of mind will need a description of the interface between information, composed of differences, the origins of the information from the stimulus events, and the "control" that information exercises over mind, brain, and actions. Information is often the result of a communication between minds, transmitted on verbal and nonverbal channels. Such communication, no matter how energetically it goes on, introduces no new energy into the system of the receiver. The energy is already there in the form of metabolic processes. Bateson (1972) argues that the activity of mind, being part of an ecosystem, can *trigger* runaway conditions in the metabolic processes. "All biological and evolving systems (i.e., individual organisms, animal and human societies, ecosystems, and the like) consist of complex cybernetic networks, and all such systems share certain formal characteristics. Each system contains subsystems which are potentially regenerative, i.e., which would go into exponential "runaway" if uncorrected" (p. 441).

An examination of the metabolic production of hormones and neurotransmitters will reveal how these metabolic processes could be triggered into exponential runaway by certain communication processes. This energy link in the complex chain of events could demonstrate how mother–infant communication can possibly be a trigger for madness. Hormones function in several different ways, and therefore their energy plays a significant role in the complex chain of events we call mind.

As Snyder (1985) tells us: "In most higher organisms there are two primary methods of communication between cells: systems of hormones and systems of neurons, or nerve cells. In both systems cells "talk" to one another by means of chemical messengers. The main difference between the two systems is the level of directness with which they act" (p. 132).

However, continues Snyder, hormones and neurons do not maintain a clear separation. There are very close links between the two major systems of intercellular communication. Both may access many of the same messenger molecules, which sometimes have a wide-ranging, global effect on many organs of the body. For example, as Carmichael and Winkler (1985) state:

> Under conditions of fear or stress a surge of the hormone adrenaline mobilizes the body for peak physical response. Flooding the bloodstream at up to 300 times the normal concentration, the adrenaline interacts with receptors on cells in various organs, increasing the heart rate and blood pressure, and prompting the release from the liver of extra sugar to fuel muscular work. (p. 40)

Snyder (1985) reminds us that hormones follow principles of feedback and control. Such steroid hormones as cortisol are formed and released when factors and hormones from the hypothalamus and pituitary stimulate the adrenal cortex. Cortisol influences nearly every tissue in the body, causing metabolic changes that increase the organism's ability to deal with continuous stress. Sometimes messenger molecules are quite specific in their effects. Functioning as neurotransmitters, they are employed to carry a message across a synapse or to take part at a very specific stage in the conversion of protohormones into hormones. Neuropeptides act both as neurotransmitters (when released by neurons) and as hormones (when secreted by endocrine glands).

The manufacture and storage of adrenaline in the adrenal medulla has been analyzed into a four-step process. Internal regulatory mechanisms control the rate at which adrenaline is synthesized. There are external "loads" on the system such that these four stages never unfold as a simple chain, but are always responsive to the external stressors. Under sudden stress there is an increase in both the number and the activity of tyrosine hydroxylase molecules, resulting in first-stage increase of the conversion of tyrosine into dopa, leading in turn to a spurt in adrenaline production. However, as Carmichael and Winkler (1985) tell us: "When stress is sustained, resulting in prolonged stimulation of the adrenal medulla through the splanchnic nerve, a different process leads to a long-term increase in the rate of adrenal synthesis" (p. 42).

Carmichael and Winkler note the correspondence between the processes of the adrenal medulla and similar chemical processes in the synthesis of neurotransmitters. It is this long-term stress and alteration of the energy systems that has such great significance for mental illness.

The adrenal medulla contains material resembling enkephalines: a group of neuropeptide molecules, previously identified in the brain, that are currently considered highly significant in both the etiology and the chemical treatment of mental illness, because of their analgesic properties. Laboratory research so far discloses that the adrenal medulla produces catecholamines and enkephalines in varying amounts, sometimes increasing both simultaneously, sometimes increasing one and not the other. Much remains to be learned about the interaction among preparation for fight or flight, endurance of sustained stress, and analgesia, as well as their combined effects on mind. However, this discussion of metabolic energy must serve to remind us that neither mind nor the energy processes that "fuel" mind are closed systems.

We are far from understanding how substances such as adrenaline and enkephalines function after their release from the adrenal medulla. If they provide some analgesia during stress, the enkephalines are probably responsible.

It is suggested that prolonged stress in the mother–infant interaction by *triggering* shifts in hormonal production and thus changes in energy may be a major factor in the disorganization of mind we call mental illness. Lifton (1983) provides a classic example of prolonged stress. Following the atomic bombing of Hiroshima the survivors lived in perpetual fear. Very likely they were producing more adrenaline for flight and more enkephalines to deaden some of their life experience as well as emotional pain. They were in a state of heightened alertness and at the same time numb. What about the prolonged stress of an infant growing up in a family that is failing to respond adequately to the infant's emotional needs? How is the prolonged production of enkephalines from the adrenal medulla (as a result of misattunement in interpersonal communication) connected with poor or indifferent object relatedness? Can enkephaline deadening be somehow related to an inability to allow people to matter? Is it conceivable that the "runaway" of both stimulation and deadening is linked to teenage suicide, teenage motherhood, teenage drug abuse, and mental illness (all increasing at an alarming rate)? Have we as a society, as a result of this prolonged condition of stress and enhanced production of enkephalines, lost our ability to become alarmed? Have we become like Bateson's frog in the slowly heating water? How can anyone claim that societal stress lies outside the proper province of the mental health professional?

As Bateson reminds us, at least two interdependent energetic systems occur in mental processes and other life forms: a system that uses energy to open or close a gate, or switch, and a system whose energy "flows through" the gate when it is open. The significance of this distinction becomes evident in such phenomena as ambivalence, or the more severe and debilitating ambivalence of confusion of contexts, which will be discussed below under Hierarchy of Logical Types.

Information from a mental process with an attitude of acceptance can place a switch in On position, and a mental attitude of rejection can place it in Off position (Hess, 1960). This has been measured in the form of autonomic nervous system responses of changes – for example, galvanic skin response, contraction of the pupils, and many other responses. Carmichael and Winkler point out how similar the sympathetic nervous system is to the adrenal medulla in its use of hormones. The energy that flows through could be triggered either by information of an external event, or by metabolic processes accompanying excitation.

The functioning of the adrenal medulla, a gland that affects other tissues and organs by discharging hormones into the bloodstream, can be described in a way that agrees closely with Bateson's model of mind. It responds to difference; it functions with energy in complex chains; it transforms the information it derives from differences; and it has a chemical "memory" that alters the chemical sensitivity as a result of both short bursts of stress and prolonged stress. The stressors function as external loads on the regulatory processes. The adrenal medulla has "intelligence." It is not mental. However, this intelligent system is definitely interacting with and a part of the complex chain contributing to mind. Indeed, I suggest that chemical runaway in the adrenal medulla, in response to prolonged stress, plays a significant role in the etiology of mental runaway processes we call mental illness. One form of information that can function as a load to trigger the energy regulatory mechanisms of the adrenal medulla in this complex chain can be labeled fear or stress. It is being suggested here that prolonged or harsh misattunements between mother and infant may qualify as prolonged fear or stress. Can attunement of excitation between mother and infant trigger changes in the energy system? The concept of attunement is discussed further in sections on complex chains and on transforms and codes. In a condition of confusion of context (criterion 6) energy is flowing in and the gate cannot determine whether to be On or Off. Could this be considered sufficient stress to stimulate the adrenal medulla into increased production? Detailed research will be required to disclose the specific nature of the misattunement that may be defined as stress capable of triggering alterations in the energy system. Is it possible to demonstrate that communication might *trigger* hormonal runaway? Could hormonal runaway *trigger* mental runaway? I suggest not only that the answers all around the chain will be yes but also that the particular nature of the communication misattunements will be describable with the sort of rigor that would make training programs possible in which parents could learn the sort of attunement that would diminish the processes of runaway in the adrenal medulla. If this should prove to be the case, would not prevention of communication mis-attunement in the first two years of life be a worthwhile, cost-effective measure for the mental health delivery system to invest in?

4.4. Complex chains

To illustrate how mental/emotional parts interact in a complex chain of self-regulating organization, Bateson (1979) provides a simple mechanical analogy, complete with flywheel, governor, fuel, and cylinder. His machine, like a person, functions in interaction with the outside world: There is energy input and load, imagined as variable and exerting weight upon the flywheel. "The machine is circular in the sense that flywheel drives governor which alters fuel supply which feeds cylinder which in turn, drives flywheel. Because the system is circular, the effects of events at any point in the circuit can be carried all around to produce changes at that point of origin" (p. 116).

The early steam engines (Bateson's machine), prior to the perfection of governor devices, suffered from problems of runaway that, as Bateson describes them, sound strikingly like the runaway phenomenon of mind we have come to label mental illness. Some machines went into runaway, exponentially maximizing their speed until they broke or slowed down until they stopped. We could almost anthropomorphize these engines into manics and depressives. Other engines resembling our schizophrenics oscillated and seemed unable to settle to any mean. The challenge is to transpose the mechanical analogy into a model of mental processes. Some significant factors to note are (1) the presence of a self-regulatory mechanism or governor; (2) that effects have repercussions throughout the complex chain of events; and (3) that mind is not to be conceived as a system closed to external sources of triggering energy. External sources (other people) can significantly refine the functioning of the governor, but contribute also to its malfunctioning.

Clark Maxwell, examining the problem of self-regulating governors in 1868, concluded that the engineers of the day (much like today's mental health professionals) erred in failing to consider time. As Bateson (1979) described it: "Every given system embodied relations to time, that is, was characterized by time constants determined by the given *whole*. These constants were not determined by the equations of relationship between *successive* parts but were *emergent* properties of the system" (p. 119).

For mental processes to be self-regulating, they require anticipation. Anticipation requires symbolization or representation of the *whole* event. Take this example. There is some load on the system (perhaps hormonal in nature) or some thoughts that require adjustment. In a model of mind as a successive chain of associations, the load takes place at time 1, while adjustment follows at time 2. However, the adjustment is now adjusting a condition that has changed since time 1, and is likely to over – or under – correct. Only anticipation can tell a mental governor what correction will be required at time 2. Any model of mind will need to include the effects of representation in some form of hierarchical "prosodic" form. Even Maxwell's simple machine required such a governor. Can we deny this to mind? Bateson described this temporal view over the *whole* event as a shift in logical types, which he describes more extensively below under Hierarchy of Logical Types. As an example, he notes that

> the steps around the circuit of the engine had the general form: A change in A determines a change in B and so on. But when the description reaches the place from which it (arbitrarily) started, there is a sudden change in this syntax. The description now must compare change with change and use the result of that comparison to account for the next step. (p. 119)

To help convert the mechanical analogue in this metatheory into a model of mental processes, we will turn next to Martin's (1972) rhythmic model for the perception and production of language. Anticipation plays an important role in this model. There is a feedforward aspect in that adjustments in the ongoing processing are based upon information about future, as opposed to present, past, or immediately successive, elements of the signal. The decisions in production are made possible because of temporal redundancies at the prosodic level. The syllables to be accented can be anticipated in real time. Attention can cycle back to previous inputs during the low-information intervals between accented syllables.

For example, in the simple nursery rhyme beginning "Old Mac-Don-ald had a farm," the first stress is on "Old," the second is on "Don," the third is on "had," the fourth is on "farm." It is apparent that some overview of the whole string is required to produce the stress in the correct place.

> A given sentence, phrase etc. can be spoken in a variety of ways, being influenced by context, mispronunciation, foreign accent, regional dialects etc. Whenever these factors affect accent placement in an utterance, the temporal pattern of the utterance is affected also. In every case a change of accent level or location requires a reorganization of the whole pattern. Greater emphasis on one syllable would require a lower relative accent on another. (Martin, 1972, p. 495)

Accented syllables emphasize some aspects of a communication and deemphasize others. Thus rhythmic structure in language carries affective weight. Verbal language in the second year of life and "body" language in the first year all have rhythmic structure and convey affective messages through giving emphasis and difference to some aspects of the message. Long before the young child knows the meaning of words the child is learning the emphatic meaning of rhythmic structure. Long before my own son had the words to convey meaning he would "speak" using gibberish that had a rhythmic structure clearly conveying how he felt. His rhythmic emphasis could be coupled with pointing and other gestures and there was a remarkable degree of communication. Thus children appropriately encode rhythmic (prosodic) information into their speech signal long before having the words. Children have to learn this rhythmic information. There have to be differences in rhythm that make a difference in the communications in the first year of life, and complex chains of mind to encode rhythmic patterns and to "plan" the time in the future sentence (even if it is made up of gibberish) at which stress accents will be selected and actualized.

So far our model depicts a mind composed of organized parts. Information for the processes (the load on the system) derives from differences that can originate from people and things in the external world and/or hormonal and neural changes. These differences trigger metabolic processes that generate changes in energy that fuel the processes. Such changes carry affective weight, slowing, speeding, and otherwise punctuating the rhythmic processes. All of these elements operate upon each other in a complex organization. The image of a chain unfortunately conjures up links strung together in sequence. Mental organization, requiring anticipation, obeys prosodic, not concatenating, laws.

Research on the earliest mother–infant interaction, as reviewed by Stern (1986), describes the development of self-regulatory systems, organized into a Batesonian type of interactional epistemology, where the parts (which Stern labels senses of self) "speak" with each other and thus have repercussions throughout the complex chain and throughout the life of the system. He argues that from birth the infant is engaged in social and cognitive organizing processes. Information about both self and other is actively sought and taken in. Stern asks: "Can the infant experience not only the sense of an organization already formed and grasped, but the coming-into-being of organization? I am suggesting that the infant can experience the *process* of emerging organization that I call the *emergent sense of self*. It is the experience of a process as well as a product" (p. 45).

He even hints that the biological need for organizing experience may be an even more powerful motivator than "oral" needs. Such an epistemological foundation would fit more closely within the philosophical tradition of Gestalt psychology and Husserl's phenomenology (Gurwitsch, 1964) than within the psychoanalytic framework. Our view of what constitutes essential survival shifts from an image of an individual in isolation (as in the Freudian image of the newborn hiding behind a "stimulus barrier" or Mahler's image of the newborn trapped in "normal autism") to a self (from the moment of birth) *embedded in an ecosystem*.

Although prelinguistic, the organization of what Stern calls experiences of substance, action, sensation, affect, and time (e.g., "prosodic punctuation of experience") in the first year may very well be considered cognitive processing. Stern points out that in order for infants to differentiate one experience from another (and there is ample evidence they do) some form of memory, as a basis of comparison, is necessary. Stern suggests what he calls "representations of interactions that have been generalized" (RIGs). Developmental psychology will need to develop a theory of this early organizational process in interactional terms. Stern states that in all regulations a dramatic shift in neurophysiological state is involved. This raises the question whether there might be some way to operationalize and measure the hormonal or neurotransmitter representations of such regulatory interactions. Is there a hormonal generalization of preverbal experiences that sets up expectations? Would a core sense of self be an aggregate of cognitive, emotional, and hormonal representations of regulatory interactions? In such a model the splitting of mind and body is reduced. We are, of course, still left with the task of describing the *relation between* the aggregate parts.

Such a representation capacity, Stern goes on, allows mother–infant interactions to regulate the infant's attention, arousal, excitation, curiosity, cognitive engagement, sense of wonder, avidity of exploration, somatic state, gratification of hunger, shift from wakeful fatigue to sleep. To illustrate how such an interaction can serve as a regulator, Stern points to a game of peekaboo in which

> the mutual interaction generates in the infant a self-experience of very high excitation, full of joy and suspense and perhaps tinged with a touch of fear. This feeling state, which cycles and crescendos several times over, could never be achieved by the infant alone at his age, neither in its cyclicity, in its intensity, nor in its unique qualities. Objectively, it is a mutual creation, a "we" or a self/other phenomenon. (Stern, 1986, p. 102)

Thus, from birth to two months old a sense of self that might even be characterized as an emergent sense of Being or existence is developing. In the first months the interactions between infant and care giver are often given over to regulating sleep/wake, day/night, hunger/satiation cycles and each other. The parents rock, touch, sooth, talk, sing, and make noises and faces. The infant and the care giver are together engaged in activities that begin to create the governors of mind. The levels of arousal and excitation need to be kept within a tolerable range. Parents attempt to seek a tolerable range of arousal for themselves as well as for the infant. Particularly in the middle of the night, a negotiating process is already encouraging the infant to develop self-regulators. The parent will either soothe the infant or leave the infant to arrive at a resolution. From this interaction the infant is already developing a sense, There is an other out there for me when I am in distress, or I am on my own, I will keep screaming, or I will give up." Not just a level of excitation, but the infant's attention, curiosity, and affective and cognitive engagement with the world are developing regulators in this interaction. A significant factor in developing a sense of agency (where the child experiences generating or being the author of actions) is the ability to regulate the level of excitation. This is a difficult negotiation, probably dependent for its outcome, in part, on other negotiations and regulations. The infant in this model is not a tension-reduction seeker as in classical psychoanalysis, but as in the model of intrinsic motivation (Hunt, 1965) a tension-regulation seeker.

These elemental experiences of action, time, and so on are organized into systems that Stern labels (1) self-agency, (2) self-coherence, (3) self-affectivity, and (4) self-history. Likewise, dimensions of the other are also formed.

Such characteristics of self and other, to conform to Bateson's model, must yet be adequately described in terms of the *relation between* self and other. Self-agency, for example, must always be mitigated by self/

communality. Bakan (1966) has argued convincingly that agency unmitigated is a source of pathology both for individuals and society. On the other hand, without a strong sense of agency both individual and society are crippled. It has been argued, for example, that the rise of Hitler was made possible by the absence of a sense of agency in German society. One might also argue that the crushing loss of a sense of agency following the Vietnam War opened the way for the wholesale ethical breakdown now being exposed in government, industry, and finance in the United States.

To have to describe an organization of self/other and agency/communality approaches the limits of clumsiness. But Bateson did warn us that we have no language for relations. Since such an organization would evolve as a consequence of continued experience, we would need a model that includes variables that facilitate or hinder the evolution of the organization. In the section on psychopathology this change aspect of systems will be addressed.

It is crucial to understand how the communication processes in the mother–infant dyad contribute to the formation of these organizations. Since all four organizations show evidence of malfunction in what has been labeled mental illness, we will not be able to treat undifferentiated mental processes unless we understand how these organizations come into being.

Psychoanalysis, observing undifferentiated organization in the minds of some adults, postulated an early, preorganizing, developmental stage to which mentally ill adults have regressed. For this reverse logic psychoanalysis required an epistemology, like that of associationism, with a nonorganized, nonorganizing tabula rasa mind. Stern argues that since intercommunication with other people is being organized throughout development, these effects should be considered contributory to the differentiation of self and other.

4.5. Transforms and codes

It is true that changes, differences, and events in the external world are not identical with the representations of the events that mind organizes and manipulates. In order to use this information, mind has to transform these external triggers into mental events. Bateson (1979) reminds us of Korzybski's famous dictum "The map is not the territory." "We see map as some sort of effect summating differences, organizing news of differences in the territory" (p. 122).

Applying the important distinction between map and territory to the mind–brain problem, Bateson generalizes it into an assertion that the effect is not the cause: This implies that mental effects are not identical with brain causes. Some transformation or coding must be accomplished in order for mind to represent and manipulate what brain causes. How does a physical cause become transformed into a mental code? Centuries of philosophical labors have thus far failed to solve the mind–brain problem. However, the present-day mental health delivery model proceeds as if it had been solved. The assumption that medication has to treat merely the physical brain implies that the map *is* the territory.

Conceptually the treatment of mental disorganization with medication is an attempt to treat a digital (on-off) brain. If you prescribe the correct dosage, you will reach the "therapeutic window" and the psychosis will be switched off. This assumes that the brain and the mind (being one and the same) are digital systems. As Bateson points out, in the early days of cybernetics there was even some considerable debate as to whether to consider brain a digital or analog system. Since the single nerve does appear to be digital (it is either firing or it is not) then the brain as a whole should be conceived of as a digital system. Recently neuropsychological split-brain research has revealed how analogical the brain's response actually is. There are several reasons for this. Hundreds of neurons are clustered together into pathways. The multiplication of those that are firing over against that percentage that are quiet yields not a binary (0 or 1) but a graded response. The right hemisphere, with its more complex interregional organization, is better able to activate the entire cortex than is the left (Goldberg & Costa, 1981), thus typically yielding an even more analogical response. As Bateson (1979) states: "In addition, the individual neurons are modified by hormonal and other environmental conditions around it which alter its threshold in a truly quantitative manner" (p. 123).

Earlier it was noted that the effects of hormones as mediators in mind-to-mind communications in the external world, as energy from metabolic processes around the body, and as neurotransmitters in the brain will require considerable attention in subsequent research.

As we have described mind, there are hormones responsive to the external world that also act as neurotransmitters, neural pathways and organizations thereof, and rhythms and patterns of thought that can plan and act as regulators. Mind is much more like an ecological system, a forest or a seashore with self-corrective properties, than a digital system. It is hard to determine what the sensors for self-correction are in such a system.

Since mind achieves patterns, plans, action sequences (Miller, Galanter & Pribram, 1960), and even a sense of self, these organizations play a significant role in altering the thresholds of neural firing. How? The answer to this may lie in the mediation of hormones, but as yet it remains unknown.

In the context of this criterion Bateson discusses a type of communication he called "ostensive." What Stern calls the development of intersubjectivity and affective attunement is important for this type of communication. Imagine speakers of different languages trying to communicate. They have to establish several things. Are they speaking languages that are comprehensible? Are there commonalities of rhythm, cadence, and so on that carry information and therefore can serve partly as ostensive communication? Do some aspects of the languages they are speaking refer to concrete things and abstract processes (e.g., I feel good, I feel excited, I am glad to be communicating)? This is, in fact, the nature of the mother–infant dyad in the first year. Ostensive communication is going on and it has to be coded. For the development of mental organization such communication and transformation are crucial. How does a child come to grasp in the first year that things do, in fact, mean what they mean? This is the level of communication Bateson was addressing with his double-bind theory (Bateson, 1972). However, it would be wrong to place this communication issue as late as the second year of life, with the development of verbal communication. It is what transpires in the first year that creates the codes that will be transformed into verbal communication. Communication in the first year could also conceivably lay the groundwork for hormonal transformations.

Stern (1986) points out that infants seeing a smiling human face can smile in response. Without knowing that they have a face or facial features, without knowing that the face they perceive is anything like the face they have, without knowing the specific muscular configuration of their own face, which is only available to them via proprioception, infants match a response to a stimulus available to them via another model; that is, visual perception. So, Stern argues, not only is this a response available by predesign, but it shows that the ability to cross over from one modality of messages to another is available by predesign. We thus conceptualize infants actively engaged in communication with the external world; that is, a form of coding that psychoanalysis calls reality testing. While the differences that Bateson asserts to be the processes of mind are not located in time or space, such processes nevertheless require a sensitivity to temporality and other change qualities in messages. The infant Stern describes is indeed tuning in to the dynamic qualities of messages, not just to finished states. Stern tells us that "the infant from early in life is exquisitely sensible of and sensitive to the temporal features of the environment" (p. 49). He points to experiments showing that infants recognize the correspondence between an auditory temporal pattern and a visually presented temporal pattern. Thus, in regard to temporal information, the infant can translate across modalities. Stern calls for investigators to demonstrate infants' capacities to transfer the properties of duration, beat, and rhythm. With this as a foundation, he argues, the infant can grasp directly the dynamic affective properties of a message. These "vitality affects" are the differences that make a difference: "These elusive qualities are better captured by dynamic, kinetic terms, such as 'surging,' 'fading away,' 'fleeting,' 'explosive,' 'crescendo,' 'decrescendo,' 'bursting,' 'drawn out,' and so on. These qualities of experience are most certainly sensible to infants and of great daily, even momentary importance" (Stern, 1986, p. 54).

What is it in the message that enlivens it? Stern compares these qualities with those that enable us to glean the meaning when a dancer or a marionnette moves. It is the vitality, the intensity, or the urgency that is the difference that we grasp directly. Likewise, Stern argues, the infant grasps these vitality affects directly. In all their minute subtlety they are far more significant transmitters of information than the "categorical affects" like anger or sadness. These vitality affects need not be intense or traumatic. In this respect Stern again differs from the classical psychoanalytic position that relegates a primary organizing role to intense emotions.

Stern describes a person getting out of a chair "explosively." The explosiveness could be related to an affect such as categorical anger or surprise, or it might just represent determination. There are a thousand ways of getting out of chairs expressing many different vitalities and combinations. How is an infant supposed to gather the information out of an ever-changing kaleidoscope of vitality affect? Yet the infant learns to distinguish an explosive joy from an explosive impatience. There are distinct enough differences in these vitality affects, which we have not yet learned to describe. The description of these vitality affects will enable us to identify the kinds of communications that promote healthy organization and those that are potentially deleterious. The social world experienced by the infant is primarily one of vitality affects rather than formal facts. These dynamic, kinetic qualities carry and organize information. They are grasped directly. "In this fashion the amodal experience of vitality affects as well as the capacities for cross-modal matching of perceived forms would greatly enhance the infant's progress toward the experience of an emergent other" (Stern, 1986, p. 59).

The infant is born into an ongoing family and social system, and mind must gain admittance into it. The challenge of regulating one's own needs with an ongoing tension system is the task of each new life in any ecosystem. Since mind develops in a community with other minds, the infant has an intersubjective task to accomplish. According to Stern, at about seven months old we see evidence that the infant recognizes not only that it has a mind, but that the "other" has a mind and a subjectivity similar to the infant's own. If we are to comprehend the meeting of minds, we will again need a description of the dynamic qualities of differences that support this growing intersubjectivity.

Mothers are actively engaged with their infants both to regulate and simply to be with them. They communicate to exchange or transmit information in an attempt to alter the infant's actions, to enliven, to quiet, to prohibit, or to restructure the interaction in some fashion. A special kind of interaction that Stern focuses attention on is what he variously calls an "interpersonal communion," an "affective attunement," a "being with" the infant. He points out that when the mother indeed achieves attunement, the infant does not orient in any noticeable way, but when the mother misattunes, whether deliberately or otherwise, the infant reacts as if to acknowledge noticing a difference in the message. Most such attunements occur across different sensory modalities. The infant's affective expression may have been vocal, while the mother's attunement may have been gestural or facial. Very often, mothers shown a taped replay of their attunements reported that they were largely unaware of the process. We can see, therefore, that messages of differences can be carried over several channels at once. The infant is decoding complex information, and has the task right from the start of decoding what sort of message that message is intended to be.

At several points throughout this discussion, I have suggested that failures of attunement and the closely related phenomenon of failures of empathy (attunement is the first essential step in the sequence called empathy) play a significant role in the complex communication chain that could lead to hormonal runaway and disorganization of mind. There is as yet no research to conclusively link these phenomena.

However, the ability to operationalize the attunement processes would bring us a major step forward.

Bateson's double-bind theory of schizophrenia is predicated on the notion that failures in the ability to classify contexts of messages are severely disorganizing to mind. The section Hierarchy of Logical Types examines the question of classification of communication.

4.6. Hierarchy of logical types

One of the most significant ideas in Bateson's writing is his insistence on context. Every message is communicated within a context. No message, under any circumstances, is that which precipitated it. There is, however, a regular, albeit never direct or simple, relation between the message and that to which it refers. A dog stretches out its front paws and puts its head down. The message being emitted to another dog is, "This is play." If the message "This is play" fails to get transmitted, the animals could wind up fighting to kill. A man meets a woman and says, "Let's go to dinner." The intended message may be, "Let's go to bed." There is a lot more regularity for the dog's message and, in this culture, sometimes a lot of directness in the man's message. There comes into existence another *class* of information, which the receiver must assimilate to tell the receiver about the coding of messages. A message of this class will not only be about the person sending or the person receiving or even about the message being transmitted. It is of another logical type. It pertains to how you go about coding transmitted messages. Bateson calls these metamessages. There is a jump from member (a single event) to class of events; from the particular to the general. It poses an interesting problem for epistemology. Associationistic learning theory would have it that this leap from the particular to the general could take place only after long exposure to many similar events. In the epistemology Bateson is suggesting, each event carries messages not only about the particular but about the class of events. The animal or infant begins to classify on the basis of a single trial. The information about the class, the metamessage, is carried in the crossmodal perception and vitality affects that Stern describes. He reports an experiment in which a very young infant was exposed to an extended series of pictures of a smiling face. The infant was then shown the same face with an expression of surprise on it. The infant's extended visual response to the surprise is an indication of the ability to *classify* difference. Stern, citing Bruner (1977) and Kagan, Kearsley, and Zelazo (1978), suggests that infants are constantly "evaluating." They "ask" how discrepant the present experience is from a previous experience. They relate, in Bateson's terminology, differences to differences.

There are several levels of messages that are important, because codes are always conditional. What has happened between members of the dyad up until now, how recently they have been in contact, whether anything has transpired to color or change the relation in the dyad, all affect how a message is to be coded. A function of the metamessage is to *classify* the messages that occur within its context – defining and making the context intelligible. The ability to classify messages into logical types is essential to human communication. Consider the great import of metamessages in the mother–infant dyad. In the development of intersubjectivity, particularly in regard to what Stern calls affective attunement, we have a situation where the infant is watching the infant watching the mother watching herself watching the infant. In all these interactions both mother and infant have to somehow convey to each other that the affective context for this communication is, for example, happy, playful excitement. Stern tells us that the metamessages are carried by various temporal attunements. This kind of mother–infant communication is always a sequence of contexts of learning in which each member is continually being corrected as to the nature of each previous context. It is easy to appreciate how many ways this communication could go awry; mother and infant have to stay in contact in order to complete any one of these sequences. Considering how many ways we in our adult-to-adult conversations break the contact – for example, by thinking about the chores that still need to be completed or about what we want to say while the other is still talking, or by turning away simply because we are tired or grumpy – it is evident how hard the mother–infant communication of affective attunement can be, and how many opportunities there are for the infant to feel misunderstood, even confused and disordered, in its mental/emotional grasp of metamessages.

Stern also describes the problem of "authenticity." The mother wanting to transmit a message of prohibition may say, "Don't do that," but with a sweet, playful voice quality, and a smiling expression in the facial/gestural channel. Which channel carries the classifying message, "This is the authentic message to be adhered to"? Probably each mother–infant dyad establishes its own means of determining classifiers through a sequence of negotiations. Disturbance sets in, according to Bateson, when the ability to classify accurately from among the messages on the several channels is markedly impaired. There are almost always multiple agendas being transmitted on different channels, so we cannot say that the inauthenticity of a single message is the pathognomonic culprit. However, there is a difference between softening a prohibition and chronically sending manipulative messages with the implied prohibition against ever classifying correctly. If a parent is committed to dissembling and obfuscation, direct contact will never be established. The question of authenticity or sincerity is a matter for classification of logical types. Is this action really what it claims to be, or is it play, or pretending, or just a minor dissembling, or perhaps a deceitful, unconscionable lie? It is not at all uncommon for people to relate some painful mishap with a broad grin and some upbeat enthusiasm, not wanting to experience the emotional impact of what their words are saying. Such ethical problems are crucial to the wholesome development of the infant. When, at two months old, the infant is excited by a new rattle, and Mommy generates a response, the infant needs to be able to experience, in the rhythms of her response, whether she is attuned to or out of synchrony with the infant's excitement. If the latter, then the infant needs to know whether the dyssynchrony is all right or not. What is the metamessage? Which of mommy's responses is a classifier of the other responses? Amazingly, the two-month-old infant is involved with this very high level of logical abstraction, as are all baby animals.

In the animal world the ability to classify the sort of message being transmitted by friend, foe, or prey has crucial survival value. Likewise, in the mating game the superior male is not just the strongest, but the one able to distinguish the trick from the actual attack maneuver of his opponent. He has to be able to anticipate. As we saw with human communication, this requires a grasp of prosodic processes (Martin, 1972) to understand the whole, and to go back and forth over the information as it unfolds. Human survival likewise requires similar classification skills. However, "food" for the human infant is emotional as well as physical substance. Without emotional food human infants wither and die. The human infant must be able to "read" the subjectivity of others. Since we do not read minds we must be able to read and classify such information as Stern's vitality affects.

The clear and unambiguous transmission of context is probably more crucial than the transmission of the message itself. How can the reader, given the sophisticated level of logic involved, believe that a newborn infant is engaged in such classification of messages? It helps to point out that even lower animals do it. We are, therefore, talking about something that mind is capable of long before conscious cognitive processing. The capacity for classifying metamessages is probably hard wired into our biology. Bateson suggests that since this sort of coding of messages – for example, "That movement over there means food" – is found so pervasively among lower animals and is so essential for survival, it does not have to be learned. Analyzed in humans, such classification looks like a high level of abstract logical thinking, and we assume it must be painstakingly learned and maybe even taught to the young by adults. When we see it in the ecology of young animals, however, we recognize that it does not have to be taught. On the other hand, confusing and distorting experiences contrived by humans can most definitely teach mistakes in the natural classification of events. At a benign level Bateson mentions humor, which depends on playing with communication at several levels simultaneously: intentional confusion. Without distortions of logical types, there would perhaps be no humor.

As a less benign example of faulty logical typing, Bateson discusses how, in our attempt to rehabilitate criminals, we address the manifest behavior rather than the underlying character of the criminal. Punishing a particular act addresses the wrong level of logical type and cannot extinguish the way in which the criminal has organized a sense of self while acting in the world. There is similarly erroneous logical typing involved in the chemical treatment of mental illness. The disordered thinking, bizarre behavior, and so on are all part of an organization of a complex chain of images of self, images of others, images of how self and other affect each other.

Many people who succumb to the schizophrenias have extreme difficulty with such classifying. Many borderline people have difficulty to a lesser degree. Such people, "concrete" or "black and white" in their classification, have difficulty grasping that some communications are to be classed as play or as metaphors, or as gestures of friendliness rather than of exploitation. The question for research that then emerges pertains to the nature of the communications by which people are taught to fail in their classification ability. Bateson suggested that "when the discrimination of levels of communication becomes confused or distorted various sorts of frustration and pathology can be the result" (p. 127).

Bateson tried to illustrate this very significant insight with his double-bind theory. Critics have suggested that distortions of communication, particularly verbal/nonverbal ambiguities that the theory addresses, are not powerful enough to account for the intractable pathology of the schizophrenias. I have tried to show how the principle of double-bind communication, applied to the developing core self and intersubjectivity in the first year of life, might be incorporated within a complex chain of hormones and neurotransmitters. Would this render the theory robust enough to account for the development of the schizophrenias and affective disorders? The research tools are available today for us to investigate messages and metamessages. We can state how communication sequences contribute to the development of accurate, and therefore wholesome, maps and how some communication contributes to the development of maps that are grossly inadequate for negotiating the territory of living with other people. Accurate maps permit a sense of agency – for example, "I am the author of my actions and my actions communicate my intent, both as to the behavior and the context of our interaction." Inaccurate maps do not permit self-regulation. The mental/emotional "governor" malfunctions and the system goes into runaway.

4.7. The objectivity of psychopathology

Taken together, the criteria of Bateson's metatheory suggest that the organization and accuracy of the conceptual map with which individual or societal mind operates are major factors in its effectiveness. If, as Bateson often reminds us, the *relation between* elements is vital to its organization, then all the ways we have of diminishing or hindering a relational management of our concepts will be detrimental to knowing and responding. Conversely, flexibility can be considered a criterion of health for an ordering system.

Throughout this discussion it has been suggested that mind is, indeed, not just a product of its environment but by its very nature continues to be in relation with its environment. An attempt has been made here to relate bodily elements, such as hormones, to mental elements, such as the preverbal vitality affects in the mother–infant interaction. Evidently we are dealing with at least a tripartite system: body, mind, and external world. Freud's tripartite model of id, ego, and superego, which likewise attempted to include body, mind, and society with its values, is familiar, but awkward, because its component parts are separately organized. For Bateson the relation between all components of a system in their initial organization is an essential feature of its functioning. To isolate one component to the exclusion of others violates its nature and necessarily provides a false representation.

For mind to formulate some knowing, either about itself as external object or about a concept such as what is to be considered psychopathological functioning, requires a complex chain of events. The original structure (body or nature) interacts with external information in the communication environment. The response and the alteration in the structure all determine the nature of the object. Therefore, there would never be an objective truth out there separate from the processes of knowing and responding. Maturana (1980), who was considered even by Bateson to be continuing these epistemological investigations, returned to a Cartesian split model. He postulated that the original internal structure *alone* determines the perception, requiring an artificial bridge between internal and external. In British associationism the external perturbation (or stimulus) determines response, and for Maturana the response is "structure determined." In his model there is no such thing as an objective reality and no information. Maturana violates the fundamental and crucial interactional nature of Bateson's epistemology.

The present-day mental health delivery system, based on the biomedical model, conceptually isolates the biological, genetic, or bodily component. This is a direct legacy of the Cartesian body–mind division. Bateson argues that the Cartesian splitting has done a great disservice to our scientific conceptualization and needs to be reversed or undone, if possible.

The concept of psychopathology in societal mind would profit greatly from a reorganization that revitalized the relation between components. Societal mind might then be in a position to deliver a more effective response. In order to organize such a new structure, some destructuring is required. The first step necessary is to examine whether the concept of psychopathology as we know it today is an eternal, elemental verity or whether it is open to reconsideration.

According to Bateson's definition, the biomedical model, by excluding the communication environment from its concept of psychopathology, is in epistemological error. The concept, however, is not readily available for reconsideration. Certain vested interests rely heavily on propagating the idea that pathology, labeled mental disease, is an objective reality. Rendering "disease" into the domain of a real "truth" that exists "out there" quite aside from the human domain of language, concepts, and values gives the mental health delivery system a propaganda advantage. People think of the currently prevailing definition of psychopathology as a timeless, culture-free, permanent truth.

Dell (1983), in a lecture given to the annual meeting of the Association for Humanistic Psychology, relates a very important argument of Bateson to the question of our definition of pathology.

> We think that language is a tool for describing the world in which
> we live, when, in fact, the world in which we live is language. To
> be human is to live in language, and to live in language, totally
> (i.e., to mistake our concepts for reality) is to be alienated in
> language – alienated from the world in which we think we live.
> (p. 6)

> The world of concepts and constructs is enormously compelling.
> Concepts and constructs make so much sense and are so helpful in
> ordering our lives that we believe them to be really real. They are
> not. (p. 5–6)

Pathology is thus a linguistic product; that is, a construct in our communication environment. Dell further illustrates how the concept of pathology and the particular societal values that shape what we deem pathological undergo a pernicious shift in meaning: From a belief that some form of mental functioning would be in the best interest of the individual and even of the society, certain interests go on to advocate compliance with a given style of mental functioning. However, as Dell and other authors (Szasz, 1961, 1970, 1971; Foucault, 1965; Halleck, 1971) have emphasized, to defend oneself against certain behaviors is not equivalent to advocating that those who exhibit them are diseased, and that the values we regard highly must be the same for all people.

Dell points out that the segment of society that is responsible for the study of the way things function, the scientific community, operates under the assumption that the universe it observes always functions perfectly according to its own laws. The only way for science to proceed, to be able to have any confidence in its observations, is to assume some form of predictable, deterministic universe.

But can human scientists, from our vantage point, ever know all the variables? For many observations there is likely to remain a high degree of uncertainty. However, modern mathematics, dealing with phenomena containing extreme variability – for example, the weather or jagged edges of a coastline – has derived formulas that force even such "chaos" into some order of predictability (Prigogine & Stengers, 1984). The more complex, irregular, and spontaneous the studied behavior, the higher the order of organization the formulas require.

The scientific community thus violates (perhaps unawares) its underlying assumption when it comes to judgments about psychopathology. Specifically, Dell points out that science accepts the universe as given and does not disagree with how it functions: Although science may not always understand the universe, it never postulates that the universe is "incorrect." The world always functions perfectly according to its nature. Likewise the objects science observes function perfectly according to their particular structure. Psychopathology, though, is said to be incorrect "nature."

Such concepts as malfunctioning, defectiveness, or incorrectness, Dell states, have no existence therefore in the universe studied by science. "These phenomena exist only for an observer who sees that a given object, system, machine, or organism is not functioning according to the criteria which he or she holds" (Dell, 1983, p. 3).

If objects always function perfectly as they are meant to function, pathology cannot be intrinsic to them. A particular form of thought organization is a perfect outcome of a given history. We may not like the outcome, but it is psychopathology only because we judge it to be so. How does the scientific community, which observes the functioning universe, come to be arbiter of acceptable and unacceptable functioning? It is puzzling to see how the meaning of values shifts as the researcher dons the hat of the clinician.

Psychopathology is not an objective fact! However, if we are to construct a model of adequate organization, the first problem is the structure of our concepts: how structures are organized into a system of interactions, how many variables can be included for consideration, the temporal framework encompassed, the ability of the structure to reorganize itself in response to what it learns from environmental perturbations. The argument put forth in this essay assumes that an adequate representation of mind requires a systemic, interactional model that includes an increased number of variables in its structure. Human mental process includes the communication environment.

Bateson's epistemological model does not begin with an internal physiology separate from the external communication environment. If this model of mind does more adequately represent mental process, then when we come to consider disorganized thought we must consider the contribution of the other. Our model of the structure of self must explain how internal physiology interacts in the communication environment with the other. Mental disorganization can no longer be considered as caused by faulty or pathological internal structure.

For Dell (1985), following Maturana, there is no such thing as malfunctioning, which exists only according to some human judgment;

that is, in consciousness. But this creates another artificial chasm that becomes difficult to bridge. There is, indeed, such a thing as malfunctioning. It belongs in that sector of mind having to do with values, emotions, and judgments. True, there is no objective *Ding an sich* pathology. But the effects of this concept, or value, have just as much reality, throughout the system of mind, as if there were. Dell tells us that the only thing that matters is that the organism not be destroyed in its structure-determined coupling with its environment, that there are many ways to exist successfully, and that the organism must simply find a way of existing that works. All of this may be the case, and there are ways of existing that work better than others at a given time in society and the life of the planet. Human consciousness makes judgments about better and worse. Not that these judgments are the "truth": I can readily entertain the hypothetical argument that some forms of maladaption or malfunctioning in today's society are indeed what the planet needs to survive, or are as yet unrecognized steps forward in consciousness. But, the judgments in regard to functioning are part of consciousness, part of mind, part of the organism's being in the world, and just as real as the material existence, even if those judgments about functioning may be wrong in a larger sphere of consideration.

If we refuse to simply exclude the possibility of pathology, then we are left with the more difficult, but, I argue, more effective, task of challenging the values upon which we as a society at a given time in history make our judgments of pathology. I am not even sure, judging by our societal responses to what is considered pathological, whether as we move through history, our judgments are in any way moving toward a closer approximation of the truth. Witch burning, holocausts, gulags, electroconvulsive shock therapy, and our current delivery of stupefying medications all reflect societal judgments in favor of political control, not objective perception of the outside reality. How can we, with any degree of ethical conscience, hold up the value of objectivity, rationality, or reality testing as an indicator of nonpathology? Anyone who believes that correct perception of the real world is the definition of nonpathology is suffering from pathological projection. Any model, based on this pathological paradigm of objectivity, therefore, is itself contributing to pathology in society. The large-scale myth founded on this paradigm of objectivity should then in itself be considered pernicious, and society should take pains to reduce the brainwashing effects of this myth.

Psychopathology and its corollary, health, are value judgments. Before we decide what we want to judge pathological, we need to examine our values in an evolving systemic context. Dell (1980) proposes some values for our consideration. These values are consistent with the model of mind Bateson suggests. Any structure, in knowing and responding to perturbations, is likely to be healthier if it has a wide and effective range of responses. Dell, using the example of families, suggests that, as families evolve, complexity, flexibility, optimum use of energy resources, and adaptation to environmental change all contribute to healthy families, since they enable the families to disrupt the coherence of their existing system and reorganize into a new coherence in response to family and environmental change. Such families become even more viable as they continue to evolve. Conversely, pathological families would be simple, rigid, entropic, often symptomatic. Since they typically respond inadequately to proposed change, they become more redundant and rigid in their functioning, avoiding both the integration of environmental changes and the incorporation of their own developmental milestones. In order to convey the evolving nature of these structures Dell borrows a term from Bohm (1969). The values he holds in high regard for healthy families have what he calls a "high order of order." The pathological families tend toward a "lower order of order." Thus he is able to convey a process model for systems as they order their order effectively or maladaptively.

When Bateson suggests that the criteria applicable for mind in any narrow sense of individual thought process are equally applicable for any large-scale system, such as an ecology or a society, which is required to know and respond to perturbations, he is urging us to address such problems as how a society can know and regulate itself. Regulations in a structure–environment interaction very likely take place in some prosodic fashion (as modeled for language by Martin, 1972). Thus to argue that psychopathology is predetermined by the genes or the internal structure alone has got to be erroneous.

Delivery systems have differed historically in their determination of what the regulatory factor should be and where in the system it should be applied. They have tended, however, to point to different single factors, and have not been systemic in their view. The burning of witches and heretics are regulatory moves within the societal system; likewise, behavior modification of children in schools, lobotomies, and large-scale administration of psychotropic drugs. As Bateson points out in criterion 4, regulatory mechanisms have reverberations throughout the system. Thus, in our exploration of values, consideration needs to be given to the nature of regulatory moves and to the proper location for their application within the system.

As this essay suggests, there are complex regulatory moves taking place in the mother–infant interaction from the moment of birth. There is a concept of prevention slowly evolving in society as an alternative to the prevailing mental health delivery system. The concept of prevention suggests that some intervention in these early regulations between self and other could effect a reduction of psychopathology. The question might be asked in the form of how people can grow up to recognize, emotionally and cognitively, that their personal, private existence does have systemic effects? In other words, is it possible to reduce a narrow, selfish, narcissistic outlook and encourage large segments of the population to acknowledge the worth and importance of the other?

But Bateson's model is after all just an armchair philosopher's model. Those scientists who have come to put their faith in the stochastic model of proof have contempt for anything that is not supported by statistical data. Fortunately, such support does exist. Indeed, throughout the country today developmental research is achieving a more accurate representation of human mental development through investigations with an interactional grounding, which observe the communication environment of mother and infant. One issue, highly pertinent to our question of mental organization, is how the infant self achieves some degree of regulation of its affective existence, as discussed in the section Complex Chains above.

Without being so presumptuous as to assume that all mental illness can be prevented by effective regulation of mother–infant interaction, the argument here stated suggests that mother–infant interaction that encourages flexibility, higher order of order, more systemic recognition of self and other, can make a significant contribution in society's search for systemic regulation.

Society would not want to mandate any particular form of mother–infant interaction. No matter how effective it may seem, such external regulation would have to degenerate into a rigid, low order of order. Witness the difficulties of the present Soviet leadership trying to extricate itself from the damaging effects of many years of an inflexible, overregulated society.

On the other hand, this caution should not deter us from an investigation of effective mother–infant interactions that could reduce society's burden of psychopathology. As an experiment, if significant numbers of families availed themselves of effective mother–infant regulatory mechanisms, society might have a statistically reliable answer after several generations. Once we can do that we can ask what sort of regulatory interactions would result in high or low order of order in the individuals and in the systems created between individuals.

Mental disorganizations are distinctly regenerative processes within the human ecosystem. As with the dying of forests from acid rain, the attempt to treat the mere symptoms – whether mental disorganization or dying trees – reveals a drastic narrow-sightedness in our epistemology. The first and most important treatment must be administered to our epistemology. This is the insight we owe to Bateson.

4.8. Wrap-up: feedback/feedforward

This discussion has been woven together from many different sources. It may have been difficult to keep the overall tapestry in view while examining individual threads that, in themselves, stir up a reaction. Certainly we must underline some of the relations between in this abductive journey.

Some may wonder why Bateson, an anthropologist, should have dedicated himself to the exploration of epistemology. The anthropologist is one who asks, "What does it mean to be a person?" If part of the answer is that a person is born into and lives out his or her life in a social context, and as a consequence of this fundamental ontology needs to know, organize the knowing, and respond within that context, affecting and being affected by that context in some organized fashion, then indeed the proper province of an anthropologist is to explore the question of epistemology. This ontological model, with both individual and context talking with and affecting each other, implies that epistemology is not just the study of how the individual absorbs information about the outside context, but of a systemic interaction. We come to recognize that the organization of the context affects the organization of the individual and vice versa.

Bateson suggests a radical departure from associationistic epistemology. Each particular knowing carries with it contextual information designed to convey what kind of message a message is. The structure of such contextual metamessages has both feedback information and feedforward anticipation, perhaps even suggestive of planning. The model of stages of development exemplified by psychoanalysis and

Piaget falls short to the extent that discrete stages encourage us to view increasing knowledge as an additive chain. The concept of metamessages sheds light on how stages may "speak with" each other as Stern suggests. Obviously, some people and systems are able to organize the feedback and feedforward information in such a way as to accommodate greater and greater complexities and develop a wide-ranging repertoire of responses to perturbations. These systems, having a higher order of order are better able to survive.

Throughout this chapter the current mental health delivery system has been challenged. It has been considered to be one historical stage of societal response to perturbations. It has been suggested that an alternative, interactional, preventative model would serve individuals and society more effectively. It has been suggested that the presently functioning model falls far short of meeting the criteria of Bateson's metatheory of mind, which was outlined here. Whatever mental health model is put forth by the professionals serves as the publicly accepted model of what constitutes acceptable or unacceptable organization of mind. As such it plays a most significant role as a context marker, a metamessage telling all of us in society how to classify revealed mind. The current model leads people to believe that mental disorganization is a disease that exists only in the isolated individual, not in the individual's relation with other. As such a metamessage, it serves as a pernicious knowing, an institutionalized stress (see Chapter 3, by Rieber and Green) within society.

One critical factor when working with a person who has organized his or her mind in a way that has been diagnosed as schizophrenic is that that mind does not seem to be reachable by the other. This can be extremely frustrating to the people who are attempting to change the organization of that mind. Indeed, I have often observed in hospital settings that professional and patient enter into a sadomasochistic dance, frustrating and being frustrated by each other. But why, we must ask, must that person's mind remain organized in such a fashion as to be inviolate? Why does it feel under attack by the very system that claims to be helping it? This is a central question, in the organization of mind. It highlights the fundamental self/other nature of mind. Mind is always concerned with both self regulation and the regulation of information from the other. It can be organized so as to be changeable, it can organize a "fixed delusion" that is impermeable, and it can organize anywhere along the continuum between.

A central epistemological model for all individuals within society, such as the mental health delivery system, cannot be treated casually.

"Oh well, so maybe we haven't yet found a way to care effectively for an increasing number of unfortunate human beings." The failure to alleviate present human suffering is certainly a source of anguish for all the caring professionals who attempt to function within the present delivery system. But that is only a small part of the anguish mental health professionals ought to be suffering. The real problem with the model is the negative effect that epistemological error has on future minds. This is why an interactional epistemology, and models developed out of such an epistemology, are so crucial.

To the extent that any societal responses are one-dimensional and monolithic, they tend toward a lower order of order and reduce the viability of the system. Particularly those epistemological forces that converge to move responses toward a lower order of order ought to be brought under public scrutiny to enable the system to enlarge its repertoire of responses. At the very least, since survival depends on a higher order of responses, society must consider allotting its resources to a diversification of delivery responses. It has been suggested here that Bateson's metatheory of mind points logically toward early intervention responses. Such education of mother–infant responses not only would be preventative of mental disorganization but also would encourage a higher order of order throughout the chain of the system. This education would have to begin with an interactional epistemology in order to encourage a mental organization in the societal system that promotes a balance between agency and communality.

Bateson intended his metatheory of mind as an illustration, not just for the complex functioning of individual human mind, but for that organ of any system that needs to know and respond to perturbations in order to survive. This discussion has crossed back and forth between these two uses of mind. By moving back and forth across these borders I intended to illustrate how individual and system speak with each other. The societal mind, in creating its organization, must know and respond to its individual minds, practitioners and clients alike, in order for it to effectively foster survival of the society it serves. The discussion across the borders of individual and system takes on a music of its own. The more that music encourages the two parties to feedback and feedforward the more flexible will be the evolving organization, and therefore the more effectively will they survive. The premise put forth in this argument is that infants are born into this world actively engaged in this dialogue with the other. It is the nature of human ontology to be knowing and responding. Both infant and care givers (mothers and societal systems) affect each other in such a dialogue. At various

historical times systems have believed that they "know The True response," and have thereby effectively cut off the dialogue. A major
factor, which motivates many systems – families, religions, governments, and mental health delivery systems – to change or suppress
individuals, arises when certain individuals organize their minds in
such a way that they are no longer open to influence. Schizophrenia,
mania, even depression, are ways in which individuals alter their
relationship with time so as to be no longer in synchrony with the
present. Only when a person and a system are in synchrony are they
able to communicate across their borders.

It is being suggested here that in order to effectively foster the
possibility of continued dialogue throughout life, society must pay
attention to the first dialogue; that is, the mother–infant attunement.
Fostering this first loving attunement will maximize the change of maintaining synchrony between individual mind and systemic mind.

References

Bakan, D. (1966). *The duality of human existence*. Boston: Beacon.

Bateson, G. (1972). *Steps to an ecology of mind*. New York: Ballantine Books.

Bateson, G. (1979). *Mind and nature: A necessary unity*. New York: Bantam Books.

Bateson, G., & Bateson, M. C. (1987). *Angels fear: Towards an epistemology of the
sacred*. New York: Macmillan.

Bohm, D. (1969). Some remarks on the notion of order. In C. H. Waddington
(Ed.), *Towards a theoretical biology, 2. Sketches*. Chicago: Aldine.

Bruner, J. S. (1977). Early social interaction and language acquisition. In H. R.
Schaffer (Ed.), *Studies in mother-infant interaction*. London: Academic Press.

Carmichael, S. W., & Winkler, H. (1985). The adrenal chromaffin cell. *Scientific
American, 253*(2), 40–49.

Dell, P. F. (1980). *Recursiveness and social pathology*. Paper presented at Society for
General Systems Research. San Francisco.

Dell, P. F. (1982). Family theory and the epistemology of Humberto Maturana.
In F. W. Kaslow (Ed.), *International book of family therapy*. New York:
Brunner/Mazel.

Dell, P. F. (1983). *Pathology: The original sin*. Paper presented at Association for
Humanistic Psychology. Toronto.

Dell, P. F. (1985). Understanding Bateson and Maturana: Toward a biological
foundation for the social sciences. *Journal of Marital and Family Therapy, 11*(1),
1–20.

Foucault, M. (1965). *Madness and civilization*. New York: Pantheon.

Freud, S. (1920). *Beyond the pleasure principle*. J. Strachey (Trans.). New York:
Bantam Books, 1959.

Goldberg, E., & Costa, L. (1981). Hemisphere differences in the acquisition and
use of descriptive systems. *Brain and Language, 14*, 144–173.

Gurwitsch, A. (1964). *Field of consciousness*. Pittsburgh: Duquesne University
Press.

Halleck, S. L. (1971). *The politics of therapy.* New York: Science House.

Hess, E. H., & Polt, J. M. (1960). Pupil size as related to interest value of visual stimuli. *Science, 132,* 349–350.

Hunt, J. M. (1965). Intrinsic motivation and its role in psychological development. *Nebraska symposium on motivation* (Vol. XIII), pp. 189–282.

Kagan, J., Kearsley, R. B., & Zelazo, P. R. (1978). *Infancy: Its place in human development.* Cambridge, MA: Harvard University Press.

Kinsbourne, M. (Ed.). (1978). *Asymmetrical function of the brain.* Cambridge: Cambridge University Press.

Lashley, K. S. (1951). The problem of serial order in behavior. In L. A. Jeffress (Ed.), *Cerebral mechanisms in behavior.* New York: Wiley.

Lifton, R. J. (1983). *The broken connection: On death and the continuity of life.* New York: Basic Books.

Mahler, M. S., & Furer, M. (1968). *On human symbiosis and the vicissitudes of individuation.* New York: International Universities Press, 1968.

Mahler, M. S., Pine, F., & Bergman, A. (1975). *The psychological birth of the human infant.* New York: Basic Books.

Marlowe, H. A., & Weinberg, R. B. (1985). Is mental illness preventable? pros and cons. *The Journal of Primary Prevention, 5*(4), New York: Human Sciences Press.

Martin, J. G. (1972). Rhythmic (hierarchical) versus serial structure in speech and other behavior. *Psychological Review, 79*(6), 487–509.

Maturana, H. R., & Varela, F. J. (1980). *Autopoiesis and cognition: The realization of the living.* Boston: Reidel.

Miller, G. A., Galanter, E. H., & Pribram, K. H. (1960). *Plans and the structure of behavior.* New York: Holt Rinehart and Winston.

Prigogine, I., & Stengers, I. (1984). *Order out of chaos: Man's new dialogue with nature.* New York: Bantam.

Sameroff, A. J. (1977). Concepts of humanity in primary prevention. In G. W. Albee & J. M. Joffe (Eds.), *Primary prevention of psychopathology: The issues* (Vol. 1). Hanover, NH: University Press of New England.

Snyder, S. H. (1985). The molecular basis of communication between cells. *Scientific American, 253*(4), 132–141.

Stern, D. (1986). *The interpersonal world of the infant.* New York: Basic Books.

Szasz, T. S. (1961). *The myth of mental illness: Foundations of a theory of personal conduct.* New York: Dell.

Szasz, T. S. (1970). *Ideology and insanity.* Garden City: Doubleday Anchor.

Szasz, T. S. (1971). *The manufacture of madness.* New York: Harper and Row.

II. Language and communication in context

5. Language, languages, and song: the experience of systems (1968)*

MARY CATHERINE BATESON

The problem to be addressed in a conference on the effects of conscious purpose on human adaptation might be summarized as follows: There is a mismatch of some sort between the nature of the universe and the conceptualization of that universe that those who build the roads and spread the insecticides and drop the bombs seem able to harbor. As they reflect upon that universe, formulate purposes, seek to achieve them, and communicate with one another about them, they make and execute decisions that–cumulatively–tend to wreck an intricate balance that their minds fail to mirror, yet that balance is the context of survival.

There is a deliberate ambiguity in the above statement, as to who is meant by "those who build the roads" and so on. It is possible that we are dealing with a general maladaptive characteristic of human consciousness, which has become urgent only as a result of the shift in the power ratio between humans and their environment caused by the technological development of the past century. If this is the case, then we must ask general questions about the nature of consciousness and the conditions of the coupling between our species and the systems in which we survive. On the other hand, it is possible that this maladaptation is associated with a particular cultural context, that aside from the facts of power it is Western or Westernized or industrial societies in

*Mary Catherine Bateson has offered for inclusion in this volume the paper she prepared for the 1968 Wenner–Gren conference in Austria, "The Effects of Conscious Purpose on Human Adaptation," responding to G. Bateson's paper of the same title (1972, pp. 446–453). The paper was designed to open lines of discussion rather than to explore them fully. For the sake of its historical interest to the contemporary reader, it has not been revised to reflect more recent work and changing terminologies and methods. M. C. Bateson did not choose to use actual excerpts from this paper in her account of the conference, *Our Own Metaphor* (Knopf, 1972), since she felt that the issues it raised emerged in the discussion in other forms, but in retrospect it can be seen to have played an important role in subsequent collaborations with her father, as well as opening consideration of theoretical issues that would repay further work.

which consciousness is organized to lead to fatal misperception of natural processes.

The question might be restated in terms of an example in Gregory Bateson's letter of March 12 to the conference participants. If the pathology with which we are concerned is what Galbraith refers to as the "conventional wisdom," a particular set of notions that can be associated with a particular time and place and with particular philosophical systems to which they gave rise, then the problem is cultural. If on the other hand the mismatch between humans and their environment results from the possession of *any* conventional wisdom – that is, from the entire pattern of learning and tradition that is central to human adaptation – then we are dealing with a human problem. It may be very tempting to blame the mismatch on Western culture, because such a verdict would tie up with a lot of half- and three-quarter truths about the difference between East and West or, on a different axis, about the primitive mind, and because it relates to so many current fads and nostalgias.

A third possibility is that "those who build the roads" and so on threaten the balance because they act as part persons, and it is here that we must consider the importance of such things as religion and poetry, totemism and bird-watching. It may be that human beings are in multiple and variable coupling with their environment and that it is this diversity that has gone awry, so that some aspects of experience are too far excluded from Western culture.

I suspect that we will find that certain processes of the mind have a built-in mismatch with the homeostatic systems in which they operate, but that there is great cultural variation in the expression and even greater variation in the place given to those more subjective processes that would tend to neutralize them.

A further question involves localizing the failure. Shall we do our best thinking by focusing on individual consciousness or on interpersonal communication or on perception? How do we visualize the crystal that polarizes information about a system into a linear pattern? Language seems to have sufficient internal structure to bring about this result and at the same time to be sufficiently pervasive. We still have no adequate account of the relationship between language and perception, language and thought, language and personality. These may be similarly structured in general (so that we can search language in general for those characteristics that might explain a general miscoupling) or in particular cases. This paper will be an effort to shed some light on the alternatives discussed above through a consideration of the following questions:

1. What are the general properties of human language as a code that make it likely to act like the crystal described above? Why is it hard to talk about systems or easy to talk in lineal terms?
2. How do languages and cultures differ in their assumptions of purposiveness and lineality? How do peoples differ in the way in which they talk and fail to talk about systems? Note that here the data are limited because few people have asked such questions, although there is a wide range of material related in a general way that I will not try to cover: material on different types of fatalism, deuterolearning, worldview, and values theory. The examples to be discussed here will try to relate language specifically to *how alternatives are presented* and *what kinds of sequences are conceived.*
3. Lastly, a very few notes on the ways in which these properties of language are neutralized in poetry and in religious ritual. How is it that when we cannot talk sense we can sometimes sing?

5.1. Lineality of human language

Language, in its primary form, speech, allows the speaker three types of feedback: an aural, a kinesthetic, and an interpersonal feedback. This is not normally true of any other part of human communication (rarely, for instance, do we see ourselves in a mirror as we carry on a conversation, and when we do it is disruptive). New material on child language learning shows that children rehearse and drill themselves in solitude (Weir, 1962), and while this is obviously very important in learning to speak, it nevertheless also allows for the temporary reinforcement of errors. Because of the multiple feedback system, it is all too easy to disconnect the interpersonal loop and listen to the sound of one's own voice. The self-sufficiency of the writer is even greater: The rate of production can be very high and the rate of interaction very low. That this happens with philosophical systems is clear, and it is one important way in which social communication deteriorates.

Language is segmental. Any spoken message can be divided at several levels into a finite set of segments, most of which follow after one another, while a very few are simultaneous or discontinuous. Opinion is divided as to the actual role of these segments in the generation and apprehension of speech,[1] and it may be that they are more important in decoding than in encoding. Therefore the spoken line may somehow be apprehended as a series of segments each of which is one of a number of possible alternatives. On the semantic level, these alternatives in turn represent points in an analysis of the universe in which continua are subdivided into mutually contrastive regions. (Thus, for example, the spectrum is subdivided in a variety of different ways in different cultures and the meaning of a term like "yellow" can be ascertained by finding out what it contrasts with.)

Closely related is the fact that language is sequential. One segment follows another. It is difficult (outside of poetry) to say two things at once; one must always be said first. Language suggests that experience is composed of discrete and ordered entities. We can make a list of "the facts," as someone generally does in a detective story. Another aspect of this sequential character, combined with the properties of the channel, is that conversation tends to involve (alternately) a speaker and a listener, whereas interaction does not. In interaction, communication continues on other bands, but if we listen only to speech we see an alternation and a sequence of speakers. This could be contrasted with a conversation carried on in sign language in which several people can "talk at once," with their hands. This property of speech certainly leads to errors in efforts to describe interaction; how many errors does it lead to in interaction itself? (And to what extent need we include interpersonal alienation with ecological maladaptation in the formulation of our problem?)

Directly related to the segmental and sequential properties of language is the fact that as far as we know all languages make some distinction between subject and predicate. English speakers learn in school to ask, "What is the subject of the sentence, what is it about?" And then, "What does the sentence tell you about the subject?" These questions reflect dimly a fact about language, but it is by no means clear that they are the best questions to ask about interaction, or that the notion that some central entity is involved in all events is a useful one. One of the difficulties of talking about a homeostatic system is that we have constantly to focus on individual parts and make these the subjects of our sentences, yet most of these sentences end up as misrepresentations, or at least commit us to describing as sequential what should be simultaneous. Our problem, which directly parallels the questions of grammar class, is the fact that we say, "What is the problem?" (insect pests, traffic jams, Red China) and "What are we going to do about it?" It may be that we ask these questions because we assume that insect pests, traffic jams, Red China, are embedded in a reality of the subject/predicate type. Similarly, in interpersonal relations we get such absurdities as "I am going to go interact with X," "Y isn't very cooperative," "Z shows a great deal of mutuality," as if one individual could *do* interaction or cooperation – or indeed love – to another.

All languages also make some sort of distinction between nouns and verbs, a distinction connected to that between entities and events/ processes. They differ greatly in what they assign to each category, and in the ease with which it is possible to move from one to the other. The noun/verb distinction and the subject/predicate distinction are clearly related to the figure/ground distinction of Gestalt psychology. Built-in is the danger of erroneous reifications – assuming all nouns do refer to entities, and that something is going on wherever there is a verb. It may be that nouns are the more dangerous of the two, with their implication of something stable, where so often a variable relationship is involved.

Lastly, language is digital, not analogic. The elements of the code are arbitrarily constituted and can be combined in novel ways to make hypotheses, nonsense, and untruth, since the spoken form is itself in no way directly isomorphic with the world it intends to describe. To borrow the usage from Hopkins, language (outside of poetry) is not in general *informed* by what it refers to. Therefore, constructing a verbal description involves a process very different from that of painting the landscape to be described, since I must have some direct participation in the form of the landscape to paint it (or dance it). My wrist must replicate the curve of the hillside, but the form of my theory of the universe need not resemble that universe.

5.2. Relating languages and cultures

Researchers trying to relate individual languages and cultures to each other have looked at almost every part of language. However, only a few aspects of language that seem likely to be related to the formulation of purposes and the conceptualization of events in progress will be discussed here. Our focus now is variations between languages, but each of the structural features to be discussed can be seen as a realization of one of the general tendencies discussed above. I will draw on Tagalog (Philippines), Trobriand, Hopi, Arabic, and English in order to look at the following: the organization of noun systems, as these represent types of segmentation with different implications for posing alternatives; verb systems, in terms of grammatical categories related to sequence, causality, and purpose; verb systems, in terms of possibilities of shifting subject and predicate; and conjunctions expressing relevant relationships.

Noun systems

The vocabulary of a language may show a variety of types of hierarchical organization. The two important types diagrammed below probably occur in all languages but in demonstrably different ratios (Bright & Bright, 1965).

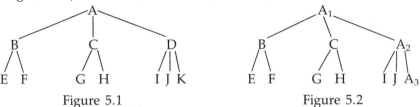

Figure 5.1   Figure 5.2

Figure 5.1 represents the type of hierarchy familiar from scientific taxonomies. Within systems of this sort, the question "Is this B?" evokes the context "or C or D?" However, for systems like that diagrammed in Figure 5.2, there is a question, "Is this A?" whose level of application and contrast is not clear, so that it offers a very different situation for decision making.

For example, if a middle-class American housewife asks her husband to pick up some bread, please, he does not know if this means A_1 (bread of any sort, anything baked from a leavened, salted dough, instead of potatoes, for instance) or A_2 (bread in some sort of loaf, of any kind, as opposed to rolls, biscuits, etc.) or A_3 (mushy American sliced sandwich bread, as opposed to French bread, rye bread, raisin bread, etc.) Unless he has some further specification, he would be wise to purchase A_3. This type of structure seems to characterize the posing of alternatives in Tagalog, and occurs even in such highly structured lexical domains as kinship.[2]

Another question of vocabulary structure that might affect decision making and posing alternatives is whether a language contains a large number of antonyms. Tagalog contains few, and there is no way in Tagalog of eliciting them, no question like "What is the opposite of X?" Dorothy Lee makes the same claim for Trobriand (Lee, 1959).

Verb systems: sequence, causality, and purpose

Some systems of obligatory categories affecting the verb (tense, aspect, mood) may be related to whether time is seen as a moving line with predictable future states (the usual characterization of the Western position) or otherwise. The question of tenses is compounded by the problem of what we called in high-school French "sequence of tenses," that is, the relationship between patterns of subordination and the selection of the appropriate tense ("He said he had had breakfast when I arrived.") Both time and aspect interlock with patterns of talking about what might have happened, what one wishes would happen, what the myths say happened, what did not happen.

According to Whorf (1956) (who can be relied on somewhat to overstate his case), two different sets of verb forms are used in Hopi, expressing:

What will occur	What really happened in the
What might occur	known past
What is hoped for	What is known to be happen-
Conjecture – the unknown	ing now
or divine	
Dim antiquity or myth	
What is just coming into being	

What is surely crucial here is the lack of the distinction that is so important in the verbalization of English decision making and in the definition of purposes, between future, subjunctive, and conditional:

He will come.

I wish he would come.

If he should come . . .

Whorf made the explicit claim that Hopi is thus more appropriate to the expression of some of the ideas of modern physics as he understood them, whatever that would mean in practical terms. Compare G. Bateson (1967): "We consider what alternative possibilities could conceivably have occurred and then ask why many of the alternatives were not followed" (p. 29). We can recast this statement about cybernetic explanation into a statement about cybernetic prediction and see how nicely Hopi fits.

Part of the difficulty seems to be that in the discussion of causal chains some languages seem to imply a temporal sequence. If we wish to consider the equilibrium of a system rather than its fluctuations, we are constantly in the position of implying that the future influences the past (that which occurs at the latter end of our description is causally related to that which occurs at the beginning, through a feedback loop); this may become the only way of recognizing that the proposed solution influences the terms of the problem. The problem may be partly alleviated in languages like that of the Trobriands, where tense is simply not an obligatory category, and sequence is avoided in the description of events. Another kind of partial solution to the problem exists in languages like Hopi, where categories of contingency or expectancy seem to cut across tenses. Another possibility (fully realized in some languages, I believe, but I can find only the partial Arabic example in my own repertoire) is to associate things that did not happen in the past with the nonpast:

kataba, "he wrote"	*lam yaktub*, "he didn't write"
yaktubu, "he writes, will write"	*lā yaktubu*, "he won't, does not write"

(But note that *kataba* may also be negated – *mā kataba*.)

Anticipating what is to be said about the language of poetry and ritual, since it will not be possible to go into such detail in that context, we might ask how people's sense of the reality of what they plan or anticipate is related to the reality of myth and prophecy that may also have special tense forms (Hopi, Hebrew).

Verb systems: subject and predicate

Virtually all languages have apparatus for shifting the figure/ground relationship – for moving an item out of the subject slot and putting something else in that position, the obvious example being the English passive voice. However, there is tremendous variation in the conditions of this shift.

English allows:

A/the man bought a/the fish (at a/the store for a/the neighbor).

A/the fish was bought (for a/the neighbor by a/the man at a/the store).

(If there is a direct object it may be moved into subject position, in which case the original subject, the actor, becomes optional. For a few verbs there is an indirect object that may also take the subject position: (A/the neighbor was bought a fish [at a/the store by a/the man].)

Arabic allows:

A/the man bought a/the fish (at a/the store for a/the neighbor).

A/the fish was bought (at a/the store for a/the neighbor).

(If the direct object is moved into the subject position, the original subject is lost; the agent may never be stated in a passive sentence.)

Tagalog allows:

The man bought a fish (at a store for a neighbor).

The fish was bought (by a man at a store for a neighbor).

The neighbor was bought-(a fish)-for (by a man at a store).

The store was bought-(a fish)-at (by a man for a neighbor).

(Almost any noun may take the subject position, usually called the focus in discussions of Tagalog grammar, but all other nouns are blurred; note that although some of the nouns marked as indefinite here may be definite for other reasons, the focus is always definite.)

This is a distinction that would seem to have a great deal of importance for the development of ideas of responsibility or of free will as opposed to determinism. Languages vary in the extent to which they allow constructions of the type, "The cookie jar got broken," and in the extent to which they imply a specified, active agent who could or should take action. Americans rail at Filipinos because Filipinos do not seem to live with the constant question, "What could/should *I* be doing about this?" Events move forward without specifically implicating a single cause or agent.

Conjunctions

The inventory of conjunctions in a language is one expression of the possible relationships between propositions in that language. What are the words of the type "therefore," "so," "whereas," "and," "but," "if," "although," and "however"? What kinds of "why" exist (as a result of what versus for the sake of what)? Trobriand is almost completely lacking in these conjunctions and yet we find them almost indispensable in verbal descriptions of systems – but perhaps only because other features of the language must be compensated for. Although these terms have a theoretical existence in Tagalog, the rarity with which they are used is striking. Terms expressing such notions as "although" and "however" are almost completely absent in conversation. Connections between ideas may be expressed in a rather more elusive way, for example:

1. An intonation pattern that identifies a sentence as a reason or excuse, perhaps best translated, "Well, you see . . ." *E Pagod na pagod ako e,* "Well, you see, I'm very tired." Sentences of this type frequently appear with no other sentence identifiable as the fact being explained (e.g., I'm going home early today . . .).
2. A particle *naman* that when inserted in a sentence identifies that sentence as in some way related to the previous one – contrasting, confirming, spelling out a result – but does not specify the relationship.

Attempts at refining logical systems concentrate very heavily on developing completely unambiguous sets of conjunctions, and yet we might ask on the other hand how many terms we have – and how many we would like to have – for relating the two propositions:

X loves Y   Y loves X

Working out the actual implications of these linguistic forms for the formulation of purpose and decision in the cultures with which they are associated would require detailed study of each, specifically related to an account of actual concepts of causation and patterns of decision making in the culture. Rather than undertake that here, we might summarize Dorothy Lee's analysis of the Trobriand codification of reality, compare it briefly with the "Western" one, and then make the same comparison in slightly greater detail for Filipino and American cultures.

Lee uses both linguistic and nonlinguistic clues, but the most important of those falling within language have already been mentioned, while others lie in the area of discourse analysis:

1. A paucity of conjunctions
2. No obligatory category of tense, time sequence
3. A paucity of formal devices for expressing relationships: comparison, contrast, transition, cause and effect
4. A vocabulary in which such relationships are not overtly expressed: lack of antonyms especially
5. A variety of lexical and idiomatic clues, corresponding to the absence of forms comparable to English "line of action," "getting your ideas straight"
6. Features of discourse that, quite aside from the absence of conjunctions, preclude their insertion (you could not go through a Trobriand narrative inserting "and so," "and then," and have it make sense)

Lee is claiming that Western codifications of reality are lineal (based on the pervasive metaphor of a line), whereas the Trobriand codification is not. This line, if it is as pervasive as she claims, is the line that underlies traditional notions of cause and effect. We could schematize her contrast as follows:

Western thought (causality and sequence):

$A \rightarrow B \rightarrow C \rightarrow D \rightarrow E \rightarrow F$

Trobriand thought (no causality, slight sequence):

A, B, F, C, E, D

(Actually, we violate her analysis here, by presenting our letters in a *line*. However, this can be associated with the inevitable sequence of narrative, because of the intrinsically sequential nature of language.)

American decision making is nicely expressed in Robert Frost's poem "The Road Not Taken:"[3]

a) Two roads diverged in a yellow wood, . . .	There exists a finite set of comparable alternatives, often a *pair*.
b) . . . And sorry I could not travel both / And be one traveller . . .	The alternatives are mutually exclusive. One *must* choose.
c) . . . long I stood/And looked down one as far as I could/ To where it bent . . .	One can mentally follow up the implications of a choice, but only to a certain point.
d) . . . knowing how way leads on to way,/I doubted if I should ever come back.	Decisions made lead to others, along a single irrevocable line.

Frost ends with lines that are part of an American ideal and more deeply part of the ambiguous identity of the poet:

e) I took the one less travelled by,
And that has made all the difference.

Two further elements, the pressure for individual decision and the tendency to see the choice as black and white (see above *two* roads), may be found in an abolitionist hymn[4]:

f) Once to every man and nation
Comes the moment to decide
In the strife of truth and falsehood
For the good or evil side.
. . . .
Then the choice goes by forever
'Twixt that darkness and that light.

If we compare these notions with informal decision making in the Philippines, we can make the following generalizations about Philippine decision making that relate to the lettered observations above:

a) There is no finite set of comparable alternatives. It is extremely difficult to elicit a list of alternatives or possible choices, or to get such a list systematically considered. Presumably this is exemplified by the difficulty in introducing electoral democracy. Instead, a possibility (one of an unexplored number) is mentioned, to be either rejected or further defined. Where Americans tend to limit consideration to two alternatives (Red or dead), Filipinos often pay attention to only one at a time. This may be related to the structure of the vocabulary, as discussed above.

b) Alternatives are not mutually exclusive and choice can be avoided.

Data on this subject are complicated by the fact that rules of courtesy constantly require that Filipinos agree to be in two places at once or say they hold two contradictory opinions. There are also serious reality constraints: Something does eventually happen. But I believe people are often rather surprised that they cannot have their cake and eat it too – the kinship system is, after all, bilateral. A related phenomenon is the absence of what might be called a delete function[5]: If in a restaurant you say, "I'll have fresh mango, please – no, I changed my mind, I'll have ice cream," you may get two desserts.

c) and d) The implications of a decision are not considered as a sequence. "I have a problem, maybe doing X will help" is rarely succeeded by "If X, then Y then Z." If X is rejected, it is rejected without a specification of its probable outcome; if this specification is made, it virtually forecloses decision, prejudicing it in favor of X. Note that in Tagalog "if" clauses and "when" clauses with present and future verbs are not distinguished. One area in which this is clearly visible is in decisions to get married; if the possibility is under discussion people may simply drift into marriage – marriage happens to them.

f) Individuals are not under pressure to make decisions for which they are responsible – "decision for Christ" revivalism has little future here. In the actual outcome, they will not necessarily see themselves as actors. What one does is what was going to be done (the cookie jar got broken), and that is the way things are. If there is a fatalism here it does not involve the will of the gods or the "system," but the unfolding of events according to their nature, and especially weak human nature. There is little room for notions of culpability, and apology is rare and uninstitutionalized in the culture, since people do not *choose* to do wrong; wrong is done by them. Indeed, since choices are not made between opposites, they are not seen as choices between right and wrong.

On the basis of interviews about the specific terminology of causality, Ronald Hines suggests that Tagalog conceptualizations of causality are as follows:

It is possible to speak of several factors converging to bring about a result:

It is possible to speak of one cause leading to a variety of effects:

$$B \longrightarrow \begin{cases} D \\ E \\ F \end{cases}$$

The commonest pattern is one in which a variety of causes lead to a variety of effects:

$$\left.\begin{matrix} A \\ B \\ C \end{matrix}\right\} \longrightarrow \left\{\begin{matrix} D \\ E \\ F \end{matrix}\right.$$

The single-cause, single-effect pattern is relatively little stressed:

$$A \longrightarrow B$$

I think we can bring this formulation more directly into the present context by stressing the relative absence of two further patterns:

$$\left.\begin{matrix} A \\ B \\ C \end{matrix}\right\} \longrightarrow \left\{\begin{matrix} \text{not-D} \\ E \\ \text{not-F} \end{matrix}\right.$$

$$A \to B \to C \to D \to E \to \text{etc.}$$

Whereas setting goals and making decisions are relatively minor activities in the culture, commanding little attention, there is a very rich repertoire of techniques for maintaining relationships, and a great sensitivity to their fluctuations.

It is worth asking here, first whether cultural notions seem congruent with the linguistic ones in these different cases, and second whether the diverse linguistic structures of the different languages may be seen as related to underlying tendencies of all linguistic codes. Some of the general features of language discussed earlier (digitality, multiple feedback) do not seem to be variable from language to language. Aspects of segmentation, sequence, and the figure/ground relationship (subject-predicate) do seem to vary. I believe that in each case tendencies may be recognized that are related to processes of goal definition and decision making, although they are played up more in some languages than in others, just as decision making is a more explicit process in some cultures than in others.

Many of the features we have looked at could simply be classed as imprecisions. They are precisely the features children may be taught to overcome as they learn to specify alternative courses, to put logical structure into discourse, and to think responsibly about the future, all useful skills. What these skills produce, however, are representations of situations or possibilities that offer striking clarity and dangerous over-simplification. They are ways of deciding to bulldoze new roads, or to spray fields with insecticides. They represent a more disciplined use of the very features of language that make it distort certain kinds of information. They provide a more perfect crystal, polarizing all that passes through it so that we tend to see lines, not loops; sequences, not systems.

We must still ask whether Whorf is right in suggesting that Hopi gives a more accurate picture of the cybernetic nature of the universe, or whether Trobriand or Filipino patterns of thought are less dangerous to the world than others. It may seem that this planet would be a more harmonious place if fewer goals were visualized and fewer decisions made, but this is only true where an ancient balance survives, as it does in very few places on the globe. Filipinos have bulldozers, and bulldozers are not devices designed for the maintenance of existing pattern and balance. Trobrianders too are acquiring bulldozers, and with the acquisition of bulldozers it is useful to have some idea of where a road is going and what it is for, to avoid half-built roads leading nowhere, a few hundred yards of concrete, like those that can be found in the environs of Manila. The cultural codifications of reality of Filipinos and Trobrianders are probably no better adapted to handle the complexity produced by the increase in the ecological dominance of the human species than the Western notions that seem to have been partially responsible for that increase. It is no more than sentimentality to dwell on the fact that they might not have been equally pernicious in producing the danger. At present no culture seems to provide a way of thinking about where to drive a bulldozer that supplies a sufficiently informed tenderness to determine a harmless course.

5.3. Poetry and religious ritual

Up to this point, we have considered the ways in which language and specific languages in cultural contexts might tend to distort our understanding of our environment. Here it is appropriate to consider some of the possible solutions. I am not going to try and explore how these can be more effectively applied, but I think that it is significant that just as we can locate in language possible correlates of the distortion, we can also locate in the uses of language by people who, in addition to making decisions, also sing, ways in which precisely these features can be suspended or brushed aside. Some of these are general and are probably shared by all human communities; these will be discussed as general categories of religious ritual and poetry. We will not undertake to explore here specific forms of ritual and poetry whereby single cultures balance specific linguistic and cultural patterns like those discussed above. Under certain circumstances, formally in poetry and religious ritual, and perhaps also in other languages of love, language is used in a way that tends to neutralize the tendencies toward lineality of language. How this neutralization acts to affect behavior outside of these spheres is not clear – indeed, both prayer and poetry have had less of an effect on human activity than might have been hoped, and yet they have a continuing effect upon human peace.

In the first section we discussed the lack of isomorphism between speech and that to which it refers, yet the language of ritual and poetry is only in a minor degree referential; both may be didactic, but neither is at its best when it becomes didactic. Each refers to a subject matter or a theology, and each expresses the speaker and implies some effect on the hearer. Yet in a more important sense, poetry is always about poetry, while ritual is always about communion; that is, poetic language is concerned primarily with the message itself, while religious ritual is phatic, communication concerned with the state of the channel. In that sense, both are informed by what they are about, and neither can misrepresent. Another way of looking at the same thing is to say that the truth value of a poem or a prayer does not depend on verification in any other sphere, but on its internal relationships.

"A poem should not *mean* but *be*."[6]

"A sacrament *effects* what it *signifies*."[7]

G. Bateson (1958) describes the *eidos* of the Iatmul people of New Guinea as characterized by an insistence that "what is symbolically, sociologically or emotionally true is also cognitively true." If in fact our ordinary cognitive systems have built-in distortions and limitations, then cognitive truth has a limited value, to be balanced by other types of truth.

Both poetry and ritual involve intense repetition in their evolution and use. The poet works and reworks the lines, so that in the finished product the end does affect the beginning. Rituals are reworked by the successive repetitions of generations. Neither poetry nor ritual is adequately experienced on a once-through basis, since the first line must be encountered again in the light of the last, and although dramatic and climactic structures occur in both, sequence and segmentation are blurred by the continual looping back. This same looping back disrupts the speaker/hearer dichotomy, as in the ancient ninefold *Kyrie:*

Priest: Kyrie eleison.	People: KYRIE ELEISON.
Kyrie eleison.	CHRISTE ELEISON.
Christe eleison.	CHRISTE ELEISON.
Kyrie eleison.	KYRIE ELEISON.
Kyrie eleison.	

The continual small modifications that occur in the composition of poetry and the evolution of ritual, as multitudes of tiny changes are made to enhance the "rightness" (or the truth?) of a passage by enhancing the internal relationships, can be studied statistically. Speech can be viewed in terms of Markoff processes, or the transitional probabilities of different forms, but the statistical distribution of all types of linguistic forms is distorted as various types of assonance or partial echoing (phonological, morphological, and syntactic) are introduced (M. C. Bateson, 1968) and the same must be true of imagery. These are the processes that give a poem or the verbal form of a ritual its quality of *unity* and *necessity.*

Lastly, the same processes that distort the sequential character of utterances also distort the grammatical function of different items within a sentence. Many of us may remember memorizing poems or prayers as children in which we mistook the functions of words, and indeed the same process that makes a unity of a line also flattens out the grammatical structure within it. Wallace Stevens is an example of a poet who often used the whole poem to make a concerted attack on the individual meaningfulness of his words and their role in the sentence, and many of the lines of Hopkins are enhanced by an ambiguity about what is noun or verb, what is subject or predicate. One of the complaints that is often made about the new and still raw translation of the liturgy being used by the Catholic Church is that individual words "stick out" – "It doesn't flow any more." I remember a conversation with a nun who was explaining how long it had taken her to get *beyond* the separate words and phrases of the new English offices so as to make a single act of worship.

In summary, we can look at the language of poetry and ritual and discover processes that give to speech a different and less lineal kind of truthfulness: a freedom from strict sequence and segmentation, a new relationship between speaker and listener, and a more complex image than the figure/ground image of our purpose and our morality. It is worth noting here that much of what has been said applies to the words of rituals of other sorts, ranging from therapy to courtship to play, all spheres in which we sometimes achieve in our communication a sufficient harmony to make transcending insights possible. We are a long way from having good structural descriptions of most of these processes, and the suggestions above are impressionistic. However, I suspect that when we have the descriptions we will find an even more strict counterpointing of those very features that give our linguistic codes their seeming precision.

There is a tension here between language as a useful tool – a crystal through which we obtain an ordered clarity that has perhaps been the essential oversimplification for humanity's analytical development so far – and language as a source of dangerous blindness, through which we see and know only in part. Ordinary language may not have sufficient complexity for thinking about the coupling of natural systems, but we may be able to live in harmony with these different systems if, in addition to the partial understanding of them we get through the ordinary linguistic processes, we also sing about them, seeking a unity of vision in prayer and poetry. Because of its structure, language seems to convey wholeness only under very special circumstances, and yet it is of wholes that we must learn to think and speak – or sing – if we are to survive.

Notes

1. This is one focus of the dispute between descriptive and transformational grammar.
2. I am indebted for many of my comments on Tagalog structures to long conversations with Ronald Hines during his research in Manila.
3. "The Road Not Taken" is used with the permission of the estate of Robert Frost, from *The Poetry of Robert Frost*, Edward Connery Latham, ed. London: Jonathan Cape Ltd. and copyright 1916 by Holt, Rinehart and Winston and renewed by Robert Frost. Reprinted from *The Poetry of Robert Frost* edited by Edward Connery Lathem, by permission of Henry Holt and Company, Inc.
4. J. R. Lowell (1845), "Ebenezer," Hymn 519 in *The Hymnal of the Protestant Episcopal Church in the U.S.A.* (New York: Oxford University Press, 1940).
5. This insight I owe to J. B. Kassarjian.
6. Archibald MacLeish, "Ars Poetica."
7. H. Denzinger, ed., *Enchiridion Symbolorum: Definitionum et rationum de rebus civii et morum*, 33rd edition (Freiburg: Herder, 1965), nos. 1606, 1639.

References

Bateson, G. (1958). *Naven* (2nd Ed.). Stanford, CA: Stanford University Press.
Bateson, G. (1967, April). Cybernetic explanation. *The American Behavioral Scientist, X*(8), 29.
Bateson, M. C. (1968). *Structural continuity in poetry: A linguistic study of five early Arabic odes.* The Hague: Mouton and Co.
Bright, J. O., & Bright, W. (1965, October). Semantic structures in northwestern California and the Sapir-Whorf hypothesis. *American Anthropologist, 67*(5), 249–258.
Gardner, W. H., Ed. (1953). *Poems and prose of Gerard Manley Hopkins.* Middlesex: Penguin Books Ltd.
Lee, D. (1959). Codifications of reality: Lineal and nonlineal. In *Freedom and culture.* Englewood, NJ: Prentice Hall.
Weir, R. (1962). *Language in the crib.* The Hague: Mouton and Co.
Whorf, B. (1956). An American Indian model of the universe. In J. C. Carroll (Ed.), *Language, thought, and reality.* Cambridge, MA: Technology Press.

6. Affective and communicative problems in young developmentally deviant language users

THEODORE SHAPIRO AND ELENA GOLDSTEIN LISTER

Language delay and deviance are prominent among the presenting symptoms of the severe disorders of early childhood, but also may be one symptom in a more complex clinical picture (Cantwell, Baker, & Mattison, 1979). Language behavior has received special research attention because it develops in well-normed sequences and is an organized structure against which variations may be readily measured. Moreover, the child-centered community has developed a number of professionals all of whom address language and speech from their own vantage. In mental retardation all developmental landmarks, including language, tend to be uniformly delayed; in cerebral palsy language may be spared while the speech motor apparatus is affected. In the pervasive developmental disorders and specifically in early infantile autism, deviant and delayed language and social withdrawal are accompanied by relatively normal motor development.

Although the language characteristics of these disorders have been well recorded phenomenologically, the relationship to brain structure and function is obscure. This leaves us in a position that Gregory Bateson (1979) might have enjoyed with the reminder that there are no neurons, pigs, or coconuts in the mind, but only ideas. This principle provides us with direction for study. We may proceed by addressing neither the substrate nor the environment but rather the structure of the minds of the children to determine if their thoughts and language are organized differently from those of normal children. Indeed, Bateson goes on to give us yet another clue by stating that "the very process of perception is an act of logical typing" (p. 190). Moreover, the outside world becomes a "source of information provided that it is incorporated

This paper was first presented in 1981 at the annual meeting of The American Academy of Child Psychiatry.

into a circuit with an appropriate network of flexible material in which it can produce change" (p. 110). It is our premise that children who develop with inbuilt problems in logical typing and lack of flexibility in shifting the verbal designators available to mind will produce deviant language forms that can be measured and typed. Children with autism and pervasive developmental disorders provide natural experiments in nature that show predictable scrambling of the normal principles. As the children develop, the linguistic productions of some are strikingly like the verbalizations of adult schizophrenics, making us wonder if the precursors to such extreme mental pathology could be studied *in statu nascendi* in these children.

Childhood schizophrenia no longer appears in the official nomenclature of the American Psychiatric Association, but child psychiatrists are directed to diagnose schizophrenia if adult criteria are met. Fish (1977) suggests that there are significant similarities in clinical phenomenology between adult and childhood schizophrenia. These include autistic withdrawal and formal thought disorder reflected in language production. She goes on to quote Bleuler's historic description: "The fragmentation of thinking is the most significant schizophrenic symptom" (Bleuler, 1911). Goldfarb (1974) also found that poor communicative speech and gross impairment in human relationships are among the four major symptoms uniformly found in his population despite the disclaimers in the third edition of the Diagnostic and Statistical Manual of Mental Disorders. Fish suggests that both of the above symptoms are necessary and sufficient for a diagnosis of childhood schizophrenia. These factors recommend that the expression of language and thought in speech ought to be a featured research interest for child psychiatrists interested in the severe disorders of early childhood. There is also recent epidemiological evidence that early language difficulties in 3-year-olds should be considered as significant to the diagnosis of concurrent disorder, and its persistence (Richman & Stevenson, 1977).

Since varied professionals attend to language and its manifest instrumentality, speech, children with language delays or deviance may first be seen by speech and hearing pathologists or special educators rather than by a child psychiatrist. Each professional views the child from a focused vantage admitting the possibility that he or she may miss the relation of the disorder or delay in language to a larger clinical picture that includes the designation of a full or part syndrome, epidemiological factors, and psychological and clinical course variables.

This fact of professional secularism provides a problem that derives from the arbitrariness of nomenclatures, something that Bateson (Schaffner, 1956) is all too aware of. If each discipline calls its population by different names, it also makes for difficulties in tracking the prevalence and course of a disorder or disease, its prognosis, and its genetics. In short, it creates a confusion in which people are lost by the artifact of reified nominalism.

Most investigators agree upon the developmental nature of language disorders (Bender, 1942; Shapiro, Huebner, & Campbell, 1974; Fish, 1977; Shapiro & Huebner, 1976) rather than espouse the view that they are functionally induced or electively supported. However, controversy remains as to whether the varied clinical pictures are best viewed as indications of specific lesions in a complex language system or as representations of a varied clinical picture of a more inclusive category. The adult literature presents extensive study of the language of schizophrenia and recently of its lack of relation to the thought disorder proposed by Bleuler. The problems center around what the empirical manifestations of thought disorder are. Language, considered by many to be the prime manifestation of thought and language disorder, has been used as evidence of thought disorder (Cameron, 1944; van Domarus, 1944; Goldstein, 1944; Kasanin, 1944). Maher's (1972) extended review of the literature on language in schizophrenia finds no syntactic problems in the studies then published, but he cites evidence of idiosyncratic use of words as determined by the Cloze technique. More recently, Rochester and Martin (1979) have found that the untrained listener could discriminate the thought-disordered patient from controls by difficulties in following sequencing of ideas. The listener experiences anticipatory frustration because of information overload, and the subjects use low-level connectives such as "and" rather than "because" or "therefore." Rutter (1979) reported similar findings using similar techniques. Johnston and Holzman (1979) take another approach in creating a thought disorder index (TDI) from a composite of productions of patients during psychological test administration. Andreason and Powers (1974), however, have found overinclusive language in a number of psychotic conditions and collapsed thought and language disorder in their analysis of speech samples and have found that schizophrenia could not be distinguished from mania by their techniques. *DSM III* (1980), because of the underemphasis in that document on thought disorder as an essential aspect for diagnosis of schizophrenia as opposed to psychosis, is consonant with their view. As recorded, each investigator's facts may be accurate, but each may labor in a different realm of discourse where the results do not exclude each other.

These facts leave the traditionally trained clinician in a relative muddle with respect to how to evaluate language disorder in relation to psychosis in children and whether old descriptions of childhood schizophrenia as found in *DSM II* still pertain. To compound the problem, once a child attains early latency, language disorder per se may be a part of the symptom cluster of several diagnostic categories and may selectively involve various aspects of the language and speech production apparatus. If clinicians are unaware of this fact they may be led astray by a surface feature of disorder that is less significant than the postulated dysfunction that gives rise to any clinical picture. For the sake of observational convenience the language system (an inferred entity) may be analyzed into its manifest behaviors featuring gestural–mimetic, vocal–articulatory, semantic–syntactic, and paralinguistic–prosodic components. Such a segmentation permits a molecular approach to the study of language.

Early studies (Shapiro & Fish 1969; Shapiro, Roberts, & Fish, 1970) examining the speech morphology and function of very young psychotic children found that the pattern of production initially helped to differentiate psychotic children from language-delayed children. In a later study of 30 psychotic children, Shapiro, Chiarandini, and Fish (1974) showed that only a small segment of that population remained nonproductive, another group did well, and a middle group maintained a significant proportion of echoic and out-of-context, irrelevant productions. The current study extends these early studies by describing six children from 4 to 10 years of age, all of whom had disturbances in an aspect of their language delivery. Some showed focal "lesions" leaving the rest of the system largely intact; others showed involvement in a number of systems. All of these children also had withdrawal from social relationships or bizarre social relationships, thus suggesting the possibility of a diagnosis of a childhood schizophrenia according to criteria set up by Goldfarb, Fish, and others. The language problem results in speech that may be deviant in only a small proportion of the total output (15 percent), yet to the auditor, they sound grossly deviant, strange – indeed, psychotic. By earlier history, three of the six children were clearly atypical or autistic. The other three had questionable autism, but clear-cut diagnosis of late-onset psychoses were made. As you may infer from this brief description, Bateson's idea about deviance in logical typing even at the onset of the developmental process may be a significant functional and mechanical factor to account for the empirical finding of deviance.

The variety of speech developmental patterns of these six children will be presented and the argument addressed that the variety of "faults" and "arrests" in linguistic production reflect different final pathways of language organization that may be construed as a more basic fault in the central nervous system and ego functioning of these children (see Shapiro & Huebner, 1976). However, as stated earlier we are not yet entitled to leap to such inferences and must be content with the realm of thought and its products. This presentation suggests that speech, because of its role in coding social and cognitive functions, can provide an observable and measurable barometer of the more remote organizations (the central nervous system and the Ego). Thus, language patterns in middle childhood may be a key behavior to diagnosing psychosis to which all practitioners ought to be alerted regardless of their training or the bias of the diagnostic system currently in use. The approach should also be considered provocative in stimulating reconsideration of the concept of childhood schizophrenia with renewed curiosity regarding its continuities with early autistic and later schizophrenic syndromes if only for a segment of the children within the pervasive developmental disorder spectrum.

6.1 Population and procedure

The children in this study (see Table 6.1 and vignettes) were selected for demonstration, and no effort at randomization was made. Six children aged 4 to 10 years were audiotaped and/or videotaped during open-ended interviews with the examiner (T.S.) during special taping sessions for a research project in progress or during clinical interview as part of a diagnostic consultation. The children were selected for the current study because they met gross clinical criteria of deviant language-production patterns and withdrawal from and/or deviance in social relationships. Only children between 4 years and prepuberty were selected. Two of the subjects were seen as inpatients at the New York University–Bellevue Psychiatric Center (Carol and Tom). One was part of a therapeutic nursery group at the Cornell University Medical College–Payne Whitney Clinic (Wendy), and three were seen in private

consultation (Barry, Perry, Fred). Table 6.1 describes the clinical characteristics of the group, and the history and course of each child is presented in the brief clinical vignettes that follow.

6.2. Clinical vignettes

Wendy

Wendy, a black child, was first evaluated at age 3 upon recommendation
of a physician responding to her mother's concern about her "abnormal
speech, screaming tantrums, and stubbornness."

The pregnancy had been marked by severe first trimester bleeding
and by a midpregnancy "sore throat." Delivery was uncomplicated and
birth weight was 6 lb, 15 oz. Wendy walked at 11 months and fed herself
by 12 months. She was toilet trained by 26 months. Her first words were
"see" and "bye," spoken at 16 months. Her language at about age 2
consisted largely of two- to three-word phrase echoes and repetition of
television commercials, the numbers 1 to 10, and items from the
"Sesame Street" program.

Wendy was born with esotropia, which required two inhospital sur-
gical procedures at 3 days and at 14 months. She continued to show
intermittent eye crossing. There was no history of head injury or convulsions.

Wendy's family history was significant in that Wendy had a brother 11
years older than she who had been diagnosed as having early childhood
autism and had not spoken until 8 years of age. She also had a sister 12
years older who had had delays in onset of speech, but was now
performing well in a normal school. Wendy's mother felt depressed and
guilty about her two handicapped children and was fearful of harm to
them by her physically violent husband.

At age 3 years, Wendy's parents first sought help for what they
described as her "oppositional behavior," which had begun at 2 years.
At that time, Wendy was seen in consultation and described as a large
energetic child with a low tolerance for frustration, insistence for same-
ness, and in frequent eye contact and caricatured affects. Her language
consisted largely of jargon with few episodes of speech to herself in
response to pleasurable activities and a few intelligible words such as
"Hello," "How ya doing?," and "Bye-bye" mainly spoken into a toy
telephone. She was placed in a therapeutic nursery school, which she
attended until 4 years.

Table 6.1. *Characteristics of Population*

	Current age	Age at onset	Dx	Language onset	Demand for sameness	Poor social relations	Affect	IQ or DQ	Neurological signs	Pregnancy complication	Disposition
Wendy	4	< 30 mo	PDD,[a] Autistic type	1.4 yr	X	X[d]	Theatrical, shallow	Gesell at 48 mo: language, social, 24 adaptive, 36 gross motor, 46		1st trimester bleeding	Special school
Carol	8	< 3 yr	CS[b]	1.6 yr		X[d]	Shallow, anxiety	WISC: V, 46 P, 58 F, 47	EEG: mild R cerebral at 8 yr	Toxemia, no eclampsia	Special school
Fred	10	< 30 mo	PDD, Autistic type	0.10 yr	X	X	Inappropriate	WISC: V, 59 P, 93 F, 74		1st trimester bleeding	Special school
Tom	8	7 yr[c]	CS	1.6 yr		X[d]	Sad, blunted	WISC: V, 79 P, 68 F, 71	Febrile, convulsions EEG: Paroxysmal disorder	Maternal alcoholic	Residence
Perry	9	< 30 mo	PDD	4 yr	X	X[d]	Variably inappropriate	WISC: V, 53 P, 53 F, 48		Threatened abortion 5 mo; Rx: Estrogen	Special school
Barry	5	< 30 mo	CS	1 yr		X[d]	Blunted	S-B, 129		Breech	Special school

[a] Pervasive developmental disorder.
[b] Childhood schizophrenia.
[c] Unreliable family history; age recorded represents first suspicion of paroxysmal disorder.
[d] Bizarre and idiosyncratic.

Wendy made progress during her 6 months in the nursery school. She developed greater frustration tolerance and began to use language more communicatively. At 4 years of age, Wendy was seen as a negativistic child with a range of sham affects, theatrically expressed. She imitated children in her environment in a ritualized way, and there was little evidence of an imaginative component to her play.

On Gesell testing at 4 years of age, Wendy's language and social personal skills placed her at the 24-month level. Her adaptive and fine motor skills were at the 30- to 36-month level, and her gross motor capabilities were close to age level. Wendy's language then consisted largely of jargon and echolalia with occasional four-word utterances and three-word sentences to communicate wishes. She could name objects and pictures, but was otherwise uncommunicative.

Carol

Carol, a black child, was first evaluated by this examiner at 8 years of age because of bizarre speech patterns. She was admitted for hospital evaluation and was described as passive and compliant, with disordered thought processes, shallow affect, concrete thinking, and poor reality testing but without hallucinations. She was reported to show a poorly delineated sense of self and avoided eye contact and had no capacity for peer relations. Often she sat alone and watched television.

Carol's mother had had toxemia during pregnancy, and Carol was delivered with the use of forceps. She achieved normal landmarks, crawled at 7.8 months, walked at 1 year. She said her first words at 18 months and read can labels at 3.4 years of age. There was no history of febrile convulsions or head injury. Relevant family history included the fact that her younger brother, 6 years of age, rocked, banged his head, and was thought to be disturbed.

Carol was first noticed as different during her third year. Neighbors asked if she spoke Spanish because of difficulty in understanding her. At 4 years her mother noticed that she did not relate normally to children her age. At 5½ years, a psychiatric evaluation at a pediatrician's request recorded a primary thought disorder and inappropriate affect. She was involved in a therapeutic nursery, but was absent frequently. From the age of 6.4 years to 8 years she stayed at home. Carol's mother was negativistic and showed signs of chronic depression and deviance and continued denial of Carol's problem. The father had never lived with the family.

On examination, Carol's speech was rapid and markedly tangential. She associated loosely to parts of questions asked, confused pronouns, and used neologisms.

Carol cooperated poorly on most tests of the WISC-R, but gave the critical impression of higher intellectual capacity, particularly in vocabulary. Her verbal IQ was 46, and a performance IQ was 58. Bender Gestalt testing showed disorganized perceptual motor functioning with poor motor control. She could read at the third-grade level, but with little comprehension. Her physical examination was normal; her EEG was minimally to moderately abnormal with indications of right cerebral wave asymmetry and dysfunction.

Carol improved on chlorpromazine in hospital and was involved in a day-care program at the children's unit. After 3 months of daily attendance, Carol showed a wariness to follow instructions, but some pleasure at performing adult-directed activities. She had improved reading skills, but still lacked in comprehension. There was some improvement in person-directed speech. Her spontaneous speech was still a loosely associated conversational stream dotted with jargon and syntactic errors.

Fred

Fred was first seen by T.S. at 10 years of age in order to reconsider his lifelong school placement as a "learning disabled child" in light of recent reports of "bizarre thought and behavior."

Fred's mother was misdiagnosed as having an ovarian cyst with mild menorrhagia. At D & C, a diagnosis of pregnancy was made and she carried to term and delivered a 7 lb, 8 oz, infant with an APGAR of 9,10. Postnatal course was uncomplicated. Fred's mother also had a high toxoplasmosis titer, but skull X ray and fundoscopic examination of Fred were negative.

Fred sat at 5 months, stood at 6 months, and walked at 12 months. He was bladder trained by 2 years, though not bowel trained until later. Nocturnal enuresis persisted. As an infant, he was considered placid and "sweet." His first word was "Mama" at 10 months. At 1½ years, he said single words such as "cookie" and "happy." He spoke phrases by 2½ years and sentences by 3 years. He was physically healthy except for recurrent otitis media. No history of convulsions or head injuries was recorded. Significant family history included the fact that Fred's father was a poor reader and nonathletic.

At age 3 years 8 months, Fred's parents first sought help because Fred did not follow directions or "talk like other children his age." A report from a major medical center at that time read, "The patient did not relate to the tester; he had extremely limited to no eye contact. . . .He did not use appropriate objects meaningfully." His language was characterized as "jargon, echolalia, and perseveration, inability to use age appropriate syntax." Visual motor problems were also noted. A series of consultations with diagnoses ensued, among which were minimal brain dysfunction, learning disability, and infantile autism.

Tom

Tom, a light-skinned black child, was first evaluated by T.S. when he was admitted to a hospital inpatient unit at the age of 8 years because of bizarre speech patterns and "liking to fantasize." Tom was the product of a full-term, normal delivery, weighing 6 lb. During pregnancy his mother drank alcohol excessively. Tom walked at 1 year, was toilet trained by 1½ years of age, said "Mama" and "Dada" at 1½ years, and put words together by 3 years. He still sucked his thumb and had episodes of enuresis. He had two known episodes of febrile convulsions at age 1 and at age 3.

Tom's mother openly stated that she resented Tom, who looks very much like his father, who left when Tom was born. There was a question of abuse and neglect by his mother, who appeared somewhat disturbed and paranoid. Tom had lived with his maternal grandmother and great-grandmother since he was 2 months old. His mother visited him a few times a week, and there was a great deal of conflict within the family about her treatment of Tom.

Tom's problem was first noticed at age 7 when he began to attend public school. Previously, he had been taught at home by his grandmother. He was expelled from public school and later private school because of inappropriate aggressive behavior and talking bizarrely. He had imaginary friends who said "crazy things."

Tom was seen as a compliant, anxious boy with an intense mock pleasantness and forced laugh. He showed disordered thought processes and a preoccupation with fantasy, but no evidence of hallucinations. He was easily distractible and lacked interest in self-care. Although he would sometimes participate in group activities, when left alone he remained at the periphery. He could not maintain eye contact. Tom's mood sometimes appeared sad, though he denied it and was evasive about feeling states.

On testing, Tom showed above average intellectual capacity. He had good vocabulary and reading skills but low comprehension, a good memory, and a large fund of general information. Nevertheless, his full-scale IQ was 71 (V, 79; P, 68). He had a paradoxically well-developed capacity for nonverbal abstract problem solving, but not abstract verbal conceptualization. Bender Gestalt testing showed problems in fine motor coordination, Gestalt integration.

On neurological exam, Tom showed poor posture, doughy muscle tone, and nonfocal neurological signs with right/left confusion and mixed peripheral dominance. His EEG was consistent with an underlying paroxysmal disorder, but no seizures were recorded.

When speaking with the examiner, Tom's responses to questions were frequently tangential and he was preoccupied with accurate naming of countries, states, and cars. He spoke in neologisms, but had no echolalia. His enunciation was "superclear." His voice overanimated.

Perry

Perry, a 9½-year-old black child, was seen by T.S. after having been in a number of special schools since nursery years. His parents had been told that he was to be reclassified from a developmental disorder to an emotionally disturbed status with recommendation for placement. The family objected and sought other opinions.

There was a threatened abortion at 5 months' gestation, which was treated with hormones. Perry went to term and labor was induced. Perry weighed 8 lb, 4 oz, and was considered to be 1 month postterm. There was no jaundice, but some questionable cyanosis. He was taken home in 5 days with no special treatment.

He slept and fed well, sat at 6 months, walked once at 12 months only to stop until 18 months, and was toilet trained by 12 months. He did not speak until 4 years. No serious illness or history of seizures or head injuries was recorded. Family history included the fact that Perry's father had one brother who was "slow to speak." Perry had one younger sibling developing normally.

When Perry was 2½ years old, his parents first sought help because he was withdrawn and uncommunicative. They were told that he was emotionally disturbed with a learning disability, and a therapeutic setting was recommended. He began a program at age 4 and remained until he was 8. At 6 years, Perry was described by his teachers as hyperactive and distractible with poor impulse control – a low tolerance for frustration and great dependency on structure. On reevaluation 1 year later, he was seen as restless, yet lethargic, and as difficult to engage in group activities. Rather, he engaged mostly in solitary perseverative play with little creativity. Only water seemed to excite him. He rarely spoke spontaneously, and sometimes echoed and spoke nonsense. By age 8, he was less restless, showing greater fine motor skills, and spoke spontaneously in full sentences and shouted when he was angry or frustrated. One year later, he was transferred to a public school special class. He was considered unable to function or make academic gains. Recommendation for placement was initiated.

On examination, Perry was seen to be negativistic and withdrawn, with perseverative play and vocalization showing inappropriate, variable affect. Testing results were deemed unreliable because of his inappropriate behavior, inability to communicate, and inattention. WISC-R full-scale IQ of 48 was recorded (V, 53; P, 53). Bender Gestalt testing showed weakness in visual perceptual organization with confused integration of body image (overelaboration of detail on figure drawings).

His speech was characterized by context deviance, jargon, echoing, and syntactic errors. There was frequent change of topic, and he often did not respond to questions and appeared disinterested and withdrawn.

Barry

Barry, a 5-year-old white child, was first evaluated at age 5 upon recommendation of his nursery school. They and his family were concerned about his garbled language and his difficulties in engaging other children. He otherwise seemed bright and was only sometimes aggressive toward his younger sister. No antenatal complications had been reported, but he was a breech presentation and was delivered by caesarean section. Birth weight was 8 lb, 9 oz, and there was no delay in discharge from hospital. The mother had been somewhat depressed during the pregnancy because her husband was in Viet Nam. Barry's developmental landmarks were normal, but his language was difficult to understand from the beginning because of the way in which he strung words together. Similarly, his peer relations were disturbed and he always remained on the periphery of groups.

There was no significant family history of mental illness or medical history noted. He had never had a full neurological examination or EEG. Diagnosis by a community service organization included the possibility of autism. He had always been considered bright. Stanford Binet at the time included an IQ of 129.

Upon examination, Barry was found to be a well-developed youngster with bright dark eyes. He had a serious demeanor, and his speech became more tangential and less understandable the longer he went on. He related to the examiner only on request and spoke with exasperated singsong prosody. His designation tasks and functional understanding of things were adequate, but his discourse was confused. It was marked by unusual association and social eye avoidance as well. His tendency to repeat variations on the verb "to know" intruded in his speech randomly. Diagnostic impression at the time was that of childhood psychosis, schizophrenic type.

6.3. Procedure

Open-ended interviews were recorded on either Sony video or audio tape recorder. Each recorded interview was transcribed and each utterance up to the first 100 utterances was counted and coded as deviant and segregated into subcategories of deviance including jargon, echolalia, context disorder, associational deviance, change of topic, and poor usage. These categories represent a modification of the two-dimensional morphological and functional analysis devised by Shapiro and Fish (1969) as appropriate to the middle childhood years. The deviance score corresponds to the earlier noncommunicative composite. Each language sample was further analyzed for syntactic form. A total percent deviant language (and percent response in each catalogued category) was calculated. A mean length of utterance omitting jargon was determined (Bloom & Lahey, 1978), and recorded as a standard measure of developmental status. Each child's speech was also studied for thematic persistence and type of question asked by the interviewer that precipitated a deviant response.

Two investigators independently coded each sample and in a subsequent meeting compromised upon those few utterances where there was disagreement. In general, the deviant production was so evident on simple audition that agreement on general deviance was not a problem. Finer categorization required compromise regrouping in fewer than 10 percent of the utterances.

The following are examples from the protocols of each type of deviance:

1. *Echolalia* (no change from the model)

Examiner: Do you have a beard? Do you know where a beard goes? Right on your chin. Put it on your chin.
Wendy: Put it on your chin.

2. *Context deviance* (material from other contexts intrudes in the theme and dominates the text)

Examiner: Oh, that's a program too? You want to tell me about it?
Fred: Um, program one and program two. It's so easy to play hair. Hair means please play the, umum, the hair, you will as I put, turn it on, the hair will start.

3. *Associational deviance* (the associational path is evident to the listener, but is unusual in following paradigmatic rather than syntactic rules)

Examiner: Now, what am I – a woman or a man? A lady or a girl or a boy?
Carol: A . . .a girl, a girl or a boy nnnn smackin' nnnn I brought you some soap powder. Pour it down on the floor in the hall.
Examiner: Carol, would you look at me?
Carol: What?
Examiner: Hi – what do you see?
Carol: The drum *crack* and *break them* and like *Diana Ross* joined the Temptations and the Supremes. It's broken.

4. *Topic change and perseveration* (clear avoidance of themes and persistent inappropriate stickiness to a perseverated here and now context)

Examiner: Did you walk into the door because you were confused or mixed up?
Tom: Yes
Examiner: What made you feel that way?
Tom: See this little girlie here?

5. *Concreteness* (tangential thematic discourse dominated by definitions and visible attributes rather than extended function)

Examiner: Why does the fireman climb the ladder?
Tom: A ladder is something that fireman use if there is a fire.

6. *Syntactic deviance* (disorders in grammatical fluency out of keeping with standard or slang usage)

Examiner: What do you like about marbles?
Barry: Well, I can do some of one of the feelings I know cause everyone should know what game I play.
Examiner: Did you hear the phone ring just now?
Carol: It's Regina. Regina's black phone, white phone. She puts some black numbers on it and puts the finger on it and put the phone on the stories.

6.4. Data and analysis

The six children (see Table 6.2) showed a mean length of utterance (MLU) ranging from 1.92 in Wendy the youngest child to 8.12 in Carol (age 8). Wendy's MLU placed her in the 24-month range, the lowest of her developmental scores on the Gesell as well. All other MLU's were above 4.37, which is well above the 40-month level. It was found that the longer utterances tended to be more problematic; that is, the more the child rambled the more evident was the deviance. Brief responses such as yes/no answers or designations tended to be appropriate.

Table 6.2. *Language Production Analysis (expressed in % of utterance total)*

	Utterances	MLU*	Total % problem	Echolalia	Jargon	Context deviance	Associational deviance	Change of topic	Syntactic deviance	Poor usage Concreteness Clang associations
Wendy	84	1.92	68	31	37	12	31		8	
Carol	100	8.12	67	8	5	5			11	
Fred	99	5.46	18	1		5		1	2	3
Tom	100	4.37	30							7
Perry	100	4.95	40	1	2	14		16	14	1
Barry	100	7.80	21			7		8	12	2

*Mean length of utterance.

The children differed as to the nature of their specific language problem. Wendy's speech was 67 percent jargon and echolalia. Carol's productions were markedly disordered in several areas, resulting in a stream of dialogue with 31 percent associational deviance and lesser percentages of jargon and echolalia, context deviance, poor usage, and syntactical errors. Syntactic structure and context disorder were the main areas of deviance in Fred's, Barry's, and Perry's speech, but Perry also changed the topic in 8 percent of his responses. Tom changed topic the most frequently, in 16 percent of his responses. He also showed problems with context (5 percent) and usage (7 percent). Regardless of the specific nature of the production disorder, each child's speech was easily recognizable as strange and bizarre, yielding a general impression of psychotic thought disorder. This was equally true when the total deviance score was as little as 18 percent, as was Fred's, or as much as the 68 percent deviance in Carol's productions.

Each child's individuality was written into his or her particular production or problem in relation to the context of the interview structure. Closer analysis showed that Tom's change of topic was not a *random* phenomenon. Rather, of the 16 percent of responses that represented topic changes, the phenomenon arose in response to open-ended questions in 6 percent and to questions concerning feeling states in 4 percent of utterances. He showed a perseverative preoccupation with fire and fire trucks. Perry responded to inquiries that may have been beyond his level of comprehension by persistently returning to references about light in the interview room. More advanced children may resort to avoidance of the question altogether in the face of questions that they cannot or will not answer. Thematic persistence then becomes a mechanism whereby the avoidance is accomplished. For the more limited child, such as Wendy, when challenged, larger productions dissolve into bizarre, shallow, and theatrical jargon showing dramatic prosody with echoes as the only mode of formed communication.

Syntactical errors were common to all five children with more advanced communicative forms and were not marked in four, Fred, Barry, Carol, and Perry. Fred had difficulty in word selection, which led him to conjugate aloud and string together possible alternative verb forms in 11 percent of his productions. Such overelaboration reflects difficulty in serial order sequencing and encoding, a deficit that contrasts with the natural automaticity of this function in normal children (Shapiro & Huebner, 1976). Twenty percent of Barry's productions contained one form or another of the verb "to know." Though not all were syntactically incorrect, 3.7 percent of his total number of words were "know" or "known." These errors in grammatical transformation result in extensive fragmentation of speech that is suggestive of Bleuler's word salad.

6.5. Discussion

In his 1972 paper "Childhood Schizophrenia Reconsidered," Rutter offered a strong summary of arguments to bolster the idea that the concept of childhood schizophrenia had outlived its usefulness (Rutter, 1972, p. 315). (He claimed that our knowledge was sufficient to distinguish infantile autism from disintegrative psychoses and schizophrenia, which is similar in symptomatology to the adult form.) He also stressed that without etiologic certainty we should adopt the World Health Organization multiaxial approach that foreshadowed the third edition of the *Diagnostic and Statistical Manual of Mental Disorders* and classify the varying clinical data at four levels to reassure clinicians that what they knew was not ignored. We must now work within a framework of syndrome and disorder until our knowledge will again permit us to reintroduce a disease concept based on firmer grounds of continuity of course, symptom profile, and etiology.

While we may yield to such a position, those whose work has centered about a concept of childhood schizophrenia argue that the childhood forms of psychosis may be continuous with adult forms and offer that the schizophrenic picture may take different forms at each developmental stage and require a nosology in accord with such principles. The work of Bender (1959), Fish (1977), and Goldfarb (1974) represents the best statements of the latter position. Recent British epidemiological reports by Wing and Gould (1979) also argue from a somewhat different vantage that autism in the narrow sense may have seen its day and that *formes fruste* should be included among the pervasive developmental disorders (thus broadening that narrowly defined sector).* It is as yet unclear that these variants will turn out to be a part of the schizophrenic spectrum. Recent reports from the University of Manitoba by Cantor (1980) have described a group of hypotonic children with thought disorder (and specific loss of peripheral muscle striation on election microscopy ascribed to cholinergic insufficiencies) that bolster Bender's and Fish's data on soft, doughy muscle tone in childhood schizophrenia. Moreover, Goldfarb's (1974) follow-up data show that his population of childhood schizophrenics had onset prior to 30 months and shared autistic features. In addition there is a recent report (Petty,

*DSM III R has absorbed these principles in the new approach to autism.

Ornitz, Michelman, & Zimmerman, 1984) that parallels our own findings that some autists show thought disorder in middle childhood.

The current study of six children suggests that whatever we mean by thought disorder it must be detected by commonsense audition of speech production. Further study by linguistic methods may permit us to tease apart just what variant components of language make for sensed strangeness. If thought disorder is but a general feature of childhood psychosis in latency, then the observable data that serve as indexes of that inference are not to be found in a single language fault. Rather, they are varied and are revealed in each of the communicational channels noted. Thus, it would be possible to classify each child linguistically and then compose a diagnostic scheme based on such an approach. The bizarre patterns may be seen as the outflow of a disordered integrative system stemming from the brain and affecting the language apparatus as only one of many behavioral sectors. The social apparatus and affective system of these disturbed children are no less deviant than their language. These facts should permit reconsideration of more global adaptive incapacity and whether the picture presented qualifies as a form of schizophrenia as it would find expression during latency. (The lack of hallucinatory and delusional symptoms should not be disturbing, though it has been used as an argument against the prior assumption.) The thought processes are so confused as expressed in language in this period that we are on safe ground in suggesting primary developmental difficulties, rather than disintegrative processes. (Moreover, there is no period of remission recorded.)

Our group of children had gross disorders in language and deviant peer and social relations, and all had been identified by their school system as needing special educational placement. Each had an onset recognized or retrospectively recognizable prior to 30 months as well as diminished IQ. (Three had been earlier diagnosed as autistic; and the remaining three would have been if they had been seen by professionals earlier.)

As clinicians, we must consider whether we are prone to rediagnose children during each epoch of life, rather than gain knowledge of the maturational process of children that will account for varied outcomes given certain initial pictures. Perhaps the children described are but one path of autism? I would suggest that such a position would place autism in the same position that childhood schizophrenia occupied in the recent past; that is, that it would be too inclusive. Invoking a thought disorder does seem suggestive of continuity with adult schizophrenia, or do all childhood psychoses show such an affliction? I will leave the issue of what to call these children and submit that there must be some way to classify them if our nosology is to be inclusive. Moreover, there may be something to gain in our understanding of schizophrenia as a disease process if we see these children as high-dose, early penetrance examples of the larger disorder. The latter could be a testable proposal. In addition, we could test mentalist and linguistic markers in such ideas as Bateson's errors in logical typing to show that they have significance to normal and deviant developmental sequences just as they may be significantly related to cross-cultural language analysis.

While we suffer from lack of etiological specificity, it should be noted that all our children had historical reports of a variety of early pregnancy complications, and two had EEG abnormalities. One child, Wendy, had an autistic sibling, and two, Carol and Tom, had one schizophrenic parent. These may be considered on axes for biological loading and taken as significant in our attempts to understand etiology.

The data as presented raise queries about our diagnostic certainties and reject any system that suggest categorically that all the answers are in concerning childhood schizophrenia. In addition to the matter of childhood psychosis, we also suggest that the fractionation of language into varying functional elements is a valuable tool that clinicians may readily use in a global nonquantitative way as a means of joining our colleagues in other professions in the diagnostic process. The latter has practical significance too because the committees on the handicapped who review educational placement for children are beset by professional sectarianism in which we who are child psychiatrists participate. Reclassification from learning and developmentally disabled to emotionally handicapped is spurious when we all agree that a primary developmental problem necessarily has emotional consequences. However, diagnoses are used to further such distinctions when not warranted. As child psychiatrists, we would direct our attention toward language in helping our dialogue with educators, psychologists, and speech and hearing professionals and not reify the name of the thing as its reason for being or as an explanation that clarifies anything.

In addition to these general professional and social issues regarding children growing up with deviant language secondary to severe mental disorders, we must also consider the psychological and social impact of such disorders of language on the developing organism, that is, the person in a social field. Bateson's own view of what linguists refer to as the pragmatics of communication is relevant because his studies of variant forms of message transmission in normal social fields reveal the rich array of nuance that is possible through combinations of vocal, gestural, and paralinguistic components of language. His analysis of the double bind provided a paradigm for one kind of misunderstanding and dysfunction in the societal field. The current analysis of the developing child with intrinsic linguistic and cognitive problems should highlight how important intact language capacity is to adequate socialization too. It also lends credence to the importance of language as a social facilitator that feeds back on emotional well-being.

We can harken back to Kanner's original notion that, whatever the origin of autism, as these children begin to speak and become more socially adept in late latency and early adolescence, they become more self-consciously aware of their social surround. However, this permits them to perceive the perplexity and rejecting attitudes of their peers without comprehending their role in precipitating those rejecting behaviors. The latter may in part account for why some of the children are reclassified as emotionally disordered rather than developmentally disabled as they mature. Thus, getting older, maturing, and increasing language skills produce a paradoxical effect of diminishing social fit in some.

One may readily imagine what it is like to grow up in a community where language is so important and where social intercourse is highly dependent on verbal exchange and on play and not be able to fully understand that one's communicational mode is incomprehensible to others. I have seen and heard of 9- and 10-year-old children who are just beginning to be able to communicate in a manner that is sufficient to keep them close to the mainstream in schooling or in a "normal" day camp during the summer only to find that the most serious problems that accrue are not in following routines, but in getting along with their peers and fitting into group sports such as baseball. Although adults may be able to make accommodations for such children, it is very difficult for normally functioning children to understand what is wrong with their developmentally disabled peers. For example, one youngster was seen standing very close to somebody he liked, almost eager to embrace him. The other youngster misinterpreted the function of the disabled child's gesture and when the child in question was rebuffed, he took the gruff tone of his peer as an ad hominem rejection rather than as a critique of his behavior that was considered "weird." There was no understanding that his unaccustomed proximity had anything to do with why his desired friend attacked him.

In other situations these children sometimes also become overly aggressive without intending to. They may approach another in a playful manner suited to a younger child, which may even be a patterned exchange sequence used at home to make contact, only to be misunderstood as their initiating a fight. Similarly, when discussing varying social functions or games, the children are led to believe they are "messing up" the games by their peers. Their categories of understanding are not quite the same, nor are they flexibly able to shift sets to less rigid ways of acting. Kanner wrote about the follow-up of one of his original cases who, although he was able to go to college and operate cognitively within the structure of that rational system, was socially inadept. For example, he cheered for the wrong team during a college football bonfire. It is this type of off-the-mark behavior that probably results from the miscategorization and the lack of understanding that these children encounter in the social arena because of their severe language and thought disorder that is characterized by a wide variety of categorical errors.

In addition to the problems of language, the problem in consequence of not being able to play or follow through on an imaginative theme in any but the most rote manner also tends to remove such children from the social milieu (Sherman, Shapiro, & Glassman, 1983). One is not ordinarily alerted to how much play and language are precursors to socialization in normal development until one sees children who are growing up with a developmental deviation. Only then is it possible to witness how inappropriately they fit and how much difficulty they have in making contact with others. These are grave consequences of faulty symbolic systems affecting communicative efficiency and social function. It is in this light that Bateson's notions of individual linguistic structures affecting social structures are so relevant.

If one miscategorizes or does not understand a category in the same way as the larger community, or one uses words in a highly idiosyncratic manner, one can predict how the behavior will affect not only the auditor, but the speaker if the speaker is self-consciously aware. The speaker must realize that he or she miscues, misdirects, and sometimes seems even rude and deviant, in order to consider change. Contrary to the opinion of many that children can be cruel, they are by and large fairly tolerant of others. Nonetheless, as they enter the late latency age, the problem of how one belongs and how one makes lasting attachments leads to experimental phenomena such as small clubs or transient affiliations that prepare for the early chumships that Sullivan has described. Obviously the medium with which this is done has to do with the transmission of ideas in a common language. Moving out of the family circle and its general protection to a peer circle that does not have a special vantage of a family is a developmental step dependent on language and play. In order to do this, children who do grow up with deviant development have a very difficult time in making this socialization step smoother. One might even be able to infer that social structure and linguistic structures are imaginative structures that are intimately linked. If one must think of the brain as having a center for language, one must also think of the brain as having a center for socialization and that adaptation in communities is the outcome of apt application of the skills that derive from these functions. It is not only that emotions are just there right from the beginning as Darwin had thought, they also are molded by the social and linguistic understanding that normal developmental processes permit. Children with pervasive developmental disorders and autism are not privy to access these skills in the usual way. Unless they are effective in the community, their problems spill over into their social life, forcing them into more isolated and removed circumstances, which is similar to the withdrawal of other psychotics. Our emotions are molded by our social and cognitive developmental achievements. The children described here provide an example of the resultant disruptions of inadequate and deviant basic biological capacity.

References

Andreason, N. C., & Powers, P. S. (1974). Overinclusive thinking in mania and schizophrenia. *British Journal of Psychiatry, 125*, 452–456.
Bateson, G. (1979). *Mind and nature: A necessary unity.* New York: E. P. Dutton.
Bender, L. (1942). Childhood schizophrenia. *The Nervous Child, 1*, 138–141.
Bender, L. (1959). The concept of pseudopsychopathic schizophrenia in adolescence. *American Journal of Orthopsychiatry, 29*, 491–512.
Bleuler, E. (1911). *Dementia praecox or the group of schizophrenias.* New York: International Universities Press, 1950.
Bloom, L. L., & Lahey, M. (1978). *Language development and language disorders.* New York: Wiley.
Cameron, N. (1944). Experimental analysis of schizophrenic thinking. In J. S. Kasanin (Ed.), *Language and thought in schizophrenia.* New York: Norton.
Cantor, S. (1980). Is childhood schizophrenia a cholinergic disease? *Archives of General Psychiatry, 37*, 658–667.
Cantwell, D. P., Baker, L., & Mattison, R. E. (1979). The prevalence of psychiatric disorder in children with speech and language disorder: An epidemiologic study. *Journal of the American Academy of Child Psychiatry, 18*(3), 450–461.
Diagnostic and statistical manual of mental disorders (DSM III). (1980). Washington, DC: The American Psychiatric Association.

Fish, B. (1977). Neurobiologic antecedents of schizophrenia in children: Evidence for an inherited, congenital neurointegrative defect. *Archives of General Psychiatry, 34,* 1297–1313.

Goldfarb, W. (1974). *Growth and change of schizophrenic children.* New York: Wiley.

Goldstein, K. (1944). Methodological approach to the study of schizophrenic thought disorder. In J. S. Kasanin (Ed.), *Language and thought in schizophrenia.* New York: Norton.

Johnston, M. H., & Holzman, P. S. (1979). *Assessing schizophrenic thinking: A clinical and research instrument for measuring thought disorder.* San Francisco: Jossey-Bass.

Kasanin, J. S. (1944). *Language and thought in schizophrenia.* New York: Norton.

Maher, B. A. (1972). The language of schizophrenia: A review and interpretation. *British Journal of Psychiatry, 120,* 3–17.

Petty, L. K., Ornitz, E. M., Michelman, J. D., & Zimmerman, E. G. (1984). Autistic children who become schizophrenic. *Archives of General Psychiatry, 41*(2), 129–135.

Richman, N., & Stevenson, J. (1977). Language delay in 3-year-olds: Family and social factors. *Acta Paediatr. Belg., 30,* 213–219.

Rochester, S., & Martin, J. R. (1979). *Crazy talk: A study of the discourse of schizophrenic speakers.* New York: Plenum Press.

Rutter, M. (1972). Childhood schizophrenia reconsidered. *Journal of Autism and Childhood Schizophrenia, 2*(4), 315–337.

Rutter, D. R. (1979). The reconstruction of schizophrenic speech. *British Journal of Psychiatry, 134,* 356–359.

Schaffner, B. (Ed.) (1956). *Group processes: Transactions of the second conference, October, 9, 10, 11, 12, 1955, Princeton, NJ.* Copyright, 1956, by The Josiah Macy Jr. Foundation, Library of Congress catalog card no. 55-11643.

Shapiro, T., & Fish, B. (1969). A method to study language deviation as an aspect of ego organization in young schizophrenic children. *Journal of the American Academy of Child Psychiatry, 8,* 36–56.

Shapiro, T., Roberts, A., & Fish, B. (1970). Imitation and echoing in young schizophrenic children. Journal of the American Academy of Child Psychiatry, *9,* 548–567.

Shapiro, T., Chiarandini, I., & Fish, B. (1974). Thirty severely disturbed children: Evaluation of their language development for classification and prognosis. *Archives of General Psychiatry, 30,* 819–825.

Shapiro, T., Huebner, H., & Campbell, M. (1974). Language behavior and hierarchic integration in a psychotic child. *Journal of Autism and Childhood Schizophrenia, 4,* 71–90.

Shapiro, T., & Huebner, H. (1976). Speech patterns of five psychotic children now in adolescence. *Journal of the American Academy of Child Psychiatry, 15*(2), 278–293.

Sherman, M., Shapiro, T., & Glassman, M. (1983). Play and language in developmentally disordered preschoolers: A new approach to classification. *Journal of the American Academy of Child Psychiatry, 22*(6), 511–524.

van Domarus, E. (1944). The specific laws of logic in schizophrenia. In J. S. Kasanin (Ed.), *Language and thought in schizophrenia.* New York: Norton.

Wing, L., & Gould, J. (1979). Severe impairments of social interaction and associated abnormalities in children: Epidemiology and classification. *Journal of Autism and Childhood Schizophrenia, 9,* 11–29.

7. A cross-cultural study of language universals: the emotional meaning of iconic and graphic stimuli

ROBERT W. RIEBER, OLIVER C. S. TZENG, and
CARL WIEDMANN*

How is a leaf on a tree, similar to a noun in a sentence? Answer: "Both grammar and biological structure are products of communicational and organizational processes."

—Gregory Bateson,
Steps Towards an Ecology of Mind

Gregory Bateson, in his essay "Style, Grace, and Information in Primitive Art" (1972), poses the question: "How is it that the artifacts of one

*The authors would like to acknowledge their debt to the following scholars, without whose collaborative effort the present work would not have been possible: Rogelio Diaz Guerrero, Ph.D., University of Mexico; Miguel Salas Sanchez, Ph.D., University of Bogota, Colombia; Bernardo Vallejo, Ph.D.; Paolo Bonaiuto, Ph.D., University of Bologna, Italy; M. Serra-Raventos, Ph.D., University of Barcelona, Spain; Florian Coulmas, Ph.D., Chuo University, Japan.
We would like to include here a statement by Dr. Coulmas regarding problems with the translation of the scales used here from English to Japanese: "When I agreed to collect the Japanese data for this study, I thought this was merely a technical matter. It was only when I got down to the actual work that I realized what I think is a fundamental problem of which the reader should also be aware. It has to do with the translation of the scales, which proved to be much more difficult than I had anticipated. Ideally, the scales on which the stimuli items were rated should be constant across languages. Since total semantic equivalence, especially with respect to connotative aspects, is rare indeed, one might settle for near-constancy of the scales across languages. If this meant a little bit of imprecision, it would not be much of a problem. However, I am inclined to think that the implications are of a more serious kind. What this element of uncertainty really means is that we don't know whether the results of the cross-cultural comparison indicate differences in the perception of the stimuli or differences that are sedimented in the semantic organization of the vocabularies in question. One example must suffice to illustrate this point. Japanese temperature adjectives are systematically divided into two sets: (1) those referring to bodily sensations and (2) those ascribing properties to objects. Thus, the Japanese equivalent of *cold* can only be the one or the other. In English it is not necessary to make a choice here. The question which arises here and which, I believe, the present study is not designed to answer, is whether differences between the English and the Japanese data on this scale are due to differences in the subjects' ratings or to differences in the organization of the semantic space in English and Japanese. It is important to add, that this is not an isolated problem, but one that concerns all scales and, in principle, any two languages."
Florian Coulmas

culture can have meaning or validity for critics in a different culture?" His answer is as follows: "If art is somehow expressed by something like grace or psychic integration, then the success of this expression may well be recognized across cultural boundaries." If we continue this line of thought we may pose a second question: If art does express a cross-culturally perceivable quality of grace or psychic integration, in what form is information about this quality encoded within the image?

Obviously, artistic images typically transmit much information, both denotative and connotative, that is readily accessible to most viewers. This is a picture of a cat, say, an angry cat getting ready to fight. But, this tells us nothing about whether it is a pleasing picture, whether it evokes a sense of awe, or of fright, or perhaps of the terrible beauty of nature. The question thus becomes what sort of additional information is encoded within the stylistic execution of the image, in its composition, in its configuration of forms, quite apart from its denotative and connotative meanings. We feel that this question is worth investigating and hope to get some valuable clues as to how to answer it in this and future studies.

7.1. Literature review: the semantics of iconography

Charles Osgood, in predicting the significance of psycholinguistic research at a lecture before the New York Academy of Science in 1975, said, "Semantics will be moving into the foreground as syntax moves reciprocally into the background." Whether Osgood's prediction will ultimately come to pass, no one knows, though there is some evidence to suggest that the general trend is Osgood's own work, and that of his associates, employing the well-known device called the semantic differential. Through factor analysis, the semantic differential technique has consistently yielded three cross-culturally valid components: evaluation (E: good/bad), potency (P: strong/weak), and activity (A: active/passive). With the use of these three components (E-P-A), the location of different concepts in a three-dimensional semantic space can be analyzed and compared. As such, the scheme gauges the emotional impact of stimulus items on the subject. The three-feature system has been shown to exist in some 30 different language–culture communities (Osgood, Myron, & May, 1975).

Insofar as research with the semantic differential typically employs a word or lexical unit as its stimulus, a limitation is imposed both in terms of the level of abstraction tested and the kind of subject used in the experiment. French (1977), in a paper entitled "Non-Verbal Measurement of Affect: The Graphic Differential," has reported an interesting study that has a bearing on this topic. French says in her study that:

the measurement of affective meaning (Osgood's three universal factors) is easily accomplished via the semantic differential. However, the verbal nature of this instrument prevents its use in many subject groups in which the measurement of affective meaning would be most interesting: illiterate cultures, verbally damaged schizophrenics, and in children younger than six. For these the present study describes the development of the nonverbal alternative to the semantic differential and assesses the statistical comparability of scores resulting from the use of the two instruments. (p. 339)

Research in this field of inquiry is important for it may help us better understand how humans' symbolic capacity has evolved as well as how it may be shaped by any particular cultural tradition. Bujas (1967) studied the "value" of pictorial opposites and found that, in many instances, one item within a pair was judged more reliably than the other. This study, however, made no attempt to relate these pictorial opposites to the E-P-A dimension. Jakobovits (1969) devised a study in which subjects rated 50 concepts against 64 photographic scales and 12 verbal semantic differential scales. An analysis of his data demonstrated rather high correlations between verbal and nonverbal scores. This was true, however, only in the evaluation of factors, not in individual protocols. Further, many of the verbal scales used in this study present problems such as the simultaneous status of affective and denotative meanings of some scales.

Our own study seeks to utilize the semantic differential technique to assess the affective impact of nonverbal, iconographic stimuli. Osgood's cross-cultural studies have tended to suggest that within a given culture both verbal and nonverbal affective meanings share the same underlying, three-factor semantic system. By implication, this suggests that the three dimensions (E-P-A) can be simultaneously represented both verbally and nonverbally. Child (1969) raises a fundamental question in this domain. He asks whether the observed agreement should be ascribed to cultural similarities or to a more fundamental basis of agreement of a panhuman nature.

In general, there is a great dearth of reliable information about the extent of intersubject agreement, if any, across cultural boundaries in the assessment of visual or auditory stimuli. One goal of the present study was to see whether the same iconographic stimuli might evoke similar or different affective ratings across different cultures. In Osgood's study (1957) of the perception of meaningful affect, the visual stimuli were kept as concrete as possible. The general approach in the study that we wish to report differs from earlier studies in many ways. In fact, you might say that it was suggested by Roger Brown's title to his critical review of Osgood and Tannenbaum's (1957) *Measurement of Meaning*. Brown's title was "Is a Boulder Sweet or Sour?" In our study we purposely chose more complex visual stimuli and systematically attempted to eliminate any possible denotative contamination.

The general purpose of this study was to see if the nondiscursive dimensions of affective meaning (within our stimuli) are independent of variations in both language and culture. We have set out to do this by going from the complex to the concrete.

7.2. Original pilot study

A number of years ago, we conducted a pilot study to establish whether any cross-culturally valid meaning space could be obtained with regard to complex visual stimuli. We compared college students in the United States with Italian students in Rome, with approximately 100 subjects in each group, matched for age, education, and sex. Sets of test booklets were constructed consisting of bound instructions to the subjects and high-quality photographs of 10 pre-Columbian art objects. We will refer to these icons as the visual stimuli. Semantic differential forms were prepared containing 15 adjective pairs. The Italian sample was administered in Rome by Dr. Paolo Bonaiuto of the University of Bologna, and his collaboration in this study is gratefully acknowledged. The translations into Italian were made under his direction, and their equivalence to the English was then checked by a professor of Italian at the City University of New York. Good agreement was obtained. Obviously our stimuli and scales (adjective pairs) had to be carefully selected. We attempted to balance E-P-A factors in the scales and to guard against denotative contamination by not using physically descriptive pairs (such as hard/soft) when the object was made of stone. We chose pre-Columbian art objects for our stimuli; these objects are familiar all over the Americas, frequently being used to decorate homes, shops, and so forth, and they have great emotional appeal for and impact on viewers.

Since "civilized" Westerners do not produce icons as substitutes for discursive languages, we felt it would be valuable to use icons as our stimuli. It is of some importance to point out that the cultures that originally produced these icons were cultures that either had no written language, or at most had only a rudimentary written language in the form of glyphs, such as the Maya or Zapotec systems. Because there is no Mesoamerican Rosetta stone, experts are still attempting to make translations of this material. The evidence seems to indicate that in ancient Mesoamerica these icons were used as a substitute for written language. (Plans are in progress to collect data from the Maya subjects in the Yucatan, since the Maya and Zapotec people are the closest living descendants of the original culture that produced these icons.) There is also evidence to demonstrate that the icons were produced in great quantities for an important purpose and with an important meaning. No one really knows what they meant, but there are bits of evidence. These icons represent symbols or images at a level of abstraction different from that of words and verbal communication. A poetic description might have it that "these are the things that metaphors, myths, and dreams are made of."

Our interpretation of data is predicated on the view that the specific lexical content of our factors is of far less importance than the fact that the relationships were clearly established between factors and across cultures. The stimuli were complex, containing the contradictory ambivalent elements that are inherent in highly symbolic works of art, especially those that are visual expressions of mythology. Our data show that the lexical content of the factors generated reflected this complexity and ambivalence. However, this should not be mistaken for a lack of order or coherence because the relationships observed in the data clearly show that there is a communality of affective responses across cultures. Further, these relationships were obtained using an investigative strategy that was highly conservative; thus, what was found is all the more likely to be a nonchance result.

A preliminary perusal of the lexical content of factors suggests the following: The first factor for the American sample seemed to be a response to the tension in the stimulus. This seemed to be true for all 10 stimuli. Factor 1 consistently loaded such adjectives as calm, relaxed, lenient, still, and loose. The Italian sample responded slightly different- ly in terms of the first factor. Italian subjects seemed to respond more strongly to the good/bad aspect of the stimulus. In the Italian sample, factor one consistently loaded such adjectives as good/bad, ugly/ beautiful, blatant/muted, obvious/subtle, and superficial/profound. This suggests that the factor in the American sample is an "uptightness" rating – that is, a rating of the perceived tension – while for the Italian subjects the first factor is a response to the stimuli of beauty/profundity (a "Mona Lisa factor"). In terms of the differences here, it is interesting that Americans responded to how relaxed the stimulus appears, or conversely, how relaxed or tense it made them feel, while Italian subjects responded to its aesthetic qualities. What is common to both samples is that to certain specific iconic stimuli (but not all) both American and Italian subjects responded to a safe/dangerous quality. We expect that in further studies this safe/dangerous evaluation will prove universal.

It is important to note that in our study, unlike Osgood's research using words as stimuli, our data show a tendency toward a dynamism rather than to the traditional E-P-A cluster of factors. This is understandable because our iconic stimuli provided a basis for a deeper feeling of emotional conflict, thus producing a tendency toward more mixed feelings in the subjects who responded to our stimuli.

7.3. Present study

The present study differs from the pilot in that we have included along with the pre-Columbian icons graphic representations of them. Insofar as our pilot study indicated, the icons did indeed carry a richer semantic meaning than is carried by less symbolic, more concrete stimuli; the question arises as to where this meaning is encoded in the icon. Working on the tentative hypothesis that this information was carried in the use of line within the objects, we constructed line drawings to capture this element while eliminating all other perceptual features (such as shading and texture).

The purposes of this study are: first, to identify the underlying semantic characteristics that people use in judging icons and graphics, and second, to compare the effects of these underlying characteristics on perceptions of individual icons and graphics from a cross-cultural perspective. These two overall goals can be decomposed into the following specific questions that can be assessed in the course of the present empirical research program:

1. Most cross-cultural research has identified three commonly found affective components: evaluation, potency, and activity. Will these also appear in the ratings of nonverbal icons?
2. If additional dimensions emerge, what will their characteristics be?
3. When subjects from different countries are analyzed jointly and separately, will the analyses yield different semantic structures?
4. How will the E-P-A dimensions be used as criteria in the judgment of

individual icons? Will all semantic features function in the same manner in the judgment of all icons. How will each indigenous culture's background and knowledge about the icons affect that culture's ratings of individual icons?

5. What are the implications of the present cross-cultural research on the psychosemantics of iconic perceptions? What are the implications of the present cross-cultural comparisons for international understanding and communication?

7.4. Measurement domains

Two domains of nonverbal stimuli were used: graphics and icons. The 10 graphics were various combinations of straight lines, circles, and waved or zig-zag lines, and were in different degrees of complexity (cf. Figure 7.1). These graphics are presumably representative of geometrical elements in humanmade and natural environments. The 10 icons were pictures (pre-Columbian art samples) in various forms of human sculptures and in different levels of complexity, ranging from a single head to extensively decorated heads and bodies. These icons are representative of sculptured human likenesses appearing in museums or archaeological displays in various countries (Figure 7.2). Each icon and graphic representation was mounted on an 8½- by 11-inch plain black paper and served as a visual stimulus for the present research (cf. Figure 7.1).

The following five countries were selected for the present study because of the interests and experiences of the researchers in the present study: Japan, the United States, Spain, Mexico, and Colombia. The icons and graphics were generally unfamiliar to the people in these five nations; this approach will enable us to identify common communication themes used in verbal and nonverbal interactions. Therefore, a group of college students were sampled from each country (however, for the present report, data on graphic ratings from the United States were not included).

7.5. Measurement instruments

For cross-cultural comparisons in ratings of the 10 graphics and 10 icons, a common set of seven-step, bipolar semantic differential (SD) scales were selected from the semantic differential literature, especially from the publications on graphic ratings (Osgood et al., 1975; French, 1977; Tzeng & French, 1985). These 21 SD scales, as shown in Table 1, contain nine markers (the first nine scales in Table 1) that represent three

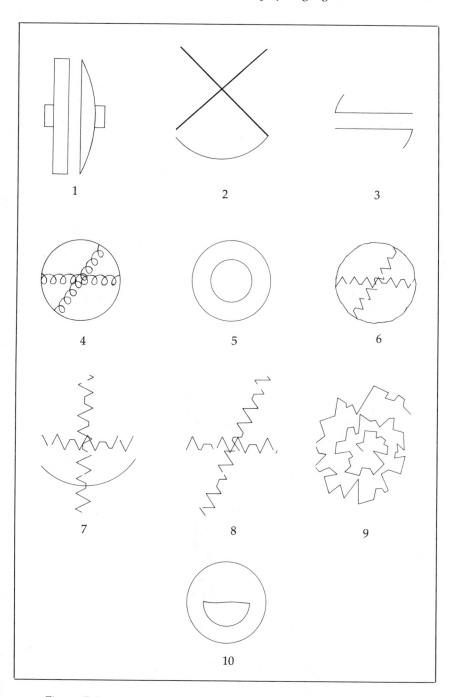

Figure 7.1.

Figure 7.2.

dominant affective dimensions (evaluation, potency, activity) found in Osgood's cross-cultural ressearch, and the 12 scales that are nonaffective adjective pairs. It was hoped that these 12 pairs would be useful in identifying dimensions unique to graphic and iconic perceptions. Before these scales were adopted as measurement tools, consultations with cross-cultural researchers and experts in the archaeological discipline in each of the five countries were made to ascertain the relevancy and representativeness of these scales.

7.6. Procedure

For ratings of each stimulus object (icon or graphic), the 21 SD scales were printed on a single sheet in the questionnaire in accordance with the usual semantic differential rating form (cf. Osgood et al., 1975). In addition, a set of questions were also asked to identify each subject's demographic information, such as age, sex, education, major, training in art, previous experiences with the icons in relation to various cultures (African, Oceanian, Pre-Columbian, Egyptian, modern, and Chinese), and previous art-related activities (painting, sculpting, drawing, and others).

For subjects in different countries, the questionnaire in English was translated into the respective indigenous languages. Within each country, the questionnaire was administered to the subjects in several group sessions. To guarantee the validity and reliability of subject responses, detailed instructions, illustrations, and pretest exercises were conducted. After the completion of ratings, all subject response protocols were screened for omissions and response settings (e.g., all 4s on the seven-point bipolar scale continuum). Those subjects with many omissions or obvious response sets were eliminated from the final analysis of data.

The method used is principal component analysis that is commonly employed for "three-mode" data of semantic differential ratings (subjects × icons × scales). Therefore, in analysis of the icons mode (i.e., computing intericon correlations), the responses from all subjects on all scales are treated as replications. Similarly, in analysis of the scale mode (computing interscale correlations), the responses of all subjects on all icons are treated as replications. Principal component analysis was then applied to the intercorrelations for the icon mode and the scale mode separately.

7.7. Results

Factor analysis of the 21 SD scales in ratings of 10 icons

Intercorrelations among the 21 SD scales computed across the 10 icons and also across the subjects from the five countries yielded five factors that account for 51.4 percent of total input variance. The salient factor loadings via VARIMAX rotation are presented in Table 7.1.

The first factor is defined by three evaluation markers, good/bad, beautiful/ugly, and nice/awful, that are followed by three general evaluative adjective pairs: safe/dangerous. ordered/chaotic, and sweet/sour.

Factor 2 is dominated by two potency markers, powerful/powerless and tense/relaxed, and followed by severe/lenient, profound/superficial, and dangerous/safe. This factor apparently connotes the intensity of affective meanings.

The third factor is defined by strong/weak, and two activity markers, active/passive and fast/slow. The inclusion of the tight/loose scale suggests that this factor would reflect the so-called dynamism connotation in the semantic differential literature.

Factor 4 is defined by agitated/calm, noisy/quiet, blatant/muted, and vibrant/still. It seems to represent more the objective (denotative) aspect of movement among icons than the affective aspect of activity in connotation. Therefore, it will be identified as a mobility factor in denoting the icons.

The fifth factor is tabbed by obvious, cold, sour, superficial, and dry on one side, and subtle, warm, sweet, profound, and wet on the opposite side. It appears to represent the nonaffective characteristics of the icons as being distinctively singular and unique, or as being general and pluralistic. Therefore, it will be called a distinctiveness factor.

Factor analysis of the 21 SD scales in ratings of 10 graphics

Intercorrelations among the 21 SD scales computed across the 10 graphics and also across the subjects from three countries (Japan, Mexico, and Colombia) yielded four distinct factors that account for 51.6 percent of the total input variance. The salient loadings from the resultant rotated factor structures are presented in Table 7.2. (Graphics were not available for Spain and the United States. These two countries were not involved in the analysis.)

Factor 1 is well defined by the three evaluation markers (good/bad, beautiful/ugly, and nice/awful). The remaining scales that were also

Table 7.1. *Salient loadings from factor analysis of 21 scales across 10 icons and five countries (Japan, Mexico, Colombia, U.S., Spain)*

Scales	Factors				
	1	2	3	4	5
1. Good/bad	.73				
2. Beautiful/ugly	.66				
3. Nice/awful	.74				
4. Strong/weak			.71		
5. Powerful/powerless		.68			
6. Tense/relaxed		.60			
7. Fast/slow			.56		
8. Active/passive			.69		
9. Noisy/quiet				.74	
10. Blatant/muted				.72	
11. Calm/agitated				−.74	
12. Superficial/profound		−.50			.44
13. Tight/loose			.55		
14. Dry/wet					.42
15. Obvious/subtle					.50
16. Cool/warm					.50
17. Dangerous/safe	−.47	.42			
18. Still/vibrant				−.67	
19. Chaotic/ordered	−.56				
20. Lenient/severe		−.71			
21. Sour/sweet	−.44				.45

Note: Five factors account for 51.4% of the total input variance.

salient on this factor were safe, ordered, lenient, and sweet associating with the positive side of evaluation and dangerous, chaotic, severe, and sour on the negative side of evaluation.

The second factor recaptured the connotation of activity with one pole being defined by such qualifiers as fast, active, noisy, blatant, agitated, and vibrant. The opposite pole was defined by such scales as slow, passive, quiet, muted, calm, and still. Those two poles clearly reflect the active/inactive nature of connotations of graphics.

The third factor is defined by three potency markers in the order of strong/weak, powerful/powerless, and tense/relaxed. The nonmarker scales that are also salient on this factor are tight/loose, severe/lenient, and profound/superficial. It seems also to indicate the intensity of the objects in connotation.

The fourth factor is defined by four scales, with dry, cool, superficial, and obvious on one pole, and wet, warm, profound, and subtle on the

Table 7.2. *Salient loadings from factor analysis of 21 scales across 10 graphics and three countries (Japan, Mexico, Colombia)*

	Factors			
Scales	1	2	3	4
1. Good/bad	−.74			
2. Beautiful/ugly	−.77			
3. Nice/awful	−.80			
4. Strong/weak			.75	
5. Powerful/powerless			.78	
6. Tense/relaxed	.48		.45	
7. Fast/slow		.62		
8. Active/passive		.68		
9. Noisy/quiet		.67		
10. Blatant/muted		.65		
11. Calm/agitated	−.43	−.61		
12. Superficial/profound			−.54	.43
13. Tight/loose			.60	
14. Dry/wet				.74
15. Obvious/subtle				.42
16. Cool/warm				.54
17. Dangerous/safe	.60			
18. Still/vibrant		−.71		
19. Chaotic/ordered	.57			
20. Lenient/severe	−.48		−.44	
21. Sour/sweet	.62			

Note: Four factors account for 51.6% of the total input variance.

opposite pole. This factor seems to differentiate the perceived icons as being either distinctively singular and unique, or general and pluralistic in association with background ecologies. In the choice of the first character, this factor is identified as the distinctiveness dimension.

Two-way MANOVA on five resultant scale factors across five cultures and 10 icons

In order to evaluate cross-cultural similarities as well as differences in attribution of the five semantic features to individual icons, the factor scores of each subject on each icon were derived by averaging each subject's ratings on the respective marker scales of each semantic feature. The mean factor score of each country on each icon was also derived by averaging the factor scores of subjects from each country. The resulting mean factor scores on all 10 icons were reported for each of the five SD dimensions separately in Table 7.3. Also reported in the table are the cultural means of the five cultures on each semantic feature computed across the 10 icons, and also the icon's means of the 10 icons on each semantic feature, computed across the five cultures.

With the variables of cultures and icons used as two independent variables, the factor scores of all subjects from the five cultures on the 10 icons were submitted for multivariate analysis of variance across the five semantic features. The results with statistical significance were also indicated in Table 3. For the evaluation, potency, and mobility dimensions, two main effects (culture and icon) and their interactions are all significant beyond the .01 level. On activity and distinctiveness dimensions, the main effects of cultures and icons are not significant, but their interactions are significant ($p < .01$).

To facilitate interpretations of intercultural differences in mean scores on each icon, the lowest cultural mean among the five countries is coded by an asterisk sign, and the mean that is greater than the lowest mean with a magnitude of 1.0 or higher is marked by a plus sign in Table 7.3. For example, on the evaluation dimension, Japan has the lowest rating of 2.66 on icon 1, whereas Spain and Colombia have 3.68 and 3.79 ratings. This may indicate that the Japanese displayed a more favorable attitude toward icon 1 than the Spanish and Colombians did. It is interesting to note that since icon 1 resembles some Japanese artwork, the Japanese rated this more favorably than the others.

7.8. Discussion

Our first question was whether the three commonly found affective components – evaluation, potency, and activity – would also appear in ratings of nonverbal icons. The answer to this question is clearly yes. We will now turn to the second and third questions and discuss them together as follows. What additional dimensions and characteristics, if any, would emerge with regard to our stimuli, and would the analyses yield different semantic structures for the various countries? To begin with, a complex interaction of icons by E-P-A scales and by cultures (Tables 7.3A–E) reveal that it is difficult to say that a particular icon is rated similarly by a culture across dimensions. The rating an icon receives depends both on the culture and the scale being used. Nevertheless, the following generalizations can be made. Icon 5 has the most mobility and icon 9 is the least mobile. Icon 6 is seen as the best and most potent as well as the least active and distinctive. Icon 1 is the least

Table 7.3. *Culture means for icons on five semantic features*

	Cultures					
Icons	Japan	U.S.	Spain	Mexico	Colombia	Icon's mean
A. *Semantic feature of mobility*[a]						
Icon 1	4.98	4.09	4.45	4.02*	4.80	4.48
2	3.57	3.51	3.07*	4.25	3.70	3.64
3	2.95*	3.46	4.98+	3.43	5.16+	4.04+
4	3.82+	4.12+	2.65*	4.55+	3.34	3.68+
5	4.04*	4.18	5.38+	4.52	5.29+	4.72
6	1.86*	3.92+	5.68+	4.08+	5.66+	4.29+
7	3.11*	3.22	3.38	3.50	3.72	3.40
8	3.15*	3.46	3.22	4.75+	3.37	3.61
9	2.28*	3.27	3.00	4.07+	3.43+	3.23
10	3.73	3.42*	4.99	4.95	4.59	4.39
Culture's mean	3.35	3.67	4.08	4.21	4.31	3.95
B. *Semantic feature of evaluation*[a]						
Icon 1	2.66*	3.28	3.68+	3.59	3.79+	3.42
2	4.61	4.61	4.03	3.62*	4.43	4.24
3	4.39	4.54	3.95	4.71	3.83*	4.27
4	3.70	3.47*	4.15	3.59	4.19	3.84
5	3.43*	3.88	3.76	3.89	4.17	3.84
6	5.59+	4.71	3.96*	3.99	4.58	4.55
7	4.14	4.60+	3.51*	4.58+	4.52+	4.27
8	5.52+	3.96	3.70	3.43*	4.24	4.17
9	5.21+	4.70+	3.89	3.65*	4.45	4.36
10	4.18	4.76	3.84*	4.02	5.02+	4.35
Culture's mean	4.34	4.25	3.85	3.91	4.32	4.13
C. *Semantic feature of potency*[a]						
Icon 1	4.53+	3.35	2.88	3.36	2.55*	3.31
2	3.93+	3.29	2.92*	3.55	3.06	3.35
3	3.08*	3.10	4.20+	3.82	3.93	3.66
4	3.81+	3.49	3.29	3.83+	2.74*	3.42
5	3.86	3.85	3.47*	3.88	3.70	3.75
6	3.33	3.18*	3.80	3.80	4.41+	3.86
7	3.75	3.16	2.92	3.22	2.91*	3.19
8	4.07	3.67	3.07*	4.17+	3.52	3.70
9	3.26	3.18*	3.34	3.71	3.59	3.44
10	3.33	3.22	3.15	3.42	2.78*	3.17
Culture's mean	3.68	3.35	3.30	3.74	3.26	3.47
D. *Semantic feature of activity*[b]						
Icon 1	4.32+	3.58	4.63+	3.12*	3.31	3.78
2	4.03	3.59	4.97	3.34*	3.37	3.85
3	2.78*	3.55	3.12	3.88+	5.06+	3.73
4	4.01+	3.53	5.38+	3.17	2.57*	3.70+
5	3.91	4.28	4.11	3.68*	4.17	4.02
6	2.71*	3.56	3.85+	4.02+	4.24+	3.70
7	4.03	3.18*	5.01+	3.25	3.35	3.77

Table 7.3. *(continued)*

	Cultures					
Icons	Japan	U.S.	Spain	Mexico	Colombia	Icon's mean
8	4.54+	3.36	4.82+	3.88	3.48*	4.03
9	2.95*	3.38	4.90+	3.41	3.36	3.60
10	3.69	3.36*	4.44	3.65	3.46	3.73
Culture's mean	3.70	3.54	4.52	3.54	3.64	3.79
E. *Semantic feature of distinctiveness*[b]						
Icon 1	3.66	3.42*	3.89	3.45	3.57	3.60
2	3.88	3.78	3.77	3.53*	3.77	3.74
3	3.47	3.80	3.18*	3.57	3.53	3.50
4	3.90	3.92	3.70	3.48	3.35*	3.65
5	3.58	4.04	3.91	3.80	3.43*	3.73
6	3.28	3.78	3.13*	3.78	3.17	3.41
7	4.29+	3.62	3.07*	3.58	3.19	3.54
8	3.75	4.00	3.65*	4.03	3.71	3.82
9	3.47	3.83	3.38*	3.67	3.56	3.57
10	4.23+	3.98	3.17	3.53	3.02*	3.55
Culture's mean	3.75	3.82	3.48	3.64	3.43	3.61

Note: Marker scales for individual semantic features are:
Mobility: noisy/quiet, blatant/muted, agitated/calm, and vibrant/still.
Evaluation: good/bad, beautiful/ugly, nice/awful, and ordered/chaotic.
Potency: powerful/powerless, tense/relaxed, severe/lenient, and superficial/profound.
Activity: fast/slow, active/passive, tight/loose, and strong/weak.
Distinctiveness: dry/wet, obvious/subtle, cool/warm, and sour/sweet.
[a]Two main effects and the interaction effect are statistically significant at the .01 level on three semantic features: mobility, evaluation, and potency.
[b]Interaction effects were significant for the activity and distinctiveness features.
*Indicates the lowest culture mean in difference from four other culture means, and + indicates a mean at least 1.0 higher than the lowest cultural means.

evaluative and icon 10 is the least potent. Icon 8 is the most active and distinctive. Icons 6 and 8 are the most sensitive to the scales. They stand out on four different dimensions, and they serve as an anchor of meaning at both ends of the scale. Icon 4 is rated good and strong by the Japanese, apparently because it appeared to be most familiar to them. Furthermore, rating across icons allows for the following generalizations to be made: (1) Colombia is the most mobile and distinctive as well as the least potent, (2) Japan is the most evaluative and least mobile, (3) Spain is the least evaluative and most active, (4) Mexico was the most potent, and (5) the United States was the least distinctive.

Our fourth question was focused on the relation of the E-P-A dimensions and judgments of the icons across different cultures. Specifically, we asked how the E-P-A dimensions would be used in framing judgments of the icons. We also asked whether the E-P-A dimensions would function in the same manner in the judgment of icons across different cultures. As well, we asked whether a culture's previous knowledge about the icons would affect that culture's ratings.

One of the most surprising results of the research was the discovery of a collapse of two of the E-P-A dimensions in the Japanese sample. Japanese raters responded to the icons with judgments that collapsed or joined the dimensions of potency and activity. This collapse was not observed with the other samples. Given that we drew our subjects from several language groups (American, Latin American, Italian, Spanish), the results suggest that the fusion of P and A is unique to Japanese culture. In effect, the icon and graphics, as the stimuli, seem to have served as a projective test eliciting a perceptive structure that is distinctive about the Japanese worldview. To be sure, the uniqueness of this collapse of the dimensions of activity and potency remains to be shown in other cultural contexts. In particular, we would like to compare the Japanese results with results drawn from other Asian cultures. Nonetheless, our own suspicion is that even after such future comparisons, the Japanese data will continue to be unique because of the unique homogeneity of the Japanese within Asia.

In interpreting this result, we must bear in mind that we are dealing with continua. The potency dimension involves both strong and weak, while activity involves both active and passive. The alignment of these dimensions in the Japanese sample thus entails a superordinate dimension with ranges from strong and active on one side to weak and passive on the other. We should expect this superordinate dimension to shape Japanese perception of various cultural contexts.

A pertinent example of the equation of potency and activity that comes readily to mind, and that is of great consequence nationally for the Japanese, is the system of rice production. As a country with limited arable land, Japan is not necessarily an agricultural power; nevertheless, it is determinedly self-sufficient in the production of rice, the basic staple of the Japanese diet. This self-sufficiency is achieved at considerable cost, and it requires an elaborate degree of social cooperation. Nonetheless, the Japanese prefer to work at it, seeing self-sufficiency in this area as an important symbol of national self-sufficiency. In short, it requires enormous activity to achieve this basic agricultural potency; the commitment to the latter includes the commitment to the former.

A similar collapse of potency and activity can be seen in the unique Japanese spirit of economic competition. Consider the race for superconductor technology. Here Japan is locked in a three-way competition with the United States and Switzerland; in all three countries, enthusiasm is high and excited researchers have been known to work through the night. But in Japan the researchers do more than work through the night. During periods of rapid advance in raising the working temperature of superconductive materials, the researchers and their student assistants literally sleep at the laboratory. Only in Japan will the assembled gathering cheer en masse as the posted temperature rises progressively higher. It is not merely that this research has become a collective enterprise in Japan. It is a question of the frame around which the group organizes its participation. The increase in working temperature signals great technical power and potentially great economic power; it is greeted during periods of rapid advance with maximum emotional and practical activity on the part of the participants. The two aspects, power and activity, are as one for the group.

The same fusion of activity and potency can be seen in the Japanese view of individual destiny. Most participants in the culture define their destiny in terms of adapting to a tightly defined social niche, low on both power and activity. In the ritual bows that form the correct gestural greeting, it is required that the lower ranking individual bow lower than the higher ranking individual; indeed, in the course of bowing the former will steal a glance just to see that this requirement has been fulfilled properly. Here, too, in a negative way, activity (bowing correctly) and potency (social status) are linked. But they are also linked at the opposite end of the scale; that is, in the national fascination with those individuals who seek to assert themselves against social restraint. Here, too, potency and activity are as one, whether embodied in the romantic form of the Samurai warrior or, to take a more recent culture hero, in the person of the devastating young American heavyweight, Michael Tyson, who has become something of a national hero in Japan. This fascination has sometimes been called, even by the Japanese themselves, the "Godzilla complex." Here let us be careful to remind ourselves that the dimension in which the hero–monster exists is independent of the dimension of evaluation: Godzilla, like Tyson, is neither good nor bad, though he is fascinating. Or to take an example from a bygone era, the farmer's son who could make the dangerous and arduous trip to gain an audience with the emperor to air the family grievances against local officials was justly acclaimed a hero, and his action led to remedial action (thus he gained power); nonetheless, he was promptly put to death, since such displays of initiative and defiance of the local authorities ran counter to the feudal code.

In seeking the social roots of this equation of activity and potency, we turn our attention to the unique Japanese family system. Male children in Japan are indulged to a degree Westerners find hard to comprehend up to approximately the age of seven. This process is called *amea ru* in Japanese. Their tempers, no less than their whims, are indulged without sanction; under the benevolent supervision of their mothers, they enjoy unlimited power and activity. Then they are suddenly ousted from their mother's care and handed over to their fathers; discipline and self-control are suddenly and determinedly enforced. American anthropologists such as Mead and Benedict found the pattern most problematical in that the child was suddenly extruded from his emotional supports, but as Professor Doi (1978) pointed out in his book, *Anatomy of Dependency*, the child is joined by his peers in this predicament and the peer cohort comes to form a new source of support. Thus the child's loss of his prerogatives is compensated for with training in how to adapt himself socially to the group.

But what of the lost paradise of male childhood? It does not disappear; instead, it resurfaces in adult sexual and familial roles. The young male who can successfully negotiate the social order finds in adulthood that he once again enjoys a kind of paradise vis-à-vis his wife, mistresses, and unique prerogatives. His needs are catered to and he can once again do what he wants.

In rough outline, what we see here is a social dynamism in which training in childhood for a privileged position in adulthood is mediated by an intervening period of enforced conformity to the group's standards. By the time the adult Japanese male recovers the prerogatives of his childhood, he is both skilled and knowledgeable in terms of the codes of social conduct. Continued observance of these codes has become both the prerequisite and the means for resuming the prerogatives of his early life. The same dynamism, we submit, is manifest in the ratings of icons: The two logically distinct dimensions of activity and potency are collapsed and become a superordinate dimension, both organizing perception and reflecting the shared Japanese worldview. In short, for the Japanese subjects *actions* give power and meaning to words in their language. This dynamic process tends to facilitate precise detailed evaluations, which in turn promote a unified cohesion of values within the culture.*

Our fifth question concerned the implications of our cross-cultural research on the psychosemantics of icon perception. On the one hand, we asked how the ratings of icons would compare with ratings of verbal concepts. Conversely, we posed the question of how differences between cultures in icon perception might be applied to issues of international communication and understanding.

The answer to both these questions revolves around the discovery of dynamisms within the data. In this respect, the Japanese sample was most striking. There the dimensions of potency and activity collapsed into a single dimension. But it was repeatedly observed that there was a distinct tendency toward the formation of dynamisms in all the samples. This was expected to occur in light of the nature of the stimuli. The greater the familiarity with the given stimulus, the more likely you are to think and speak about it on a cognitive level. On the other hand, the less familiar the object, the greater the probability to attach a deeper affective meaning to it. From the onset, the icons tend to tap deeper areas of emotional resonance and of potential emotional conflict than do most verbal stimuli. Put simply, they are the sort of thing dreams and myths are made of. The observed dynamisms in our data – the tendency for response dimensions to move in the direction of unique cultural patterns – are entirely in keeping with this presupposition. Here let us note, however, that these dynamisms varied across cultures.

References

Bateson, G. (1972). Style, grace, and information in primitive art. *Steps to an ecology of mind.* New York: Ballantine Books.

*Chie Nakane discusses how democracy as a symbolic idea developed in Japan immediately after World War II. Although this was an Americanization process, it took place in the typical Japanese fashion with activity and potency playing major roles. The following quote illustrates this point: "It is in this sociological and psychological soil that the imported term 'democracy' has developed its specific Japanese connotation. It is used particularly as a charge against the monopoly of power by a privileged sector or a stronger faction in an organization. It is interesting to observe, however, that the form in which this charge is stated is identical with that through which authoritarian power has been exercised. The change from feudalism to democracy is not structural or organizational; it is rather a change in the direction of the motion of energy within the same pipeline, this energy exerted by the same kinds of people."

Bujas, Z. (1967). Graphic form of Osgood's semantic differential. *Acta Institute of Psychology*, 49–63:5–12
Child, I. L. (1969). Aesthetics. In G. Lindzey and E. Aronson (Ed.), *Handbook of Social Psychology*, 2nd Ed. (Vol. 3), pp. 395–449. Reading, MA: Addison-Wesley.
Doi, T. (1981). *Anatomy of Dependence*. New York: Kodansha.
French, P. (1977). Non-verbal measurement of affect: The graphic differential. *Journal of Psycholinguistic Research*, 6(4), 337–347.
Jakobovits, L. A. (1969). The affect of symbols: Towards the development of a cross-cultural differential. *International Journal of Symbols 1*, 28–52.
Nakane, C. (1987). Japanese Society. *Bunkyo-ku*. Tokyo: Tuttle.
Osgood, C., & Tannenbaum, P. (1957). *The Measurement of Meaning*. Urbana, IL: University of Illinois Press.
Osgood, C. E., Myron, M. S., & May, W. H. (1975). *Cross-cultural universals of affective meaning* Urbana, IL: University of Illinois Press.
Osgood, C. E. (1975). A dinosaur caper: Psycholinguistics, past, present, and future. In D. Aaronson & R. Rieber (Eds.), *Developmental Psycholinguistics and Communicative Disorders. Annals of the N. Y. Academy of Sciences, 263*, 16–26.
Tzeng, O., & French P. (1985). *Journal of Psycholinguistic Research, 14(3)*.

8. Machine dreams: computers in the fantasies of young adults

JOHN M. BROUGHTON

Norman sat down at the computer.
He placed his apple on top of the terminal.
He thought of taking a byte of his apple and laughed.
But maybe the fruit is forbidden, he thought.
Second thoughts flooded his mind.

The narrative above is a fantasy story constructed collaboratively by five young adult subjects. In this chapter, I would like to make use of a number of such fantasies to illuminate the shadowy universe of symbolic phenomena that, beneath the level of awareness, is associated with the microcomputer. In so doing, it is my intention to question the authority of computational technique and, by so doing, take a byte out of the area that has come to be known recently as "political psychology."

Specifically, I want to suggest one way in which we might begin what Gregory Bateson called a "metalogue" on the dynamic meaning of high technology in the contemporary cultural unconscious. This meaning seems to me to be at one and the same time both personal and social, and at both levels to be of exceptional significance to our historical self-awareness and our possible future. But we should be prepared for the fact that, in the words of our subjects' story above, examination of this meaning may release a flood of second thoughts about computer technology.

8.1. Mind, self, and society

Bateson is celebrated for many things in particular but one overarching contribution in general: the synthesis of approaches from genetics, ethology, anthropology, epistemology, and family sociology through cybernetics to yield a comprehensive, evolutionary, systems-theoretical worldview for the social and ecological sciences (Bateson, 1972, 1979).

191

He even wrote about worldviews themselves (Bateson, 1968). Not content with mere metatheory, he argued the merits of his vision in terms of specific issues and studies. Five of his major preoccupations were the relation between mind and body (Bateson, 1976, 1980), the question of self or agency (Bateson, 1970, 1971), the importance of relationship and dialogic interaction (Bateson, 1972; Ruesch & Bateson, 1951), the problem of power (Bateson, 1974, 1978), and the possibilities of transcendence (Bateson, 1970, 1982; Bateson & Bateson, 1987).[1]

The research to be reported below recapitulates these same old philosophical chestnuts. It does so opportunistically, taking advantage of the extraordinary contemporary technological and cultural phenomenon centered upon the microcomputer. It is my conviction that high technology is a new kind of prism as well as a new kind of prison. The dark side, the creation of more deeply entrenched and preemptive structures of social discrimination and control, has been expertly documented and explicated (Weizenbaum, 1976; Dreyfus, 1979; Greene, 1985; Solomonides & Levidow, 1985; Noble, 1985; Olson, 1985; Sloan, 1985; Sullivan, 1985). On the bright side, the construction of sophisticated mechanisms for the manipulation of symbols has brought with it a less visible but nonetheless real semiotic potential. Between the lines, at the level of unconscious symbolism, the technology of microcomputers suggests a fresh discursive matrix in which old philosophical problems such as psychophysics, subjectivity, intersubjectivity, and immanence–transcendence are refracted in novel ways, emerging in a vivid spectrum of fresh images. The creative imagination embodied in the technology bursts out in unintended ways, generating deeper and more powerful visions of the relations between mental and material, self and other.

It would hardly be guesswork to assume that, as one of the earliest and most active proponents of the metaphoric power latent in the language of the information and communications sciences, Bateson would have been much stimulated by the recent events of the "electronic revolution." He was certainly not reticent to borrow metaphors from the world of computing (Bateson, 1972, p. 454; M. C. Bateson, 1972, pp. 52–53). Also, given his researches in psychiatry (e.g., Bateson, Jackson, Haley, & Weakland, 1956; Bateson, 1960, 1966) and his interest in fantasy (Bateson, 1955, 1973), the psychodynamic drift of the following analysis is not far from his bailiwick. What would have piqued his curiosity, I hope, is the notion that, rather than the application of cybernetic metaphors to psychiatry, we need the converse, a psychiatric approach to computing (cf. Faber, 1984).

8.2. The symbolic meaning of computers

Because the computer now represents the very essence of symbolic mastery, and programming the propaedeutic human skill, we tend to forget that the computer itself has a meaning that is not necessarily reducible to formal organization or the manipulation of information. What it *does* fails to exhaust what it *is*.

Although programming efficiently generates consistency, there is still something imprecise about it – the aura that it takes on in the public imagination. One only has to think of the polymorphous and ambivalent way in which computers have been taken up into the sphere of popular culture, in mass-market feature films, music videos, advertising, even in robotic styles of dance, and metallic clothing materials.

One of the most profound meanings that the computer has for us, then, is the very uncertainty of what it means to us. In the technical domain, its performance conforms well to the modern ideal of infinite utility and functional stability. In the alternative, but equally "real" cultural realm, it appears to be strictly mercurial, capturing in an exquisitely poignant way the potential for polarizations, reversals, and ruptures of meaning. Here, the system seems to be at the mercy of the unsystematic. If its reality in the one world is the power of action, in the other it is the power of passion. The capacity for simulation residing in the computer has been much touted. But insofar as the computer conceals the deep ambiguity of its own existence with the guise of pure practicality, it reveals to the attentive eye its equal capacity for dissimulation.[2]

The discourse of desire lurking under the thin disguise of electronic rationality has received little attention in the scientific community. I can think of only two exceptions (see Turkle, 1984, and Faber, 1984). If the microcomputer, this technological paragon of objectivity, expresses at the same time a certain cultural subjectivity, then an important new role opens up for the research psychologist: the illumination of that suppressed zone of sensitivity in which the personal meaning of the new technology is at play.

8.3. An exploratory study of computer fantasies

The research to be described has the status of an exploratory study. The aim was to pilot one particular technique for eliciting imaginative constructions centered on the microcomputer. The method employed for this study had three major features: It was of the "projective" type, it employed a game format, and it required group rather than individual performance.

In the middle of an academic term, a heterogeneous class of 88 graduate students was persuaded to comply with a procedure for generating multiple fantasy narratives around computer use. The subjects selected for the study were participants in a popular graduate course in social thought at a graduate school of education in a major East Coast urban center.[3] It was assumed that young adult subjects were a suitable population to sample in this way, since they represent the first generation confronting the new work world so extensively transformed by high technology.

The materials consisted of 88 sheets of paper (8 by 11 inch) at the top of which was the first line of a "story." Half the stories started with the sentence "Joy sat down at the computer." The other half began, "Norman sat down at the computer."[4] The instructions given (verbally) to the subjects were as follows.

> Each of you has a sheet of paper with the first line of a "story." Please write underneath that sentence a second sentence that could be the next part of the story. Then fold the top of the paper over to cover up the first sentence, so that the next person can see only the sentence that you have just written. Then pass the folded sheet four seats to your left. Whenever you receive a sheet, make sure that only the last sentence is showing, and then write another sentence of the story, and repeat the procedure I just described. Please relax and enjoy yourself as much as possible, and allow your imagination to run free. Don't think too long about your contributions – just write the first thing that comes into your mind.

The sheets circulated for about 5 minutes, enough time to thicken the plots. The completed stories averaged six to seven lines in length. Not coincidentally, this coincides with the optimum length for very short stories (Alldis, 1985).

The format of a projective test (Bell, 1948; Frank, 1949; Anderson & Anderson, 1951) was adopted on the grounds that it is ideally suited to the illumination of "primary process," that is, unconscious dynamic material, typically appearing in the form of quasi-narrative themes (Schafer, 1948; Rosenzweig, 1949; Holt, 1967). The present approach blends two successful standard projective approaches, association and completion (Rotter, 1951).[5]

In order to make a preliminary assessment of the validity of the method, the fantasy narrative data were reviewed informally with respect to Auld, Goldenberg, and Weiss's (1968) Scale of Primary Process Thinking. The majority of the narratives appeared to fall above the minimum level in Auld et al.'s scale, exhibiting features that can be legitimately called unusual (level 2) or contradictory, obviously symbolic, or slightly uncanny (level 3). This observation provides at least provisional reassurance that the story completion task stimulated primary process phenomena.

Although quantitative analyses can be applied to projective data in general (Cattell, 1951) and to fantasy themes in particular (Symonds, 1949; see Zayas and Broughton, 1988), the presentation of the data here is confined to the identification and illustration of qualitative themes and patterns in the stories. The interpretive technique employed draws on the tradition of content analysis as used widely in the social sciences (Lazarsfeld & Baran, 1951; Berelson, 1952; Pool, 1959; Holsti, 1969; Krippendorf, 1980) but resembles most the methods described and validated by Cicourel (1964) and Glaser and Strauss (1967). The identification of specific themes was modeled after the methods of Murray (1938), Symonds (1949), and Gould (1972).[6]

8.4. Thematic content of the fantasies

The predominant thematic dimension of the sagas was the hedonic continuum, from pleasure to pain, with a distinct bias in content toward the latter. The most frequent scenarios were not concerned with achievement, productivity, or empowerment. If mastery seems to be the dominant issue at the level of conscious thought, it is displeasure that would appear to reign in the unconscious and preconscious. The dysphoric experiences mentioned in the stories crossed the spectrum from boredom to terror, including feelings of compulsion, physical discomfort, torpor, uncertainty, confusion, frustration, inadequacy, anxiety, depersonalization, dependence, and outright fear.

Euphoria without ambivalence was rare. Wherever pleasurable experiences were mentioned, they were typically associated with a dysphoric context, as in the following example:

1: Joy sat down at the computer.
   She has a fun.
   In the event of fire, though, she knew they would all have to leave.[7]

We will consider first the milder displeasures, and "progress" toward the more sinister ones.

The dysphoric experience

Compulsion. The predominant picture of computer work emerging from the stories is of something one is driven to, rather than as an autonomously willed choice.

> 2: In fact she wasn't sure if she wanted to do this particular
>   program.

In some stories, the operator of the computer seems to lose agency as the syntax lapses into the passive voice:

> 3: Brow furrowed, a new entry was made.

The theme of involuntary work, in one particular case, was linked to the theme of the exploitation of women. The outcome of this vignette is a relational distancing of the protagonist:

> 4: Joy sat down at the computer.
>   She was learning computers.
>   But she wasn't learning fast enough to suit her boyfriend who
>   was dependent upon her for helping him out.
>   So she began to resent her boyfriend and began to find him less
>   sexually attractive.
>   As a result, they became less sexually active.
>   That was terrible.

Compulsion appears not just in coerced behavior but also in the fascination with the computer and the resulting need or desire for it:

> 5a: She was mesmerized about all the gadgets she saw.

> 5b: Joy likes computer very much.
>   She was getting addicted by computer.

A negative consequence of the magnetic quality of the computer and the compulsive features of computer use is their interference in human relationships:

> 5c: When he got up the next morning, he went right over to the
>   computer and turned it on.
>   His wife was quite annoyed.

Aversion. The majority of subjective states attributed to the protagonist express a general discomfort with the computing experience. It is not always clear what the occasion of aversion to working at the computer is. In one case, the dysphoria was not even experienced directly, but vicariously, as though under the sway of the defensive maneuver that Freud and the ethologists have called "displacement":

> 6: Joy sat down at the computer.
> And formatted a days worth of discs.
> Little did he suspect that there were clouds on the horizon.
> He began to think of his mother.
> His mother was not feeling well in the morning.

Frequently, there are enervating or devitalizing effects of computer use. The mildest and most obvious of these is sheer tedium:

> 7a: Joy sat down at the computer and thought, What another boring day.

> 7b: Storing information could be a bore!

> 7c: After half an hour she was bored.
> Because the material was not challenging or interesting.
> So she trashed the whole thing.

A similar reaction, but in response to the quantitative rather than the qualitative character of the work, more time related than content related, is fatigue:

> 8a: Guess she had worked a little too late on that program.

> 8b: It was all he could do tonight.
> He had already been at the computer for 14 hours.

> 8c: My eyes are heavy, I feel like sleeping.
> But I still have a paper to complete.

> 8d: He learned how to operate it and then went to sleep.

There was mention of trips for coffee:

> 9a: The program being loaded was involved and complicated.
> She got a cup of coffee.

> 9b: She went to get a cup of coffee.

This suggests that computer use is felt to diminish alertness, so that sustained performance requires an auxiliary stimulant.

Discomfort is not always strictly a function of tiredness or mere work load, however. There are allusions to feeling *stifled* by computer work:

> 10a: She got up from her desk and walked outside.
> She needed to get a breathe [sic] of fresh air.

Many stories allude to such an impetus toward the outside, into the open air:

> 10b: She decided to go out for a walk.

10c: He wished he could go out into the sunshine.
But he had a lot of work to do at the computer.

10d: What a weird toy – She decided to leave.
She went out into the street and started walking.
She thought about all the work she had to do at home.
She really could not work at the computer all day.

Here, the computer is associated with a closed and constricted space; its image is claustrophobic. Its gravitational attraction restricts one's orbit; it keeps one in when one could be going out:

10e: He wondered why he always got stuck working on weekends.
He'd rather be dancing at Chippendale's.

One is inclined to ponder the possibility that the way in which microcomputers encourage the translocation of labor into the domestic space and into nonworking hours may have compromised the traditional retreat into the haven of the home and the possibility of enjoying spare time there.

Not only the imagery of constricted space but also the imagery of light is implicated. In the chiaroscuro of the fantasy images, the room is a "shade-haunted space,"[8] which is offset by the charm of natural illumination in the outside world:

11a: Joy sat down at the computer.
"It was that time of the year again," she thought.
And outside the wind was blowing, the shine shining [sic],
the birds singing.

The syntagmatic slip from "sun" to "shine" only serves to emphasize the sensuous vividness of solar irradiation. But, in contrast, there is the paradoxically injurious quality of natural light:

11b: I may as well put the shades down to cut down the screen glare.

In the cathode ray microworld, natural light is proscribed in favor of purely artifical light by virtue of a medicalized rationale. The light from the inside needs protection against the light from the outside; fluorescence supersedes illumination.[9] Shades of Blake's "dark satanic mills."

Despite the assiduous task orientation of 10b, movement away from the computer generally predominates over movement toward it. While the micro is consistently the center of attention, its human operators seem subject to a centrifugal tendency. Physical locomotion seems to be a popular form of relief. Being an ambulatory creature is somehow an effective antidote to being a sedentary operator. One might say that, while the sitter appears to be doing all the spelling, the walker is actually spelling the sitter. Activation of the body is revitalizing – the antithesis of the retreat into sleep. Gross bodily movement seems liberatory and brings the individual closer to nature, while keyboard operation entails a constriction – what neurophysiologists call "fine motor control."

Perambulation, in turn, can lead to other, clearly pleasurable activities:

12: He decided at that point to go to a bar for a drink.

This example encourages speculation as to whether the magnetic, centripetal power of the computer may be experienced as somehow opposed to pleasure. Certainly, on occasion, the centrifugal tendency appears peremptory and unprovoked, as though there were a spontaneous aversion to the computer. For example, the line following 2 above was:

13: So she stopped what she was doing and pulled the plug.

What is the origin of this aversion? Most, if not all, of the excerpts so far are compatible with the hypothesis of a general aversion to work; labor may always be experienced as more or less involuntary. However, 14 suggests two other possibilities.

14: Joy sat down at the computer.

And wished she was some place else.

Hoping to met [*sic*] someone usual.

The last line here encourages the speculation that the aversion has to do with the computer *not being a person,* or not being "usual"; that is, there is something disquietingly unusual or peculiar about the computer. What this might be we shall come to in a moment.

What we can say by way of a summary so far is that there appear to be certain dynamisms in the primary orientation of the computer user. First, there is the dispositional transformation from passive to active, down to up, sedentary to ambulatory, and mental to physical. Second, in the realm of the spatial, there are the vectors of proximity to distance, internal to external, and containment to release. Third, there is the ontological transition from mechanical to natural. Fourth, there is a motivational dimension from duty to inclination and tension to relief. Fifth, there is a reparative change from dark to light and devitalization to revitalization.

The overall vector dominating the imaginative constructions seems to be from pain to pleasure, or even from reality to fantasy – from the reality principle of the computational device to the compensatory rewards of primary process. At the same time, there is an overall flavor of the shift from attachment to autonomy, reminiscent of Mahler's phases of infant and childhood "separation–individuation" (Mahler, 1972a, 1972b; Mahler, Pine, & Bergman, 1975). One cannot help noticing the value dimension to these transitions, suggesting that the centrifugal tendency represents a movement from wrong to right, a drift toward the morality of righting wrongs. The imaginative mind detects in computer work some distinctly aversive quality for which psychological and physical distancing from the computer – retreat from consciousness and escape from the room – are alternative remedies.

Computing itself may represent not so much a healthy attraction as a negation of the exercise of will. The price of the computer may no longer be prohibitive but, in fantasy, the computer itself remains a prohibitive object. In one story, Joy decided to go get a cup of coffee and

15: The computer said, "Don't move!" (cf. Figure 8.1)

Anxiety. Among the dysphoric state themes, the most frequently mentioned experience is anxiety – so much so that it warrants its own subsection here. The word "anxiety" itself appeared regularly, although related conditions, such as being confused, perplexed, ambivalent, dismayed, tense, panicked, or paralyzed, have also been included in this category.

At the mild end of the spectrum, there is mention of confusion and perplexity:

16a: Where did all this come from?
I am getting confused.

16b: Norman sat down at the computer.
He found himself totally confused.

16c: Joy sat down at the computer.
She said I am so confused.
Where do I start.

16d: Norman sat down at the computer.
He stared at it perplexed.

Typically, the reference is to a more incapacitating state of anxiety, manifest as worry, dismay, or paralysis. In a number of cases, this anxiety appears more or less spontaneously, apparently as a function of the situation of being with the computer rather than in reaction to something the computer does:

17a: He was so worried about writing the program.
He had to count up to 10 first in order to relax.

17b: Norman sat down at the computer.
Then began to think of what to write.

Figure 8.1. Photograph reproduced with permission of Barbara Kruger.

His mind went completely blank.
He then became anxious.

17c: Joy sat down at the computer.
    And regarded it with a mixture of dismay and determination.
    As time went on the stress made her ill.

17d: Joy sat down at the computer.
    And her body froze.
    The icicles came down from her arms.

17e: Joy sat down at the computer.
    The tension was overwhelming and she passed out.
    She had to be revived by her brother.

In other cases, it is not entirely clear what precipitates the anxious reaction, or at least what agent is responsible for the anxiety-provoking event:

18a: Norman sat down at the computer.
    This was the first time, he has ever worked on one.

He searched for the on-off switch.
It went on immediately and he looked at it.
And had an anxiety attack.

18b: Norman sat down at the computer.
He punched up the program he had been working on.
But he discovered the computer program has been erased.
He became very anxious – the program had been vitally important.
Suddenly he vomited all over the terminal.

In one case only (19, line 3) is the computer implicated explicitly in the origin of the anxiety, but even here, this is offset by the fact that the previous association (lines 1–2) indicates that the anxiety was self-generated:

19:    He made a mistake.
There was a moment of anxiety.
When the computer flashed an unpredictable light.

A psychologist might argue that the arousal at low levels of anxiety is a helpful and necessary part of skilled performance. However, this does not fit with the narratives obtained: The anxieties are more or less disabling. In only three cases was this not so, and two of these involved ignoring or overriding the anxiety rather than putting it to good use.

20a: Joy sat down at the computer.
She turned on the monitor, the disk drive, and the printer.
She felt an inward groan of anxiety about this machine.
Yet, she began to do her work.

20b: Even though he had a mild fear of computers.
He decided to give it a try anyway.
He furrowed his brow in concentration.

20c: Joy sat down at the computer.
She was hoping that this was a better way to write.
She found, however, that her mastery of the machine was not what she thought.
"What shall I do?" she panicked.
Suddenly she remembered what she had learned the previous week.
And that was to use the save key when storing information.

Later, we shall return to the topic of how anxieties arising in the use of the computer are ignored, avoided, or defended against. For the moment, we need to pursue the question of what exactly it might be about operating such a device that is so frightening. What we will find is that, even though the computer does not necessarily do anything in particular to precipitate anxiety, there is something about its general appearance and "presence" that is nevertheless disturbing.

The alien mechanism

Reification. Considering that so much of the anxiety appearing in the fantasy stories is unprovoked and so little is ameliorated, one is led to inquire of Norman and Joy, "Why so apprehensive?" Many of the stories focus on a state of high anxiety without accounting for its origins. However, this should not be taken to imply that the computer itself escapes critical scrutiny – far from it. In many of the vignettes, there is more of a focus on the objective events than on the protagonist's subjective states, and negative qualities are attributed directly to the computer. The thematic content of these stories suggests that what triggers a malaise may be something about the computer itself – not what it does, but what it is.

A significant aspect of this reaction is the extent to which the computer as object is reified. This is evidenced by the common appearance in the stories of what Marx (1844, p.311) called "petrified relations," as in the use of the substantive form "learning computers" (see example 4 above) rather than the more subjective, process-oriented verb conjugations "learning to compute," "learning computing," or "learning how to compute." Reification is reflected in the general tendency, throughout the stories, to emphasize the hardware and to ignore the role of software in mediating the relationship between computer and user.[10]

This "thingification" of technology manifests itself also in the use of the term "machine" rather than "computer."[11] In several instances this transformation is associated with what appear to be positive experiences of mastery and excitement:

21a: She was intrigued with the machine.

21b: She felt very exhilerated [*sic*] with the power the machine gave her.

21c: But she was more powerful than the machine.

Nevertheless, reification appeared more frequently in scenarios where negative affect predominated, as in 19a and the following:

22a: She hesitated and looked at the grey machine sitting in front of her.

22b: She thought the machine was as frustrating as her sex life.

22c: It didn't seem to be offering a cue about what to do next with this machine.

22d: She thought "Damn machines I hate them."

22e: Then the machine started to go crazy.

Here, labeling the computer as a mere "machine" could be construed as derogatory. In one story, to be analyzed below, Joy dismisses her micro as nothing more than a "gadget."

How are we to make sense of what seem to be conflicting meanings – pejorative and nonpejorative – attached to the examples of reification? A possible reconciliation of the excerpts in 21 with those in 22 would be achieved if we were to understand the "mechanization" to occur whenever what is being sought is an objectification of the relationship between self and computer, either through an affective distancing or a reduction of the interface to a purely instrumental connection. As will emerge below, the magnetic appeal of the computer and its promise of thrilling power reflect an underlying rigidification of the human relationship to it, one that Turkle (1984) has shown to have distinctly compulsive features. Under this interpretation, the apparently euphoric form of objectification may turn out to be a reaction against an unconsciously dysphoric experience.

The use of the generic, superordinate term "machine," whether as a means to rise above the computer or to subordinate oneself to it, seems designed as a leveling ploy, reducing the computer to a merely mechanical device. At this level, there emerge objections to the complexity of the instrument, as in the following:

23: It had so many buttons!
   She was horrified.

For one Joy, the complexity of the instrumentation was sufficient to elicit what would seem to be a defensive act of denial:

24: Joy sat down at the computer.
   The keyboard looked like the cockpit of a Boeing 747.
   It was not intimidating at all.

However, "technophobic" reactions were typically couched in more or less clichéd expressions of antipathy toward mechanical things, as in, "They are so complicated," or "Machines are too complex."

The sinister. In 14 above, we witnessed the elliptical suggestion that the computer may be aversive because it is unusual – sufficiently so to make Joy wish she were "some place else." What we learn from the derogatory connotations attached to calling the computer a "machine" is that anxiety may not be just a function of some internal problem of the self but instead may reflect qualities inherent in the computer itself. Such a shift of emphasis from the subject to the object allows the tedium of computer work, detailed above, to be reified as a quality of dullness inherent in the computer itself, as suggested, for instance, by the "grey machine" of example 22a. Similarly, the retreat from the computer may be less a function of subjective states of alienation than a result of something alienating in the technology itself.[12]

In the fantasies, a number of remarks seem to imply an aversively alien or deviant character to the computer. For example, in 10d, Joy exits rather hastily because the computer is "weird" and, in 14, she wishes she could escape the computer to meet "someone usual." The inauthentic character of the computer was intimated by one writer who protested, "User-friendly? Fiction, mere fiction." In another story, Joy feels that "the impersonality was alienating." Conceivably, then, the variety of aggressive impulses visited upon the mechanical hardware itself, as witnessed in 13 and 18b – not to mention the various verbal expressions of anger, as in "Damn machines, I hate them" (example 22d) – may be a consequence of alien qualities perceived in the technological object. We tend both to fear and to attack the foreign (Frank, 1967; Allen & Broughton, 1987).

We noted earlier the implicit equation of computer with darkness, with the "shade-haunted space." If the Prince of Darkness is the Devil, then it should come as little surprise that various evil qualities are attributed to the computer. In the fantasy stories, it appears to take on a variety of disturbing characteristics, ranging from the uncanny to the ugly and repulsive. It is almost as if the very responsiveness of the keyboard to a light touch sharpens awareness of the computer's darker side. On the one hand, there is the dextrous instrument, but on the other, there is the sinister device:

> 25a: Norman sat down at the computer.
>> He looked for the switches with which to control the instrument.
>> The screen glowed ominously.
>> It was green and bilious hued.
>> And I wanted to change the color but the command button was stuck.

25b: Joy sat down at the computer.
  And prepared to log on.
  But the computer went off.
  And began to make strange noises.
  She believed that the noises came from the room.
  She's disturbed by the noises.
  She opened the door slowly and saw a dim light at the bottom
    of the stairs.
  "Hello, who's there?" she cried out.
  The only response was a printed command.

Here, the computer no longer asserts its authority passively or indirectly, by its evocation of states of hypnosis or addiction, but actively and directly. The tool becomes the author; the slave turns into the master. But it is a wicked rather than a beneficent master, a dictator rather than a provider, recalling again the earlier machinery of Blake's "dark satanic mills."

The mechanism no longer responds to commands, preferring to issue them itself. The demands of computer work pass over into commands. The commander is in deadly earnest:

26: Norman sat down at the computer.
  It was as if death was at hand.

The computer not only devitalizes but also immobilizes, as in the scene where Joy gets up to go for some coffee and the computer says, "Don't move!" (Figure 8.1). The protagonist, faced with this implacable commander and experiencing diminution in her own volition, may retaliate. Self-defense seems justified, even to the point of cutting off the life-support system of this other. To cite in full the segment previously quoted in 2 and 13:

27: In fact, she wasn't sure that she wanted to do this particular
    program.
  So she stopped what she was doing and pulled the plug.

But, as we saw in example 25b, the computer displays a mysterious degree of autonomy. It possesses its own power, and so can operate even without electrical current.

The authority of the computer is not merely political. It has an epistemic genesis. With this comes the sense of taboo, the proscription of desire attached to knowledge itself, the second thought following rapidly upon the heels of the first (cf. Thorner, 1983). Computer corporations were not slow to capitalize on this central theme in the cultural power of high technology – hence the name "Apple":

28: Norman sat down at the computer.
    He placed his apple on top of the terminal.
    He thought of taking a byte of his apple and laughed.
    But maybe the fruit is forbidden, he thought.
    Second thoughts flooded his mind.

If we review 25, 26, and 28, what is impressive is a differential in initiative. In the face of the superior intelligence that is the ultimate judge, the operator feels relatively powerless. The machine no longer responds. To borrow Sartre's (1953) terms, it is an "in-itself" and a "for-itself," not a "for the other." In proportion to the magnificent independence of the computer, Joy and Norman become all the more dependent. Following the normal dynamics of dependence (Kovel, 1978), to the extent that the machine does not need them, the salience of their need for the machine approaches a maximum.

Danger. From our review of the fantasy stories, the relationship to the computer would appear to be not only one of subjection, but also one in which there is a constant potential for danger, a threat implicit in the self-sufficient potency that the computer appears to possess. The malignancy of power ruptures the constructiveness of work.

29a: Joy sat down at the computer.
    She put her belongings on the floor beside her.
    She switched on the power.
    The light suddenly came on and she physically recoiled.

29b: With a wicked smile, he proceeded to turn on the power switch.
    Lightning flashed across the screen.[13]

The dark side of the computer reveals itself most dramatically in fantasies that transgress the merely uncanny, sinister, or even authoritarian, stepping behind scenarios of conflict or subordination to locate images of preemptive disruption and injury. In the imaginary, the ideal rationality of the machine casts a tragic shadow in which lurk irruptions of irrationality, often in a violent form. The calculated and lawful functioning of the system brings with it the unexpected accident. The quickness of the machine is matched by the suddenness of the calamity.

30a: Norman sat down at the computer.
    One of the legs on the chair broke.
    He landed on his behind and cursed and kicked the terminal.

> 30b: Joy sat down at the computer.
> As she crossed her legs to get comfortable, she split her nylon tights.
> She became angry at her stupid mistake and swore and struck the computer.
> When she struck the computer, she hurt her hand.

Some of the accidents are more punitive than others. "It was as if death was at hand" – Norman's ominous intuition upon sitting down at the computer (example 26) turns out to be more than mere fancy. The terminal is, for some, aptly named:

> 31a: Norman sat down at the computer.
> With swift, sure keystrokes, she began typing the opening paragraph of her dissertation.
> She was very excited because she was just beginning her project.
> Then all of a sudden the whole thing exploded.

> 31b: My eyes are heavy, I feel like sleeping.
> But I still have a paper to complete.
> I think I'll explode.
> Help me, I need a degree.
> Help yourself!
> She got electrocuted.

In the first of these tragedies, the "punishment" follows directly upon euphoric aspiration, reminding us of how intimately related pleasure and danger are, at least in the subjective realm (cf. Vance, 1984). In the other story, the retribution appears to be a consequence of petitioning the machine for help. Here, the micro is Thomas Hardy's malignant deity incarnate.

It is important to note that in these various sorry tales, the mishaps occur without any overt provocation. In only one case was the "accident" consequent upon an unsolicited act of aggression on the part of the operator:

> 32: Norman sat down at the computer.
> So what?
> She opened up the back of the computer and ripped out the wires.
> She gave herself electric shock therapy.

Nevertheless, it is interesting to note, on occasions, a certain indeterminacy about the precise location of the danger. To return to examples 31a and 31b, for example, it is noticeable that in one case it is "the whole thing" that explodes, while in the other, it is the self that threatens to explode. Similarly, in example 29b, it is the operator, not the machine, that sports the wicked smile. These observations suggest that it may be the situation of computer use or the human–computer relationship that is malignant or explosive, rather than the computer itself.

The fantastic subject

Reverie. There is a sense in which everything that we have discussed so far amounts to primary process of some kind, since all the protocols are fantasy narratives. However, it is noticeable in the stories how frequently the protagonists, Joy and Norman, themselves experience primary process as a moment of their own subjectivity.

Primary process enters into the computer narratives as a subjective state in a variety of ways. What is noticeable is that it is so frequently treated negatively. Often it is treated impersonally as an undesirable distraction from the task at hand. We have already seen examples of this in 6, where rather than using the formatted diskettes, Joy lapses into a daydream about her or his mother, or in 11a, where, upon sitting down to work, Joy's fancy immediately turns to thoughts of nature and the seasons. In another instance, reverie is at first used in a task-oriented way, but soon passes over into a mere interference, the possible personal significance of the remembrance being dismissed:

33: He slowly began to dream about a program.
He remembered some things from childhood that interrupted his concentration.

In addition to parents, nature, and childhood, the altered states of consciousness that we have already encountered include a variety of concerns or attitudes, ranging from a hypnotic attachment to the hardware (5a) to morbid states, as in Joy's preoccupation with incendiary disaster (1) and explosion (31b) and Norman's presentiments of death (example 26). Overall, one is hard put to avoid the pervasively puritanical attitude toward reverie that manifests itself in the stories. For example, humorous and alimentary imaginings are confronted with a stern taboo (28). In addition, dream thoughts are dismissed as epiphenomena:

34a: She thought about last night's dream, when computers danced in her head.
Guess she had worked a little too late on that program.

Sexual fantasies come up against the harsh reality of marital promises:

> 34b: Norman sat down at the computer.
> He took a deep breath.
> And began to fantasize about that morning's happenings.
> She fantasized about her favorite lover.
> She's in a good mood.
> The thought of her impending wedding made her think about John.
> And his memory made her jittery.[14]

And terpsichorean daydreams are dismissed as merely mind-trips into the light fantastic:

> 34c: He soon started fantasizing about being a go-go dancer.
> But knew it was only a dream.

Fantasy is permitted only a brief flight; it is quickly made an occasion of self-control, a restoration of the authority of reason. The oneiric, the mythopoetic underworld of consciousness, is set up in this way as not only unreal but also illicit, especially in the workplace, and perhaps even dangerous. This stern attitude – "Daydreaming is all very well, *but* . . . " – appears again in the following two cases:

> 35a: What milestone would he make today in his program.
> Perhaps he would invent a shortcut to Shangri La.
> But he'd have to figure out the program first.

> 35b: He was ready to play Pac Man.
> He wanted to get over 15,000 points.
> But he was too slow and stupid.

Here, the protagonist does not stray so far from the relationship to the console, but he lapses into idealistic exaggeration, only to sober himself up sharply with a cold splash of realism. No punitive reminder from the computer itself is required here. Authority is internalized and self-control occludes the limitless horizon of desire.

Play. Much as reverie is the counterpoint to concentration, the opposite of work is play – a more extended form of fantasy than daydreaming and one implying that the protagonist is physically "off task" as well as mentally so. Play was the predominant form in which primary process made its appearance in the stories. In its mildest form, there was a desire or attempt to weld the ludic impulse to the constraints of the computer, downgrading the machine to the level of a mere toy (cf. 10d), or using it in a game-playing (example 35b) or graphics mode:

36a: She couldn't wait to try it.
    She had nothing to lose; it was just a new toy, a game.
    So we started playing with it.

36b: He wished it was a video game instead.

36c: Joy sat down at the computer.
    She decided to play a game.

36d: She began to use color lights and develop a pattern.

Play serves defensively as a diversion, an escape from work and work-related difficulties, as depicted in the following:

37a: So he took out the instruction manual.
    It wasn't very helpful.
    So he decided to give up the computer and take tennis instead.

37b: Norman sat down at the computer.
    He was so worried about writing the program.
    He had to count up to 10 first in order to relax.
    Thought he'd start with a group of graphs.
    Then he thought he'd just play a game.
    So he looked through his pile of discs and found one called Stary Night [sic].

The simultaneous and paradoxical relations of continuity and mutual exclusion between work and play are captured in the next example, which is actually the full story behind 36b above.

38: Norman sat down at the computer.
    He wanted to write a story and would use his word processor.
    But suddenly he realized to use finger paint and not the word pro.
    So he went to the playroom and got the watercolors.
    He started to mix some paints.
    And came up with an extraordinary computer graphic.
    It was something that would change the face of previous graphics.
    He wished it was a video game instead.

This last narrative possesses two additional features of interest. First, the expressive function of play seems to be exaggerated, perhaps with the intention of putting it in sharp relief against the background of the instrumental activity of word processing. The expressive mode chosen is one that is characteristic of children's play, suggesting that, subjectively, the relation of expressive to instrumental may implicate the tension between the immature or regressive and the mature or progressive (cf. 33). The reference to using the hand for spontaneous daubing rather than in its mode of precisely controlled digital manipulation underlines the oppositions of controlled/uncontrolled, skilled/unskilled, work/fun, scientific/aesthetic, or even analog/digital (if the pun may be excused).

On the other hand, example 38 reveals ways in which there may be transitional zones between the poles of these oppositions. After all, in this story, the word processor was first invoked creatively, as a means to writing a story. Moreover, in a paradigm instance of symbolic condensation, the mixing of paints merges into the creation of computer graphics, bringing the prodigal Norman back home to his travail again. The grandiose and flowery sequela – "It was something that would change the face of computer graphics" – returns us to a stress upon the functional, goal-directed nature of artistic activity with the computer: Art *is* science, or play *is* work. The next sentence adds a further twist: Even graphic uses of the computer are still serious, and not playful enough for some. Finally, it should be noted that, according to the plot, finger painting was first conceived as a substitute for the word processor – presumably a means to the same or a similar end. Of course, there is a certain irony here since, from the point of view of the subjects themselves, what the finger-painting theme is doing is precisely the writing of a story!

We are certainly at risk, here, of overinterpreting a single example. However, all of these observations appear to converge upon an interesting moral lesson: Between the poles of instrumental and expressive, between "playing and reality," there lies not a vacuum but a versatile space of transitions. At least one author (Winnicott, 1971) has found that it is precisely along this seashore that the imagination litters its joyful experiments. In the liminal zone, alternations of fusion and fission generate a manifold of diverse possibilities of experience. It is out of this amphibious world of symbolic condensations and displacements that the dream and the substance arise, not only of subjectivity but also of culture and communication (Buck-Morss, 1987).

Rhythm. The surplus of work finds its antithesis in the catharsis of music and dance. The rigorous Apollonian life of intellectual labor and learning, with its tenuous promise of delayed gratification, pales in comparison to the carnivalesque glow of Dionysian revelry, with its rich and immediate satisfactions. In the words of Marx (1844) – referring to the alienation of labor, not the anticipation of a visit by his in-laws – "Those petrified relations must be forced to dance by singing to them their own melody" (p. 311).

> 39: Joy sat down at the computer.
> She decided to play a game.
> Oh boy, now I'll have some fun, she thought.
> The lights were bright the music blasting, she was very excited.
> She started dancing.
> She couldn't stop.
> It was an uncontrollable impulse.

Such uninhibited revelry provides a stark contrast to the computer sweatshop, and stimulates the centrifugal tendency, as in the following story:

> 40: Norman sat down at the computer.
> Norman turned on the computer.
> He wondered why he always got stuck working on weekends.
> He'd rather be dancing at Chippendale's.
> He soon started fantasizing about being a go-go dancer.
> But knew it was only a dream.
> Nevertheless it bothers me.

The strife between work and play echoes that between accomplishment and pleasure, duty and inclination, that has been a repeated theme in our analysis above. The subjective reality of that strife is nowhere better captured, however, than in the following story:

> 41: Joy sat down at the computer.
> He's touching the key board.
> And the music was full and low.
> Would the tiny click click of the keys destroy the mood.
> It is unlike the silent gliding of ink on paper.

In 41, the rich aesthetic textures in "full and low" are artfully juxtaposed with the impoverished mechanical tonality that is small and high; the substantial and sensuous is contrasted with the diminutive and hollow. Moreover, mechanized sound is attributed the power to spoil the pleasurable sensations evoked by music. Finally, in the last line, we have a poignant nostalgia for the traditional forms of literacy, denigrating the din of machines that traffic in script.

Despite this wistful critique of Joy's, the hope of harmony between person and machine is not entirely given up:

> 42a: Joy turned on the machine.
> She sat and watched the screen, listening to its hum.
> She then began to hum the Battle Hymn Republic [sic].
> As she hums she wants the figures on the screen.

42b: Joy sat down at the computer.
    She was mesmerized about all the gadgets she saw.
    I want to have a rock and roll time.
    Rock and roll is better than computers.
    I love rock and roll, but I also love input and output.
    No-one cared why she got up and began dancing to the
        music, but she was happy listening to the beat mingling
        with the hum of the computer.

In these examples, the moment of aesthetic release follows immediately upon the initial engagement with the apparatus: The Dionysian follows upon the Apollonian. Following the interpretation of tedium and fatigue above, we might suspect that primary process is a more or less desperate reaction to the deleterious effects of excessively demanding intellectual labor on the stable organization of the mind. For example (cf. 5b and 34a above):

43: Joy likes computer very much.
    She was getting addicted by computer.
    She thought about last night's dream, when computers danced
        in her head.
    Guess she had worked a little too late on that program.

This story suggests that primary process appears reactively and is more a result of stress or fatigue than creative imagination. Such an interpretation fits with the popular view that "fantasy is now recognized as serving many useful functions" (Brody, 1986, p. 8). Yet what is recognized is only the objective instrumentality of fantasy; the playful subject goes unacknowledged. Play is a haven in a heartless world, a temporary escape from work that nevertheless confirms the reality of its regimen. In the words of Adorno, "He who whistles at the world does not realise that he whistles its tune." It is true that there is a need for the renewal provided by sensuous activity and it is precipitated by the alienation of computational labor. The intent to make a joyful noise and the desire to salve rational coherence in a different kind of consistency – the unity of rhythm – act to rescue whatever vitality feels deadened in the Apollonian quest.

Nevertheless, in the words of Benjamin (1955), "In the image of happiness there whirls, inalienably, the image of redemption" (p. 693). We need to amend the opposition between time "on task" and time "off task" suggested earlier. What would appear to be at work is something other than a simple opposition. It is not merely a case of "R & R" compensating an overtaxed laborer. Rather, rhythmic release of the body and its senses acts to redeem the worth of the rational deliberations and formal constructions at work in intellectual operations.

Admittedly, in 42, certain oppositions are again implied: visual and auditory appreciation versus instrumental activity, happiness versus causal explanation. Yet there are also signs of reconciliation, a parallel compromise to that which we identified in 38 above. The musical and the mechanical are reconciled insofar as a continuity is perceived at the level of sound and its pure rhythmicity. Note that it is at the level of the common denominators, motion and energy, that the synthesis emerges. The mediation is enhanced in one case by equating the abstract, recursive cybernetic loop of "input and output" with the repetitive physical oscillation of "rock and roll" – in and out with to and fro. In the other case, the mediation is enhanced by stressing, on the side of the computer, the electrical rather than the mechanical and, on the side of the human, the physical resonance or percussive sensitivity of the body. It may not be coincidental that this conciliatory manner of speaking is reminiscent of the discourse of sexual intimacy. "I sing the body electric," and all that.

The ambiguity of terms like "hum" (42a) and "keyboard" (41) serve to remind us again that there are highly permeable loci in the boundaries between art and science, play and work, as indeed there would have to be in order for these couplets to have a vital connection of any kind, rather than being merely arbitrary pairings.

The impulsive moment

We have become accustomed to the conventional picture of conscientious individuals applying themselves to the rigorous but enjoyable task of acquiring skilled performance at the keyboard. It pervades not only computer advertising but also the noncommercial literature of educational, psychological, and other technological journals. Nevertheless, this icon of mental labor exists in tension with images from another domain, a nether level of nonintellectualized need. The fantasy narratives appear to provide the romantic opportunity: Out of the interstices of calculated computational life bursts the polymorphous life of sexual and aggressive impulse. Genital and oral imagery predominates but anal and urethral themes make their presence felt between the lines.

Aggression. Abusive behavior toward the computer was a common event in the stories. The abuse was sometimes confined to the verbal form, as in 22d and the following:

44a: "Damn these computers!"

44b: "I hate computers."

44c: She hit the switch look again [*sic*] and cursed.
Cursed in a language the spell check did not contain.
She did it again.
And again, and again and again.

Verbal abuse was often accompanied by physical aggression, as we have seen: "He . . . cursed and kicked the terminal" (example 30a); "She . . . swore and struck the computer" (30b). Physical aggression also appeared on its own, varying from the relatively mild, "She . . . pulled the plug" (27), to the relatively violent, "She opened up the back of the computer and ripped out the wires" (32).

The spontaneity of the aggressive impulse is indicated by the fact that, in each of these cases, the aggression was not provoked by the computer. Where, by contrast, the aggression is reactive, it is either in the form of a preemptive strike (example 45a, cf. 26) or a disproportionately vindictive, even sadistic response (45b):

45a: It was as if death was at hand.
He prepared to launch an attack.

45b: He started pressing the keys to see what would happen.
Then the machine started to go crazy.
So he kicked the crap out of it.
And became a homosexual.
He wasn't into this and became bisexual.[15]

Genitality. Genital sexual themes appeared with roughly the same frequency as aggressive ones. We have already been privy to Joy's sexual secrets in 34b. Two more explicitly sexual themes emerged as follows:

46a: Everything had gone wrong that day, and working with the machine was frustrating.
She thought the machine was as frustrating as her sex life.
So she started playing forcefully with the keys and really turned it on.

46b: This is an important aspect of programming.
But she still decided to go to bed alone.

When we add 4 above to this group, and perhaps 5c as well, the overall tenor of the genital sexual themes appears one of dissatisfaction, frustration, and anxiety, resulting in maneuvers of a more or less defensive kind. Only in 46a is there any semblance of gratification, but here it is still a compensatory maneuver, one suffused with surplus aggression. The computer's role is variously defined: as interfering in sexual relationships or as implicated in the decline of desire; as stimulating sexual fantasies or arousing sexual feelings inappropriately; or as a surrogate object of desire. There is a certain congruence here with the drift of 44, too, where the disruption in the relationship to the computer precipitates instability in the protagonist's sexuality.

Orality. Food and beverages were frequent visitors to the folded pages. We have already seen the role of imbibing stimulants in examples 9a, 9b, and 12: "The program being loaded was involved and complicated. She got a cup of coffee." "She went to get a cup of coffee." "He decided at that point to go to a bar for a drink." Often, these cases of distraction and leaving the field are reactive: They constitute responses, more or less defensive in nature, to difficulties in the work itself. Nevertheless, there is an immediacy about appetite itself:

> 47: Joy sat down at the computer.
> She began to think of food.

Here, one might psychologize the issue and describe Joy's behavior as impulsive. However, there is another possible interpretation, a more ontological account that stresses the valence of the immediate objective environment (cf. Lewin, 1935). In concrete terms, appetite seems to be switched on by the very fact of being situated in front of the computer – before the operations of computation commence, and even before the machine itself has been switched on.[16]

In another scenario, yet again a time out from computer operation, the salience of bodily function in general is expressed by combining the need for ingestion with the need for elimination.

> 48: He rose from his seat.
> He went to the bathroom, grabbed a beer and a bag of doritos, and went back to the terminal.

The body as an input–output system, with its own operational characteristics and maintenance imperatives, is set up in parallel with the computer – the substance-processing system over against the information-processing system. When we consider the systems terminology of "feedback" and "feedforward," it would appear that such analogies are built into the very foundation of computing discourse (Faber, 1984).

Often, the quest for oral satisfaction, like the search for sexual gratification, is not fulfilled or is even directly frustrated:

49a: Joy sat down at the computer.
She wished she had something to eat.
Her tastebuds tingled with anticipation.

49b: Joy sat down at the computer.
She took a bite from her stale bagel.
It must have been lunch time.
She went to the corner diner.
Where she ordered your basic steak and eggs.
But the oven just wouldn't work.

Here, there appears to be some implicit parallel – whether analogy or opposition – between the computer and the oven, drawing closer the symbolic juxtaposition of the system of information flow and the system of nutrient flow. The introduction of the oven may represent an awareness that there is more than a parallel at stake: Digestive operations necessarily depend upon technology (Levi-Strauss, 1969) so that, cybernetically, machinery is incorporated into the system of basic human survival. Not only does the machine "digest" its input in a manner comparable to that of the human; at the experiential level, it also enters into and participates in the human digestive process as a functional component.

There is a theme of delay of gratification running through many of the stories. As 49b reminds us, to err is not only human: The potential of the computer for malfunctioning presents an intrinsic threat to human survival. It is not just that technology is introduced into the digestive cycle, but that this technology fails, deferring satisfaction, and leaving the tastebuds in the lurch, probably tingling even more from frustration. There is a moral dimension to this involuntary curbing of appetite: Witness 28 above. That story of the apple made the ambivalent connection of eating to knowing apparent, as does the following (an expansion of 47):

50: Joy sat down at the computer.
She began to think of food.
Bananas is her favorite food.
How do I began [sic] to digest this gadget?

This example suggests that another possibility in the alimentary symbolic domain is that the computer itself may be experienced as aliment. Joy's and Norman's preoccupation with eating and drinking may be something more than just resistance to technology, a disruption of its field of influence, or a compensation for the deprivations of the body caused by the escalation of intellectual labor. In addition or instead, it may be a reflection of the continuity, more or less problematic, between mechanical and organic function.[17]

If both the computer and food need to be digested, one can see why they might stand in opposition. Although digestion may act as a common denominator uniting the nutritional and informational, physical and mental sustenance would then be in essential disharmony. The one tends to exclude the other insofar as they are both competing for the same "final common path." The impulsive quality of oral need may then be less a comment on the psychic makeup of the protagonists than it is a reflection of this binary dichotomy. Phasic demands from the body appear in reaction to the chronic demands of computational labor.[18]

The dominating relationship

Mastery. A number of descriptions in the stories bear witness to the significance of personal control:

    51a: Norman sat down at the computer.
       He was determined to master the word processor.
    51b: Joy sat down at the computer.
       She placed her hand on the instrument of the keyboard,
         ready to begin.
       Fingers flying, she "keyed on" and began her program.
       She felt exhilerated [sic] with the power the machine gave
         her.
    51c: She felt very inadequate.
       But she decided to rally forth by trying to overcome it.
       She would not be mastered, she would be the one
         to control it.

Certainly, these examples testify to the need for mastery, and to the hope that the machine will lend its power to the operator. However, at the same time, the phrasing of these excerpts raises the question of how unhealthy and compulsive that need may be. The concern for control may be driven, 51c suggests, as emerging not from a spontaneous desire to achieve a specific goal but in reaction to a negative self-image, a feeling of being "very inadequate." The focus is not on using the computer as a tool to get something done but on sheer conquest: "trying to overcome it." The relationship between self and computer is conceived not just in instrumental but also in adversarial terms. It is a matter of the best defense being a good offense – an attitude of "control it before it controls you" (see Mahler et al., 1975, p. 181). The outcomes of this zero-sum game are polarized in terms of two opposite extremes:

> 52: The impersonality was alienating.
>
> The loneliness of being number 1.
>
> And the agony of defeat!

The determined quest for control is motivated as much by the aversive image of subjugation as by the ideal image of synergy. Narrowly escaping defeat frequently gives rise to a brief intoxication: Joy's "exhilerated" [sic] feeling or "flying" sensation (78), in which the "high" subliminally promised by applying to modern electronic commodities the rubric "high technology." Turkle (1984) has described this craving for control as "mastery in the service of the desire to operate just on the edge of disaster" (p. 175), and Balint (1959) and Lichtenberg (1984) have demonstrated how such thrill seeking represents a defensive psychological regression.[19]

The defensive, antidepressant nature of this kind of excitement is reflected in its transitory and illusory quality: The sense of control need not necessarily be an indication of real learning or competence at the keyboard (Broughton, 1985). Between the sensation and the mastery falls the shadow. The impression of being in control is deceptive and tends to lull the subject into a false sense of security:

> 53a: Joy sat down at the computer.
>
> She was hoping that this was a better way to write.
>
> She found, however, that her mastery of the machine was not what she thought.
>
> 53b: The light suddenly came on and she physically recoiled.
>
> But she was more powerful than the machine.
>
> Well, at least she felt she was more powerful.
>
> She started wondering whether in fact the computer was more powerful than she.

In 53b, the reactive, self-protective nature of the delusion is apparent: Joy's empowerment of her self-image occurs in response to the computer's activity, the shocking simplicity of "the power coming on." Like most defenses, the feeling of mastery is only a temporary one, an intoxicating assertion of independence, a brief protest against dependence upon a powerful other before sobering up and returning to its charge again (cf. Bateson, 1971). As Mahler (1972a), Mahler et al. (1975, pp. 128–129), Eichenbaum and Orbach (1983), and others have suggested, a phasic feeling of independence is not incompatible with a chronic state of dependence. To the clinical mind, what at first glance appears to be admirable perseverance, at second glance seems closer to perseveration; persistence is revealed as resistance, action as reaction. The counterphobic defense belies the phobia. Hyperactivity signals the dread of immobilization (Adorno, Frenkel-Brunswik, Levinson, & Sanford, 1950, pp. 405, 428; Mahler et al., 1975, p. 137). When a subject in hot pursuit of control (like Norman in 51a above) proclaims how determined he or she is, it becomes clear how *determined* he or she is. Dependent variables prefer to cloak themselves in the garb of independent variables.

A certain kind of dedication or addiction to mastery, then, can be a form of subservience:

54: Norman sat down at the computer.
And began to punch in data.
The computer received it obediently.
And the equally obedient "master" was triumphant.
Until the word "error" appeared.

This example expresses the realization that gaining control over technology does not necessarily entail freedom from dependence; even successful mastery over the computer can constitute a subjection to its order.

Dependence. The line of argument pursued above uses the fantasy data to call into question the common assumption that there is a natural, healthy, and straightforward human need for control. Rather, the desire for mastery should be interpreted as both compulsive and defensive: a flight into an illusory independence triggered by threatening feelings of dependence. On this account, when the beleaguered individual seizes upon the emblems of autonomy – self-direction and individual control – we should take this not as the apotheosis of the will but as its symbolic capitulation; the involuntary is struggling to signal its absence through the tokens of the voluntary. In this regard, the findings of the present study converge with the research results reported in various areas of the psychological literature that have unmasked the ulterior motives of the drive toward mastery. These include studies in the areas of personality psychology (Adorno et al., 1950), clinical psychology (von Gebsattel, 1958; Khan, 1983; Shapiro, 1981; Strauss, 1948), child psychology (Weininger, 1975), feminist social psychology (Benjamin, 1987; Bragonier, 1985; Dinnerstein, 1976), education (Miller, 1983; Walkerdine, 1985), and political sociology (Habermas, 1975; Kontos, 1975; Memmi, 1966). Similar conclusions have been reached in other interpretive disciplines (Bourdieu, 1977; Charney, 1981; Derrida, 1979; Lacan, 1977; Ricoeur, 1970).

This reinterpretation of mastery as defense, as a foreclosure of freedom rather than a successful attempt to purchase it, may help us to understand better the pervasive anxiety in the fantasy data that we noted earlier in this chapter. It is the expressive, not the defensive, responses to experiences of failure and feelings of intimidation that illuminate the underlying emotional significance of computing. If we inspect the fantasies in which states of anxiety, confusion, and need are acknowledged rather than suppressed, we find that these states are frequently associated with a condition of dependence. The awareness of ignorance or incompetence leads to reliance on an auxiliary for instruction or assistance:

55a: Now he didn't know how to fix it so he went to call for help.

55b: Joy sat down at the computer.
And attempted to enter the computer system.
The computer responded in machine language and the operator looked around for help.

55c: He wanted to learn how to use it.
He turned it on, but was stymied as to what to do next.
So he took out the instruction manual.
It wasn't very helpful.

55d: Joy became so frustrated because she couldn't even log on.
She located an instruction booklet.
She opened to the first page.

55e: She looked around to ask someone for help.
Nobody responded.
She gave it a perplexed glance and looked for someone to help her.
After all, the booklet wasn't the easiest thing to follow.
It needed to be made user-friendly.
That was always the promise. User-friendly? Fiction, mere fiction.

55f: Norman sat down at the computer.
He immediately stood up and went to the computer consultant for help.
However, he was out to lunch.
I will wait 20 mins. max for him to return from lunch.
She waited and waited, but he did not return.

55g: The cursor blinked endlessly.
It didn't seem to be offering a cue about what to do next with this machine.
Back to the manual!

55h: He found himself totally confused.
So he read "How to Operate the Computer in Five Steps" manual but it still didn't help.

So he called over a friend to help.
His friend got him out of his bind.
There's nothing like a close friend!

What is interesting about these examples is not only the degree of felt dependence occasioned by the computing experience but also the lack of anything or anyone to depend on. According to these episodes, it would seem that neither the machine itself nor the immediate human context associated with computing is nurturant. Expert advice is inaccessible or inadequate. It is hard to get to first base with the consultant and hard to get past page 1 or step 1 in the book. The impersonal nature of expertise, its failure to provide what is needed, and the frustration that results are captured succinctly in the following refrain:

56: They always do.
   Teach you the commands after you need them.
   That's a hell of a thing!

It is as though the technology were designed to foster precisely those needs that it is incapable of satisfying. The computer is a rugged individualist, inclined to be intolerant of the nonindependent (i.e., nondefensive) user. To recap the climax of story 31b above, the more desperate the plea for assistance, the less sympathetic the reply: "Help me, I need a degree. / Help yourself! / She got electrocuted."

Apparently, from the above examples, there is little in the way of succor to be had from the world of computing; only personal intimacy – in its human form – provides any solace. In one case (17e), as we have seen, Joy, overwhelmed by her own inadequacy, "had to be revived by her brother." The timely proximity of the competent, helpful friend or sibling stands in opposition to the rejecting computer, on the one hand, and the dilatory, desultory, and distal object of consultation, on the other. The contrast between "person-friendly" and "user-friendly" is underlined.

Despite the unfriendly character of the computer and the satellites in its orbit, the protagonist typically sustains the relationship to them and their attractiveness may even intensify. One wonders why it is that Norman's or Joy's typical response is not simply to sever the connection. However, such is the characteristic dynamic of the relationship between the needy and the powerful, the interior dialectic that makes psychology indispensable to any analysis of political domination (Kovel, 1978). As demonstrated by political thought from Hegel and Marx to Arendt, Sartre, Fanon, and the Frankfurt School, and critical literature and drama from Kafka to Orwell, Genet, and Pinter (Kontos, 1975), dependence participates in dominion via the attachment of the dependent agent to the dominant one – what amounts to an active collusion on the part of subjects in their own subjection.

The archetype of dependence is the infant (Jung, 1940). The madonna, smiling beneficently at the helpless babe in arms, is a persistent icon in the semiotic twilight of Western consciousness (Kristeva, 1980). But our wishful recollections of that momentous relationship should not distract us from the uglier lessons of world history. In that larger dyad of the "developed" nation and the "underdeveloped" one, dependence goes hand in hand with colonization; the embrace tends to pass over into the grip (Memmi, 1968). In his latest work, Memmi (1984) has underlined the tight connection between the dialectic of providing–dependence and that of domination–subjection.

Joy and Norman do not appear always to be enslaved to the computer, but this does not mean that they are not embroiled in a relation of domination. "Subjection is the totality of ways, both active *and passive,* in which those who are dominated can respond to the aggressive behavior of those who are dominating them" (Memmi, 1984, p. 181, emphasis added). Joy and Norman hardly seem to be in a state of subjection when they strive for mastery over the computer. However, as the examples above suggest (particularly 54), we are already intuitively aware in our fantasy life how our behavior with the computer tends to play into the mystification of high technology. The appearance of innocuous tool use and its accompanying technical language of objectified "instruments" and "operations" conceal the subtlety with which our voluntary participation in an already assembled order is co-opted. Our sense of autonomy feeds off an implicit heteronomy. It is precisely the tendency to place ourselves in the hands of the authoritative other that denies in practice the "neutrality" that, in theory, that other maintains.

Infantilization. As Ihde (1975) has pointed out, man–machine relations require a certain deindividuation at the interface, a dissolution of identities and a subjective merging between the human and mechanical elements. The very term "interface" evokes the bizarre imagery of a merger of bodies and a sharing of sensitive surfaces normally considered discrete. Small surprise, then, that there are marked analogies between the way in which our subjects fantasized about the initiation of the user at the "man–machine interface" and the way in which psychologists have recently been describing the early relationship between infant and primary caretaker, prior to the subjective differentiation of the former from the latter.

Throughout the story excerpts reported above, there has been a distinct tendency to anthropomorphize the microcomputer. However, the dynamics of domination and dependence suggest that, in fantasy, the computer is more than just "an other" – it is the primal and propaedeutic (M)other (see Garner, Kahane, & Sprengnether, 1985). The operator is positioned in relation to the technological device in a way that evokes the original experience of heteronomy, one that fuses a need for care with a desire for the other's power.[20]

The parallel between the two dyads, computer–user and infant–caretaker, is suggested by fantasies such as the following:

57: Norman sat down at the computer.

He punched up the program he had been working on.

But he discovered the computer program had been erased.

He became very anxious – the program had been vitally important.

Suddenly he vomited all over the terminal.

His Mom came in and looked at the mess.

She couldn't believe he had done it.

There are even cases where the computer stands in for the parent:

58: Joy sat down at the computer.

And formatted a days worth of discs.

Little did he suspect that there were clouds on the horizon.

He began to think of his mother.

His mother was not feeling well in the morning.

He thought he'd take it out on the computer.

There are vignettes suggesting blissful union and completion:

59. Joy sat down at the computer.

To her surprise her program ran.

She was delighted with herself.

Her feet felt warm and cosy.

She was very content.

So she turned the computer off.

Such states of satisfaction we have encountered already in the sections on music, dance, and play, where the rhythmicity of relation to the other was celebrated. Csikszentmihalyi (1975) has called such euphonious states "flow" experiences, and has argued that they are particularly characteristic of sensuous and playful relating between lovers or between mother and child (Csikszentmihalyi & Massimini, 1985, p. 127). In such loving interactions, there is a partial dissolution of boundaries, harking back to psychic states prior to the differentiation of the infant self from the other (see Freud, 1930; Chodorow, 1978; Fliess,

1961; Silverman, Lachman, & Milich, 1982), where there is a "mutual preverbal empathy" (Mahler et al., 1975) dependent on "vocal or kinetic rhythm" (Kristeva, 1984, p. 24). Following this line of interpretation, Joy's sensuous, bodily explorations of sound in 41, 42a, and 42b would be homologous with the kinetically and sonically based syntheses between infant and maternal activity demonstrated empirically by Condon and Sander (1974), Trevarthen (1975), and Stern, Jaffe, Beebe, & Bennett (1974), among others.

At this preverbal level, visual interaction is also charged with significance:

    60. Joy sat down at the computer.
        She saw some big green eyes.
        Pushed a button and it smiled.

It is not just the satisfaction of corporeal needs that is important to the infant's healthy development but the establishment of a reliable and communicative gestural interaction in the face-to-face situation, what Stern (1974a) has called "the mutual maintenance of a level of attention and arousal" (p. 404). This type of face-to-face orientation and mutual excitation is identifiable at all ages, as in adult conversation (Stern, 1974b). It would appear to manifest itself in that adult "conversation" occurring at the "interface" between person and computer.

However, as in the earlier material, the dysphoric is always nigh. The fluidity of communication gives way all too frequently to disruptive moments of what infant psychologists call "relationship disturbance," which we have witnessed already in 41 and can see again in the following:

    61a: Joy sat down at the computer.
         She switched on the terminal.
         And called up her program.
         Something unprintable.
         Came from the monitor; the computer was spewing garbage
             once again.
    61b: The machine bleeped and "Error" printed out on the screen.
         The cursor blinked endlessly.
         It didn't seem to be offering a cue about what to do next with
             this machine.
    61c: She asked for her last program.
         However, the screen remained blank.
         After she checked to insure it was plugged in, she again tried
             to enter.
         She did not realise that computer learning could be so . . .
             frustrating.

61d: Joy sat down at the computer.
   And stared at the blank screen.
   What to do?
   Concentrating furiously, she tried a new tack.
   It failed completely.
61e: He started pressing the keys to see what would happen.
   Then the machine started to go crazy.
61f: Joy sat down at the computer.
   She looked for the on-off switch.
   She turned it on and waited.
   And the computer printed the date.
   This was as much as anyone could expect.
   Although she expected much more.
   She felt disappointed.

These scenes parallel closely the clinical and empirical findings on the disruptions occurring in expressive relations between infants and their mothers (Spitz, 1945, 1965; Fliess, 1961; Stott, 1962a, 1962b; Mahler, 1968; Tronick, Adamson, Wise, Als, & Brazelton, 1978; Stern, 1977, 1985; Murray, 1980).

In the absence of responsiveness in the mother, even the sense of a shared communicative medium disappears, and the defense of narcissistic isolation comes into play (cf. Mahler, 1968), with its illusory promise of self-satisfaction:

62: Joy sat down at the computer.
   She positioned her fingers on the keys.
   She began typing.
   She called on her last program.
   But the code she had used before no longer worked.
   So she made up her own code and began to work.
   "Some day I'll write my own computer language,"
      she muttered.
   "I'll call it Joytalk," she said to herself.

The loss of meaning to the exchanges interrupts the "flow" in the relationship, which regresses to its starting point. As Klein (1945) and Bion (1967) have so graphically described, the frustration and helplessness in the face of failure foster intolerable aggression that, in fantasy, tends to be split off and projected into the visible world in the form of fragmented persecutory objects, such as lurking insects:

63: Joy sat down at the computer.
   She incerted [sic] her flop [sic] disk into the disk drive and
      stared at the screen.

> The screen stared back at her and then flashed an
>   incomprehensible "A".
> Back to the drawing board.
> The bugs had not yet come out.

Segal (1964), like Klein (1975; cf. R. Klein, 1983), finds that in infantile fantasy the craving for the goodness of the other and the fear that she is withholding things can lead to sadistic forays into the mother's body, with disturbing outcomes:

> 64: It was an uncontrollable impulse.
>   How on earth could he resist the desire to examine the inside.
>   What a mess it must be in there. Meaningless.

In auspicious circumstances, such visions of the damaged maternal interior may inspire guilt and then reparative desires, though still loaded with ambivalence, as we saw in the solicitous but angry concern for the mother's welfare in 58 above.[21]

Conclusion

> Nature has no Outline, but Imagination has. Nature has no Tune, but Imagination has. Nature has no Supernatural, and dissolves: Imagination is Eternity.

> William Blake, *The Ghost of Abel*

In our trip through the primary process of young adults, we have found a variety of ways in which, as Bateson would have predicted, fantasies about technology repeatedly raise such Batesonian topics as mind–body, self, agency, relationship, dialogue, power, and transcendence. One might say, then, that we have illustrated some fundamental concerns of Batesonian theory in a new context. But the fantasies raise these concerns in a way that cannot be acounted for by a cybernetic epistemology such as Bateson's. Thus, the corpus of data reported here also sheds light on some of the limitations of Bateson's approach.

There appear to be two specific shortcomings in Bateson's worldview that our findings bring to light. First, as Dell's (1985) review concludes, "Bateson delineated an epistemology, but never clearly developed a corresponding ontology" (p. 1). This weakness is best exemplified in his last book (Bateson & Bateson, 1987), where the attempt to answer metaphysical questions in epistemological terms is all too transparent. Bateson's commitment to neofunctionalism precludes his access to the issues of being that are repeatedly raised in the computer narratives, and that call for an existential phenomenology of the subject. Such an interpretive stance toward subjectivity stands directly in opposition to cybernetic theories, which center on system control via the objective medium of information (Broughton, 1981).[22]

Second, the very exclusion of conscious instrumental reason and problem-solving strategies from the fantasy themes bears witness to the significance of unconscious symbolic processes, for which evolutionary cybernetics and information theory have no place. Although Bateson toyed with dynamic phenomena, his concern was always to reduce them to principles of system organization, thereby removing their symbolic quality. In so doing, as Habermas (1973, 1975) has pointed out in another context, neofunctionalism (just like the traditional functionalism from which it is descended) removes the possibility of understanding identity formation. The stress on functional organization for instrumental action has a doubly homogenizing effect: Both psychological and cultural specificity are occluded. Individual life history (Blasi, 1983), on the one hand, and social identity formation (Habermas, 1971, 1974; Döbert, Habermas, & Nunner-Winkler, 1987), on the other, lose their significance. The systems approach simultaneously dismantles self and culture, assisting precisely that collapse into biology on the one hand and bureaucracy and technology on the other that is so desirable from the position of authority (Gouldner, 1970; Winner, 1986; Broughton, 1987).

In brief, the fantasy narratives about computers that we have witnessed help to define the limitations of the systems approach as a general paradigm for the human sciences. It is as though once one presses an investigation of information technology far enough into the poetics of its symbolic penumbra, the technology loses its power to provide the root metaphor for our theoretical thinking.

Bateson's oeuvre remains most conducive to insight at those junctures where he allowed his Romantic suspicion of rationality to blossom, as illustrated by his dialogues with his daughter (e.g., Bateson, 1969, excerpted in M. C. Bateson, 1972, pp. 9–12) and this exchange during the 1968 Wenner-Gren conference in Gloggnitz, Austria:

Gregory Bateson: "It's not that the machines get closer and closer to us, but . . ."
Gertrude Hendrix: ". . . but we get closer and . . ."
(M. C. Bateson, 1972, p. 224)[23]

He understood, and managed to convince others, that technology is a means of our self-expression as well as a product of our ingenuity, and that we therefore run the risk of idealizing the device to obscure its, and our own, vices.

Not just our factual, level-headed selves are condensed in the circuitry and programs of computer technology. Rationally, we may enter the microworld, gratefully accepting and celebrating technological progress. But beneath that compliant surface, even the few fantasies reported here reveal a dense mythopoetic underworld, the deeply conflicted psychic jungle of the imagined machine – the truly *personal* computer. The invention and its potential are truly fantastic.

As an instrument, the computer may well be one of the great products of human imagination. It needed to be produced by us precisely because it has no imagination itself. Nevertheless, as we have discovered, we are equipped and eager to use it as the instrument of further imaginings. In so doing, we draw attention to precisely that domain in which the computer is impotent: the realm of the sensuous and expressive. Here, we do not need its help – it needs ours. Its pretensions to the infinite are largely a cover for its shortcomings in all but a single, narrow sphere. It is the master in the medium of decontextualization: analytic reasoning, formal structures, functional computations, and recursive programs. In this domain, it corresponds to the perfection of bureaucratic organization, assuming the same posture of unquestionable authority. But outside the calculus of the system it is abjectly dependent on human beings; it leans heavily on the resources of our symbolic unconscious for the restoration of context. It was in this situation that our young adults so eagerly and easily undertook the charitable task of enriching the impoverished, giving information meaning, placing the dissociated object back in the field of the subject – telling the story. They put the rhythm back into the algorithm.

However, as we have seen, these same enterprising subjects are not just delightful commentators. They are intrepid voyagers, confronting a dark and misanthropic underworld. Computer lobbyists have informed us (although without presenting any evidence) that the subjective impact of computing is to be understood in terms of "empowerment" – a purely rational affect, of course. However, the subjective constructions manifesting themselves in the narratives of our graduate students do not confirm this psychological claim.[24] Instead, on our trek through the corpus of fantasies, we have encountered a variety of reservations, suspicions, and fears.

1. The computer does not elicit spontaneous motivation. We are driven but not by our own drives. It uses the captive energy of our computational minds to exert a gravitational drag on our bodies. The spontaneous reaction is resistance: a centrifugal desire for release from its containment and for the liberation of the noncognitive faculties. The computer signifies darkness and compulsion rather than enlightenment and mastery.

2. The computer, rather than inspiring its users, provokes their anxiety and insecurity. It is peculiarly resistant to control. Rather than facilitating work, it escalates labor to new levels of tension and stress. Its mastery over nature is not experienced as natural. Instead, it stands over against us and opposes our nature.

3. The computer evokes our dependence but fails to fulfill its promise to provide. It reminds us of a living other, but its vitality is unpredictable and disruptive. It offers to satisfy needs that we do not yet experience and frustrates those that we already feel. Its presence is alien, sinister, and even deadly. It substitutes force for meaning. It is coercive and threatening, to the point of being injurious.

4. We struggle to restore a rhythmic and fluid relationship. But it obstructs our efforts and makes us fail. It specializes in setbacks and shortfalls. It feeds us the wrong food and rejects our advances. It withdraws from interaction, closes itself off, speaks in its own language. It evokes feelings of disappointment, helplessness, and rage. If it is a parent, it is so by law, not love. The invention is the mother of necessity.

The general interpretation that has been pursued in this chapter is that the primary effect of the computing situation on individuals, in fantasy, is that of infantilizing them. The propaedeutic power of the computer lies in its capacity to simulate, but what has not been hitherto acknowledged is that, in order to exercise this power in the cognitive sphere, it first has to simulate *the initial grounding of the cognizant being*. This position has been taken up increasingly by the more adventurous members of the artificial intelligence community (e.g., Winograd, 1980; Winograd & Flores, 1985; Dreyfus, 1979, 1982). However, what those authors have not considered is the possibility that the presimulation of being entails *revisiting the developmental foundations of the psyche*.

However, the implication of this is not that we naturally have to learn how to be and think again, at the generous breast of the micro. The caretaking imagery is deceptive. There is something profoundly wrong with the new orthodoxy centered on Stern, Brazelton, Trevarthen, et al. (1974). The reappearance, in the fantasies about computers, of the phenomena that they describe is therefore a disturbing one. What is unwittingly promoted by the researchers cited is a modernized Orwellian vision of the infant–mother relationship as a cybernetic communication system, electronically conceived as a networking of mutual tunings and calibrations designed to guide the organism through transitions from one state to another. The states are ordered sequentially in terms of purely bureaucratic criteria of increasing differentiation and integration, which are then argued to be natural and necessary because biologically grounded. As documented in detail by Harris (1987) and Kaplan and Broughton (1989), it is a prescription for the production of the compliant child as subsystem in the family organization and for the reproduction of the traditional mother as sole caretaker and emotional manager. In this manner, political socialization for bureaucracy and rational authority has co-opted both the imagery of the blissful madonna–child dyad and the flashy instrumentality of gentrified technology.

Of course, issues of external and internal validity (cf. Campbell & Stanley, 1963) remain. Regarding the former, one can hardly generalize from a handful of graduate students to universal claims. Regarding the latter, we still do not know whether the fantasies explored here apply specifically to computers or more broadly to high technology, electronic devices in general, and so on. For example, could it not be that in either the past or the present the reception in fantasy would have been the same for the electric typewriter? Moreover, we do not know whether the misgivings about the micro are a function of unfamiliarity. It is also possible that certain features of the narratives have to do with the form of narrative itself. Work remains to be done.

The purpose of this outing has been to raise the possibility of second thoughts. Should it turn out that the corpus of themes summarized here cannot be dismissed as a special case or as sheer artifact, then a legitimate query will have been raised about the one-sided, denarrativized view of the "information revolution" we have received. If the public euphoria is matched by a private dysphoria that remains to be given voice, it behooves us to inquire not only into the subjective apprehensions themselves but also into the ways in which their voice tends to be silenced.

Acknowledgments

It is rare that one can learn from and count on the same person. I dedicate this chapter to my *camarade de chambre,* Jacques Vonèche. I can count on him to be faintly amused by it, and I have learned from him two things: that in cognitive psychology lurks a certain false consciousness, while in biology awaits a subject worthy of the attention of even a social theorist.

I would like to express my gratitude to a variety of other people who have influenced the present work. First, my undying thanks to Colin MacGillivray (subsequently architect of the Sarawak Hilton) who, around 1960, made me read a paperback novel called *Last Man on Earth,* thereby introducing me to a blessed generation of science fiction writers, particularly A. E. van Vogt, Philip K. Dick, and Fredric Brown. It was through popular literature that the diffuse intellectuality of that re-pressed young adolescent first became focused on the fantasy of science and on the strange relationship between humanity and technology.

During my late adolescence, my father, Ralph Broughton, was in-strumental in bringing my attention to electronics, while in the college years, my brother-in-law, Richard Slee, encouraged me to sally forth into programming. My mother, Doris Broughton, taught me that even art involves technique, and so can redeem it.

Dr. John Gedye, in giving me my first job (at the University of Essex), is responsible for having got me excited about the medical dimension of the relation between people and machines. David Ingleby taught me mechanistic psychology with a sense of irony whose signal has not gone undetected. Liam Hudson made me think for the first time about the connection between scientific technology and personality. I remain mindful that Bernie Kaplan and Robert Young made me think historical-ly and philosophically about life and mechanism.

With regard to the oeuvre of Bateson, I am much indebted to the guidance and sage counsel of Ray McDermott, Hervé Varenne, and Michael Watts, all of whom have made available to me "their own metaphors."

In addition to the generous subjects of my studies, a variety of stu-dents, colleagues, mentors, and friends have specifically fostered my recent interest in computers and technology: Eric Amsel, Michael Black, Paul Chevigny, Maxine Greene, Howard Gruber, Joan Gussow, Mar-garet Honey, Clifford Hill, Richard Kitchener, Alkis Kontos, Joel Kovel, Pat Lee, Robbie McClintock, Doug Noble, Bill O'Donnell, Michael O'Loughlin, Paul Olson, Seymour Papert, Roy Pea, Bob Rieber, Doug Sloan, Jonas Soltis, Tom Southwick, Ed Sullivan, Bob Taylor, Michael Timpane, Valerie Walkerdine, and Philip Wexler. I thank them all from the bottom of my cardiac mechanism.

For specific comments on a draft of this chapter, much gratitude to Vivien Blackford, Carla Bluhm, Dale Dannefer, Madeleine Grumet, Helen Haste, Rich Ryan, Bob Steele, Marta Zahaykevich, and the "Tree-house" study group.

The Graduate School of Education and Human Development at the University of Rochester was generous in its provision of facilities for my work, and Debby Mathinos was kind enough to assist me in obtaining word-processing facilities.

Finally, I am grateful for generous invitations from the Center for Children and Technology at the Bank Street College of Education and the Center for the Humanities at Wesleyan University that made it possible for me to present some of my ideas and receive invaluable, informed commentary.

Notes

1. It is perhaps no coincidence that, looking back over the trajectory of my own concerns, I find similar preoccupations with the functioning of systems (Broughton, 1981, 1983; Broughton & Zahaykevich, 1982), the mind–body problem (Broughton, 1980), the concept of the self (Broughton, 1978, 1986a), the role of dialogic relationships (Berkowitz, Gibbs, & Broughton, 1980; Broughton, 1982), the issue of power (Broughton, 1986b, 1987a, 1987b; Broughton & Zahaykevich, 1980), and the religious vision of transcendence (Broughton, 1986c). In a recent fit of masochism, I reread the theoretical chapter of my own dissertation on self, mind, and body (Broughton, 1975) and rediscovered that Bateson's views on these topics had been seminal in the emergence of my own obsessions.

    It would be hubris indeed to attempt to compare my own work with his. I am afraid to admit that, feeling uncomfortable with the political implications of systems theory (see Gouldner, 1970; Habermas, 1975), I have remained in permanent theoretical limbo, unable to formulate a more satisfactory *Weltanschauung*, or any general worldview for that matter. But I owe a considerable debt of gratitude to Bateson for legitimating the pursuit of such grand questions by nonphilosophers, and showing, in his inimitable style, how they could be the occasion of considerable fun. (See, for example, M. C. Bateson, 1972.)

2. In arguing for the existence of a hidden dimension to our contemporary technology, I am hardly engaged in anything original. The structure of my argument runs closely parallel to that of Walter Benjamin's (1936a, 1936b, 1939) analysis of the eclipse of one level of experience ("involuntary" memory) by another (intellectual or "voluntary" memory) involved in the technological and cultural transition to modernism. Bateson himself might well have traced this tradition further back to his favorite William Blake, for whom "without contraries, there is no progression."

    The tacit dimension of microcomputers is brilliantly expounded by Heim (1987), in a volume that was published too recently for me to be able to include its insights in the present chapter.

3. In addition to a concern for sample size, the particular course selected for the study was chosen on the grounds of its emphasis on class discussion and cooperative work. The study was conducted sufficiently late in the term to allow for the development of at least a minimal degree of group identity, and at a point where the instructor judged group morale to be at a relatively high level. Up to this point, the class had not been involved in discussions of computers or high technology, although the conduct of the study did stimulate subsequent discussion of these issues.

4. These names were chosen in the light of a desire not to initiate the fantasy narrative with a character whose ethnic identity was immediately obvious. Both genders were included for the sake of equity and with a view to examining the effect of protagonist gender on response, an analysis that remains to be done.

5. The disjunctive association technique (obscuring the beginning of the story) was preferred to a continuous one (in which the whole of the story to date is visible) because of pilot work suggesting that this reduced the tendency to "rationalize" the structure of the plot – to make the characters behave rationally and to regulate the narrative in terms of norms of logical coherence.

6. The particular approach used here in the presentation of the material is distinctly literary, being influenced especially by three interpretive classics of psychological analysis: Freud's *Psychopathology of Everyday life* (1901), Propp's *Morphology of the Folktale* (1968), and Adorno's "Stars Down to Earth" (1974). All three traditions – psychoanalysis, structuralism, and critical theory – depart from the positivist concern for frequency counts and probability estimates and rely instead upon a dialectical construction of the totality of relations between whole and parts (Jameson, 1971). Thus, despite a concern to identify prevalent themes, there is an interest in less frequent themes whenever these permit a lucid illustration of a particular phenomenon (see Allport, 1954). In this, I merely apply the principles of cognitive prototypes (Rosch, 1975). Rather than conceal the identities and differences within the corpus of fantasies that I have collected by means of arcane mathematical devices, I have tried to demonstrate that "identity of identity and difference" that exists in the results by laying out most of the data for public scrutiny in these very pages.

7. Throughout, the illustrative examples are predominantly excerpts from the complete narratives, since the unit of analysis here is the theme, and there was a strong tendency for each story to feature several themes. Some excerpts therefore overlap with others. The excerpts presented are quoted verbatim; they are completely unedited, with the exception that an occasional period has been inserted to punctuate the end of a line.

8. The phrase is Bachelard's and is purloined from his splendid phenomenology of space, interiors, and the home (1964, p. 216).

9. See Abrams, 1971, p. 173.

10. This is all the more remarkable given that we know from the work of Basseches (1984) and Irwin (1985), as well as my own research (Broughton, 1978, 1982b), that the concepts of relation, process, and interaction are not at all beyond the cognitive grasp of the graduate student. It remains to be seen whether the reification observed reflects a preoccupation with the "hard" in preference to the "soft," as a function of the semantic differential in gender connotations between these terms (see Keller, 1985; Haste, 1987; Broughton, 1987).

11. Sheldrake (1972) has pointed to a historical trend toward an increasingly impersonal stance toward computing and, in parallel, an increasingly mechanical understanding of the computer.

12. It is perhaps no coincidence that the professionals concerned with detecting extraterrestrial aliens are predominantly computer scientists (see Minsky, 1985; Regis, 1985).

13. On the violence of light, already foreshadowed in 11b, see Derrida (1978).

14. The hiatus here between the flight of fantasy and the act of being brought down to earth leads one to believe that the overall impact of this particular example may be partially or wholly an artifact. However, this story still testifies to the puritanical flavor of the computer narratives, a general suspicion of pleasurable experience.

15. I was gratified to see this particular example since elsewhere (Broughton, 1983), I had suggested, using as a fetish the recent work of Chasseguet-

Smirgel (1984, see also 1985 and Honey & Broughton, 1986), how high
technology has an intrinsically perverse dimension that embodies such
anal sadistic tendencies. Joel Kovel (1985) has made a related argument.
Freud made a relevant observation: "The instinct for knowledge can actually take the place of sadism . . . a sublimated offshoot of the instinct for
mastery."

16. This elicitation of desire by the mere situation of person in relation to
screen is reminiscent of the hypothesis of Metz (1975) that, in modern life,
the screen has come to be a master signifier of the oral provider, an
occasion for the sudden subjective registering of absence and lack. Working within a different framework, Memmi (1984) has recently made the
compatible argument that there is a continuity in the age of advanced
technology between need for provision of basic satisfactions and need for
televised material.

17. This issue of the interpenetration of organism and mechanism is a common
focus of concern in modernity. It was prefigured in relation to the industrial
era by Marx, in the 1844 manuscripts (Fromm, 1961). It preoccupied Bateson on many occasions (e.g., 1971). I have tried elsewhere to show how
it takes on an especially intractable form in the emergence of computer technology and the educational demand for "computer literacy"
(Broughton, 1985).

18. Faber (1984) has pointed to the binary oppositions inherent in the feeding
situation. We might note also that the early emergence of behavioral and
then verbal affirmation and negation is closely tied to the infant's feeding
experiences (Spitz, 1957).

19. Bateson (1979–1980) himself referred to compulsive risk taking as a species
of "schismogenesis," a spiraling system of "threats," each of which served
as a "fix [for] . . . staving off the feelings of deprivation" (p. 23; cf. Bateson
& Bateson, 1987, p. 12).

Although I cite here the second of the two famous communiques to the
University of California Board of Regents, as the reader may discern, my
analysis throughout this section is indebted to Bateson's (1971) highly
original interpretation of addictive devices, which he worked out first in
terms of alcoholism, and only later brought to bear on the international
military situation. This connection is made again in the last work (Bateson
& Bateson, 1987, ch. 12).

20. Harris, in talking of adults (1981) as well as infants (1975), reminds us that
all learning takes place in an instructional context, in relation to a maternal
other – however symbolic – who mothers the learner into existence. In a
similar way, in an analysis of the dynamics of pedagogy, Portugues (1983)
has suggested that it is precisely this copresence of learner and teacher that
reevokes the separation-individuation process, with all the vestiges of its
first, infantile instantiation.

21. In a personal communication, Bob Steele has suggested to me that the
suppressed subtext in the caretaking imagery is *the father* who controls the
mother–infant relationship, much as it is the masculine world that controls
the computer–user relationship. If Steele is correct, then it would seem that
the fantasies regarding interaction with the mother constitute a kind of
refuge from the unassailable power of the rational computer–father and a
denial of his function as interrupter of the dyadic mother–child bond (cf.
Lacan, 1977). Steele's suggestion raises the interesting question of why the
triangular imagery of the oedipal situation does not make its presence felt

in the fantasy data, while the preoedipal, dyadic images are quite prominent.
22. Of course, it is possible that Bateson himself was aware of this desideratum, and had he lived longer he might have taken steps to rectify the lack.
23. Bateson departed, here, from the more typical liberal vision, according to which the technological transformation of human beings is not necessarily to be lamented (see, for example, Bolter's *Turing's Man* (1984) and Lee's (1984) commentary on it).
24. As Chomsky (1972) points out, we recognize the point at which empirical psychology passes into ideology by the fact that claims are made by fiat or appeal to the self-evident and the support of empirical evidence is no longer considered to be relevant (cf. Pea & Kurland, 1984).

References

Abrams, M. H. (1971). *Natural supernaturalism: Romance and revolution in nineteenth-century literature.* New York: Norton.

Adorno, T. W. (1974). The stars down to earth. *Telos, 19,* 13–90.

Adorno, T. W., Frenkel-Brunswik, E., Levinson, D., & Sanford, N. (1950). *The authoritarian personality.* New York: Norton.

Alldis, B. (Ed.) (1985). *The book of minisagas.* Gloucester, England: Alan Sutton.

Allen, J., & Broughton, J. M. (1987, April). Purity and danger: Polarization in the discourse of psychology and nuclear threat. Paper presented at the 58th annual conference of the Pacific Sociological Association, Eugene, OR.

Allport, G. W. (1954). The use of personal documents in psychological research. *Bulletins of the Social Science Research Council, 49.*

Anderson, H. H., & Anderson, G. L. (1951). *An introduction to projective techniques.* New York: Prentice-Hall.

Auld, F., Goldenberg, G. M., & Weiss, J. V. (1968). Measurement of primary-process thinking in dream reports. *Journal of Personality and Social Psychology, 8*(4), 418–426.

Bachelard, G. (1964). *The poetics of space.* Boston: Beacon.

Balint, M. (1959). *Thrills and regressions.* New York: International Universities Press.

Basseches, M. (1984). *Dialectical thinking and adult development.* Norwood, NJ: Ablex.

Bateson, G. (1955). A theory of play and fantasy. *Psychiatric Research Reports, 2,* 39–51. Reprinted in Bateson, 1972.

Bateson, G. (1960). Minimal requirements for a theory of schizophrenia. *Archives of General Psychiatry, 2,* 477–491.

Bateson, G. (1966). Communication theories in relation to the etiology of the neuroses. In J. H. Merin (Ed.), *The Etiology of the Neuroses.* Palo Alto, CA: Science & Behavior Books.

Bateson, G. (1968, August). *The logical categories of learning and communication, and the acquisition of world views.* Paper presented at the Wenner-Gren Symposium on World Views, Gloggnitz, Austria.

Bateson, G. (1969). "Daddy, what is an instinct?" In T. A. Sebeok & A. Ramsay (Eds.), *Approaches to animal communication.* The Hague: Mouton.

Bateson, G. (1970). Form, substance and difference. *General Semantics Bulletin, 37,* 221–245.

Bateson, G. (1971). The cybernetics of self: A theory of alcoholism. *Psychiatry, 34,* 1–18.

Bateson, G. (1972). *Steps to an ecology of mind.* New York: Ballantine.

Bateson, G. (1973). Style, grace, and information in primitive art. In A. Forge (Ed.), *A study of primitive art.* New York: Oxford University Press.

Bateson, G. (1974). Scattered thoughts for a conference on "Broken Power." *Co-Evolution Quarterly,* Winter, 26–27.

Bateson, G. (1976). Mind–body dualism conference position paper. *Co-Evolution Quarterly,* Fall, 56–57.

Bateson, G. (1978, August). Time is out of joint. Memorandum to the Regents of the University of California. Reprinted in Bateson, 1979.

Bateson, G. (1979). *Mind and nature: A necessary unity.* New York: Dutton.

Bateson, G. (1979/80). Letter to the Regents of the University of California. *Co-Evolution Quarterly, 24,* 22–23.

Bateson, G. (1980). Mind and body: A dialogue with Robert Rieber. In R. W. Rieber (Ed.), *Body and mind.* New York: Academic.

Bateson, G. (1982). They threw God out of the garden. *Co-Evolution Quarterly,* Winter, 62–67.

Bateson, G., & Bateson, M. C. (1987). *Angels fear: Towards an epistemology of the sacred.* New York: Macmillan.

Bateson, G., Jackson, D. D., Haley, J., & Weakland, J. (1956). Toward a theory of schizophrenia. *Behavioral Science, 1,* 251–264.

Bateson, M. C. (1972). *Our own metaphor: A personal account of a conference on the effects of conscious purpose on human adaptation.* New York: Knopf.

Bell, J. E. (1948). *Projective techniques: A dynamic approach to the study of personality.* New York: Longmans.

Benjamin, J. (1987). The decline of the Oedipus complex. In J. M. Broughton (Ed.), *Critical theories of psychological development.* New York: Plenum.

Benjamin, W. (1936a). The work of art in the age of mechanical reproduction. In *Illuminations.* London: Cape, 1970.

Benjamin, W. (1936b). The story-teller and artisan cultures. In *Illuminations.* London: Cape, 1970.

Benjamin, W. (1939c). On some motifs in Baudelaire. In *Illuminations.* London: Cape, 1970.

Benjamin, W. (1955). Über den Begriff der Geschichte. In *Gesammelte Schriften,* Vol. 1. Frankfurt: Suhrkamp, 1974.

Bentham, J. (1931). *The theory of legislation.* London: International Library of Psychology.

Berelson, B. (1952). *Content analysis in communication research.* Glencoe, IL: Free Press.

Berkowitz, M., Gibbs, J. C., & Broughton, J. M. (1980). The effects of homogeneous versus heterogenous peer dialogues on moral judgment development. *Merrill-Palmer Quarterly, 26(4),* 341–357.

Bion, W. (1967). *Second thoughts.* London: Heinemann.

Black, M., & Worthington, R. (1985). Democracy and reindustrialization: The politics of technology in New York State. In P. T. Durbin & C. Mitcham (Eds.), *Research in philosophy and technology.* Greenwich, CT: Jai.

Blasi, A. (1983). The self and cognition. In B. Lee & G. G. Noam (Eds.), *Developmental approaches to the self.* New York: Plenum.

Bolter, J. D. (1984). *Turing's man: Western cultures in the computer age.* Chapel Hill: University of North Carolina Press.

Bourdieu, P. (1977). *Reproduction: In education, society and culture.* Beverly Hills, CA: Sage.

Bower, T. G. R. (1977). *A primer of infant development.* San Francisco: Freeman.

Bragonier, P. (1985). The psychological differentiation of latency age boys in traditional and non-traditional families. Unpublished doctoral dissertation, Teachers College, Columbia University.

Brody, J. E. (1986, August 27). Personal health: Researchers say that sexual fantasy is almost universal. *New York Times*, p. C8.

Broughton, J. M. (1975). The development of the epistemological self in the years 10-26. Unpublished doctoral dissertation, Harvard University.

Broughton, J. M. (1978). The development of concepts of self, mind, reality, and knowledge. In W. Damon (Ed.), *New Directions in Developmental Psychology: I – Social Cognition*. San Francisco: Jossey-Bass.

Broughton, J. M. (1980). Genetic metaphysics: The developmental psychology of mind–body concepts. In R. W. Rieber (Ed.), *Body and mind*. New York: Academic.

Broughton, J. M. (1981). Piaget's structural–developmental psychology, III: Function and the problem of knowledge. *Human Development*, 24(4), 257–285.

Broughton, J. M. (1982a). Cognitive interaction and the development of sociality. *Merrill-Palmer Quarterly*, 28(3), 369–378.

Broughton, J. M. (1982b). Genetic logic and the development of philosophical concepts. In J. M. Broughton, & D. J. Freeman-Moir (Eds.), *The cognitive-developmental psychology of James Mark Baldwin*. Norwood, NJ: Ablex.

Broughton, J. M. (1983). The psychological origins of nuclear war. *Forum International*, 3, 73–106.

Broughton, J. M. (1985). The surrender of control: Computer literacy as political socialization. In D. Sloan (Ed.), *The computer in education: A critical perspective*. New York: Teachers College Press.

Broughton, J. M. (1986a). Piaget's concept of the self. In P. Eisendrath Young & J. Hall (Eds.), *The book of the self: Subject, ego, and identity*. New York: New York University Press.

Broughton, J. M. (1986b). The genesis of moral domination. In S. Modgil & C. Modgil (Eds.), *Lawrence Kohlberg: Consensus and controversy*. Lewes, England: Falmer.

Broughton, J. M. (1986c). The political psychology of faith. In C. Dykstra, & S. Parks (Eds.), *The Faith Development Theory of James Fowler*. Birmingham, AL: Religious Education Press.

Broughton, J. M. (1987). The masculine authority of the cognitive. In B. Inhelder & D. de Caprona (Eds.), *Piaget today*. Hillsdale, NJ: Erlbaum.

Broughton, J. M., & Zahaykevich, M. K. (1982). The peace movement threat. *Teachers College Record*, 84(1), 152–173. Reprinted in D. Sloan (Ed.), *Education for Peace*. New York: Teachers College Press.

Buck-Morss, S. (1987). Piaget, Adorno, and dialectical structures. In J. M. Broughton (Ed.), *Critical theories of psychological development*. New York: Plenum.

Campbell, D. T., & Stanley, J. C. (1963). *Experimental and quasi-experimental designs for research*. Chicago: Rand McNally.

Cattell, R. B. (1951). Principles of design in "projective" or misperceptive tests of personality. In H. H. Anderson & G. L. Anderson (Eds.), *An introduction to projective techniques*. New York: Prentice-Hall.

Charney, M. (1981). *Sexual fiction*. New York: Methuen.

Chasseguet-Smirgel, J. (1984). *Creativity and perversion*. New York: Norton.

Chasseguet-Smirgel, J. (1985). *The ego-ideal*. London: Free Associations Books.

Chodorow, N. (1978). *The reproduction of mothering*. Berkeley: University of California Press.

Chomsky, N. (1972). Psychology and ideology. *Cognition*, 1(1), 11–46.

Cicourel, A. (1964). *Method and measurement in sociology.* New York: Free Press.

Condon, W. S., & Sander, L. S. (1974). Neonate movement is synchronized with adult speech. *Science, 183,* 99–101.

Csikszentmihalyi, M. (1975). *Beyond boredom and anxiety.* San Francisco: Jossey-Bass.

Csikszentmihalyi, M., & Massimini, F. (1985). On the psychological selection of bio-cultural information. *New Ideas in Psychology, 3*(2), 115–138.

Davies, M. M. (1984, July 14–20). The eyes have it: Interview with T. G. R. Bower. *Radio Times,* pp. 20–23.

Derrida, J. (1979). *Spurs: Nietzsche's styles.* Chicago: University of Chicago Press.

Derrida, J. (1978). *Writing and difference.* Chicago: University of Chicago Press.

Descombes, V. (1980). *Modern French philosophy.* New York: Cambridge University Press.

Dinnerstein, D. (1976). *The mermaid and the minotaur.* New York: Harper & Row.

Döbert, R., Habermas, J., & Nunner-Winkler, G. (1987). The development of the self. In J. M. Broughton (Ed.), *Critical theories of psychological development.* New York: Plenum.

Dreyfus, H. L. (1979). *What computers can't do* (2nd Ed.). San Francisco: Freeman.

Dreyfus, H. L. (1982). *Husserl, intentionality, and cognitive science.* Cambridge, MA: MIT.

Eichenbaum, L., & Orbach, S. (1983). *Understanding women.* New York: Basic Books.

Erikson, E. (1976). Dr. Borg's life cycle. *Daedalus, 105*(2), 1–28. Reprinted in E. Erikson (Ed.), *Adulthood.* New York: Norton.

Faber, M. D. (1984). The computer, the technological order, and psychoanalysis. *Psychoanalytic Review, 71*(2), 263–277.

Faber, M. D. (1985). Computers and education: A response to Papert. *New Ideas in Psychology, 3*(3), 293–296.

Fairbairn, W. R. D. (1943). The repression and the return of bad objects. *British Journal of Medical Psychology, 19*(3–4), 156–178.

Fliess, R. (1961). *Ego and body ego.* New York: Schulte.

Foucault, M. (1972). *The archaeology of knowledge and the discourse on language.* New York: Harper & Row.

Frank, J. D. (1967). *Sanity and survival: Psychological aspects of war and peace.* New York: Random House.

Frank, L. K. (1949). Projective methods for the study of personality. In R. I. Watson (Ed.), *Readings in the clinical method in psychology.* New York: Harper.

Freud, S. (1901). *The psychopathology of everyday life.* Standard edition of the complete works (Vol. 6). London: Hogarth.

Freud, S. (1915). *Instincts and their vicissitudes.* Standard edition of the complete works (Vol. 14). London: Hogarth.

Freud, S. (1930). *Civilization and its discontents.* Standard edition of the complete works (Vol. 21). London: Hogarth.

Fromm, E. (1961). *Marx's concept of man.* New York: Frederick Ungar.

Fuller, L. L. (1964). *The morality of law.* New Haven: Yale University Press.

Garner, S. N., Kahane, C., & Sprengnether, M. (Eds.) (1985). *The (m)other tongue: Essays in psychoanalytic interpretation.* Ithaca, NY: Cornell University Press.

von Gebsattel, V. E. (1958). The world of the compulsive. In R. May (Ed.), *Existence.* New York: Simon & Schuster.

Glaser, B. G., & Strauss, A. L. (1967). *The discovery of grounded theory: Strategies for qualitative research.* Chicago: Aldine.

Gould, R. (1972). *Child studies through fantasy: Cognitive–affective patterns in development.* New York: Quadrangle.

Gouldner, A. (1970). *The coming crisis of western sociology.* New York: Basic.

Greenberg, J., & Mitchell, S. (1983). *Object relations in psychoanalytic theory.* Cambridge, MA: Harvard University Press.

Greene, M. (1985). Philosophy looks at microcomputers. *Computers in the Schools, 1*(3), 3–11.

Guntrip, H. (1971). *Psychoanalytic theory, therapy, and the self.* New York: Basic.

Habermas, J. (1971). Theorie der Gesellschaft oder Sozialtechnologie? In J. Habermas & N. Luhmann, *Theorie der Gesellschaft oder Sozialtechnologie.* Frankfurt: Suhrkamp.

Habermas, J. (1973). *Theory and practice.* Boston: Beacon.

Habermas, J. (1974). On social identity. *Telos, 19,* 91–103.

Habermas, J. (1975). *Legitimation crisis.* Boston: Beacon.

Harris, A. E. (1975). Social dialectics and language: Mother and child construct the discourse. *Human Development, 18,* 80–96.

Harris, A. E. (1981). Radical pedagogy. *PsychCritique Newsletter, 1,* 5–6.

Harris, A. E. (1987). The rationalization of infancy. In J. M. Broughton (Ed.), *Critical theories of psychological development.* New York: Plenum.

Haste, H. W. (1988). Legitimation, logic, and lust: Review of Keller, "Gender and science." *New Ideas in Psychology, 6*(1), 137–146.

Heim, M. (1987). *Electric language: A philosophical study of word processing.* New Haven: Yale University Press.

Holsti, O. R. (1969). *Content analysis for social sciences and humanities.* New York: Addison-Wesley.

Holt, R. R. (1967). The development of the primary process. In R. R. Holt (Ed.), *Motives and thought.* New York: International Universities Press.

Honey, M., & Broughton, J. M. (1986). Feminine sexuality: An interview with Janine Chasseguet-Smirgel. *Psychoanalytic Review, 72*(4), 527–548.

Ihde, D. (1975). A phenomenology of man–machine relations. In W. Feinberg & H. Rosemont (Eds.), *Work, technology, and education.* Urbana: University of Illinois Press.

Irwin, R. (1985, June). A critique of the proposed stage of dialectical thinking. Paper presented at the Second Conference on "Beyond Formal Operations." Harvard University.

Jameson, F. (1971). *Marxism and form.* Princeton, NJ: Princeton University Press.

Jardine, A. (1985). *Gynesis.* Ithaca, NY: Cornell University Press.

Jung, C. G. (1940). *The psychology of the child archetype.* The collected works of C. G. Jung (Vol. 9, Part I). Princeton: Princeton University Press, 1960.

Kaplan, M. M., & Broughton, J. M. (1989) The mother herself: Reproduction, resistance, and subjectivity in women's development. Unpublished manuscript, Teachers College, Columbia University.

Keller, E. F. (1985). *Gender and science.* New Haven: Yale University Press.

Khan, M. M. R. (1983). *Hidden selves: Between theory and practice in psychoanalysis.* New York: International Universities Press.

Klein, M. (1945). The Oedipus complex in the light of early anxieties. In *Love, guilt, and reparation.* New York: Delta, 1975.

Klein, M. (1975). *Envy and gratitude.* New York: Delta.

Klein, R. (1983). In the body of the mother. *October, 23,* 66–75.

Kohl, H. (1982, September–October). Should I buy my child a computer? *Harvard Magazine,* pp. 14–21.

Kohon, G. (1986). *The British school of psychoanalysis: The independent tradition.* London: Free Associations Books.

Kontos, A. (1975). *Domination.* Toronto: University of Toronto Press.

Kovel, J. (1978). Rationalization and the family. *Telos, 37,* 5–21.

Kovel, J. (1985). *Against the state of nuclear terror*. Boston: South End Press.

Krippendorf, K. (1980). *Content analysis: An introduction to its methodology*. Beverly Hills, CA: Sage.

Kristeva, J. (1980). Motherhood according to Giovanni Bellini. In *Desire in language*. New York: Columbia University Press.

Kristeva, J. (1984). *Revolution in poetic language*. New York: Columbia University Press.

Lacan, J. (1977). *Ecrits*. New York: Norton.

Lacan, J. (1978). *The four fundamental concepts of psychoanalysis*. New York: Norton.

Lazarsfeld, P., & Baran, A. (1951). Qualitative measurement in the social sciences: Classification, typology, and indices. In D. Lemen & H. D. Lasswell (Eds.), *The policy sciences*. Palo Alto, CA: Stanford University Press.

Lee, P. C. (1984). Review of Bolter's "Turing's man." *Computers in the Schools*, *1*(4), 29–34.

Levi-Strauss, C. (1963). The structural study of myth. In *Structural anthropology*. New York: Basic Books.

Levi-Strauss, C. (1969). *The raw and the cooked*. New York: Harper & Row.

Lewin, K. (1935). *Dynamic theory of personality*. New York: McGraw Hill.

Lichtenberg, J. (1984). Continuities and transformations between infancy and adolescence. In D. D. Brockman (Ed.), *Late adolescence: Psychoanalytic Studies*. New York: International Universities Press.

Mahler, M. (1968). *On human symbiosis and the vicissitudes of individuation*. New York: International Universities Press.

Mahler, M. (1972a). On the first three subphases of the separation–individuation process. *International Journal of Psycho-Analysis*, *53*, 333–338.

Mahler, M. (1972b). Rapprochement subphase of the separation–individuation process. *Psychoanalytic Quarterly*, *41*, 487–506.

Mahler, M., Pine, F., & Bergman, A. (1975). *The psychological birth of the human infant: Symbiosis and individuation*. New York: Basic.

Marx, K. (1844). *Die Frühschriften*. Stuttgart: Kroner, 1953.

Memmi, A. (1966). *Dominated man*. Boston: Beacon.

Memmi, A. (1968). *The colonizer and the colonized*. Boston: Beacon.

Memmi, A. (1984). *Dependence*. Boston: Beacon.

Merleau-Ponty, M. (1962). *The phenomenology of perception*. London: Routledge & Kegan Paul.

Metz, C. (1975). The imaginary signifier. *Screen*, *16*(2), 14–76.

Miller, N. K. (1983). Mastery, identity, and the politics of work: A feminist teacher in the graduate classroom. In C. Portugues (Ed.), *Gendered subjects*. Amherst: University of Massachusetts Press.

Minsky, M. (1985, April). Communication with alien intelligence. *Byte*, 127–138.

Murray, H. (1938). *Explorations in personality*. New York: Oxford University Press.

Murray, L. (1980). *The sensitivities and expressive capacities of young infants in communication with their mothers*. Unpublished doctoral dissertation, University of Edinburgh, Scotland.

Noble, D. (1985). Computer literacy and ideology. In D. Sloan (Ed.), *The computer in education: A critical perspective*. New York: Teachers College Press.

Olson, C. P. (1985). Dream and practice in education: A response to Papert. *New Ideas in Psychology*, *3*(3), 297–308.

Osgood, C. E., Suci, G. J., & Tannenbaum, P. H. (1957). *The measurement of meaning*. Urbana: University of Illinois Press.

Pea, R., & Kurland, M. (1984). On the cognitive effects of learning computer programming. *New Ideas in Psychology*, *2*(2), 137–168.

Piaget, J. (1954). *The construction of reality in the child.* New York: Basic.

Polanyi, M. (1983). *The tacit dimension.* Magnolia, MA: Peter Smith.

Pool, J. (1959), *Trends in content analysis.* Urbana: University of Illinois Press.

Portugues, C. (1985). The spectacle of gender: Cinema and psyche. In M. Culley & C. Portugues (Eds.), *Gendered subjects: The dynamics of feminist teaching.* Boston: Routledge and Kegan Paul.

Propp, V. (1968). *Morphology of the folktale.* Austin: University of Texas Press.

Regis, E. (1985). *Extraterrestrials: Science and alien intelligence.* New York: Cambridge University Press.

Ricoeur, P. (1970). *Freud and philosophy.* New Haven, CT: Yale University Press.

Riley, D. (1983). *War in the nursery.* London: Virago.

Rosch, E. (1975). Universals and cultural specifics in human categorization. In R. Brislin, S. Bochner, & W. Lonner (Eds.), *Cross-cultural perspectives on learning.* New York: Halsted.

Rosenzweig, S. (1949). Fantasy in personality and its study by test procedures. In R. I. Watson (Ed.), *Readings in the clinical method in psychology.* New York: Harper.

Rotter, J. B. (1951). Word association and sentence completion methods. In H. H. Anderson & G. L. Anderson (Eds.), *An introduction to projective techniques.* New York: Prentice-Hall.

Ruesch, J., & Bateson, G. (1951). *Communication: The social matrix of psychiatry.* New York: Norton.

Sartre, J. -P. (1953). *Being and nothingness.* New York: Philosophical Library.

Schafer, R. (1948). *The clinical application of psychological tests.* New York: International Universities Press.

Segal, H. (1964). *Introduction to the work of Melanie Klein.* New York: Basic.

Shapiro, D. (1981). *Autonomy and rigid character.* New York: Basic.

Sheldrake, P. (1972). People, animals and things. *Center for Research in the Educational Sciences Occasional paper No. 11.* University of Edinburgh, Scotland.

Silverman, L. H., Lachmann, F. M., & Milich, R. H. (1982). *The search for oneness.* New York: International Universities Press.

Sloan, D. (1985). Introduction: On raising critical questions about the computer in education. In D. Sloan (Ed.) *The computer in education: A critical perspective.* New York: Teachers College Press.

Solomonides, T., & Levidow, L. (1985). *Compulsive technology: Computers as culture.* London: Free Associations Books.

Spitz, R. A. (1945). Hospitalism: An inquiry into the genesis of psychiatric conditions in early childhood. *Psychoanalytic Study of the Child, 1,* 53–74.

Spitz, R. A. (1957). *No and yes: On the genesis of human communication.* New York: International Universities Press.

Spitz, R. A. (1965). *The first year of life.* New York: International Universities Press.

Stern, D. (1974a). The goal and structure of mother–infant play. *Journal of American Academy of Child Psychiatry, 13,* 402–421.

Stern, D. (1974b). Mother and infant at play: The dyadic interaction involving facial, vocal and gaze behaviors. In M. Lewis & L. A. Rosenblum (Eds.), *The effect of the infant on its caregiver.* New York: Wiley.

Stern, D. (1977). *The first relationship: Infant and mother.* Cambridge, MA: Harvard University Press.

Stern, D. (1985). *The interpersonal world of the infant: A view from psychoanalysis and developmental psychology.* New York: Basic.

Stern, D., Jaffe, J., Beebe, B., & Bennett, S. L. (1974). Vocalizing in unison and in alternation: Two modes of communication within the mother–infant dyad. *Annals of the New York Academy of Science, 263,* 89–100.

Stott, D. H. (1962a). Abnormal mothering as a cause of mental subnormality, I. *Journal of Child Psychology and Psychiatry and Allied Disciplines, 3,* 79–93.

Stott, D. H. (1962a). Abnormal mothering as a cause of mental subnormality, II. *Journal of Child Psychology and Psychiatry and Allied Disciplines, 3,* 133–148.

Strauss, E. W. (1948). On obsession. *Nervous and Mental Disease Monographs, 73,* 3–92. (Reprinted by Johnson Reprint Co., New York, 1968.)

Sullivan, E. V. (1985). Computers, culture, and educational futures: A critical meditation on "Mindstorms." *Interchange, 16*(3), 1–18.

Sumrall, L. (1978). *Alien entities: Beings from beyond.* Tulsa: Harrison House.

Symonds, P. M. (1949). *Adolescent fantasy.* New York: Columbia University Press.

Taylor, R. P. (1980). *The computer in the school: Tutor, tool, tutee.* New York: Teachers College Press.

Thorner, H. A. (1983). Notes on the desire for knowledge. In J. S. Grotstein (Ed.), *Do I dare disturb the universe?* Croydon, England: Meadway.

Trevarthen, C. (1975). Early attempts at speech. In R. Lewin (Ed.), *Child alive.* London: Temple Smith.

Trevarthen, C. (1979). Communication and cooperation in early infancy: A description of primary intersubjectivity. In M. Bullowa (Ed.), *Before speech: The beginning of interpersonal communication.* New York: Cambridge University Press.

Trevarthen, C. (1980). The foundations of intersubjectivity. In D. R. Olson (Ed.), *The social foundation of language and thought.* New York: Norton.

Tronick, E., Als, H., Adamson, L., Wise, S., & Brazelton, B. (1978). The infant's response to entrapment between contradictory messages in face-to-face interaction. In M. Bullowa (Ed.), *Before speech: The beginning of interpersonal communication.* New York: Cambridge University Press.

Turkle, S. (1980). Computer as Rorschach. *Society, 17*(2), 15–24.

Turkle, S. (1984). *The second self: Computers and the human spirit.* New York: Simon & Schuster.

Vance, C. S. (Ed.). (1984). *Pleasure and danger: Exploring female sexuality.* Boston: Routledge & Kegan Paul.

Walkerdine, V. (1985). Science and the female mind: The burden of proof. *PsychCritique: The International Journal of Critical Psychology and Psychoanalysis, 1*(1), 1–20.

Wallon, H. (1941). *L'évolution psychologique de l'enfant.* Paris: Armand Colin.

Weininger, O. (1975). Dominance and children. In A. Kontos (Ed.), *Domination.* Toronto: University of Toronto Press.

Weizenbaum, J. (1976). *Computer power and human reason.* San Francisco: Freeman.

Werner, H., & Kaplan, B. (1963). *Symbol formation.* New York: Wiley.

Winner, L. (1986). *The whale and the reactor.* Chicago: University of Chicago Press.

Winnicott, D. W. (1965). *The maturational processes and the facilitating environment.* New York: International Universities Press.

Winnicott, D. W. (1971). *Playing and reality.* London: Tavistock.

Winograd, T. (1980). What does it mean to understand a language? *Cognitive Science, 4,* 209–241.

Winograd, T., & Flores, F. (1985). *Understanding computers and cognition.* Norwood, NJ: Ablex.

Zayas, L. H., & Broughton, J. M. (1988). Dream content and themes in first-time expectant fathers. Unpublished manuscript, Teacher's College, Columbia University.

III. Mind and paralinguistic communication

9. In search of coronary-prone behavior

ARON W. SIEGMAN

This essay is concerned with the role of psychological variables, especially emotions, in coronary heart disease. That psychological variables, especially emotional upsetness, can affect health, is an idea that goes back to antiquity. However, from the beginning, scientific medicine, although conceding a role for psychological variables in mental illness, insisted that only "physical" processes could play a role in physical illness. Perhaps the first to challenge this dualism in modern times were Freud and his students, who postulated causal relationships between specific neurotic conflicts and a variety of physical diseases. Thus, repressed dependency was implicated in ulcers, and repressed hostility in heart disease. However, despite clinical support for some of these hypotheses, empirical support for such highly specific connections between psychological factors and illness remained spotty at best. Also, the psychoanalysts failed to specify the mechanism by means of which the psychological conflicts became translated into disease processes. In recent years, however, evidence has been accumulating in support of the hypothesis that psychological factors are indeed causally involved in a variety of disease processes. Perhaps the evidence for such a relationship is best documented for coronary heart disease (CHD). Most importantly, we now have at least some reasonable speculations and even some supporting data as to how psychological events could be transformed into disease processes. As a result, we may very well be witnessing a Kuhnian paradigm shift concerning the body–mind relationship. At the very least, these recent developments in psychosomatic medicine require that we reformulate the body–mind relationship in more holistic terms. It is of interest to note that even before these recent de-

The writing of this paper and the studies reported herein were supported by research grants HL-28591 and HL-32585 awarded to the author by the National Heart, Lung and Blood Institutes of the National Institutes of Health.

velopments in psychosomatic medicine, Gregory Bateson rejected the dichotomy between "body" and "mind," advocated a holistic approach, and struggled toward a new definition of mind (e.g., Bateson, 1972). A discussion of recent findings on the role of behavioral factors in CHD is, therefore, entirely appropriate for a festschrift dedicated to Gregory Bateson's memory.

9.1. The type-A behavior pattern and CHD

That behavioral variables are implicated in CHD is no longer a matter of controversy. Smoking, obesity, and a high cholesterol level – all of which involve, at least in part, behavioral factors – are among the recognized risk factors for CHD. What is controversial is whether specific personality traits and/or emotional experiences are also independent risk factors for CHD. Recently, there has been considerable discussion both in the scientific and in the popular literature regarding the role of the Type-A behavior pattern (TABP) in CHD. The TABP has been defined by Friedman and Rosenman (1974), the two cardiologists who are primarily responsible for the TABP construct, as consisting of intense job involvement, competitiveness, time urgency and impatience, hostility and anger. In more general terms, Type-A individuals have been described as being in constant competition with their fellow humans and with time. By way of contrast, Type-B individuals are perceived to lead a much more relaxed life-style. Perhaps the most convincing evidence for the proposition that the Type-A behavior pattern is a significant risk factor for CHD emerged from the Western Collaborative Group Study (WCGS). This was a large-scale prospective study in which Type-As were found to be about twice as much at risk for myocardial infarctions (MIs) as Type-Bs independent of the traditional risk factors such as smoking, overweight, and cholesterol level. (Rosenman et al., 1964; Rosenman, et al., 1975). The TABP was also found to correlate significantly with angiographically documented coronary artery disease (CAD) (Blumenthal, Williams, Kong, Shamberg & Thompson, 1978; Frank, Heller, Kornfeld, Sporn, & Weiss, 1978; Friedman, Rosenman, Straus, Wurm, & Kositchek, 1968; Williams et al., 1980). Recently, however, a number of studies have failed to obtain significant relationships between the TABP and CHD, or between the TABP and CAD. Of special significance in this regard are the results of the Multiple Risk Factor Intervention Study (MRFIT) study, which like the WCGS was a large-scale prospective investigation, yet failed to replicate the relationship between Type-A designation and the incidence of CHD (Shekelle et al., 1985). Other studies failed to replicate the relationship between TABP and severity of coronary occlusion (Arrowood, Uhrich, Gomillion, Popio, & Raft, 1982; Dembroski, MacDougall, Williams, Haney, & Blumenthal, 1985; Dimsdale, Hackett, & Hutter, 1979; Krantz, Sanmarco, Selvester, & Matthews, 1979; Scherwitz et al., 1983; Siegman, Feldstein, Tommaso, Ringel, & Lating, 1987d).

The major objectives of the present paper are (1) to suggest possible explanations for the inconsistent findings and (2) to propose alternative formulations of the relationship between behavior and CHD.

9.2. On the assessment of the TABP

The TABP can be assessed either by means of objective paper-and-pencil questionnaires, such as the Jenkins Activity Survey, or JAS (Jenkins, Zyzanski, & Rosenman, 1971), or by means of a structured interview (SI) that was developed by Rosenman (1978). The SI consists of questions concerned with hard-driving, competitive, time-urgent, impatient, and hostile behaviors. From the beginning, Rosenman (1978) was quite clear that the SI is to be administered in a challenging manner, although the original article was not very specific on how to implement this challenge, besides indicating that occasionally the interviewer should interrupt the interviewee and challenge the interviewee's responses with statements such as "Why?" and "Why not?" More specific guidelines were provided in a subsequent article by Chesney, Eagleston, and Rosenman (1980). According to this article, the questions in the SI are to be asked in a crisp, abrupt, and staccato style, and the challenging remarks, which are designed to evoke competitiveness and self-justification, are to be presented in a rapid-fire manner. The rationale for conducting the interview in such a highly confrontational manner is that it is designed to elicit a behavioral sample of the interviewee's response to challenge (Chesney et al., 1980). However, the scoring of the SI is based not so much on the content of the interviewee's responses as on the interviewee's expressive vocal behavior, or vocal stylistics, during the SI. The scoring criteria include short response latencies, loud speech, explosive speech, rapid accelerated speech, and frequent interruptions of the interviewer. By way of contrast, when one's behavior type is derived from the JAS, or other paper-and-pencil instruments, it is, of course, based exclusively on content. The advantage of these paper-and-pencil instruments is their reliability and economy. Unfortunately, however, the data linking the JAS or other paper-and-pencil instruments with CHD and CAD are less persuasive than are the data for the SI (Blumenthal et al., 1978; Brand, Rosenman, & Jenkins, 1978). A recently completed metaanalysis of all extant prospective studies on the Type-A–CHD link concludes that this association emerges only when the Type-A–CHD link is measured by the SI, and not when it is measured by the JAS (Matthews, 1988). Rosenman and Chesney (1982) have suggested that the JAS and other questionnaire-type self-assessments of the TABP are not reliable predictors of CHD because Type-A individuals tend to deny their Type-A behaviors. This may very well be the case. However, findings obtained in our laboratory indicate that at least for males the SI too may not be completely free from the social desirability response bias (Siegman, Dohm, Lating, & Wilkinson, 1988b). Other problems concerning the SI involve its administration and scoring.

The role of interviewer challenge

As has been pointed out earlier, the SI is supposed to be administered in a challenging manner, but there are no clear-cut criteria for the precise level of interviewer challenge that is to be used in the SI, nor is it at all clear that different interviewers, even when trained by the same person, use comparable levels of challenge. In fact, there is evidence to the contrary. For example, Scherwitz (1989) has noted systematic differences in the vocal stylistics of the interviewers in the MRFIT project. These differences involve the very variables that define the level of the interviewer challenge. The differences obtained even though great efforts were made to ensure that the interviews be administered in a uniform manner. Of interest in this context, and of obvious relevance to the contradictory findings between the WCGS and the MRFIT studies, is the claim by Scherwitz, who had access to both the WCGS and the MRFIT interviews, that at least some of the interviewers in the latter study were more highly challenging than the interviewers in the WCGS study.

Although it seems reasonable to assume that variations in an interviewer's level of challenge will affect an interviewee's level of Type-A behavior in the SI, we must ask whether there is any empirical evidence that such is in fact the case. Results obtained in our laboratory indicate that the answer to this question is clearly in the affirmative. In an early study (Siegman, Feldstein, Simpson, Barkley, & Kobren, 1984) with 48 college students, each of whom participated in two SIs, one of which was administered in a challenging manner and the other in a neutral manner, we found that the challenging interviews were associated with significantly higher Type-A scores than the nonchallenging ones. In a subsequent study (Siegman, Feldstein, & Lating, 1987c) in which we used a similar design with 76 college students, we found that interviewees responded with shorter latencies and more interruptions (both manifestations of the Type-A behavior pattern) in the challenging than in the nonchallenging interviews. Also of interest is the finding that the challenging interviews were significantly shorter than the nonchallenging ones. Some interviewees responded to the highly challenging interviewer questions with one- or two-word answers (i.e., a refusal to self-disclose). In the absence of sufficient scorable material, such individuals could easily be misclassified as Bs. It should be noted that in both studies, interviewer challenge did not substantially alter the rank order of the participants' Type-A scores. However, in a more recent study (Siegman et al. 1987d) with 52 angiographic patients who were administered one-half of the SI in a nonchallenging manner and the other half in a moderately challenging manner, the correlation between the behavior type scores that were obtained from the two interview segments was only .56, when using a four-point TABP classification (A1, A2, X, and B), and only .38 when using a three-point classification (A, X, and B). Five patients who were classified as Type-Bs or Type-Xs on the basis of the nonchallenging interview segment became Type-As on the basis of the challenging interview segment. Three patients moved from A to B, and another five from A to X. As pointed out earlier, some Type-As "clam-up" and refuse to self-disclose when confronted with a very challenging interviewer. Their very brief responses can cause such individuals to be misclassified as Xs or Bs. More importantly, in the same study, interviewees' speech stylistics (loudness and frequency of interruptions) predicted severity of CAD much better when these stylistics were derived from a nonchallenging SI than from a challenging SI (Siegman, Feldstein, & Ringel, 1986a; Siegman et al., 1987d). Similarly, Scherwitz (1989) reports that in the MRFIT study, the less challenging interviews were more predictive of clinical CHD endpoints than the more challenging ones.

It may very well be, then, that the recent spate of negative findings as far as SI-derived Type-A and coronary disease are concerned, is a result of an escalation in interviewer challenge. That there has been such an escalation is suggested by the fact that the SIs in the earlier WCGS were administered in a less challenging and confrontational manner than the SIs in the more recent MRFIT study (Scherwitz, 1989). Clearly, we need a definitive study on which type of SI–nonchallenging, moderately challenging, or highly challenging–is the most predictive of coronary disease. If a nonchallenging SI is as predictive, and perhaps even more predictive, of coronary disease than a challenging one, as the available evidence seems to suggest (Siegman et al. 1987d), then there should be little difficulty in standardizing the administration of the SI. While it is difficult to calibrate interviewers so that they administer the SI with identical levels of challenge and provocation, it is not too difficult to train interviewers to simply avoid challenging behaviors.

The scoring of the SI

From the very beginning Rosenman (1978) has stressed that in scoring the SI, primary attention should be given to voice stylistics and other expressive behaviors.[1] There is reason to suspect, however, that while some scorers ignore content almost completely (Scherwitz, Berton, & Leventhal, 1977), others give it some weight (Matthews, Krantz, Dembroski, & MacDougall, 1982). Moreover, there are no rules for precisely how much weight should be assigned to the various stylistic components. Although it is entirely possible to train scorers to assign similar weights to the various stylistic (and content) components, and thus achieve exceedingly high levels of reliability, there is no evidence that such high levels of agreement do in fact exist across studies. Although these considerations probably do not account for the discrepancies between the WCGS and the MRFIT studies, because efforts were made to achieve comparable scoring procedures in these two studies, they may explain the inconsistencies among the various angiographic studies. Whatever the explanation may be, no one can question the need for a more objective procedure for assessing coronary-prone behavior.

9.3 Toward the objective measurement of coronary-prone behavior

Much of our own research in the area of coronary-prone behavior has focused on the identification of objective, computer-scorable indexes of such behavior.

From the very beginning, Friedman and Rosenman emphasized the role of expressive behavior in the assessment of the TABP. Thus, in describing the scoring of the SI, Friedman and associates point out that "the assessment of the behavior pattern actually is determined far more by the stylistics in which the interviewee responds than by the content of his responses" (Friedman, Brown, & Rosenman, 1969, p. 829). Despite the recognition of the central role of expressive behavior in behavior typing, relatively few efforts were made to apply the rapidly emerging technology for the objective measurement of expressive behavior to the assessment of the TABP. That such objective indexes of expressive behavior can be applied to the assessment of the TABP was demonstrated by Howland and Siegman (1982), who employed a semiautomated system to score 66 taped SIs that were used by the Rosenman group for training purposes. These SIs were scored by Howland and Siegman by means of this semiautomated system for reaction time, silent pause duration, volume, simultaneous speech, and several productivity indexes. In a regression analysis in which the interviewees' objective speech indexes served as the independent variables and the five-point TABP ratings that were assigned to them by Rosenman as the dependent variable, reaction time and volume emerged as significant sources of variance, which together accounted for 47 percent of the variance of the respondents' TABP ratings. Furthermore, using regression equations that were obtained from one-half of the sample, and using cutoff points that were selected to minimize misclassifications, Howland and Siegman were able to correctly identify the subjectively arrived at TABP classifications of 89 percent of the remaining subjects. The basic findings of this study have since been replicated in our laboratory with college students and patients, although the specific vocal indexes that predict Type-A diagnosis vary somewhat from study to study.

Ultimately, of course, we are not so much interested in predicting Type-A diagnosis as in predicting CHD. Specifically, can objective computer-scorable indexes of expressive vocal behavior predict CHD? Beyond that, by focusing on the expressive correlates of coronary-prone behavior, we should gain a more precise understanding of the emotions and personality tendencies that are involved in such behavior. Over the past two decades, considerable progress has been made in identifying the expressive vocal correlates of trait and state anxiety, trait and state anger, and depression (Siegman, 1985, 1987a,b). It should be noted that expressive vocal behaviors, as well as other expressive behaviors, are viewed not as mere external correlates of emotions, but as integral parts and determinants of the emotional experience, on a par with the physiological and cognitive dimensions of emotional experience (Buck, 1987; Plutchik, 1984; Epstein, 1984). Specifically, we now know that anger arousal is associated with an increase in loudness, speech rate, and the frequency of interrupting one's speaking partner (Siegman, 1985; Siegman & Kruger, 1988c). Under certain specific circumstances, anxiety arousal, too, is associated with an accelerated speech rate, but unlike anger arousal, it does not appear to be associated with an increase in loudness and a struggle for "floor time" (Siegman, 1985, 1987b). By way of contrast, depression is associated with a decrease in speech rate, which is due to longer silent pauses (Siegman, 1987a). Thus, careful analysis of the expressive vocal correlates of the coronary-prone individual can help clarify precisely which negative emotional experiences are risk factors for CHD.

The purpose of our next study (Siegman & Feldstein, 1985), then, was to determine which objectively measured vocal indexes, if any, are also associated with CHD. In that study, 35 patients undergoing diagnostic coronary arteriography were administered an expanded version of the SI. The first half of the interview was administered in a nonchallenging style, the other half in a moderately challenging style. Both halves of the interview were computer scored by the means of the Automatic Vocal Transaction Analyzer, or AVTA (Jaffe & Feldstein, 1970), for the following speech variables: response latency, average duration of silent pauses, speech rate, and frequency of interruptive speech. The patients' responses were also rated for loudness, but these involved subjective judgments. The problem with such judgments is that they are confounded with the speaker's speech rate (Bond & Feldstein, 1982). In the present study, therefore, speech rate was always used as a covariate for the loudness ratings. A highly qualified cardiologist, who was blind to the patient's TABP status, assigned each patient an occlusion score on the basis of the patient's arteriogram, according to the Gensini (1975) method.

The results of a regression analysis, which included traditional risk factors such as the patient's age, gender, weight, and blood pressure as covariates, showed that in the nonchallenging part of the interview, loudness and frequency of interruptive speech accounted for as much as 35 percent of the variance of the patients' coronary occlusion scores (loudness for 18 percent and interruptive speech for 17 percent). In the challenging part of the interview, frequency of interruptive speech and loudness also accounted for 35 percent of the variance of the patients' Gensini scores (interruptive speech for 31 percent and loudness for 4 percent). In this study, then, the nonchallenging interviewer style and the challenging style were about equally effective in predicting severity of CAD. Overweight and blood pressure accounted for another 20 percent. Altogether, then, in this study we were able to account for about 55 percent of the variance of the patients' severity of coronary occlusion scores. It is important to point out that in this study there was no significant relationship between the patients' global Type-A scores and severity of CAD.

Considering the small number of patients in this study, and the fact that in the regression analyses there were a large number of independent variables for a sample of only 35 subjects, it was felt that the findings needed to be replicated before they could be accepted with any degree of confidence. The replication (Siegman, Feldstein, Ringel, Tommaso, & Salomon, 1986b) was conducted in another hospital that serviced a patient population of a somewhat higher socioeconomic status. Altogether there were 44 patients in this second study, 29 males and 15 females. Separate analyses were performed for the male and the female patients. In the male group, the frequency of patients' interruptive speech scores and their loudness scores in the nonchallenging interview segment correlated significantly with their coronary occlusion scores, as determined by the Gensini (1975) method [$r(27) = .39$ and $.35$, respectively]. Between them, the two stylistic indexes accounted for 29 percent of the variance in the male patients' Gensini scores – which is comparable to what we found in our first study. In this second study, however, none of the vocal indexes that were obtained from the challenging interview segment correlated significantly with the patients' Gensini scores. Although we cannot conclude on the basis of these findings that a nonchallenging interview is superior to a challenging one, given that the order of interviewer style was not counterbalanced, it is nevertheless reasonable to conclude that interviewer challenge is not essential for eliciting the relationship between the speech variables and severity of CAD. As pointed out earlier, this is encouraging news as far as introducing greater standardization in the administration of the SI is concerned, for it is much easier to standardize a nonchallenging interview than a challenging one. Finally, it should be noted that in this second study, too, there was no significant relationship between the patients' SI-derived global Type-A scores and their severity of CAD scores.

How are we to interpret these findings regarding the relationship between expressive vocal behavior and CAD, and what do they imply about the role of emotions in CHD?

The Role of Hostility in CHD

It has been pointed out by a number of investigators (Dembroski & MacDougall, 1985; Dembroski et al., 1985; Matthews, 1982) that the

TABP construct, as originally defined by Friedman and Rosenman (1974), is a multidimensional construct, consisting of many behavioral tendencies, such as competitiveness, time urgency, impatience, hostility, and anger. However, not all of these components necessarily constitute coronary-prone behavior; some may, others may not. These considerations have led some investigators to advocate a component scoring approach to the SI, in which each behavioral component that contributes to the global Type-A score is separately assessed for its relationship to CHD (Dembroski & MacDougall, 1983). Using this component scoring approach, Dembroski and MacDougall (1983) and MacDougall, Demobroski, Dimsdale, and Hackett (1985) found a significant relationship between SI-based potential for hostility ratings and severity of atherosclerosis. Using a self-report measure of hostility, Williams and associates (e.g., Williams, Barefoot, & Shekelle, 1984) also found significant relationships between hostility and CHD. Given that loud and interruptive speech are uniquely related to expressive anger and hostility (Siegman, 1985), we can conclude that our findings regarding expressive vocal behavior and severity of CAD in males implicate expressive anger and hostility in CHD. Taken together, the results obtained by Dembroski, MacDougall, Williams, and associates and the results of our own studies suggest that expressive anger and hostility is indeed a, if not the, toxic agent in the relationship between the TABP and CHD.

Let us now turn to the findings regarding expressive vocal behavior and severity of CAD in the female sample. In this group, neither loudness nor interruptive speech correlated significantly with the Gensini scores (in fact, the correlations were in the opposite direction from those obtained in males). However, two other correlations approached significance: the higher the patients' Gensini scores the shorter their silent pauses and the longer their responses during the SI. This pattern of expressive vocal behavior suggests anxiety arousal (Siegman, 1987b) rather than hostility. Our findings, then, suggest the possibility that different negative emotional experiences are related to CHD in females than in males; that is, expressive hostility in the case of males and anxiety in the case of females. This is an intriguing hypothesis that we are pursuing in our current studies.

9.4. Components of hositility and the severity of CAD

Although a number of studies point to hostility as the "toxic" factor in the relationship between the TABP construct and CHD, at least as far as males are concerned, there are also some negative findings. For example, two recent studies failed to obtain a significant positive correlation between scores on Spielberger's Trait Anger Scale (TAS) (Spielberger, 1980) and angiographically documented occlusion (Shocken, Worden, Greene, Harrison & Spielberger, 1985; Smith, Follick, & Korr, 1984), and yet a third study found a significant negative correlation between TAS scores and severity of CAD (Spielberger, personal communication, October, 1986). Perhaps hostility is not less a multi-dimensional construct than the TABP, with only some dimensions being related to coronary disease. We decided to explore this issue further by comparing the relationship of the experience of anger and hostility versus overt–reactive hostility to coronary disease. A number of years ago, Buss and Durkee (1957) constructed several theoretically based hostility scales. Factor analyses of these scales yielded two factors, with the resentment and suspicion scales loading on one factor, and the assault and verbal hostility scales loading on the second factor, (Musante, MacDougall, Dembroski, & Costa, in press). The first factor would seem to be a measure of the experience of anger and hostility. Given that indexes of the experience of anger and hostility correlate fairly highly–as much as .7–with neuroticism indexes (e.g., Sarason, 1961; Siegman & Gjesdal, 1987e), they could be viewed as measures of neurotic hostility. By way of contrast, the second factor seems to be a measure of frustration-induced, reactive hostility and aggression, or expressive hostility. In a recent study, we investigated the relationship of these two dimensions of hostility – that is, the experience of hostility and expressive hostility – with CAD (Siegman, Dembroski, & Ringel, 1987b). The participants were 72 patients, 51 males and 21 females, scheduled for coronary angiography. In addition to the Buss–Durkee Hostility Inventory (BDHI), they were also administered Bendig's (1956) abbreviated form of the Taylor Manifest Anxiety Scale (MAS) – an index of neuroticism. In younger patients – up to the age of 60 – the patients' expressive hostility scores correlated positively and significantly with the CAD endpoints. On the other hand, the patients' experience of hostility scores correlated negatively and significantly with the severity of coronary occlusion. It is of interest to note that in this group of younger patients ($N = 36$), not only the experience of hostility but neuroticism, too, as indexed by the MAS, correlated negatively and significantly with severity of CAD (partial r, with gender partialled out, $= -.35$, $p < .05$). An item analysis was conducted in order to identify the specific BDHI items that correlated significantly with severity of occlusion in the below age 60 group. The results show that patients with significant occlusion affirm items that suggest impulsive, reactive hostility and anger and deny items that suggest neurotic concerns, such as chronic resentment and suspiciousness. (See table 9.1)

These results can help us understand why previous investigators failed to obtain significant positive correlations between scores on Spielberger's TAS and coronary disease. In an evaluation of this scale, Costa and McCrae (1985) conclude that it "is perhaps two-thirds neuroticism and one-third antagonism." Given our findings, it is not likely that personality tests that also measure neuroticism and trait anxiety will correlate positively with severity of CHD. Depending on the level of confounding, the correlation can even be significantly negative.

The positive correlation between overt–expressive hostility and severity of CAD was, of course, expected. However, the significant negative correlation between the experience of hostility and severity of CAD was not expected and needs explanation, as does the significant negative correlation between neuroticism and CAD. One possibility is that these negative correlations are an artifact of how patients get selected for coronary angiography. Neurotic individuals may be prone to hypochondriacal anginalike pains, although they have perfectly clean arteries (Costa, 1986). When such individuals are selected for coronary angiography because of their repeated complaints about their chest pains, we are likely to obtain a wholly artifactual inverse relationship between neuroticism and severity of CAD.

Alternatively, the negative relationship between measures of the experience of hostility, or neurotic hostility, and the severity of CAD can be explained if we assume that measures of neurotic hostility tap primarily attitudes rather than affect, that is, levels of anger arousal, which is tapped by measures of reactive hostility. Although it may be the case that individuals who hold hostile attitudes are easily angered, it is not necessarily the case that they become excessively aroused. Also, as pointed out elsewhere (Siegman, 1987b), we need to distinguish between the effects of state and trait measures. In relation to anxiety, the evidence is quite clear that state and trait anxiety have different consequences. Whereas state anxiety, at least in moderate dosages, is typically associated with disruptive speech, relatively high productivity, and relatively short silent pauses, trait anxiety has no such effects. In fact, measures of trait anxiety tend to be associated with relatively long silent pauses (Siegman, 1987b). This discrepancy can be explained if we assume that chronically anxious individuals become habituated to or de-

Table 9.1. *Buss-Durkee Hostility Scale items that correlate significantly[a] with CAD endpoints in patients aged 60 and younger (N = 36)*

Items affirmed	Items denied
I lose my temper easily but get over it	I don't get what's coming to me
When people yell, I yell back	I feel resentful when I look back
I am capable of slapping someone	If I am made fun of, my blood boils
I have not had a temper tantrum	Being forgiven for my sins concerns me
I raise my voice when arguing	
People push me so far, we come to blows	People have a hidden reason for doing something nice
	I feel I get a raw deal out of life
	I would rather concede than argue

[a]$p < .05$.

velop compensatory mechanisms to cope with low levels of anxiety arousal. This distinction between state and trait measures may also explain the inverse relationship between trait hostility and severity of CAD. In this context, it should be recalled that in our study trait anxiety also correlated negatively with severity of CAD. This explanation has also been invoked to account for the otherwise puzzling inverse relationship between neuroticism and cancer reported by Eysenck (1985) and Grossarth-Maticek, Kanazir, Schmidt, and Velter (1985).

Additional explanations for the discrepant findings regarding the TABP and CHD

In relation to the findings summarized above, it is important to point out that the positive relationship between expressive hostility and severity of CAD was significant only in the 60 and younger group, not in those 60 and older. Similarly, the relationship between expressive vocal behavior and severity of CAD discussed earlier also occurred only in the 60 and younger group (Siegman et al., 1987d). Also, in a subgroup of this patient population on whom we had information regarding the frequency of MIs, we found a positive relationship between the patients' SI-derived global Type-A scores and number of MIs, but this relationship too occurred only in the relatively younger patients (Siegman, Feldstein, & Ringel, 1986a). Apparently, behavioral variables like the TABP and hostility are most salient in relatively younger patients. Older patients may represent "hardy survivors" in whom behavioral and psychosocial variables are only marginally or not at all relevant to disease status. This finding has obvious methodological implications. Nonsignificant findings obtained in populations that include older patients may become significant when the interaction with age is taken into consideration. In fact, the inconsistent findings of the different studies mentioned in the beginning of this chapter may very well be a result of differences in the age distributions in the respective studies.

Others (e.g., Matthews, 1988) have suggested that differences in the health status of the participants in the different studies may be yet another factor that can account for the discrepant findings. Thus, the participants in the WCGS were healthy middle-aged males, in contrast to the MRFIT study whose participants were at risk for CHD. Of course, the patients in the angiographic studies represent a sick population, and some are quite sick.

Another reason for the inconsistent findings in the CAD studies may be the different criteria for coronary occlusion that are being used in the different studies, such as number of vessels with 50 percent occlusion, number of vessels with 75 percent occlusion, and the Gensini method. Although these measures correlate very highly with each other (about .75 and better for number of vessels affected and Gensini scores), there are consistent differences in how they correlate with the risk factors for CAD and CHD.

Yet another possible explanation for the negative results in recent studies is the high percentage of Type-As in these studies. In the WCGS, there were about 50 percent Type-As, but in recent studies, there have been as many as 70 percent Type-As. In our two studies, about two-thirds of the patients were classified as As. Such a preponderance of Type-As may not be unreasonable in a group of coronary patients, but it is likely to attenuate the chances of obtaining a significant correlation between Type-A scores and CAD, even if there is such a relationship. On the other hand, we did obtain significant correlations between our patients' stylistic variables – whose distributions were much less skewed than the Type-A scores – and their coronary occlusion scores.

9.5. Components of the TABP, hostility and physiological reactivity, and testosterone production

The early evidence suggesting a link between the TABP and CHD prompted speculations about the mechanisms whereby such behavior is translated into coronary disease. Of course, such speculations must involve biological processes that underlie atherogenesis and/or the precipitation of acute coronary events. The leading hypothesis in this re-gard postulates excessive cardiovascular and neuroendocrine respon-siveness (reactivity) on the part of Type-As, compared with Type-Bs, to challenging or provocative situations. Chronic exposure to such situa-tions is believed to cause initial injury to the lining of coronary arteries, making them susceptible sites for atherogenic lesions. Furthermore, chronic physiological arousal could enhance the development of atherogenic lesions by mobilizing circulation lipids and by increasing blood clotting (Williams, Friedman, Glass, Herd, & Schneiderman, 1978). Recent reviews of the relevant literature conclude that the TABP, when assessed by the SI, is indeed associated with heightened car-diovascular reactivity, although some studies have failed to obtain the expected postive relationship (Contrada & Krantz, 1988). However, as pointed out earlier, the TABP is a multidimensional construct, and it is important to establish precisely which of its components is related to cardiovascular reactivity. The results of the relatively few studies that have looked at this question suggest that both hostility and vigorous speech stylistics manifested during the SI show positive correlations with measures of challenge-induced physiologic reactivity (Contrada & Krantz, 1988). Given our findings in relation to hostility and CAD, we wanted to ascertain whether the distinction between expressive and neurotic hostility that obtained in relation to CAD also holds in relation to physiologic reactivity. These, then, were the questions that were the focus of our study (Siegman, Dohm, & Gjesdal, 1988a; Siegman et al., 1988b) on the components of the TABP and cardiovascular reactivity: (1) Precisely which component of the SI or combination of components are related to heightened cardiovascular reactivity? (2) What is the relation-ship between the two components of hostility – expressive and neurotic hostility – and cardiovascular reactivity? One other major focus of this study was the role of gender in the above relationships. The generaliza-tion that was made earlier, that most of the studies that looked at the relationship between the TABP and physiologic reactivity found positive correlations, is limited to males. Relatively few studies examined this relationship in females, and of those that did the majority obtained null results. Contrada and Krantz (1988) suggest that these null findings in females may be due either to an inappropriate assessment of the TABP – by means of the JAS, which is not related to reactivity even in males – or to the use of challenging tasks that may not have been sufficiently engaging or may have appeared too difficult to the female participants. They suggest that challenges of an interpersonal nature may be more appropriate for women than tasks involving mathematical computations or rapid psychomotor responses. In our study, therefore, we used both kinds of challenges: a moderately challenging SI and a serial subtraction task. In addition to these two tasks, the participants (male and female college students) were also administered the SI and the two sets of hostility scales that were used in our CAD study, one measuring expressive hostility and the other neurotic hostility. The SI provided the basis for yet another measure of expressive hostility.

The following is a summary of our findings regarding the relationship between components of the SI and of hostility and cardiovascular reactivity in young adult males and females. However, prior to presenting these findings, we will first review the findings on gender differences in physiologic reactivity.

Gender and reactivity

It is generally accepted that there is a gender difference in susceptibility to CHD, with males being more at risk than females (Rice, Hing, Kovar, & Prager, 1984). However, none of the established behavioral and biological risk factors for CHD can account for this gender difference in CHD morbidity and mortality (Wingard, Suarez, & Barret-Connor, 1983). Recently, researchers have become interested in gender differences in physiologic reactivity to stress, because if it could be shown that males are more reactive than females, we might have an explanation for the gender difference in CHD morbidity and mortality (Matthews, 1988). Frankenhauser (1983) and colleagues report that women show higher urinary catecholamine excretion during stress than do men. Stoney, Matthews, McDonald and Johnson, (in press) obtained similar findings in regard to lipoprotein cholesterol. In the same study, males obtained higher systolic blood pressure scores and lower heart rates than did females during the stressful tasks.

Turning now to our study, we, too, found that the male participants exhibited significantly greater systolic reactivity[2] relative to the female participants during the SI task, but the female participants obtained significantly higher heart rates during the SI than did the males. By and large, then, our findings parallel those obtained by Stoney et al. (in press).

However, in our study, the gender difference in relation to systolic blood pressure reactivity during the SI occurred only in individuals with high defensiveness scores, as measured by the Marlowe–Crowne Social Desirability Scale (Crowne & Marlowe, 1964). A similar interaction between gender and defensiveness occurred in relation to systolic blood pressure reactivity during the math task. These interactions suggest that the male participants' heightened systolic reactivity during the SI and the math task should not be attributed solely to biological factors.

Finally, although the male participants manifested greater systolic blood pressure reactivity than did the females, they also manifested significantly faster recovery rates. Traditionally, the focus has been on the role of physiologic reactivity in CHD, with very little attention being paid to the role of recovery rate. It may very well be, however, that the hemodynamic processes that contribute to CHD are more complex than has been assumed heretofore, and they may involve *both* reactivity and recovery rates.

Components of the TABP and cardiovascular reactivity.

Consistent with the results obtained by previous investigators, we, too, found that Type-A individuals (as determined by the SI) were more reactive than Type-Bs. Type-As obtained significantly higher systolic reactivity scores during the SI, and significantly higher diastolic reactivity scores during the math task, than Type-Bs. However, these relationships between the TABP and cardiovascular reactivity obtained only in males. Of course, this does not preclude the possibility that Type-A women, too, are more reactive to challenge and stress than Type-B women. However, in women this hyperreactivity may express itself in physiological parameters other than blood pressure and heart rate, such as corticosteroid production and cholesterol level. In fact, the results of a recent study (Stoney, Matthews, McDonald, & Johnson, 1988) indicate that different individuals exhibit different patterns of reactivity to challenge and stress, with some individuals primarily showing heightened adrenalin and cardiovascular responses and others primarily showing heightened lipid responses, with women clustering in the latter group and men in the former group.

In our study, as in previous studies, vigorous speech stylistics during the SI and SI-derived potential for hostility scores correlated significantly with challenge-induced cardiovascular reactivity. The participants' SI-derived potential for hostility scores correlated significantly with heart rate reactivity during the SI, but not with systolic or diastolic reactivity. On the other hand, rapid accelerated speech correlated positively and significantly with systolic reactivity and with a slow recovery during the SI and with heightened diastolic reactivity during the math task. Additionally, short response latencies correlated significantly with systolic reactivity during the SI. It would appear, then, that the positive correlation between SI-derived global Type-A scores and systolic reactivity that has been found in a number of previous studies is mediated primarily by vigorous speech stylistics.

The usual interpretation for the positive relationship between TABP scores and physiologic hyperreactivity is that it is cognitively mediated; that is, that Type-A individuals are more responsive to challenging and anger-arousing situations than are Type-B individuals, and hence their physiologic hyperreactivity. However, as pointed out by Contrada and Krantz (1988) and by Williams (1989), several recent reports suggest a biological basis for the TABP. For example, Kahn, Kornfeld, Frank, Heller, and Hoar (1980) found that Type-A individuals manifested greater cardiovascular reactivity than Type-Bs even during general anesthesia, suggesting that both the TABP and the associated cardiovascular hyperreactivity reflect an underlying hyperresponsive sympathetic nervous system. However, the finding, in our study, that the relationship between the TABP and physiologic reactivity was limited to highly defensive individuals is most consistent with a cognitive interpretation. On the other hand, the two interpretations – the cognitive and the biological – are not necessarily mutually exclusive, and both factors may play a role in the relationship between the TABP and hyperreactivity.

Components of hostility and cardiovascular reactivity.

It will be recalled that in an earlier study with angiographic patients (Siegman, Dembroski, & Ringel, 1987b), we found a significant positive correlation between an index of expressive hostility and severity of CAD and a significant negative correlation between an index of the experience of hostility, or neurotic hostility, and severity of CAD. Two hypotheses were suggested for the unexpected negative relationship between neurotic hostility and severity of CAD. According to one hypothesis, this inverse relationship is artifactual, a consequence of how patients get selected for angiographic examination. According to the second hypothesis, the inverse relationship between neurotic hostility and severity of CAD is a consequence of the fact that chronically anxious or hostile individuals become inoculated against stressful or challenging situations, or develop strategies to cope with such situations. If so, we could expect a significant negative correlation between chronic, neurotic hostility and cardiovascular reactivity. In the present study, we did indeed obtain a significant negative correlation between the participants' neurotic hostility scores and systolic reactivity during the SI.

Furthermore, in males there was a significant negative correlation between neurotic hostility and diastolic reactivity during the math task, and between neurotic hostility and heart rate reactivity during both the SI and the math tasks (the latter restricted to nondefensive individuals). Clearly, then, the present study confirms that there is an inverse relationship between chronic, neurotic hostility and cardiovascular reactivity, especially in males, that cannot be explained away as an artifact of how the participants were selected for this study.

By way of contrast, the findings of this study suggest a positive correlation between expressive anger-hostility and cardiovascular reactivity. The participants were administered two measures of expressive anger-hostility: one based on the BDHI (the assault and verbal hostility scales) and another based on the SI. Although there was no significant correlation between the former and cardiovascular reactivity, we did find a significant positive correlation between the latter and heart-rate reactivity (partial $r(35) = .42$, $p < .01$). Moreover, in another study with a similar group of male college students, we obtained a significant positive correlation between the participants' Framingham anger-out scale scores (Haynes, Feinleib, & Kannel, 1980) – which is yet another measure of expressive anger-hostility (Musante et al., in press) – and their systolic reactivity scores ($r(41) = .34$, $p = < .05$). By and large, then, our findings suggest that in males, there is a *positive* correlation between reactive anger-hostility and cardiovascular reactivity and a *negative* correlation between neurotic hostility and cardiovascular reactivity.

Components of hostility and testosterone production

Another hypothesis concerning how behavior gets translated into CHD involves the production of testosterone (Williams, 1989). Moreover, there are a number of findings that suggest that testosterone production may mediate the relationship between behavioral risk factors and CHD. For example, there is evidence to suggest that under challenging conditions Type-A men produce more testosterone than Type-B men. Also, Zumoff et al. (1984) found elevated daytime urinary excretion of testosterone glucuronide in Type-A but not Type-B men. There was no corresponding difference in the testosterone glucuronide levels of Type-A and Type-B men during the times of day when people are less involved in competitive, time-pressured activities. A particularly attractive feature of the testosterone hypothesis is that it also accounts for the fact that men are significantly more at risk for CHD than are women. However, if there is any validity to the contention that hostility is the "toxic" component in the TABP, we should be able to demonstrate a relationship between hostility and testosterone production. Moreover, this relationship should be limited to reactive hostility. There is, in fact, evidence to that effect in a study undertaken more than 17 years ago by Persky, Smith, and Basu (1971) on the role of testosterone in aggressive behavior in men without the authors being aware of the implications of their findings for the role of aggression in CHD. They found a significant positive correlation between overt, reactive hostility, as measured by the appropriate Buss-Durkee (B-D) hostility scales, and plasma testosterone levels [$r(16) = .52$, $p < .05$] and testosterone production rate [$r(16) = .69$, $p < .001$] in a group of 18 young males. By way of contrast, the experience of hostility, or neurotic hostility, as measured by the appropriate B-D scales, barely related to testosterone production rate at the 5 percent level. Furthermore, in a regression analysis, in which these two measures of hostility plus two other indexes of overt–reactive hostility were entered as independent variables and testosterone production rate as the dependent variable, both types of hostility contributed significantly to the variance in the participants' testosterone production rates, but in opposite directions: overt–reactive hostility positively, and the experience of hostility negatively. Between them they accounted for 82 percent of the variance in the participants' testosterone production rates. Similar findings were obtained more recently by Olweus (1983, 1986) and associates in a group of boys aged 15 to 17 years. Two scales measuring reactive–expressive aggression correlated significantly with the boys' testosterone levels [$r(56) = .41$, $p < .01$]. A detailed item analysis revealed that only items that involve a response to provocation, including threat or unfair treatment, showed a relationship with testosterone levels (Table 9.2). It is of interest to note that both these items and the items that predicted severity of CAD in our angiographic study seem to measure reactive–expressive hostility. By way of contrast, a scale measuring aggressive attitudes – that is, the experience of anger and aggression – showed no significant correlation with the boys' testosterone levels (Olweus, 1983).

It would appear, then, that overt–reactive hostility and the experience of hostility relate differentially not only to the severity of CAD but also to cardiovascular reactivity and to the production of testosterone.

9.6 The biological context of human communication: speech and cardiovascular reactivity

The relationship between loud and interruptive speech and severity of CAD that obtained in our study of angiographic patients was explained

Table 9.2. *Correlation between testosterone levels and individual items from the verbal and physical aggression scales* (N = 58)

Item	Correlation coefficient (r)
Verbal aggression (5 items)	
1. When an adult is unfair to me, I get angry and protest.	.18
2. When an adult tries to take my place in line, I firmly tell him or her it is my place.	.24
3. When a teacher criticizes me, I tend to answer back and protest.	.33
4. When a teacher has promised that we will have some fun but then changes his or her mind, I protest.	.19
5. When an adult tries to boss me around, I resist strongly.	.33
Physical aggression (5 items)	
6. When a boy starts fighting with me, I fight back.	.33
7. When a boy is nasty with me, I try to get even with him.	.37
8. When a boy teases me, I try to give him a good beating.	.15
9. I fight with other boys at school.[a]	.05
10. I really admire the fighters among the boys.[a]	.11

[a]These items do not contain a clear element of provocative challenge.

in terms of the mediating role of expressive hostility. However, there may be a more direct relationship between speech and CHD. This is suggested by a study (Friedman, Thomas, Kulick-Chiffo, Lynch, & Suginohara, 1982) in which the authors raised subjects' blood pressure simply by instructing them to read more rapidly than they normally do. Additional support for the hypothesized relationship between speech style and cardiovascular reactivity comes from a study in which we monitored changes in blood pressure and heart rate of 36 male undergraduates as they responded to an abbreviated SI. The results of regression analyses, in which measures of the participants' vocal behavior during the SI served as independent variables and their cardiovascular reactivity scores during the SI as dependent variables, showed significant positive relationships between the participants' productivity scores, loudness levels, and frequency of interruptive speech and their heart rate reactivity scores (the respective F values were 10.74, 4.99, and 3.28; the reactive p values were $p < .01$, $p = .05$, and $p < .10$ in a two-tailed test). It is interesting to note that the same two speech variables that were related to the severity of CAD in angiographic patients (i.e., simultaneous speech and loudness) are also implicated in heightened cardiovascular reactivity in male college students. Perhaps the chronic surges in cardiovascular activity that are associated with this speech style cause damage to the coronary arteries and lead to the development of arterial plaques and CHD.

Of course, the two hypotheses – the hypothesis emphasizing reactive hostility and the hypothesis emphasizing an excessively emphatic speech style in the genesis of CHD – are not mutually exclusive. To the contrary, the two may reinforce each other, perhaps even in a synergistic fashion. As people get angry they experience an increase in cardiovascular reactivity, raise their voices, interrupt their partner, and probably accelerate their speech, which in turn may further heighten their reactivity and their anger. Speaking with an angry voice about frustrating experiences is likely to exacerbate the emotional and cardiovascular reactions to those experiences. Thus, Ekman, Levenson, and Frieson (1983) have shown that by simply putting on an angry face one can produce feelings of anger and the corresponding ANS arousal. The same may occur when one speaks with an angry voice. In fact, in a recently completed study (Siegman et al., 1989), we found that speaking about anger-provoking experiences in a loud and rapid manner increases one's angry mood. Moreover, the male participants rated themselves as significantly more angry even when discussing neutral topics in a loud and rapid manner as opposed to a soft and slow speech style. Kearns (1987) too found that speaking loudly about a neutral topic raises one's anger level. A more detailed schematic illustration of this vicious cycle is represented in Figure 9.1. This model needs to be complemented, however, by the listener's responses. There is considerable evidence for conversational congruence or synchrony in which participants in dyadic interactions match each other's speech style, including loudness level (Feldstein & Welkowitz, 1978). Thus, as an angry speaker raises his or her voice, so will the speaker's partner. Furthermore, we now have some preliminary evidence suggesting that angry speech also heightens the listener's cardiovascular reactivity. This, of course, is likely to increase the listener's anger, which in turn will affect the angry speaker, and so on. This model accounts nicely both for the escalating and the contagious nature of anger.

The modification of cardiovascular reactivity

Given the findings reported thus far, we next addressed ourselves to the question whether it is possible to raise and, more importantly from our perspective, to lower a person's cardiovascular reactivity in the SI by instructing the respondent to speak more loudly and quickly or more softly and slowly than usual. Should it be possible to reduce blood

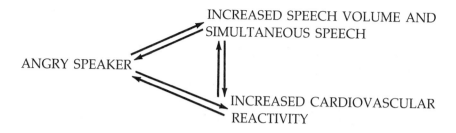

Figure 9.1. Schematic representation of the reciprocal interactions of anger, speech, and cardiovascular reactivity.

pressure by speaking slowly and softly, such findings could have important implications for the behavioral control of essential hypertension and perhaps even coronary-prone behavior. In a study designed to answer this question, 40 normotensive college students were administered an expanded version of the SI that was subdivided into three parts. Standard instructions preceded the first part of the interview. Before each of the other two parts, the participants were instructed either to speak more loudly and rapidly or more softly and slowly than usual. We used a within-subjects, or crossover, design, so that each subject participated in all three conditions: normal speech, loud and fast speech, and soft and slow speech. The participants' systolic (SBP) and diastolic (DBP) blood pressures, as well as their heart rates, were monitored during a baseline period and throughout the SI. A comparison of the participants' cardiovascular reactivity scores in the three conditions revealed significant differences for SBP $[F(2,76) = 19.57, p < .001]$ and HR $[F(2,76) = 5.80, p < .05]$ but not for DBP. The participants evidenced significantly lower SBP scores $[F(1,39) = 26.23, p < .001]$ and lower HRs $[F(1,39) = 5.11, p < .05]$ in the "soft and slow" condition as compared to the standard interview condition (133 vs. 138 for SBP and 77.6 vs. 79.6 for HR). Analogous results were obtained when the analyses were based on the participants' delta (differences from baseline) scores. However, none of the "loud and fast" versus "standard speech" comparisons were significant. Information obtained from the participants during the debriefing sessions revealed that although most participants had little difficulty in following the instructions that they speak softly and slowly, some found it difficult to speak more rapidly and loudly than usual.

In the preceding study, loudness was confounded with speech rate. When subjects were instructed to speak loudly, they were also instructed to speak rapidly. Conversely, when subjects were instructed to speak softly, they were also instructed to speak slowly. We cannot tell, therefore, whether it was slow speech or soft speech that was associated with reduced systolic blood pressure and heart rate reactivity. In our next study (Siegman, Crump, Dembroski & Gjesdal 1987a), therefore, we made an attempt to unconfound these two speech parameters. Furthermore, we took steps to ensure that the participants would indeed speak at the intended rate and volume level. In this study, instead of responding to an interview, the participants were asked to read a series of children's stories. Each subject participated in three distinct conditions: either soft, normal, and loud speech or slow, normal, and fast speech. When speech rate was manipulated, volume, or loudness, was held constant at a moderate level, and when loudness was manipulated, speech rate was held constant at a moderate level. To ensure that the participants would indeed read the passages at the intended volume and rate, they were asked to "shadow" a trained actor. Manipulation checks indicated that the passages were indeed read at the intended rate and loudness levels. Participants who could not match the actor's rate or loudness were eliminated from the study. Twenty-four females participated in the manipulation of rate condition, another 24 in the manipulation of volume condition. Soft speech was associated with significantly lower systolic blood pressure reactivity than either normal or loud speech (116 vs. 120 vs. 124), and slow speech was associated with significantly lower diastolic blood pressure than either normal or fast speech (79 vs. 83 vs. 84). Most important, from the perspective of modifying cardiovascular reactivity by means of reducing speech rate and/or loudness level, is the finding that slow speech was associated with significantly lower systolic, diastolic, and heart rate reactivity than fast speech, and soft speech with significantly lower systolic and diastolic reactivity than loud speech. It would appear, then, that both slow and soft speech are associated with reduced cardiovascular reactivity, when compared to fast and loud speech.

Our next study (Siegman & Kruger, 1988c) in this series specifically addressed the question whether slow (and by implication soft) speech can reduce cardiovascular reactivity even if the speaker is engaged in an anger-arousing communication. In this study, 24 students at the University of Würzburg, Germany, described a series of neutral events and a series of anger-arousing experiences. The speakers used their normal speech rate in describing one-third of the events – both neutral and anger arousing – a fast speech rate for another third of the events, and a slow speech rate for yet another third of the events. Systolic and diastolic blood pressure measures were obtained immediately following each description. The speech-rate manipulation had a significant effect on systolic blood pressure, with the participants obtaining lower blood pressure during the slow speech condition relative to the fast speech condition, whether they talked about anger-arousing or neutral topics. It should be recalled that a soft and slow speech style also attenuates one's angry mood.

Taken together, our findings suggest the feasibility of reducing cardiovascular reactivity by training people who speak fast or loud to speak more slowly and/or more softly. However, our studies thus far have involved only short-term modifications of a speaker's speech style. We are now trying to establish the feasibility of long-term changes in coronary-prone speech styles, and the effects of such modifications on cardiovascular reactivity in both normotensive and hypertensive individuals.

Summary and conclusions

1. It is suggested that recent failures to confirm earlier findings of a causal relationship between the TABP and CHD are, at least in part, a result of conceptual problems with the TABP construct, and of methodological problems with the SI as an assessment instrument.

The TABP is a multidimensional construct not all of whose components are necessarily coronary prone. Some may be, others may not, and still others may be protective. Clearly, we need to distinguish between the TABP and coronary prone behavior – the two are not identical. Moreover, there is a discrepancy between the conceptual definition of the TABP, which focuses on competitiveness and related behaviors, and its operational definition by means of the SI, which focuses primarily on vigorous speech stylistics. All this argues strongly for a component analysis approach, in which each of the components that contributes to the global Type-A score is separately assessed for its relationship to CHD.

The methodological problems of the SI involve a lack of standardization in its administration and subjective scoring procedures.

2. Results of studies using a component analysis approach suggest that hostility is a, if not the, toxic component of the TABP construct as far as its relationship with CHD is concerned.

3. We need to distinguish between reactive–expressive hostility and the experience of hostility (or neurotic hostility). Whereas the former correlates positively with the severity of CAD, the latter correlates

negatively with severity of coronary occlusion, cardiovascular reactivity, and the production of testosterone during challenging tasks. It is suggested that we need to distinguish between state and trait anger as we need to distinguish between state and trait anxiety. Chronically hostile and anxious individuals may become "immunized" or develop compensatory mechanisms to cope with challenge and stress. However, we still need prospective evidence to confirm the hypothesized negative relationship between neuroticism and CHD.

4. Objective, computer-scorable indexes of expressive vocal behavior, specifically, loudness and simultaneous speech, were shown, in replicated findings, to account for as much as 38 percent of the variance in patients' severity of occlusion scores, even in the absence of a significant relationship between SI-derived global Type-A scores and severity of CAD. Vigorous speech was also identified as the SI component that accounts for the positive relationship between the TABP and systolic reactivity in male subjects. These findings are consistent with the proposition that expressive hostility is the toxic factor as far as CHD is concerned, since both of these speech indexes are correlates of expressive hostility. This augurs well for the objective measurement of coronary-prone behavior. Future studies should look for additional objective, vocal, and nonverbal expressive correlates (e.g., facial expressions and body movements) of expressive anger, and thus hopefully further improve the predictability of coronary events.

5. Given the fact that males are more at risk for CHD than females, it is of considerable interest whether a similar gender difference also exists in relation to physiologic reactivity, which presumably is a major mediating mechanism in the behavior–CHD link. A number of studies, including our own, suggest that males are indeed more reactive than females. However, there is also contradictory evidence, and this whole issue needs further investigation.

In our study, males showed not only greater systolic reactivity relative to females but also more rapid recovery rates. Traditionally, researchers have emphasized the role of cardiovascular reactivity in CHD and have ignored the role of recovery rate. However, the relationship between behavior and CHD may in fact be mediated by complex hemodynamic processes involving both reactivity and recovery rates. For example, a very high reactivity level combined with a quick recovery rate may constitute an especially bad combination because of the damaging effect of "shear stress." Other mediating mechanisms – for example, testosterone production – were also discussed.

6. The evidence indicates that the coronary-prone speech style – loud and interruptive speech – is associated with heightened cardiovascular reactivity. It is not unreasonable to speculate about a synergistic interaction between speech style and hostility during angry interactions. Expressive anger is likely to be associated with loud and interruptive speech, which in turn is likely to heighten the speaker's cardiovascular reactivity, which in turn is likely to increase the speaker's anger and "coronary-prone speech style," and so on.

7. The evidence suggests that by getting people to speak softly and slowly, we can reduce their cardiovascular reactivity and feelings of anger, even during angry intereactions. Future research will need to look at the long-range effects of such modifications on people's risk for CHD and essential hypertension.

8. In conclusion, although there may be only a very weak relationship between the TABP, as measured by the SI, and CHD, the evidence is much stronger regarding the expressed anger–CHD link. Future research will need to identify more precisely which dimensions of anger and hostility are related to CHD and the mediating mechanisms that are involved in these relationships.

Notes

1. These other expressive behaviors involve gestures and facial expressions presumably associated with competitiveness, anger, and other components of the TABP. However, because the SI is scored from audio recordings, these nonverbal indexes have been ignored in most subsequent studies.
2. Cardiovascular reactivity is usually measured by obtaining the difference between a person's systolic and diastolic blood pressure and heart rate in a challenging or stressful situation and that person's resting or baseline cardiovascular response. Given the statistical problems associated with difference scores, we partialled out baseline responses by means of multiple regression analyses and partial r's.

References

Arrowood, M., Uhrich, K., Gomillion, C., Popio, K., & Raft, D. (1982). New markers of coronary-prone behavior in a rural population. *Psychosomatic Medicine, 119*, 44–119 (Abstract).

Bateson, G. (1972). *Steps to an ecology of mind.* New York: Ballantine Books.

Bendig, A. W. (1962). The development of a short form of the manifest anxiety scale. *Journal of Consulting Psychology, 20*, 384.

Blumenthal, J. A., Williams, R. B., Kong, Y., Schamberg, S., & Thompson, L.

(1978). Type A behavior and angiographically documented coronary disease. *Circulation, 58,* 634–639.

Bond, R. N., & Feldstein, S. (1982). Acoustical correlates of perception of speech rate: An experimental investigation. *Journal of Psycholinguistic Research, 11,* 539–557.

Brand, R. J., Rosenman, R. H., & Jenkins, C. D. (1978). Comparison of coronary heart disease prediction in the Western Collaborative Group Study using the structured interview and the Jenkins Activity Survey assessments of the coronary-prone Type A behavior pattern. *American Heart Association CVD Epidemiological Newsletter, 24.*

Buck, R. (1987). The psychology of emotion. In J. E. LeDoux & W. Hirst (Eds.), *Mind and brain.* Cambridge: Cambridge University Press.

Buss, A. H., & Durkee, A. (1957). An inventory for assessing different kinds of hostility. *Journal of Consulting Psychology, 21,* 343–348.

Chesney, M. A., Eagleston, J. R., & Rosenman, R. H. (1980). The Type A structured interview: A behavioral assessment in the rough. *Journal of Behavioral Assessment, 2,* 255–272.

Contrada, R. J., & Krantz, D. S. (1988). Stress, reactivity, and Type A behavior: Current status and future directions. *Annals of Behavioral Medicine, 10*(2), 64–70.

Costa, P. T. (1986). Is neuroticism a risk factor for CAD? Is Type A a measure of neuroticism? In T. Schmidt, T. Dembroski, & G. Blumchen (Eds.), *Biological and psychological factors in cardiovascular disease.* New York: Springer-Verlag.

Costa, P. T., & McCrae, R. R. (1985). *Personality assessment in psychosomatic medicine: The value of a trait taxonomy.* Unpublished manuscript, Stress and Coping Section, Gerontology Research Center, N.I.A., Francis Scott Key Medical Center, Baltimore, MD.

Crowne, D. P., & Marlowe, D. (1964). *The approval motive: Studies in evaluative dependence.* New York: Wiley.

Dembroski, T. M., & MacDougall, J. M. (1983). Behavioral and psychophysiological perspectives on coronary-prone behavior. In T. M. Dembroski, T. H. Schmidt, & G. Blumchen (Eds.), *Biobehavioral bases of coronary heart disease.* New York: Karger.

Dembroski, T. M., & MacDougall, J. M. (1985a). Beyond global Type A: Relationships of paralinguistic attributes, hostility, and anger-in to coronary heart disease. In T. Field, P. McCabe, & N. Schneiderman (Eds.), *Stress and coping.* Hillsdale, NJ: Lawrence Erlbaum Associates.

Dembroski, T. M., MacDougall, J. M., Williams, R. B., Haney, T., & Blumenthal, J. (1985b). Components of Type A, hostility and anger-in: Relationship to angiographic findings. *Psychosomatic Medicine, 47,* 219–233.

Dimsdale, J. F., Hackett, T. P., Hutter, A. M. (1979). Type A behavior and angiographic findings. *Journal of Psychosomatic Research, 23,* 273–276.

Ekman, P., Levinson, R. W., & Frieson, W. V. (1983). Autonomic nervous system activity distinguishes between emotions. *Science, 221,* 1208–1210.

Epstein, S. (1984). Controversial issues in emotion theory. *Review of Personality and Social Behavior, 5,* 219–238.

Eysenck, H. J. (1985). Personality, cancer, and cardiovascular disease: A causal analysis. *Journal of Personality and Individual Differences, 6,* 535–556.

Feldstein, S., & Welkowitz, J. (1978). A chronography of conversation: In defense of an objective approach. In A. W. Siegman & S. Feldstein (Eds.), *Nonverbal behavior and communication.* Hillsdale, NJ: Lawrence Erlbaum Associates.

Frank, K. A., Heller, S. S., Kornfeld, D. S., Sporn, A. A., & Weiss, M. B. (1978).

Type A behavior pattern and coronary angiographic findings. *Journal of the American Medical Association, 240*, 761–763.

Frankenhauser, M. (1983). The sympathetic adrenal and pituitary-adrenal response to challenge: Comparison between the sexes. In T. M. Dembroski, T. H. Schmidt, & G. Blumchen (Eds.), *Biobehavioral bases of coronary heart disease.* Basel: Karger.

Friedman, M., Rosenman, R. H., Straus, R., Wurm, M., & Kositchek, R. (1968). The relationship of behavior pattern A to the state of the coronary vasculature: A study of 51 autopsied subjects. *American Journal of Medicine, 44,* 525–549.

Friedman, M., Brown, M. A., & Rosenman, R. H. (1969). Voice analysis test for detection of behavior pattern. *Journal of American Medical Association, 208,* 828–836.

Friedman, M., & Rosenman, R. (1974). *Type A behavior and your heart.* New York: Knopf.

Friedman, E., Thomas, S. A., Kulick-Chiffo, Lynch, J. J., & Suginohara (1982). The effects of normal and rapid speech on blood pressure. *Psychosomatic Medicine, 44,* 545–553.

Gensini, G. G. (1975). *Coronary arteriography.* Mt. Kisco, NY: Future.

Grossarth-Maticek, R., Kanazir, D. T., Schmidt, P., & Velter, H. (1985). Psychosocial and organic variables as predictors of lung cancer, cardiac infarct, and apoplexy: Some differential predictors. *Journal of Personality and Individual Differences, 6,* 313–321.

Haynes, S. G., Feinleib, M., & Kannel, W. B. (1980). The relationship of psychosocial factors to coronary heart disease in the Framingham study: III. Eighth year incidence of coronary heart disease. *American Journal of Epidemiology, 771,* 37–58.

Howland, E. W., & Siegman, A. W. (1982). Toward the automated measurement of the Type-A behavior pattern. *Journal of Behavioral Medicine, 5,* 37–54.

Jaffe, J., & Feldstein, S. (1970). *Rhythms of dialogue.* New York: Academic Press.

Jenkins, C. D., Zyzanski, S. J., & Rosenman, R. H. (1971). Progress toward validation of a computer-scored test for the Type A coronary-prone behavior pattern. *Psychosomatic Medicine, 33,* 198–202.

Kahn, J. A., Kornfeld, D. S., Frank, K. A., Heller, S. S., & Hoar, P. F. (1980). Type-A behavior and blood pressure during coronary bypass surgery. *Psychosomatic Medicine, 42,* 407–414.

Kearns, L. R. (1987). *The role of speech rate and loudness in cardiovascular responsivity.* Master's thesis. Catonsville, MD: Department of Psychology, University of Maryland Baltimore County.

Krantz, D. S., Sanmarco, M. I., Selvester, R. H., & Matthews, K. A. (1979). Psychological correlates of progression of atherosclerosis in men. *Psychosomatic Medicine, 41,* 467–476.

MacDougall, J. M., Dembroski, T. M., Dimsdale, J. E., Hackett, T. P. (1985). Components of Type A, hostility and anger-in: Further relationships to angiographic findings. *Health Psychology, 4,* 137–152.

Matthews, K. A. (1982). Psychological perspectives on the Type A behavior pattern. *Psychological Bulletin, 91,* 293–323.

Matthews, K. A. (1988). *Behavioral antecedents of CHD.* Paper presented at the annual meeting of the American Psychological Association, Atlanta, August 1988.

Matthews, K. A. (1988). CHD and Type A behaviors: Update and alternative to the Booth-Kewley and Friedman quantitative review. *Psychological Bulletin, 104,* 373–380.

Matthews, K. A., Krantz, D. S., Dembroski, T. M., & MacDougall, J. M. (1982). The unique and common variance in the structured interview and the Jenkins Activity Survey measures of the Type A behavior pattern. *Journal of Personality and Social Psychology, 42*, 303–313.

Musante, L., MacDougall, J. M., Dembroski, T. M., & Costa, P. T., Jr. (in press). Potential for hostility and dimensions of anger. *Health Psychology.*

Olweus, D. (1983). Testosterone in the development of aggressive antisocial behavior in adolescents. In K. Van Dusen & S. A. Mednick (Eds.), *Prospective studies of crime and delinquency.* Boston: Klever-Nijhoff.

Olweus, D. (1986). Aggression and hormones. In D. Olweus & J. Block (Eds.), *Development of antisocial and prosocial behavior: Research, theories and issues.* New York: Plenum Press.

Persky, H., Smith, K. D., & Basu, G. K. (1971). Relation of psychological measures of aggression and hostility to testosterone production in men. *Psychosomatic Medicine, 33*, 265–227.

Plutchik, R. (1984). Emotions: A general psychoevolutionary theory. In K. R. Scherer & P. Ekman (Eds.), *Approaches to emotion.* Hillsdale, NJ: Lawrence Erlbaum Associates.

Rice, D. H., Hing, E., Kovar, M. G., & Prager, K. (1984). Sex differences in disease risk. In E. B. Gold (Ed.), *The changing risk of disease in women.* Lexington, MO: Collamon Press.

Rosenman, R. H. (1978). The interview method of assessment of the coronary-prone behavior pattern. In T. Dembroski, S. Weiss, J. Schillar, S. Haynes, & M. Feinlieb (Eds.), *Coronary prone behavior.* New York: Springer–Verlag.

Rosenman, R. H., Friedman, M., Straus, R., Wurm, M., Kositchek, R., Hahn, W., & Wethessen, N. T. (1964). A predictive study of coronary heart disease: The Western Collaborative Group Study. *Journal of the American Medical Association, 189*, 15–22.

Rosenman, R. H., Brand, R. J., Jenkins, C. D., Friedman, M., Straus, R., Wurm, M. (1975). Coronary heart disease in the Western Collaborative Group Study: Final follow-up experience of 8½ years. *Journal of the American Medical Association, 233*, 872–877.

Rosenman, R. H., & Chesney, M. A. (1982). Stress, Type-A behavior and coronary disease. In L. Goldberger & S. Breznitz (Eds.), *Handbook of stress: Theoretical and clinical aspects.* New York: Free Press.

Sarason, I. G. (1961). Intercorrelations among measures of hostility. *Journal of Clinical Psychology, 17*, 192–195.

Scherwitz, L. (1989). Type A behavior assessment in the structured interview: Review, critique and recommendations. In A. W. Siegman & T. M. Dembroski (Eds.), *In search of coronary-prone behavior: Beyond Type A.* Hillsdale, NJ: Lawrence Erlbaum Associates.

Scherwitz, L., Berton, K., & Leventhal, H. (1977). Type A assessment and interaction in the behavior pattern interview. *Psychosomatic Medicine, 39*, 229–240.

Scherwitz, L., McKelvain, R., Laman, C., Patterson, J., Dutton, L., Yusim, S., Lester, J., Kraft, I., Rochelle, D., & Leachman, R. (1983). Type A behavior, self-involvement, and coronary atherosclerosis. *Psychosomatic Medicine, 45*, 47–57.

Shekelle, R. B., Hulley, S., Neaton, J., Billings, J., Borhani, N., Gerace, T., Jacobs, D., Lasser, N., Mittlemark, M., & Stamler, J. (1985). The MRFIT behavior pattern study: II. Type A behavior pattern and incidence of coronary heart disease. *American Journal of Epidemiology, 122*, 559–570.

Shocken, D. D., Worden, T., Greene, A. F., Harrison, E. E., & Spielberger, C.

(1985). Age differences in the relationship between coronary artery disease, anxiety, and anger. *The Gerontologist, 25*, 36.

Siegman, A. W. (1985). Expressive correlates of affective states and traits. In A. W. Siegman & S. Feldstein (Eds.), *Nonverbal behavior: A multichannel perspective*. Hillsdale, NJ: Lawrence Erlbaum Associates.

Siegman, A. W. (1987a). The pacing of speech in depression. In J. D. Maser (Ed.), *Behavioral assessment of depression*. Hillsdale, NJ: Lawrence Erlbaum Associates.

Siegman, A. W. (1987b). The telltale voice. In A. W. Siegman & S. Feldstein (Eds.), *Nonverbal behavior and communication* (2nd ed.). Hillsdale, NJ: Lawrence Erlbaum Associates.

Siegman, A. W., Feldstein, S., Simpson, S. M., Barkley, S., & Kobren, R. (1984). *Content and stress in the interview method for the assessment of Type A behavior*. Paper presented at the annual meeting of the Eastern Psychological Association, Baltimore, April 1984.

Siegman, A. W., & Feldstein, S. (1985). *The relationship of expressive vocal behavior to severity of coronary artery disease*. Symposium paper presented at the Society for Behavioral Medicine meeting, New Orleans, March 1985.

Siegman, A. W., Feldstein, S., & Ringel, N. (1986a). *Type-A behavior and coronary disease*. Paper presented at the annual meeting of the American Psychological Association, Washington, DC.

Siegman, A. W., Feldstein, S., Ringel, N., Tommaso, C., & Salomon, J. (1986b). *Expressive verbal behavior and coronary artery disease: A replication*. Paper presented at the annual meeting of the Society of Behavioral Medicine, San Francisco, March 1986.

Siegman, A. W., Crump, D., Dembroski, T. M., & Gjesdal, J. (1987a). *Speech and cardiovascular reactivity*. Paper presented at the annual meeting of the Society for Behavioral Medicine, Washington, DC.

Siegman, A. W., Dembroski, T. M., & Ringel, N. (1987b). Components of hostility and the severity of coronary artery disease. *Psychosomatic Medicine, 49*, 129–135.

Siegman, A. W., Feldstein, S., & Lating, J. (1987c). *The effects of interviewer style in the structured interview on Type-A behavior pattern scores*. Paper presented at the annual meeting of the Society for Behavioral Medicine, Washington, DC.

Siegman, A. W., Feldstein, S., Tommaso, C., Ringel, N., & Lating, J. (1987d). Expressive vocal behavior and the severity of coronary artery disease. *Psychosomatic Medicine, 49*, 545–561.

Siegman, A. W., & Gjesdal, J. (1987e). *Neurotic hostility and cardiovascular reactivity*. Paper presented at the annual meeting of the Society for Behavioral Medicine, Washington, DC.

Siegman, A. W., Dohm, F. A., & Gjesdal, J. M. (1988a). *Components of hostility and cardiovascular reactivity*. Symposium paper read at the ninth annual meeting of the Society of Behavioral Medicine, Boston, April 27–30, 1988.

Siegman, A. W., Dohm, F. A., Lating, J., & Wilkinson, J. (1988b). *Components of the Type-A behavior pattern, hostility and cardiovascular reactivity: The moderating effects of gender and defensiveness*. Paper presented at the annual meeting of the American Psychological Association, Atlanta.

Siegman, A. W., & Krüger, H. P. (1988c). *Expressive and physiological correlates of anger-arousing communications*. Unpublished manuscript, Catonsville, MD: Department of Pyschology, University of Maryland Baltimore County.

Siegman, A. W., Krüger, H. P., Herbst, J., & Berger, T. (1989). *Angry voices: Physiological and mood correlates*. Unpublished manuscript. Catonsville, MD:

Department of Psychology, University of Maryland, Baltimore County.

Smith, T. W., Follick, M. L., & Korr, K. S. (1984). Anger, neuroticism, Type A behavior and the experience of angina. *British Journal of Medical Psychology*, 57, 249–252.

Spielberger, C. D. (1980). *Preliminary manual for State-Trait Personality Inventory (STPI)*. Tampa, FL: University of South Florida Human Resources Institute.

Stoney, C. M., Matthews, K. A., McDonald, R. H., & Johnson, C. A. (1989). *Are there different types of reactors to stress?* Paper presented at the ninth annual meeting of the Society of Behavioral Medicine, Boston, April, 1988.

Stoney, C. M., Matthews, K. A., McDonald, R. H., & Johnson, C. A. (in press). Sex differences in lipid lipoprotein, cardiovascular and neuroendocrine responses to acute stress. *Psychophysiology*.

Williams, R. B., Jr. (1989). Biological mechanisms mediating the relationship between behavior and coronary heart disease. In A. W. Siegman & T. M. Dembroski (Eds.), *In search of coronary prone behavior: Beyond Type A*. Hillsdale, NJ: Lawrence Erlbaum Associates.

Williams, R. B., Jr., Friedman, M., Glass, D. C., Herd, J. A., & Schneiderman, N. (1978). Section summary: Mechanisms linking behavioral and pathophysiological processes. In T. M. Dembroski, S. M. Weiss, J. L. Shields, S. J. Haynes, & M. Feinlieb (Eds.), *Coronary-prone behavior*. New York: Springer Verlag.

Williams, R. B., Jr., Haney, T. L., Lee, K. L., Kong, Y., Blumenthal, J. A., & Whalen, R. (1980). Type A behavior, hostility, and coronary atherosclerosis. *Psychosomatic Medicine*, 42, 539–542.

Williams, R. B., Jr., Barefoot, J. C., & Shekelle, R. B. (1984). The health consequences of hostility. In M. A. Chesney, R. H. Rosenman, & S. E. Goldstein (Eds.), *Anger, hostility and behavioral medicine*. New York: Hemisphere/McGraw-Hill.

Wingard, D. L., Suarez, L., & Barret-Conner, E. (1983). The sex differential in mortality from all causes and ischemic heart disease. *American Journal of Epidemiology*, 117, 165–172.

Zumoff, B., Rosenfeld, R. S., Friedman, M., Beyers, S. O., Rosenman, R. H., & Hellman, L. (1984). Elevated daytime urinary excretion of testosterone glucuronide in men with Type A behavior pattern. *Psychosomatic Medicine*, 46, 223–225.

10. Two principles of communicative functioning

NORBERT FREEDMAN

The opportunity to contribute to this volume dedicated to the work of Gregory Bateson offers me a chance to revisit my own past. It was in 1947 that I viewed Mead and Bateson's presentation of *Der Hitler Junge Quex* at the American Museum of Natural History in New York. As a German Jew who had recently emigrated to America, I was, of course, well acquainted with the movie and with the turmoil in German society from 1929–1933. However, it was Bateson's commentary that allowed me to reconstruct the roots of Nazism as they can be found, in part, within the German family structure. And, further, as I reflect upon my early professional life, I wonder whether Bateson's incisive analysis affected the direction of my own investigative work. Let me cite some reminiscences.

During the Nazi era in Germany, certain body movements while one was talking were verboten. Obvious body movements or gestures during everyday conversational discourse were considered to be a characteristic of Jews and other "inferior races," whereas motionless speech was considered a mark of the ethnic elite. I recall a ritual in which Jewish boys, when they inadvertently made a clearly visible gesture, could expect punishment in the form of a punch in the stomach delivered by one of their buddies. I, too, was a victim of such punching by my friends, and I have spent a good part of my professional life trying to understand the function and meaning of body movements during discourse.

Today we know that there is no such thing as motionless speech – bodily acts during spoken discourse are a universal phenomenon. However, their function is poorly understood. With the tremendous

This work was supported in part by grant #MH-07336 from the United States Public Health Service.

279

advance during the 1960s in technology for recording behavior, cameras, videotapes, zoom lenses, and monitors became available, making it possible to capture the fleeting observations of motor behavior during discourse on tape so that permanent records could be available. It was at this time that Birdwhistell proposed that it would be feasible to develop a language of kinemes just as linguists had developed a language of phonemes. Coming from an ethnological background, Birdwhistell (1970) was of necessity qualitative and descriptive in his approach. We are attempting to demonstrate that in the motor manifestations that accompany language, there may be found some of the mainsprings of creative thought. It is believed that in the efficacy of the muscular system, there is something more basic than signs or symbols – there are ongoing regulators of cognitive processing that have their roots in earliest infancy but constantly emerge even in the most mature dialogue.

Recorded behavior samples present an infinite range of opportunities for analysis. Nonverbal behavior can be, and indeed has been viewed as, a continuous stream of rhythmic motions – a dance. Yet, such a behavioral stream, while apparently rich in content, offers little basis for conceptually guided study. In order to gain some understanding of functional regularities, we tried various experimental interventions. One of these was an attempt to alter thought organization in selected psychiatric inpatients. The intent was to create conditions that would promote either primary process or secondary process "reality-oriented" thought. A psychiatric patient suffering from a persecutory delusion was selected, and his communicative behavior was observed under two interview conditions: (1) expressive and primary process dominated, and (2) reality focused and secondary process dominated. The patient, Mr. G., was suffering from the delusion that he had been poisoned by a mysterious gas while sitting on a park bench with his girl friend. He felt harassed by an unknown persecutor. He was eager to tell his story, and did so in the expressive phase of the interview. He was then asked to talk about "reality" – the daily activity program on the ward, the food, his fellow patients, and so forth.

The videotaped records emerging from these two conditions presented dramatically different pictures (Freedman & Hoffman, 1967). The differences could be discerned even with the sound turned off. In the primary process portion, Mr. G. looked alive, his hand moving in rhythmic motions with the beat quality of his speech, his head moving in unison, his eye gaze fixed on the interviewer, and his voice volume up. In the reality-focused phase, his gaze was downcast, his speech was monotone, and his head was motionless; both hands engaged in continuous repetitive self-stimulation, sometimes caressing his thighs, and sometimes fingering each other while resting in his lap. Dramatically different communicative organizations were observable on the kinesic and postural, as well as on the vocal and lexical levels. In these organizations, the hands assumed a pivotal part. To describe the actions of the hands as indicators of broad communicative organizations, we introduced the terms object- and body-focused movements. Object-focused movements are movements directed away from the body, rhythmic, sometimes depictive, sometimes emphatic, but always phased in with the beat of speech. Body-focused movements involve continuous touching of the body surface by the hands, and appear unrelated to speech. Whereas object-focused movements are single events, body-focused movements are continuous events. The two patterns of manual activity offered a visible and measurable index for the objective study of kinesic behavior during discourse.

Although for us this had the air of discovery, the phenomena encompassed by object- and body-focused activity had been reported earlier. Krout (1954), presenting his experimental subjects to conflict-producing interview conditions, made a distinction between autistic gestures and communicative gestures; Sainsbury (1958), tracing variations of patients' behavior in the course of psychiatric interviews, made a distinction between expressive behavior and self-manipulatory behavior; Mahl (1968), creating the face-to-face and back-to-back condition (in which patients could neither see the other nor feel they were being seen), distinguished, like Krout, between autistic and communicative gestures. Finally, Ekman and Friesen (1969), in their classification of hand activity, distinguished between illustrators and self-adaptors, a classification that roughly overlaps with certain categories reported here. What holds these distinctions together is behavior indicative of "towardness" and "awayness," which can be noted in any dialogue.

What is at issue is not the phenomenon, but its interpretation. After the first observations of Mr. G, a systematic effort was made to discover and delineate the psychological functions served by the variety of object- and body-focused movements. A motor act may take place in different kinds of psychological space, and it is the "spatial" context that determines its meaning. It is this recognition that the evolution of personal meanings always proceeds through successive patterns through time or contexts that is at the heart of Bateson's work (Bateson, 1980). Thus, as we shall see, a movement may occur in interpersonal space, in personal space, or in linguistic space. In each of these spatial contexts, the understanding of kinesics in communication becomes sharpened, and so does the understanding of the communicative process itself.

10.1. Principles of communicative functioning

Communicative behavior tends to be biphasic not only in states of speaking or listening but also in important fluctuations within phases of speaking. There are moments of expansion marked by reaching, contacting, or representing ideas, and there are phases of contraction, mostly but not necessarily taking place in pauses marked by reflection, planning, or consolidation of thought. It is this biphasic activity of expansion and retrenchment that is visible in the successive or alternating appearance of object- and body-focused movements.

The biphasic organization of communicative behavior can be found in the behavior of organisms interacting with the environment across the phylogenetic spectrum. It was Schneirla (1959) who showed that the biphasic principle is observable in species ranging from paramecia to birds, to primates, and to humans, and constitutes the most fundamental manifestations of that which impels and sustains behavior. According to Schneirla, these motivational aspects of behavior are encompassed by the concepts of approach and withdrawal. Approach refers to any behavior in which the organism reduces the distance between itself and the source of stimulation (the object). Withdrawal refers to behavior in which the organism creates a maximum distance or barrier between itself and the source of stimulation. The principles of approach and withdrawal are adaptive in the sense that a balance between the two guarantees traffic with the environment, and after all, communication is the process by which such traffic is maintained on the symbolic level.

The biphasic organization of communicative behavior becomes reinterpreted when we study the communication of humans. Human communication involves communicative intent and the construction of inner representations that make communication possible. What shifts in the development of organisms are not only the means, the vehicles for transmission, but an increasing reliance upon goal-directed behavior – a shift that Bruner (1969) described as "finding what was intended rather than coming to rest on what is merely encountered" (p. 226). From a cognitive point of view, awayness and towardness become the intention to receive and transmit.

In an interactive model, communication occurs in actual space, but in a cognitive model, communication takes place in the construction of an inner space. Body movements become tools for the maintenance and implementation of these constructions. Three dimensions of spatial constructions have emerged in the course of our work, and these appear to form an essential prerequisite for any human discourse. First, there is the construction of interpersonal space – the awareness of the existence of "me." Second, there is the construction of personal space – the cognitive representation of a self with definable boundaries and of personal objects having an independent existence. Third, there is the construction of linguistic space – the construction and selection of symbols appropriate to the stream of imagery and thought. The relationship between these spatial dimensions is transitive.

Our research had indicated that although bodily acts may be similar in appearance, when viewed in various contexts, their functions shift. In interpersonal space, that function is contact; in personal space, the function entails boundary definition; and in linguistic space, the function of action involves the control of symbols.

Reaching and disengaging

In our early studies on kinesic activity in the clinical setting, we viewed bodily actions in interpersonal space. The biphasic manifestations within this interpersonal space are reaching and disengagement. From this vantage point, bodily activity is a nonverbal statement of a person's communicative intent. We regarded the organization of object-focused behavior as a sign of an intent to reach, and body-focused activity was viewed as a sign of an intent to disengage. It should be recognized that the motions of the body are but an analogue of the basic wish. The wish is literally to touch the other or simply to hide; yet, such a wish is rarely carried out in discourse. Reaching and disengaging are indeed acted out in early child development, and such action sequences become cornerstones in the development of the self. Note the search-and-dodge sequence of the 3-month-old with his mother as described by Beebe and Stern (1977), or the repetitive clinging as the toddler moves in concentric circles, always staying close to his schizophrenic or depressed mother (Bateson, Jackson, Haley, & Washland, 1956). Those are actual enactments of the original intent vis-á-vis the object. Watzlawick, Beavin, and Jackson (1967) have stressed that all nonverbal behavior is governed by the analogic code, according to which the original intent is displayed in the actions of the body. Open legs are an analogue of the wish for openness, banging one's head, an analogue of the wish for self-destruction, and so forth.

The view that object- and body-focused organizations may, on the level of description, constitute an analogue of the wish to reach or disengage was found to be indicative of the communicative patterns of certain pathological states. The polarities of paranoia and depression offer a strategic point to begin our studies concerning the role of kinesic behavior in communication. Paranoia and depression are both states of acute distress, yet the patient's mode of coping with aggressive impulses differs in each condition. Paranoia involves projection; depression involves introjection. On the surface, paranoid patients are concerned with the danger "out there." Patients in a depressed state feel either helpless or hopeless. The object that has injured them is within themselves. They have given up the effort to reach, and they thus create a shield that must not be penetrated.

We compared two small groups of patients, four schizophrenic patients with paranoid (delusional) symptoms, and four nonschizophrenic patients with depressive symptoms. The clinical interviews of all patients were video recorded at the time of intake while they were in an acute clinical state, and a second interview was recorded about 3 months later at the point of clinical remission. The kinesic activity of the patients in the acute state, seen only in 5-minute samples, showed dramatic differences between the two groups. The paranoid patients showed a predominance of object-focused hand activity as they articulated their grievances. These movements were only part of a broader nonverbal communicative structure. The paranoid patients revealed more direct eye-to-eye contact, had an erect posture, and higher vocalization volume. This constellation fits the notion of an intent to reach. In contrast, the depressed patients engaged both their hands simultaneously in continuous self-stimulation, often a stroking of arms and legs. Their gaze was focused downward, and their voice volume lower. This constellation seems to reflect an intent to disengage.

We were thus able to discern structures of kinesic activity reflecting clinical states. The use of a clinical polarity in which two groups were observed before and after treatment afforded an opportunity not only to determine differences in initial clinical states but to trace variations within an individual over time. Thus, in tracing changes in object- and body-focused movements over the 3-months' course of treatment, we noted that paranoid patients still showed a predominant use of object-focused movements, and depressed patients showed a predominant use of body-focused movements. What had shifted, however, was the structure of the kinesic activity. Object-focused movements, which are speech related, became increasingly directed to the word rather than to the object of presence (i.e., they were symbol linked). Body-focused movements became increasingly circumscribed and patterned. These initial observations of clinical change led us to define stages or levels of object- and body-focused activity.

A coding system was developed that discriminated levels of object- and body-focused activity (Freedman, 1972). The quality of object-focused movements can be further defined by the relationship of the gesture to speech. The movements may substitute for the verbal utterance, they may supplement what is being verbalized, or they may be subordinate to the verbal message. Three levels of object-focused movements were identified on the basis of their level of integration with the verbal message: (1) *speech primacy movements,* the rhythmic and emphatic gestures having no content or depictive qualities, movements that are subordinate to speech; (2) *representational movements,* also rhythmic movements, but depicting, in content, some unverbalized aspect of the verbal message, movements that serve a supplementing function: and (3) *nonrepresentational movements,* a category at that time defined as movements involving the concretization of feelings or major qualifiers, in which the gestures bear little evident relationship to speech, movements that serve a substitutive function. It was also possible to discriminate levels of body-focused activity. Since body-focused movements are manifestly unrelated to speech, we looked at the morphology and structure of the movements, their directness, and the extent to which they are patterned – for example, whether hands explicitly are used as agents upon the body as object. (Another important parameter, namely, laterality of self-touching, was not yet discovered at that time, and will be discussed later.) Three levels of self-touching were identified: (1) *finger–hand movements,* the touching of one hand upon the other or one hand upon itself, essentially unpatterned and continuous; (2) *continuous body touching,* one or both hands acting upon a specific body part (continuous, lasting more than 3 seconds), legs, arms, cheek, neck, or extensions of the body, such as necklace, tie, shoe; and (3) *discrete body touching,* either direct or indirect body touching, but having a specific instrumental quality such as relieving an itch or closing a button. These movements were time limited in nature, lasting 3 seconds or less.

Over the course of 3 months of treatment, systematic changes in the structure of object-focused movements were observed in the paranoid patients. Initially, object-focused activity was predominantly nonrepresentational or representational in nature. That is, motor action was relatively autonomous from speech. Object-focused movements seemed to reflect a wish to reach, expressed by an analogic code. With clinical improvement, nonrepresentational movements almost disappeared, representational movements declined, and speech primacy movements predominated. Motor action was closely phased in with the symbolizing process. Among the depressed patients, we observed a transition with clinical improvement. During the acute state, self-touching involved continuous and massive stroking of major areas of the body surface. The effort to create a barrier between self and object may be taken as a sign of an intent to disengage. With improvement, movements became indirect, discrete, and circumscribed. They also appeared to have an instrumental quality that no longer suggested a total disengagement from the surround. The possibility was suggested that self-touching may entail not just a shielding from the enviroment but a transitory retrenchment, a preparation for possible engagement. The classifications of object- and body-focused movements in terms of levels of organization became a framework for our subsequent studies.

The discovery that with a change of internal state there also occurs a shift in the structure of movements has major implications. With object-focused movements, the shift is in the direction of focus – from an object of presence to an object of representation. The movement becomes subservient to a symbol rather than to a person. This transformation means that the speaker must have a representation of someone out there who understands him or her. Movements thus become involved in representing as well as in reaching. With body-focused movements, the increasingly more functional use of self-stimulation with clinical improvement suggests that a shift occurs from total disengagement to a protective maneuver involving some segment of body or self. This would indicate that the description of the kinesic organization, as an analogue of the intent to reach or disengage, is an incomplete one.

This sort of observation has underscored the limitations of viewing, as many writers have, all nonverbal behavior as serving the analogic code. The overwhelming majority of movements, little wiggles and touches, are not depictive in nature, and become increasingly phased in with the symbolizing effort. Many movements, as Dittmann (1971) has noted in his critique of Birdwhistell's work, do not fit the criterion of a code. They are continuous in nature, and are not marked by a clearly definable onset and termination. And, finally, the absolute dichotomy between digital–verbal and analogic–nonverbal codes does not seem to hold. Rather, as we have seen, there is a gradual transition in which one becomes increasingly coordinated and subordinated to the other. The most palpable demonstration of the relevant independence of object-focused movements from the immediate presence of the other was provided by both Mahl's (1968) and Hoffman's (1968) studies. When subjects were seated back to back, when they could neither see the other nor feel they were being seen, object-focused movements still persisted. These movements appear to be better conceptualized in part as processes that sustain an inner cognitive activity. It is this information-processing interpretation of kinesics in communication that marked the next phase of our research efforts.

Regulating self and object representations

In the construction of personal space, the biphasic principle is concerned with the maintenance of self versus object representations. We recognized early that an inner representation of a sense of self is a psychological structure that creates barriers and a kind of distance that is essential for communciation. An inner representation of the self is a psychological structure that makes approach behavior and sharing possible. In the context of this reinterpretation of communicative behavior, limb actions constitute a continual reaffirmation and nourishment of these inner representations.

Freud noted in his "Formulations on the Two Principles of Mental Functioning" (1911) that it is in the efficacy of the muscular system that we can distinguish between an "inside" and an "outside." It is in the efficacy of motor actions that we can also sustain the self and object representations. Thus, body-focused activity may be regarded not only as disengagement behavior but as a transitory protective maneuver acting to fortify the boundaries between self and nonself. Object-focused movements may be concerned not only with reaching but with confirming representations in the object world.

We employed the "method of individual differences" to make inferences about the regulating mechanism implied by this view of kinesic behavior. We first contrasted field-dependent (F-D) and field-independent (F-I) normal subjects who could be presumed to manifest clear differences in their organization of self and object representations. We then returned to observations of psychopathology, comparing clinical groups for whom similar types of assumptions could be made. The behavior of individuals engaged in discourse can be regarded as a prism reflecting a beam of light. If their motor activity reflected the kind of organization we would associate with a given self or object representation, then our ideas concerning the function of motor action would seem to be supported.

Observations on the dimension of field dependence–independence. Several successive studies were conducted in which F-I and F-D individuals were engaged in monologue and dialogue and their kinesic behavior was video recorded (Freedman, O'Hanlon, Oltman, & Witkin, 1972; Sousa-Posa, 1974). In each study, care was taken to control such variables as ethnic background, sex, socioeconomic status, and the social demand characteristics of the interview situation. Thus, any differences that emerged could then be traced to the individual's capacity for processing information. All studies revealed differences traceable to cognitive style. Motor activity is clearly a part of cognitive processing. Our goal, however, was a more ambitious one; namely, to show how different levels of object- and body-focused activity may play a role in the establishment of self-representations and object representations.

In introducing these studies in 1972, we advanced the following rationale:

> The hypothesis that kinesic expression is related to an individual's level of psychological differentiation derives directly from our conception of motility during speech. From the moment we grant that movements are not just discharge acts but part of the symbolizing process, questions regarding individual differences in the capacity to symbolize and represent arise. If, as Werner and Kaplan (1967) suggested, the process of representing follows the development of the differentiation of the self from the external world, then it may be that individual differences in the style of representing are related to the dimension of psychological differentiation as developed by Witkin et al. (1962), which includes as one of its core concepts the sense of separate identity. An estimate of an individual's capacity for symbol formation is provided by the perceptual manifestation of psychological differentiation, that is, the variable of field dependence. (pp. 239–258)

Field independence is an attribute of a person's ability to create experiences of segregation and separateness. There is a large body of data to indicate that the F-I person, in contrast to the F-D individual, has more articulated body boundaries (Witkin, Dyk, Faterson, & Karp, 1962), employs more elaborate mechanisms of defense, and has a more clearly defined sense of self-esteem (Witkin & Goodenough, 1976). This literature demonstrates a direct bearing on the field-independence dimension of an individual's capacity to engage in an interchange. In spite of its emphasis on sharing, all discourse requires the selective capacity for distancing. Body-focused movements are one mechanism by which such distancing is achieved. The question, then, was whether, under communicative stress, an F-I individual in contrast to an F-D individual is able to achieve an adaptive form of separating, while simultaneously allowing the maintenance of the reciprocal flow of information.

The role of self-stimulation in the establishment of adaptive self-boundaries was shown in two experimental studies. In one study, we induced withdrawal behavior by confronting the subjects (volunteer college students) with a cold and rejecting interviewer who asked them to talk about a personally meaningful experience without his interruption. This interviewer appeared disinterested and, at times, even hostile. (A contrasting condition was with a warm and receptive interviewer who gave the same instructions. This condition was designed to create approach behavior.) The subjects all complied superficially by giving their verbal associations, yet their wish to withdraw was evident in various forms of body-focused activity and postural adjustments regardless of cognitive style. The organization of bodily activity of F-D and F-I subjects was dramatically different in the face of a cold and rejecting interviewer. The F-D subject engaged in continuous finger–hand motions, which, as will be recalled, are stereotyped, unpatterned motions of finger upon finger or hand upon hand, with hands often held at the midpoint. The subject dutifully delivered an essay, but the very repetitive and arhythmic act by which hand movements were unrelated to the verbal flow suggested that the bodily adjustment was split off, and thus disengaged from the symbolizing process. The subject was clearly unable to establish a sense of separateness from the interviewer's demands, and the bodily organization portrayed this. The F-I subjects, in contrast, revealed more differentiated levels of self-stimulation, both continuous and discrete forms of body-focused activity. Discrete body touching is similar in its structure to continuous body touching, but as will be recalled, is time limited in nature to 3 seconds or less and has an instrumental quality.

What is most significant is the condition created by the communicative context, which gives rise to the use of such patterned self-stimulation. Looking at the data from subjects with the cold and

rejecting interviewer in comparison with that from subjects encounter-
ing a warm and accepting interviewer, we saw that it was specifically the
F-I subjects who employed discrete body touching in the face of the
rejecting interviewer. Thus, it is the selective use of patterned self-
stimulation during an associative monologue that suggests that kinesics
become a kind of regulatory emergency maneuver to protect the integrity of the associative process under stress.

The field-dependence dimension also suggested hypotheses concerning the role of object-focused activity in the establishment of object
representations. In the second phase of the study, the warm interview
condition, which was expected to elicit approach behavior as mentioned, the subjects in the communicative setting were confronted with
a friendly and supportive interviewer who gave the same instructions as
before. In such a supportive context, the physical as well as the psychic
distance between the participants was reduced; that is, the warm interviewer tended to lean forward and nodded in synchrony with the
subject's articulation. Object-focused movements were prevalent in both
cognitive style groups, but the question posed was whether such activity involved motor or speech primacy movements. However, the expected predominance of speech primacy movements in the F-I subjects
did not materialize. We concluded from these data that although a low
level of differentiation clearly indicates a difficulty in establishing object
representations, a high level of differentiation does not necessarily indicate the attainment of such representations. This suggests that giv-
en a high level of differentiation, a large repertoire of choices is available for the attainment of object representation. Which of these choices
subjects implement depends on factors other than their cognitive
style.

These studies, using the dimension of field independence as a method
for understanding the role of movement behavior in discourse, have
firmly established that kinesics are linked to the information-processing
capacities of the speaker. In all these studies, replicable differences
emerged between F-I and F-D subjects. These studies have also shown
that under conditions of communicative stress, self-stimulation may be
used as a strategy to create more clearly defined adaptive boundaries.
Yet, the role of object-focused movements for establishing object representations and hence the capacity for a more sensitive dialogue was left
unsettled.

Observations of psychopathology. It has been our research strategy to start
with clinical observations as a method for generating hypotheses, to test

these hypotheses in experimental studies, and then to return with the knowledge gained to clinical observations to enhance our understanding of the clinical process. The syndromes of paranoia and depression provided us with a contrast in our first clinical observations. In subsequent comparisons, we contrasted the depressive syndrome with that of chronic schizophrenia, and in yet another study, a comparison was made between two groups of schizophrenic outpatients – isolated and belligerent. In each case, the clinical condition was used as an accident of nature, and constituted a paradigmatic comparison to highlight our understanding of the role of kinesics in communication. Grand, Freedman, and Steingart (1973) in a study of the representation of objects in schizophrenia, compared two groups of schizophrenic outpatients who clearly differed in their social competence. Isolated nonbelligerent chronic patients were compared with nonisolated and more belligerent chronic patients. The comparison afforded a contrast of individuals different in their object relationships, and afforded an opportunity to evaluate how such manifest behavioral differences may be reflected in the organization of communicative behavior.

In regard to self-stimulation, the isolated patient was observed to engage in continuous unpatterned finger–hand motions often lasting throughout the entire interview segment. In view of the continuous and arhythmic quality of the movements, motor discharge was truly split off from the linguistic representational function. This is a pattern that we have already noted in F-D subjects, but there it was elicited under conditions of communicative stress (cold interview). In the isolated patients, it emerged even with communicative support. The difficulty seems to stem not from social withdrawal per se, but from an internal deficit in the representational process. The nonisolated belligerent patients (such as the F-I subjects) used significantly more discrete body touching and patterned, lateralized, and instrumental self-stimulation. In line with the earlier discussion on field independence, we might say that the social competence of the two groups of schizophrenic patients was rooted in more or less clearly defined self-boundaries.

Did such self-definition necessarily imply more internalized object representations leading to a more sensitive awareness of the object world? Here the findings concerning object-focused movements were again tenuous. Although representational object-focused movements tended to be greater among the nonisolated aggressive patients, this finding did not reach significance. The kinesic manifestation of object representations as a condition for sensitive dialogue was left to be demonstrated.

In summary, when F-I subjects create a transitory tactile barrier between themselves and their interlocutor, or when schizophrenic patients treat their bodies as injured yet cohesive objects, they are maintaining their personal integrity or separateness when threatened by fusion. This need to draw a line of demarcation, which is essential to all discourse, was poetically stated by William James (1890):

> One great splitting of the whole universe into two halves is made by each of us; and for each of us almost all of the interest attaches to one of the halves; but we all draw the line of division between them in a different place. When I say that we all call the two halves by the same names, and that those names are "me" and "not-me" respectively, it will at once be seen what I mean. The altogether unique kind of interest which each human mind feels in those parts of creation which it can call me or mine may be a moral riddle, but it is a fundamental psychological fact. (p. 289)

Whereas body-focused movements have been clearly implicated in the establishment of self-boundaries, object-focused movements, in the data represented, have not been clearly linked to object representation. Measures of cognitive style, as we have noted, reflect the potential for cognitive processing; measures of language are indicative of the effort delivered in the here and now. It is this recognition that led to the third phase of our research program: kinesics and language.

Linguistic representation and the regulation of attention

In the next phase of research, bodily activity was viewed in linguistic space. Linguistic space, of course, is cognitive space as well, but it refers to those aspects of cognition that deal with shared symbolic thought, and hence with the verbal delivery of ideas. In studies of cognitive style, it was possible to link body movements to the cognitive structure of a person. In studies on language, it becomes possible to link movement to the process of unfolding thought, the moment-to-moment fluctuations in the verbal representation of experiences. Such moment-to-moment fluctuation affords a glimpse of bodily activity as information-processing activity prior to or during linguistic encoding. The linking of movement to language constituted another step in our understanding of movement in communicative thought. Motor activity that at first was seen to signify the nonverbal expression of a wish, now became a catalyst in the verbalization process. Nonverbal behavior becomes a part of verbalization behavior.

The biphasic principle governing linguistic space is that of symbolizing and attention filtering. These are two fundamental processes that a speaker must utilize in any dialogue. Symbolizing – that is, the transformation of image into word – is the central task of communication and may be regarded as the communicative act proper.[1] It is approach behavior by symbolic means. It assumes that there is an image or idea in focus that must be converted into shareable thought, and thus deals with the delivery aspect of communication. However, before such representing can take place, before an image is ready to be encoded, an entire series of relatively peripheral cognitive processes are called upon that bring the image into focus. This is the process of attention filtering. The production of an idea requires work before it can be shared, work that takes place either during listening or during pausing. It is during the silent moments of speech that we are most likely to call up relevant images or thoughts from memory, that we establish priorities of relevance, and that we buttress our incipient ideas against intrusion from within or from without. The work of symbolizing appears to be facilitated by object-focused activity; the work of attention filtering by various patterns of self-stimulation.

Testing of the foregoing formulations would not be possible without recent technologial advances in the audio and video recording of behavior. From audiotapes and videotapes, we can glean a sample of spontaneous speech and a record of the stream of ongoing motor activity. Even though this method has become commonplace, it is worthwhile to view its development in a historical perspective. It was Bateson, in collaboration with Margaret Mead, who pioneered the annotated analysis of film segments in the study of Balinese character (Bateson & Mead, 1942). On the transcript of such spoken language, we can superimpose kinesic events that determine where the movement precedes, occurs with, or follows an utterance.

We chose two approaches, each appropriate to our major hypotheses: the method of content analysis, using Gottschalk, Winget, and Gleser's (1969) scoring system and the method of language construction developed by Steingart and Freedman (1975). In the study of language construction, we chose a grammatical unit, the clause within a sentence. For the study of meaningfulness of language output, we used Gottschalk's method of unit analysis. Gottschalk relies upon continuous 5-minute speech samples, and then selects major content themes (e.g., hostility, anxiety) as scorable units. Rather interestingly, for both approaches, the unit tends to comprise about five words, the number of words that can be uttered comfortably between breaths.

The subjects were female volunteer college students who were asked to talk to a psychiatrist who wanted to inquire about their current interests. The scale used was that of hostility. However, what was evaluated was not whether the subjects were hostile or not hostile, but rather how well they were able to articulate the hostile promptings – whether the hostility was direct and overt, indirect and covert, or ambivalent. That is, assuming the subject experienced hostile promptings, how adequately were these represented in language?

The findings established fairly systematic relationships between the kinds of object-focused movements used and the explicitness of the verbal message. With one exception, there was no relationship between body-focused activity and language content, and indeed, we did not expect such findings. There was an ordinal and predictable relationship between explicitness of hostility and the quality of speech-integrated movements. When motor activity showed a primary rhythmic integration with speech, the intended representation appeared in explicit verbal form. The more the motor activity was depictive and arhythmic, the less strong was its relation the verbalization. It would appear that it is specifically the rhythmic and beatlike component in object-focused movements that makes the greatest contribution to the verbal transmission of thought.

The most general conclusions from these data indicate that object-focused movements bear a systematic relationship to the more or less adequate encoding of verbal content. The relationship is particularly intimate for rhythmic speech primacy movements in which activity is closely phased in with speech rhythm.

The method of language construction developed by Steingart and Freedman (1975) sought to derive a language score that reflected formal organizational rather than content aspects of speech. The flow of linguistic utterances was divided into sentence units, and each sentence was, in turn, classified as either fragmented, narrative, specified narrative, complex portrayal, or complex conditional.

The relationship between these forms of language construction and kinesic activity was explored by casting an increasingly fine net. The grossest discrimination was obtained by a factor analysis based on correlations between a person's language and movement scores during 5 minutes of speech.

Three major factors were extracted: Factor 1, termed object-focused movement–speech productivity, failed to bring out any essential connection between levels of object-focused movements and complexity of language construction. Factor 2, labeled continuous body touching–

narrative construction, revealed a positive link between continuous body touching and this particular form of language. Factor 3, labeled discrete body touching–complex conditional construction, also emphasizes the potentially facilitating role of certain classes of self-stimulation in language construction. The largest loading in factor 3 was traceable to scores in complex conditional construction, and the largest loading of any of the kinesic behavior variables is traceable to discrete body touching. Discrete body touching, the most internalized form of tension regulation, seems then to be part of a process that facilitates the encoding of the most complex (i.e., conditional) language forms.

The validity of factors 2 and 3 was then checked by peak–trough and sequence analysis. A peak–trough analysis revealed that for any of the individuals studied, a peaking of continuous body touching was accompanied by an upsurge of narrative language forms and especially a more elaborate average words per sentence (AWS) count of language, whereas during trough periods of motor activity, word selection was more barren. Similarly, a peak–trough analysis concerning discrete forms of self-touching indicated that in periods of peak activity, there was greater word selection in complex conditional clauses, whereas during trough periods, language became more sparse. Finally, we studied the localization of movement–language sequences. Here, we discovered an envelope: Discrete body touching tended to precede the onset of the language unit and an object-focused movement terminated the verbal utterance. There appear to be truly rhythmic sequences in which the verbal clause, usually a complex conditional one, is enveloped by a discrete touch prior to verbal onset and an object-focused movement at its terminal juncture. Such a patterned and rhythmic deployment of self-stimulation is consistent with the hypothesis that prior to actual representation, there must occur a process of selection and sorting, and certain forms of body-focused activity appear to have an instrumental role in this process. It may be added that when we examined pause–clause sequences without considering movements, it was not possible to link pausing with quality of language.

The self-stimulation–attention hypothesis was given an important boost by concurrent work on communication in schizophrenia conducted by Grand, Freedman, Steingart, and Buchwald (1975). It has been part of the pattern of our investigation to create a continuing feedback loop between observations on normal subjects in experimental situations and studies of clinical states. Grand et al. (1975) reexamined the data from the isolated and nonisolated schizophrenic patients mentioned earlier, but now they attempted to interpret the significance of the movement behavior from the vantage point of an attention–arousal hypothesis. A systematic relationship between the different forms of self-stimulation and formal aspects of language was also observed. The isolated schizophrenic outpatients had not only continuous bilateral finger–hand motions, but their language production revealed a saliency of relatively barren and restricted narrative. In contrast, the nonisolated and more belligerent patients used discrete forms of self-stimulation embedded in complex conditional language. A body of literature has emerged concerning the central information-processing deficit in schizophrenia. The interpretation of our kinesic–linguistic observations in the light of recent knowledge casts the meaning of the communication phenomena observed here into a new perspective. If self-stimulation is a manifestation of arousal, which in turn affects levels of attention, then we have a new vantage point for understanding the potential regulatory role of kinesics in attention.

The observation in schizophrenia together with the earlier observations of language construction not only provides a psychological interpretation of the role of self-stimulation in attention regulation, but suggests a mediating physiological mechanism as well. In the language construction studies, we speculated that patterns of self-stimulation may direct the breadth of attention deployment, and hence affect the organization of language units. From the studies on schizophrenia, we would surmise that the attentional shifts take place precisely because they also involve shifts in levels of physiological arousal. Here, we turn to the principle of transitionality as a guide to the understanding of motor phenomena. At one moment they may be discharge phenomena reflecting a reduction of tension, yet at other moments, they may also be regulatory phenomena that modulate arousal and facilitate the adaptively effective construction of thought. In either case, these observations provide us with provisional support for the attention-regulating role of body-focused activity. The very common phenomena of stroking cheeks, hair, arms, or legs while talking, appear to have an intrinsic feedback function necessary for the organization or form of communicated thought.

We have now established two organizations of communicative behavior manifest by motor activity. The two forms of kinesic acts appear to play a different role in the production of linguistic planning. Object-focused movements may be said to have a role in semantic encoding, and body-focused activity in those aspects of language construction having to do with syntax formation.[2]

We can now return to the video recording of Mr. G., but with a new interpretive perspective. His use of object-focused movements during the time he related his delusional experiences was a reflection of the close and nonconflicted connection between his private image and his verbal utterance. His single-minded purpose allowed no interference to enter consciousness; his thoughts were there ready to be encoded. The only task was to find an optimal "fit" between image and word, and object-focused movements facilitated this task. His body-focused activity during the reality-oriented phase of his interview reflected the continual attentional struggle to suppress the interfering impact of his delusional images. The requirement to focus on reality, made difficult by his being constantly subjected to interference from internal delusional images, required the regulatory support of self-stimulating activity (reinforced by a corresponding heightening of physiological arousal) that could shield the adaptive task from his delusional and powerfully intrusive thought process.

Conclusion

The studies reviewed have depicted a network of empirical relationships reflecting two basic communicative structures. Yet, if we take literally the notion that object- and body-focused movements constitute a motivational force that lends cohesiveness to these structures, then we are led to two regulatory principles. The first is the principle of *rhythmic motor actions* in the establishment of representation. This principle holds that rhythmic bodily activity (involving various body parts) is an essential building block in shared communicative thought. The activity derives this special function by virtue of its role in the image-to-symbol link, and by virtue of its directionality, reducing the distance between self and object. The second is the principle of repetitive tactile self-stimulation as a condition for information filtering. This principle holds that if attention filtering is a requirement for effective discourse, then various forms of patterned self-stimulation function as regulatory strategies creating conditions of optimal innervation. Both principles suggest that body movements function as kinesic strategies regulating the cognitive apparatus during ongoing communication.

The two principles of communicative functioning do not operate in isolation, but rather in close coordination with one another. Only under conditions of extreme pathology or stress would we note a total absence of representing activity or information-filtering activity. Optimal functioning requires an integration of the two principles. We thus tend to look for oscillation and rhythmic alternations occurring in the sequence of any communicative flow. It is these patterns of oscillation and their disruption that become very evident in various communicative settings: talking, listening, normal discourse, psychopathology, and sensory deficit.

The human being's possession of a pair of adaptable hands equipped with a rich reservoir of sensory and motor innervation, is a prized evolutionary asset (Stone, 1961). From the point of view of the ability to communicate, the hands are probably rivaled only by the vocal apparatus. The variegated use to which manual activity is put is suggested by the range of functions outlined in this paper.

The basic motivational mechanism, that of approach and withdrawal, cuts across all levels of observations. What changes is the object of focus. Thus, the simple approach reaction of the lower organisms evolved into an intent to reach the person of presence, to confirm the inner object representations, and finally, to represent by arbitrary symbols. Similarly, the mechanism of withdrawal became an intent toward disengagement, a wish to maintain boundaries between self and nonself, and finally, the filtering out of intrusive or disruptive ideas. The earlier functions have not become irrelevant; the later ones simply became grafted onto earlier ones. However, the impelling motivational force, implicit in the earliest approach and withdrawal reactions, remains throughout life. It is in this way that object- and body-focused activity, as a manifestation of motivational activity, provides continuing cohesiveness to ongoing discourse.

Acknowledgment

I would like to express my appreciation for the valuable and creative work by Mrs. Caroline Apolito in the preparation of this manuscript.

Notes

1. In Bateson's terms, the image to be encoded has the status of a thinglike property. For him, I believe, the process of transformation entails a synonymous language. We have generally thought of these preparatory steps in transformation as precursors, since they precede the "thing" in time. The logical status of precursors is beyond the scope of this contribution (Bateson, 1980).
2. For an experimental application of these hypotheses, see Bucci and Freedman (1978) and Barroso, Freedman, Grand, and Van Meel (1978).

References

Barroso, F., Freedman, N., Grand, S., & Van Meel, J. (1978). Evocation of two types of hand movements in information processing. *Journal of Experimental Psychology: Human Perception and Performance, 4,* 321–329.

Bateson, G. (1980). *Mind and nature: A necessary unity.* New York: Bantam Books.

Bateson, G., & Mead, M. (1942). *Balinese character: A photographic analysis.* Special Publication of New York Academy of Sciences.

Bateson, G., Jackson, D., Haley, J., & Washland, J. (1956). Toward a theory of schizophrenia. *Behavioral Science, 1,* 251–264.

Beebe, B., & Stern, D. N. (1977). Engagement-disengagement and early object experiences. In N. Freedman & S. Grand (Eds.), *Communicative structures and psychic structures.* New York: Plenum.

Birdwhistell, R. (1970). *Kinesics and context.* Philadelphia: University of Pennsylvania Press.

Bruner, J. S. (1969). Eye, hand, and mind. In D. Elkind & J. H. Flavell (Eds.), *Studies in cognitive development.* New York: Oxford University Press.

Bucci, W., & Freedman, N. (1978). Language and hand: The dimension of referential competence. *Journal of Personality, 46,* 594–622.

Dittman, A. (1971). Review of R. Birdwhistell, Kinesics and context. *Psychiatry, 34,* 334–342.

Ekman, P., & Friesen, W. (1969). The repertoire of nonverbal behavior: Categories, origins, usage, and coding. *Semiotica, 1,* 49–98.

Freedman, N. (1972). The analysis of movement behavior during the clinical interview. In A. W. Siegman & B. Pope (Eds.), *Studies in dyadic communication.* New York: Pergamon Press.

Freedman, N., & Hoffman, S. P. (1967). Kinetic behavior in altered clinical states: An approach to the objective analysis of motor behavior during clinical interviews. *Perceptual and Motor Skills, 24,* 525–539.

Freedman, N., O'Hanlon, J., Oltman, P., & Witkin, H. A. (1972). The imprint of psychological differentiation on kinetic behavior in varying communicative contexts. *Journal of Abnormal Psychology, 79,* 239–258.

Freud, S. (1911). Formulations on the two principles of mental functioning. *Standard edition* (Vol. 12, pp. 218–226). London: Hogarth Press, 1958.

Gottschalk, L., Winget, C., & Gleser, C. (1969). *Manual of instructions for using the Gottschalk-Gleser Content Analysis Scales: Anxiety, hostility, social alienation–personal disorganization.* Berkeley: University of California Press.

Grand, S., Freedman, N., & Steingart, I. (1973). A study of the representation of objects in schizophrenia. *Journal of the American Psychoanalytic Association, 21,* 399–434.

Grand, S., Freedman, N., Steingart, I., & Buchwald, C. (1975). Communicative behavior in schizophrenia. The relation of adaptive styles to kinetic and linguistic aspects of interview behavior. *Journal of Nervous and Mental Disease, 161*(5), 293–306.

Hoffman, S. P. (1968). *An empirical study of representational hand movements* (doctoral dissertation, New York University). Ann Arbor, MI: University Microfilms, no. 69-7960.

James, W. (1890). *The principles of psychology* (Vol. 1). New York: Dover Publications, 1950.

Krout, M. H. (1954). An experimental attempt to produce unconscious manual symbolic movements. *Journal of General Psychology, 51,* 94–120.

Mahl, G. F. (1968). Gestures and body movements in interviews. In J. Shlien

(Ed.), *Research in psychotherapy* (Vol. 3). Washington, DC: American Psychological Association.

Sainsbury, P. (1958). Gestural movement during psychiatric interview. *Psychosomatic Medicine, 17,* 458–469.

Schneirla, T. C. (1959). An evolutionary and developmental theory of bi-phasic processes underlying approach and withdrawal. In M. R. Jones (Ed.), *Nebraska Symposium on Motivation* (Vol. 7, pp. 1–42). Lincoln: University of Nebraska Press.

Sousa-Poza, J. F. (1974). *Effects of different communicative tasks and cognitive style on verbal and kinesic behavior.* Unpublished doctoral dissertation, State University of New York, Downstate Medical Center.

Steingart, I., & Freedman, N. (1975). The organization of body-focused kinesic behavior and language construction in schizophrenic and depressed states. *Psychoanalysis and Contemporary Science.* New York: International Universities Press, 4, 423–450.

Stone, L. (1961). *The psychoanalytic situation.* New York: International Universities Press.

Watzlawick, P., Beavin, J., & Jackson, D. (1967). *Pragmatics of human communication.* New York: Norton.

Werner, H., & Kaplan, B. (1967). *Symbol Formation.* New York: Wiley.

Witkin, H. A., Dyk, R. B., Faterson, H. F., & Karp, S. A. (1962). *Psychological differentiation.* New York: Wiley.

Witkin, H. A., & Goodenough, D. R. (1976). *Field dependency revisited.* Educational Testing Service, Princeton, New Jersey, Research Bulletin.

IV. Dialogues and dialectics

11. Gregory Bateson (1904–1980) and Oscar Wilde (1854–1900): A heavenly discourse

PETER OSTWALD

A singular expression of Gregory Bateson's genius was what he called his "metalogues," imaginary conversations about some problematic subject. His seven metalogues, appearing in *Steps to an Ecology of Mind* (1972), are pithy arguments between a father and a daughter. Each deals with a special problem in communication.

The "heavenly discourse" presented here is considerably longer than a metalogue, and its protagonists go into much greater depth along the lines of family dynamics and personality structure. Moreover, Bateson no longer interacts with a child. Here he matches imaginary wits with Oscar Wilde, one of the most brilliant and provocative raconteurs of the Victorian era. Wilde not only shares with Bateson an interest in metaphorical and paradoxical thinking but also discloses having had some of the same problems that Bateson attempted to resolve through his concept of the double bind (Kavka, 1975). Both men wrestled with ambiguities inherent in the social definition of crime, deviance, and disease.

Although they were separated by half a century, Wilde and Bateson may be compared for the intellectual stimulation they gave at times of very rapid social change. Many of the attitudes and values regarding human behavior that they challenged have subsequently undergone serious reexamination. For example, medical destigmatization of what used to be considered sexual perversion owes a great deal to Oscar Wilde's philosophy (Bayer, 1980). Similarly, today's furor over changing concepts of legal insanity would be inconceivable without the pioneering work of Gregory Bateson (Insanity Defense Work Group, 1983). Let us eavesdrop on these extraordinary men.

BATESON: Now that we are finally in the same place, I can listen to that wonderful voice of yours, which has been described as uniquely "warm," "full," "mossy," and "caressing" [Pearson, 1954, p. 205].

WILDE: How kind of you to say so. Men of genius like the two of us are seldom appreciated for the things that truly make a difference.

BATESON: It's a great pity, Oscar, that your voice was never recorded – we might have been able to analyze it scientifically.

WILDE: Oh, it was actually, on an early Edison cylinder. But you know how I abhor science. Nevertheless, I must admit that it was my voice that led to so much success, as well as my notoriety. A friend of mine thought I sounded like "pure cello," and my biographer Hesketh Pearson wrote that I made "exquisite music" whenever I spoke, like "a musician on his instrument, conscious of its range, commanding its scale, causing it to sing, to linger, to rise and fall, with never a false note struck, all in perfect harmony with the spoken words. Thus [I] could make the slightest story sound delightful, and those who had heard [me] speak a parable found it cold and lifeless when they read it in print" [p. 205].

BATESON: What a remarkable confirmation of my belief that we do most of our communicating in personal relationships with paralinguistic and kinesic signals [Bateson, 1972, p. 370]. In your written work, Oscar, you don't come across as a real person at all.

WILDE: Thank you for saying so, Gregory. It was always my intention to disguise myself as completely as possible through my art. I hate realism in literature. "One's real life is so often the life that one does not lead."

BATESON: That is one or your famous epigrams. Paradoxical statements of this kind illustrate my theory of the double bind perfectly.

WILDE: Then you would be able to understand why people often found it was so difficult to catch my meaning. When I told the truth they thought I was lying, and when I lied they believed in what I said.

BATESON: Hmm. I can well imagine the ensuing complications.

WILDE: It was a terrible problem in my famous libel action against the Marquess of Queensberry, father of young "Bosie" Douglas. When Bosie's father left a calling card at my club with the insulting words "Oscar Wilde, posing as a sodomite," I thought surely it would be quite simple to defeat such a horrid brute in court. Queensberry had threatened me repeatedly and was treating his son despicably. But as I soon discovered, law courts are not like drawing rooms. One cannot speak to entertain or to delight, but only to defend oneself. Wit and reason did not suffice to reduce Queensberry's malignant hostility toward me; nor did I convince the judge, the jury, or the public of my innocence.

BATESON: You should never have allowed yourself to get involved in a trial, Oscar. Why didn't you just tear up Queensberry's silly card and forget about the whole thing?

WILDE: It was impossible to do that, Gregory. My desire to go down to posterity by participating in a famous lawsuit was an adolescent fantasy, stimulated by a wish to emulate my father [Hyde, 1975, p. 10]. He was a very famous man, you know.

BATESON: How's that? So was my father. I didn't realize we have that in common: a tendency to question our worthiness in reference to our forebears. My father was a famous zoologist, a Cambridge professor, who hoped that at least one of his three sons would follow in his footsteps. I'm afraid I disappointed him in that.

WILDE: My father was Sir William Wilde, a famous surgeon, and an amateur anthropologist. (Perhaps that is one reason why I am so drawn to you.) But what he expected from his children never seemed very clear. Sir William immersed himself so deeply in scholarship and writing that there was little time left for his family. In addition, he sired a number of illegitimate children, one of whom, Henry Wilson, studied medicine and helped him in his practice. Thus, some of us legitimate ones appeared to be rather superfluous.

BATESON: I never felt close to my father. He often seemed distant and intimidating. I hated him at times, and came to resent authority in general.

WILDE: "Fathers should neither be seen nor heard. That is the only proper basis for family life."

BATESON: Surely this quip from your play *An Ideal Husband* reveals something about your own experience as a father.

WILDE: There were many similarities and certain differences between me and my father. He adored women, and loved them promiscuously. I also adored women, but I loved men more passionately. And he, like me, was ruined by a trial in a court of law.

BATESON: How did that happen?

WILDE: Foolishly my father became intimate with one of his patients, a woman named Mary Travers. The affair deteriorated after she began writing lurid newspaper articles about it and then pestering my mother unmercifully with accusatory letters. My mother finally retaliated with a harsh letter of her own. Mary Travers showed this letter to her father, himself a medical doctor, who advised a libel suit. It destroyed Sir William Wilde financially and damaged his reputation irreparably. Hence, in my adolescent idealism, I vowed to gain notoriety and hopefully revenge by also doing legal battle one day with Queen Victoria.

BATESON: If I'm not mistaken, you did follow your father's footsteps in a certain way, Oscar.

WILDE: It was necessary for my self-esteem, Gregory. You see, I resembled my mother, both physically and mentally. She was called Speranza. Mother had been a feminist and Irish liberationist who towered over my father and was given to a highly melodramatic style of behavior. She wrote copiously and well. Much of my literary talent must have stemmed from her influence. My mother yearned to have a daughter, and I, her second son, was surely a disappointment, which she tried to disguise with her engulfing possessiveness. Also, she dressed me as a girl and pretended I could fulfill all of her wishes.

BATESON: We seem to have the makings of a transvestite here!

WILDE: Much worse, Gregory. When I was 3 years old my mother became pregnant again, and this time she had a girl, which made me superfluous, a person of no importance.

BATESON: How tragic! Yet this theme of the unwanted, abandoned, or lost child is one that you dramatized repeatedly in your great society plays, for example, *A Woman Of No Importance*. Was this not a way of telling the world that you wanted love and craved recognition?

WILDE: Precisely. But you must remember that all of these plays – my most successful literary works – were written under the spell of Bosie, that enchanting and androgynous aristocrat whom I pampered and who allowed me to assume of the role of an adoring, all-giving mother, while he behaved like a neglected child.

BATESON: Hmm, a double bind reminiscent of the temporary stabilities I've often observed in social relationships between unstable partners. But what actually happened when you were 4 years old and found yourself displaced in your mother's love by a sister?

WILDE: My mind went briefly to pieces, or, as you schizophrenia experts would put it, underwent a split. Part of me sided with my mother and adored the child, my sister, who was named Isola. Another part of me hated Isola and wished to see her dead. This ambivalence toward females also contaminated my relationship with my wife, Constance.

BATESON: "The man who killed the thing he loved, / And so he had to die" – how eloquently you wrote of this in *The Ballad of Reading Gaol*, the last great work you created.

WILDE: Ah, but I had begun coupling love with death at a much earlier stage of my literary career. You see, a fantasy that Isola must die came tragically true in my adolescence. My sister lived only 9½ years, and her death when I was just entering puberty sealed my fate. It plunged my mother into a perpetual state of mourning, while I, now doubly bereft of a sister and a mother, was left in a brooding state of melancholy.

BATESON: What a muddle. How did you deal with it, Oscar?

WILDE: First of all by adopting a character style that became my trademark. I would pretend to be happy, and try to make other people happy through my wit and verbal talent. Second, I turned inward and drew out of myself the prose and poetry that has made me immortal. While mourning for my sister, for example, I wrote "Requiescat."

> Tread lightly, she is near
>   Under the snow,
> Speak gently, she can hear
>   The daisies grow.
>
> All her bright golden hair
>   Tarnished with rust,
> She that was young and fair
>   Fallen to dust.
>
> Lily-like, white as snow,
>   She hardly knew
> She was a woman, so
>   Sweetly she grew.
>
> Coffin-board, heavy stone,
>   Lie on her breast,
> I vex my heart alone,
>   She is at rest.
>
> Peace, Peace, she cannot hear
>   Lyre or sonnet,
> All my life's buried here,
>   Heap earth upon it.

BATESON: Such a magnificent expression of sorrow, and an excellent example of the principle, known to artists for centuries but only recently articulated by behavioral scientists, that the loss of someone very close to you may stimulate poetry, music, or other symbolic expressions [Pollock, 1978]. Let me tell you a little of my own personal history. I had two older brothers. Both died. John Bateson was killed on a French battlefield in World War I. Martin Bateson shot himself in the middle of London beneath the statue of Eros on Piccadilly Circus. For my family these tragedies were unbelievable, and much of my own anguish, as well as my restless desire to invent new ideas, stems from this double sibling loss [Lipset, 1980].

WILDE: I had no idea that behind that peaceful facade of yours lay such deep experience with violence. Why did your brother Martin commit suicide?

BATESON: He aspired to be an actor, but my parents disapproved of that ambition. Also, Martin wanted a young woman to love him who did not have it in her power to do so.

WILDE: How sad. It's a pity that I was not able to speak with your brother. Perhaps I could have lifted him out of his depressive rage and helped steer him toward a new and more positive realm of thinking. I was always regarded highly for the beneficial effects of my conversation, you know. If my style of social interaction were to be analyzed today, it would probably be called "therapeutic."

BATESON: Very likely. I know of one description that suggests you were an excellent group psychotherapist:

> [Wilde] watched his listeners closely, noted the smallest sign of restiveness, and promptly switched to a new theme. He seemed to know by instinct whether people wanted to be amused or impressed, to talk or to listen. If they wanted to talk he brought them into the conversation [so that] by the time he had finished with it they were delighted by their own brilliance or profundity. This unegotistical quality made him the most attractive of companions, for in the midst of his elaborate flights of eloquence he was always ready to stop and hear someone else, paying equal attention to lord and commoner, child and adult, notability and nonentity. Moreover, he never talked of his own affairs except to intimates, never laid down the law, never contradicted, never pretended to

be an authority on anything (except, occasionally, manners), was always pliant and considerate, would join heartily in a laugh against himself, and gave the whole of his genius to supply the pleasure of the moment, whether the company consisted of one or two friends or a large and distinguished party. [Pearson, 1954, p. 207]

WILDE: (tears in his eyes) Oh Gregory! How kind of you to remember those delightful words. As you must know, my reputation among clinicians has not been exactly positive. Even before my downfall, a German psychiatrist in his textbook about degenerates spoke of me as someone who wore "queer costumes" merely so that I would be able to "occupy the attention of the world [and] get talked about" [Nordau, 1895, p. 317]. And more recently the British neurologist Macdonald Critchley described what he thought were my "histrionic style and behavior, flippancy, shallow emotivity and lack of awareness of the gravity of a situation" [1957, p. 201].

BATESON: What do you expect from the spokesman of a science that tries to locate the origin of every human action inside somebody's brain?

WILDE: He accused me of having "wholly inadequate insight," when in fact my conduct always was a carefully studied pose, designed to place me at the center of the universe!

BATESON: You really were an attention getter, Oscar.

WILDE: It takes one to know one, Gregory. You would be noticed by dressing down, wearing baggy pants and rumpled sweaters, and walking around in torn sandals, sometimes without socks – an excellent way to attract attention. I on the other hand dressed up as a dandy.

BATESON: "It is exactly because a man cannot do a thing that he is the proper judge of it."

WILDE: How charming! One of my best epigrams. You and I were unable to conform to social hypocrisy. I never could tolerate the deceptions of Victorian morality; you could not accept the make-believe of dualistic science. Both of us tried to rise above our doubts, and in doing so we became judgmental, and ultimately unpopular among our peers.

BATESON: You, Oscar, defied the status quo almost too aggressively. Did your Irish heritage have anything to do with that?

WILDE: I suppose so. Ireland is a crazy place, you know.

BATESON: Now what do you mean by that?

WILDE: I mean that my native land has an unusually high incidence of psychosis, at least twice that of England or the United States [Torrey et al., 1984], which is frightening. And being brought up, as I was, by eccentric parents made me fear madness even more. Fortunately I was shielded from the abrasiveness of other children by having private tutors until I was 9. But after that I went to a public school in Dublin where my intellectual aggressiveness quickly pushed me ahead of my peers.

BATESON: Were you a lonely child, Oscar?

WILDE: Very lonely, Gregory. My sister had been my only playmate, and after her death I turned to my imagination for companionship. I invented characters and situations to play with. Scholarly pursuits, poetry, and art were my other sources of vicarious gratification.

BATESON: And of social approval as well, I would imagine.

WILDE: Indeed. A brilliant student, I was awarded a scholarship to Dublin College at the age of 17. That is where I succumbed to the spell of John Mahaffy, an extraordinary young history professor who turned my head toward antiquity. We admired each other tremendously, and after I'd entered Oxford University, we traveled together to Greece and Italy. John asked me to write a chapter about Greek male homosexuality for his famous textbook (though he tried to deny my influence later on.)

BATESON: Hmm. Oxford must have had a strict double standard in those days.

WILDE: It was possible to talk endlessly about male beauty and the charms of androgynous love, but only in the context of myths, fairy tales, poems, or aesthetic portrayals from ancient history. But actually to be "so," as one called it with raised eyebrows, would invite social ostracism. Some students were provocative. But since I was big and very strong, few of them were able to intimidate me, and in a number of brawls I defended myself quite well. My vulnerability for masculine affection did not remain undetected, however, and under the guise of what was then called the Aesthetic Movement I would champion pagan ideals, to the delight of my friend Sir Ronald Gower, who opened the door to a certain segment of society for me.

BATESON: Gower introduced you to Frank Miles, your first male lover, isn't that so?

WILDE: Not the first, but certainly the most important at that time. Frank was an artist who later went mad. After I left Oxford, we lived together in rooms off the Strand. I adored getting all dressed up, going to the theater, and inviting the most glamorous actresses to come over for parties. Frank would make drawings for the fashion magazines while I wrote poems about them.

BATESON: Haven't you been parodied? Rupert Croft-Cooke said that as a young Londoner you were a "charming and promiscuous, witty, and imaginative queer, whose seemingly predestined fate it was to bring down the whole temple of Victorian propriety on [your] shoulders" [1972, p. 28].

WILDE: I won't deny the queerness, but the idea of predestination rings hollow.

BATESON: As a young man you seem to have adjusted rather successfully to the ambiguities of Victorian culture.

WILDE: Ah, but nothing demonstrates my versatility better than my success in the United States, at the age of 27, when I was invited to give lectures to promote Gilbert and Sullivan's comic opera *Patience*. I created a sensation by appearing in costume, wearing tight pants, a velvet jacket, a flowing green necktie, silk stockings, and rouge on my face. "I have nothing to declare, gentlemen, except my genius" was my studied greeting of the New York customs officials, after which you couldn't keep the crowds away, and I soon became a darling of high society and the press.

BATESON: Oscar, you remind me of "Beatlemania," a more recent form of public hysteria imported from the United Kingdom.

WILDE: I made a fair amount of money in America, which allowed me to spend nearly half a year in Paris. I indulged myself, learned to speak French fluently, and tried to impress the local intelligentsia.

BATESON: Edmond de Goncourt called you "an individual of doubtful sex who talks like a third-rate actor" [Croft-Cooke, 1972, p. 80].

WILDE: That man was such a snob. But André Gide liked me well enough. In Paris I also met Robert Gerard, who developed a life-long fascination in me and wrote books about me. Poor boy, he never did understand the seamy side of my character.

BATESON: Your marriage may have fooled him.

WILDE: A contributing factor, perhaps. Constance and I were truly in love, at least for a while, until the competitiveness in our relationship destroyed it. I wanted to be both husband and wife. I designed her dresses, organized our parties, and arranged the household. Our home in Tite Street was a showplace. James MacNeill Whistler decorated our exquisite rooms. But who was to pay for all this? Going to work regularly bored me. Fortunately Constance had inherited some money, one of the reasons no doubt that my mother urged me to marry her. But her personality left a great deal to be desired.

BATESON: "She was sentimental, pretty, well-meaning and inefficient," observed one of your friends. "She would have been very happy as the wife of an ornamental minor poet, and it is possible that in marrying Wilde she mistook him for such a character" [Hyde, 1975, p. 102].

WILDE: Very well put. My wife definitely had literary aspirations, and that increased the competitiveness in our relationship.

BATESON: How very awkward. I had a similar problem with my first wife. She too was an anthropologist.

WILDE: One should never marry a person who shares one's interests. "The only proper basis for marriage is mutual misunderstanding" [Redman, 1954, p. 97].

BATESON: Oh, but Margaret was a very capable woman, terribly well organized and not like your Constance, who seemingly had "a passion for leaving things alone, broken only by moments of interference badly timed" [Hyde, 1975, p. 102].

WILDE: Worse yet, my wife had no sense of humor!

BATESON: How was she in bed?

WILDE: Rather tepid and terribly Victorian. Women, well-bred ones that is, were too refined for enjoyable sex in those days. They tended to be passive and expected the man to excite them. I did that for a while, but soon lost interest.

BATESON: Is that why your marriage failed?

WILDE: Not exactly. My disappointment with Constance increased after she became a mother. We had a son, Cyril, whom I adored. Next I wanted a girl child – a replacement for my long-lost sister. We had already decided on the name Isola for her. To my horror Constance produced another boy, whom we named Vyvyan.

BATESON: Years later Vyvyan remarked that you lived in "an artificial world . . . in which the only things that really mattered were art and beauty in all their forms" [Holland, 1960].

WILDE: But wouldn't you agree, Gregory, that art and beauty are vastly preferable to the drabness of everyday life?

BATESON: I would agree that the magnificence of your creative output – for example, shimmering fairy tales like "The Happy Prince" – contrasts with the cruelty you later inflicted on your wife and children by indulging so openly in homosexuality.

WILDE: Don't make me feel guilty, Gregory!

BATESON: You forget that I worked within the American mental health establishment for many years, and that my wife, Margaret Mead, was overtly homosexual at times [Bateson, 1984].

WILDE: Which confirms my generally low opinion of America, a thoroughly philistine country. I understand that some Americans are shamelessly using my name in order to market a new beer for the "gay community." How disgusting!

BATESON: But not nearly as degrading as your conduct with gay men.

WILDE: Sir, I resent that remark. In the first place, "gay men" is a highly artificial pseudocategory. All living creatures have a number of potentials for acting with and upon each other for purposes of pleasure, mutual growth, and reproduction.

BATESON: I would add communication.

WILDE: Precisely, and we humans exhibit the greatest variability in our behavior, which can be restricted or made to flourish according to the dictates of society. To consider affectionate intimacy between members of the same sex a basis for classification – a sort of typology of human conduct – seems illogical.

BATESON: Quite illogical, I would have to agree.

WILDE: Which brings me to my second point. The way I behaved with men was never dirty or degraded. Bosie, my most intimate companion, was quite explicit on this point. We may have enjoyed "familiarities" that resemble the everyday practices of boys in public schools – nowadays it would be called "safe sex" – but of "the sin which takes its name from one of the Cities of the Plain there never was the slightest question" [Douglas, 1940, p. viii.].

BATESON: Hadn't Bosie already embraced the Roman Catholic faith when he made that statement?

WILDE: Yes, he confessed his "solemn word before God" because he hoped "to be saved."

BATESON: I consider that to be utterly hypocritical. Surely both of you had contacts with other men, under conditions where the restraint and purity Bosie claimed were not possible. Several male prostitutes in London swore to that during your trial.

WILDE: Perjurers! Mischief makers! Bosie's father paid these ruffians to testify against me; furthermore, they were threatened with prosecution under the Criminal Act of 1885 if they refused to do so. Who can blame those poor wretches for wanting to protect themselves while making a little profit on the side.

BATESON: You were always very generous toward thieves and criminals, weren't you, Oscar?

WILDE: I see little difference between thievery and the profit motive that generates conventional business. Besides, underworld characters can be utterly charming. Some even helped me to imagine *Lord Arthur Savile's Crime*, the *Picture of Dorian Gray*, and other stories that tantalized the British public.

BATESON: I believe that you were a sort of subjective cultural anthropologist, observing human behavior by participating in it directly and describing your findings with wit and imagination. We have that in common. It is a healthy antithesis to scientific objectivity.

WILDE: Yes, Gregory, but you have always posed as a scientist, someone who is held accountable for data, hypotheses, and conclusions. By contrast, I posed as an artist, one who may invent truths as well as falsehoods.

BATESON: A dangerous profession, if I may say so.

WILDE: But no less risky than science, and equally important for our survival as civilized human beings.

Epilogue

A famous psychotherapist, in moments of calm but unhappy contemplation, would occasionally remark that "we're just big messes trying to help bigger messes, and the only reason we can do it is that we've been through it before, and have survived" (Rako & Mazer, 1980, p. 16). The dialogue we've just witnessed is a case in point. In it one detects certain features of a psychotherapy interview: the positive mutual interest, the probing for delicate information, the supportiveness, the analytic approach, the free association, the fluctuating emotional tension, the catharsis, the open-endedness.

Bateson began by complimenting Wilde on the favorable qualities of his voice. He did not focus attention, however, on Wilde's keen intelligence and superior reasoning ability, the ingredients necessary for directing a voice, by means of language, to convey meanings and thus make symbolic communication possible. Wilde surely was a master of persuasion; he used his voice most effectively to entertain, to cajole, to seduce, and, as was mentioned, to heal. Even when his message was hostile or nonconformist, he could successfully employ double meanings and humor to make Victorian society listen and if possible even to enjoy and accept his barbs. Bateson, unlike Wilde, did not achieve notoriety. Having to be scientific and philosophical, he would adopt an intellectual tone, using his voice to question, to instruct, and to enlighten. Bateson had wit and brilliance to burn, but he played down the exhibitionistic elements, often muting his sarcasm in favor of the studious probing for knowledge.

One would have liked to *see* them in dialogue, to observe the kinesic dimensions that animate a vocal interaction. Both men were tall and somewhat clumsy. Wilde would stuff his anomalous girth into vivid plaids, gaudy jackets, loose shirts, and striking neckwear. Bateson also defied sartorial tradition, but more in the manner of an understatement, wearing casual, rumpled clothes that sometimes resembled hand-me-downs. Wilde's face was fleshy, his hands gigantic, and his posture somewhat imperious. Bateson, by contrast, had a softer look and an elegant slouch, a subdued manner ever mobile with doubts and contradictions.

During their dialogue, Wilde reacted with impatience and even some annoyance whenever Bateson tried to be objective, as if wanting to study his subject scientifically, like a specimen to be measured and analyzed. Deliberate scrutiny tended to offend Wilde's sense of privacy, and objectivity could be a threat to his narcissism, which craved constant adulation. His approach to life was that of an aesthete who prefers the taste of immediate experience and believes that the only way to know a thing is to relish it. Truth, for Wilde, lay in immediate gratification of the senses. As for the rest – well, it was better to tell lies (Wilde, 1889).

In attempting to interview Oscar Wilde, Bateson very quickly evoked a fatherly transference from this conflicted man. Almost immediately, Wilde started complaining about the despicable behavior of the Marquess of Queensberry, who had tried, vengefully and finally with considerable success, to put a stop to Wilde's relationship with Queensberry's son, Lord Alfred Douglas. Unable to maintain therapeutic neutrality in the face of such a tantalizing story, Bateson responded with some criticism of Wilde's behavior, and even tried giving him advice. He went so far as to talk about his own father, a further transgression of therapeutic neutrality, and one that took the spotlight away from Wilde.

However, as the insatiable Wilde burst forth with memories of his childhood, the distilled oedipal wisdom of Sophocles, Shakespeare, and Freud seemed to flow into his dialogue with Bateson. Now attention was given to Sir William Wilde, a famous Irish surgeon, anthropologist, and womanizer, whose trial and public disgrace had brought silent anguish to his wife. (She was not entirely blameless, having sent a tactless letter to the father of her husband's mistress, thus triggering the libel suit that ultimately ruined the entire family. A revealing book has been written about Oscar Wilde's extraordinary parents [White, 1967]; they must have been a difficult act for him and his siblings to follow.) Oscar spoke with particular compassion about his beloved sister, Isola, whose death when he was a young adolescent had instilled deep mourning and also stimulated his poetic imagination. Wilde always liked to display the picture of a nubile girl in his room, and until the day he died he carried with him an envelope containing strands of her hair, an example of what Volkan called a "linking object" to the dead (Volkan, 1983). Wilde's most imaginative artistic representation of simultaneous attraction and repulsion for an immature, erotic, aggressive, and destructive girl was his Biblical play *Salome*, written in French and translated into English by Lord Alfred Douglas.

Not quite as dramatic a family situation, but certainly a very complicated and compromising one gave birth to Gregory Bateson's genius. His professorial father provided a model for the patterning of ambitions among his children, while their loving mother did her best to regulate their affections. But disappointment in the expected orderly conduct of human affairs drove Gregory, the third and only surviving son, into an attitude of considerable disenchantment with the status quo. The first World War, with its impersonal slaughter of young men and the particularly senseless destruction of Gregory's gifted oldest brother, had plunged all survivors of this outstanding family into depressive grief. Soon they were engulfed in another, and a more personal, horror: the flamboyant public suicide of Gregory's second brother. But as in the case of Oscar Wilde, early sibling loss and recovery from mourning seems to have activated, perhaps even vitalized, his considerable talent. Bateson's originality and audacity continues to amaze us, as does his willingness to think, to produce new ideas, to look above and beyond immediate reality for ingenious solutions to human problems. And, like Wilde, he was somewhat alienated from the social mainstream by his dissatisfactions and nonconformity.

Greater historical perspective – Wilde died nearly a century ago – allows a more objective view of his difficulties than of Bateson's. Wilde's eroticism did not seem to fit comfortably with his moral attitudes, and his physical attraction to other men, especially, led to anxiety, which he tried to reduce in different ways. Alcohol was always helpful, but the drinking would too often lead to social embarrassment and occasional brawling. In his youth, Wilde had sought to become a Catholic, which might have increased his self-control; his father strongly disapproved and threatened to disinherit him. (Only on his deathbed, in Paris, did Wilde confess his "sins" and join the church.) His literary talents and creative ability had made it possible for him from an early age to externalize and thus neutralize some of the preoccupations churning within, for example the obsession with love resulting in death (Grinstein, 1980).

During a trip to Greece with Prof. John Mahaffy, and while helping him with his book about the social life of the ancient Greeks (Mahaffy, 1875), Wilde discovered how to deal with the topic of male homosexuality more intellectually, as a form of sublimation. But, despite his brilliant academic record, he could not long employ this defense against the anxiety generated by inner conflicts over physical intimacy. Wilde was too undisciplined to pursue a university career, and the gay friendships he made at Oxford and in London's theatrical circles proved to be too seductive for him to lead a conventional life. In addition, his widowed mother held him in what Bateson would surely have called a double bind. Speranza always talked about matrimony for Oscar, and she even selected possible partners, including the woman he finally did marry. At the same time, she regularly used the brilliant and witty Oscar as a stellar attraction for guests attending her famous London salons, which inevitably attracted numerous gay artists, writers, and actors.

Only after he began his love–hate affair with Lord Alfred Douglas, did Wilde, so far as we know, avail himself of the rough and criminal elements in London's underworld. That style of covert socialization was symptomatic of the hypocrisy that characterized so many sexual attitudes during the Victorian period, and it can still be observed when the fear of stigmatization, ostracism, and punishment drives sexual minorities "into the closet" (Marmor, 1980). In addition, illicit thrill-seeking probably aggravated what today would most likely be called Oscar

Wilde's narcissistic character structure, wherein his anxious and depressed core personality was disguised and became distorted by an inflated, grandiose facade (Kernberg, 1975). Incongruities between these two aspects of the self produced inner tension and also led to observable eccentricities in Wilde's behavior. He managed to negotiate these difficulties fairly successfully so long as the social environment provided support for his grandiosity and applauded his exhibitionism. But when these reinforcements were withdrawn and the law against homosexuality was invoked to humiliate and punish Wilde, he became deeply depressed, and his psychological defenses began to crumble.

Psychiatry has been attempting for some time to elucidate the connections between biological factors responsible for the sort of mood disorder that affected Oscar Wilde (as well as other members of his family), and the social experiences that give rise to narcissistic character deformations. A useful method of research is psychobiography, in which the life of an individual can be explored in great detail, beginning with the family and cultural background and ending with the autopsy findings (Ostwald, 1985). There is a serious limitation in this method, however, since psychological hypotheses cannot be refuted or validated when the central character of the study is dead. On the other hand, the direct, clinical study of living patients can result only in brief, fragmentary glimpses into personality structure and psychopathology because of the limited time spent together and the effects of the observer on the subject.

Gregory Bateson's belief, that "action, if it be planned at all, must always be planned upon an aesthetic base,"(Bateson, 1972) ought to be a guiding principle for psychobiographical research, especially when the subject is someone like Oscar Wilde. The investigator then would be obliged to explore the organizing principles of poetry, dance, music, drama, painting, or other higher-order patterning of behavior, along with the activities of individuals who dare to impose their will on an aesthetic pattern. With his uncanny appreciation for the interplay between biology, beauty, and brains, Bateson had hoped to be able to apply his ideas about third-order learning to the understanding of those mental functions that result in organization (creativity) as well as in disorganization (psychosis).

By agreeing with Wilde, at the end of this heavenly discourse, that art can be as dangerous a profession as science, Bateson seems to have acknowledged his fundamental respect for those men and women of superior intellect who habitually strive for the truth, only to discover that the closer they come to their goal the further it recedes. We can be grateful that both of these great men had the capacity to maintain their sanity, as well as their sense of humor, while they were grappling with so painful a paradox.

References

Bateson, G. (1972). *Steps to an ecology of mind: Collected essays in anthropology, psychiatry, evolution, and epistemology.* San Francisco: Chandler Publishing Company, 1972.
Bateson, M. C. (1984). *With a daughter's eye: A memoir of Margaret Mead and Gregory Bateson.* New York: Morrow.
Bayer, R. (1980). *Homosexuality and American psychiatry: The politics of diagnosis.* New York: Basic Books.
Brémont, A. (1911). *Oscar Wilde and his mother.* London: Everett & Co.
Critchley, M. (1957). Oscar Wilde, a medical appreciation. *Medical History, 1,* 199–210.
Croft-Cooke, R. (1972). *The unrecorded life of Oscar Wilde.* London: W. H. Allen.
Douglas, Lord A. (1940). *Oscar Wilde: A summing-up.* London: The Richards Press.
Grinstein, A. (1980). Oscar Wilde. *American Image, 37,* 125–179.
Holland, V. (1960). *Oscar Wilde and his world.* New York: Charles Scribner's.
Hyde, H. M. (Ed.). (1956). *The three trials of Oscar Wilde.* London: Hodge.
Hyde, H. M. (1975). *Oscar Wilde.* New York: Farrar, Straus and Giroux.
Insanity Defense Work Group. (1983). American Psychiatric Association Statement on the Insanity Defense. *American Journal of Psychiatry, 140,* 681–688.
Kavka, J. (1975). Oscar Wilde's narcissism. *The Annual of Psychoanalysis, 3,* 397–408.
Kernberg, O. F. (1975). *Borderline conditions and pathological narcissism.* New York: Jason Aronson.
Lipset, D. (1980). *Gregory Bateson: The legacy of a scientist.* Englewood Cliffs, NJ: Prentice-Hall.
Mahaffy, J. P. (1875). *Social life in Greece from Homer to Menander.* London: Macmillan.
Marmor, J. (Ed.). (1980). *Homosexual behavior.* New York: Basic Books.
Nordau, M. (1985). *Degeneration.* New York: D. Appelton & Co.
Ostwald, P. (1985). *Schumann: The inner voices of a musical genius.* Boston: Northeastern University Press.
Pearson, H. (1954). *The life of Oscar Wilde.* London: Methuen & Co.
Pollock, G. H. (1978). On siblings, childhood sibling loss, and creativity. *The Annual of Psychoanalysis, 6,* 443–481.
Rako, S., & Mazer, H. (1980). *Semrad, the heart of a therapist.* New York: Jason Aronson.
Redman, A. (1954). *The epigrams of Oscar Wilde.* New York: John Day Company.
Torrey, E. F., McGuire, M., O'Hare, A., Walsh, D., & Spellman, M. P. (1984). Endemic psychosis in western Ireland. *American Journal of Psychiatry, 141,* 966–970.
Volkan, V. (1983). *Linking objects and linking phenomena.* New York: International Universities Press.
White, T. D. (1967). *The parents of Oscar Wilde: Sir William and Lady Wilde.* London: Hodder and Stoughton.
Wilde, O. (1889, January). The decay of lying. *The Nineteenth Century.*

12. Mind and body: a dialogue

GREGORY BATESON AND ROBERT W. RIEBER

RIEBER: What is the so-called mind–body problem?

BATESON: Alright, for example, I have end organs in my fingers. And "I touch the tabletop." The question that we are up against is: What are we going to do with that pronoun "I." Do we need it? A dog may touch the tabletop with his nose. Does he have a pronoun? I would suspect that this split between "I" and the rest is rather late in evolutionary development. You don't have to start with a split between mind and body. The split between mind and body is something which occidental culture and perhaps other cultures have invented and played with and built up language around. And so on.

RIEBER: Then why did we develop the different words "body" and "mind" if the split is, as you implied, artificial, unnecessary?

BATESON: I think it is even counterproductive. It may also be productive, but it is very heavily counterproductive.

RIEBER: Then why did the two words emerge (in occidental culture) in the first place?

BATESON: Well, they were going fairly well by the time of the ancient Greeks.

RIEBER: I think there was certainly a distinction. In language, I am not sure about the words, because I don't know the original Greek language that well.

BATESON: Well, they had pronouns no doubt. But what they meant when they talked and used the pronouns, I wouldn't really know. The "body" for example? Yes, but what many peoples use for the

This chapter first appeared in Robert W. Rieber (ed.), *Body and Mind: Past, Present, and Future* (New York: Academic Press, 1980). It is reprinted here, with minor changes, by permission of the publisher.

self or the other person are not pronouns. They usually use names of relationships, outside themselves.

RIEBER: Perhaps the real breaking point was at the beginning of the seventeenth century. This probably comes out of some kind of a commitment to Baconian principles.

BATESON: Yes, and it comes out of Descartes, of course, too. I think that Descartes both invented the Cartesian graph and went screwy on the mind–body split or the mind–matter split. Those two inventions seem to be very closely related. It's the split of coordinates.

RIEBER: Well, why did he split mind from body? Wasn't it an arbitrary, capricious sort of thing? Or was he trying to achieve something? I suppose he was trying to shake somebody up.

BATESON: He was trying to shake somebody up, no doubt. And he was trying to do things unambiguously. And what he succeeds in saying, you see, is that the variables are to be handled separately.

RIEBER: Which variables? Or what were the variables?

BATESON: Oh, whatever. When you make a graph of temperature or of the rate of falling of a body, or whatever it is, you have time as a horizontal coordinate and whatever variable you want as a vertical. The temperature "rises," as we say, and "falls." It doesn't rise but that's the word for it.

RIEBER: Whenever you have matter on the one hand, you must then have its opposite.

BATESON: Yes, when you have matter, you have its opposite!

RIEBER: Apparently, whatever was opposite to matter was mind to Descartes.

BATESON: Yes.

RIEBER: And it was necessary to have something opposite to matter to account for something like one's intention.

BATESON: The question is, is body alive? You see, the split comes out of saying matter is not alive. And the moment you say organized matter is not alive then to handle purpose, humor, etc., you've got to invent a ghost of some kind.

RIEBER: The brain is matter, and the brain is alive.

BATESON: But the matter is not alive.

RIEBER: By alive, you mean what?

BATESON: Let's say you have a string, and you've got one end and I've got the other, and I give you a pull and you wake up or jump or whatever. Is the string alive?

RIEBER: No. it's not.

BATESON: But, does the string carry a message?

RIEBER: Perhaps!

BATESON: And similarly, neurons are a little bit more alive than a string in the sense that they carry messages. But the string is sort of a passageway to carry the messages but doesn't create the energy to transmit it. It depends on my pulling the string. The neuron responds from the energy of its breakfast.

RIEBER: So it's what these neurological mechanisms do that gives the organism's intention.

BATESON: But, you see, the subject of the verb was the neurons. To talk about the interface between the neuron and what the neuron does would be very awkward, wouldn't it?

RIEBER: Yes.

BATESON: That's the interface that I objected to at the beginning of our dialogue, when I objected to saying, "I touch the table."

RIEBER: There's a distinction between what one means by body and what one means by mind that I would like to refer to, namely, the difference between such a distinction made about something in the past versus something in the present.

BATESON: Yes, but the thing doesn't change much from paramecium to human.

RIEBER: But, as you said before, it is rather late; that is, the distinction between mind and body is rather late in its appearance from an evolutionary point of view. It's late because humans are late in the development on the phylogenetic scale.

BATESON: It's late because natural language is late in its development.

RIEBER: Is that dependent upon the development of consciousness in humans?

BATESON: I don't know. Maybe I use the word "consciousness" differently from the way you do. For example, if I look at that artifact on the wall, I *consciously* see a dance shield. I am totally *unconscious* of the process by which I see that dance shield. I see only the product of that process.

RIEBER: But you're conscious of yourself seeing that dance shield.

BATESON: I'm conscious of the *product* of seeing that dance shield.

RIEBER: But you're conscious of your being separate from the dance shield, and you are also conscious of yourself perceiving the dance shield in your own way.

BATESON: I don't know. Somehow, you see, I've got to make something in me. I have got to make an image of that thing. Right? Of that process, I'm totally unconscious.

RIEBER: You're probably better off if you're not conscious of it.

BATESON: Right. I wouldn't believe the shield was there if I were conscious of the process of making it. If you think about it, you discover there is a process between you and the shield that's making the thing – the image – that enables you to perceive the object. Three dimensions, color, etc., etc. This is a psychological product. That is to say, you really don't see the shield per se.

RIEBER: So, you don't see that shield. What do you see?

BATESON: What you see is your image of the shield.

RIEBER: In other words, the thing is not the same as your perception of the thing. Just like the word you use is not the thing that it stands for.

BATESON: That helps account for the fact that we don't all see it in the same way.

RIEBER: So, how does this tie in with the mind–body problem? The matter is what you're perceiving on the wall. Perception of the shield is the matter, then?

BATESON: The shield is matter by virtue of my perception of it.

RIEBER: You then seem to be extrapolating something from matter. It's giving life to matter.

BATESON: You can say that, but I'm not sure that you mean the same thing that I would mean by that.

RIEBER: What I mean is that you conceptualize it, therefore you give life to it.

BATESON: This is my hand, right? It is part of me? And I learned a lot from it.

RIEBER: Yes.

BATESON: How do I know it's a part of me? Did I teach it anything?

RIEBER: No, because it is a part of you. But that's animism, isn't it?

BATESON: Ah ha. [Laughs.]

Now let's take a look at a much different way of approaching this. What is the personality of the Balinese character in the middle of this illustration (Figure 12.1)? He is animated in every joint. Now, this gentleman, he lost his head (Figure 12.2). But his body is still animated.

RIEBER: In Figure 12.1, every joint has a head, right. What does that mean?

Figure 12.1. Illustration no. 4, p. 94, in the *Balinese Character* by Gregory Bateson and Margaret Mead (New York: New York Academy of Sciences, 1942).

Figure 12.2. Illustration no. 3, p. 94, in the *Balinese Character* by Gregory Bateson and Margaret Mead (New York: New York Academy of Sciences, 1942).

BATESON: It implies that each part is separately alive.

RIEBER: That's certainly animism, isn't it? But what does it tell us about the mind–body problem?

BATESON: It tells us that the Balinese don't have to think the way the occidentals think about bodies and minds. We're illustrating this with the Balinese, because we want to open up all of the ways of approaching this subject.

RIEBER: In other words, the dualism is unnecessary. You don't have to talk about bodies and minds at all in this context. Let's suppose that there were a few scholars who were really interested in discovering the truth about human existence and tackled the question of mind and matter mainly for that purpose. They felt, perhaps, that if they conceptualized a piece of matter like the body that they experience and a piece of something like antimatter called the mind that they could proceed to investigate them by elementalizing them and isolating their properties.

BATESON: But, now look, seriously, for instance, if you take a page of newsprint, the words are not there, you know.

RIEBER: What do you mean not there?

BATESON: On the page.

RIEBER: You mean you put the words there. Is that it?

BATESON: Yes. When I read, I, *in imagination*, put the words there. And so you see I wouldn't like to talk about the split between that ink and the word on the page, right?

RIEBER: I suppose we will have to, won't we? The distinction of body–mind implies there is something that has a space–time dimension relationship.

BATESON: Is there a relationship between the imagined word-on-the-page and the ink?

RIEBER: I suppose there was at one time, but I'm not sure there is one now.

BATESON: Where is the space between them, and where is the time?

RIEBER: Doesn't everything have to have some spatial and temporal dimension in the real world?

BATESON: I don't think so. Most things don't.

RIEBER: What does not have spatial and temporal factors associated with it?

BATESON: The difference between that shield and the wall.

RIEBER: That's a high level of abstraction, isn't it? I'm not referring to abstractions, I'm referring to real things. I can't perceive the word "difference."

BATESON: You can't perceive anything but difference.

RIEBER: But difference is just a word, isn't it? I never bumped into a difference on the street, have you?

BATESON: Difference is a mental event. The only thing that can get into your retina is information about a difference. The lowest level of mental operation is the perception of a difference.

RIEBER: When I said that I couldn't understand how anything in the real world would not have some kind of temporal or spatial aspects to it, you disagreed, right? So, you claim that difference is something that has no temporal or spatial aspect to it, and I said difference is only an abstract idea and you agreed. So, it seems then that what we have been talking about is a state between ideas and ways of describing human thought processes or cognition.

BATESON: Right. But you cannot have an interface between matter, on the one hand, and mind, on the other.

RIEBER: Well, I suppose so, but it depends on your definitions.

BATESON: Well, when you pull them apart, that's already a step toward a definition. Having pulled them apart and given them a totally different nature, mind being an abstraction and matter being an abstraction, but arranged in such a way that they can't meet each other. And then when you attempt to understand how they are interfaced with each other, you are up against a blank wall.

RIEBER: So the split between body and mind is a fruitless affair, because you're trying to pull something apart which is already an integrated whole in order to see how it comes back together again. It's like Humpty-Dumpty not being able to be put back together again.

BATESON: Yes, it's like trying to take the print away from the words on the page.

RIEBER: Maybe that's the message intended in Humpty-Dumpty – at least one of the messages.

BATESON: Yes, perhaps it is one of the things that is meant in Humpty-Dumpty. Essentially, Humpty-Dumpty is negative entropy. He is a gestalt pattern, and if you randomize him all the king's horses and all the king's men couldn't put him back together again.

RIEBER: Ergo, you can't split body and mind. Now, if we take it one step further and ask the following question: What gives us the power to know that we exist as an entity separate from anything else?

BATESON: I know that me touching a book is different from me touching your knee. Is that what you mean by "separate entity"?

RIEBER: Partially. But it goes further than that. For instance, suppose you wake up in the morning, and you feel that it's good to be alive and you're happy that you exist, and you feel your separate existence in a way that completely isolates you from anything else. On the other hand, you may wake up at another time and say that you're not happy to be alive, you do not value your life and do not wish to carry it on, and you wish you could self-destruct. Obviously, these two conditions are dependent upon the way you experience yourself both qualitatively and quantitatively at a given point in time and in a particular circumstance. In other words, what has given us the ability to experience this human condition? It seems to me that the human species is the only one that has the ability to experience this. And if that's true, how did this ability come about?

BATESON: I don't know. But I've given you the first step: the difference between the I that touched the book on the table and the I that touched your knee. Is that not the first step that one has to make toward what you want?

RIEBER: Yes, I suppose it is. Let me reword this by asking what it is about the development of the human organism that enables us to have this rather unique capacity.

BATESON: Obviously, it comes from the ability to distinguish the difference between the book and the knee.

RIEBER: Yes, but how does that capacity grow to the proportion that I described earlier?

BATESON: Are time and space useful abstractions when talking about mind? No.

RIEBER: Then what is a useful abstraction when you're talking about mind?

BATESON: Difference.

RIEBER: What do you mean by "difference"?

BATESON: Difference means an appeal to irritability. I can feel that edge of the table. This is an appeal to irritability. And short of that appeal to irritability, I do not receive information.

RIEBER: Difference has to make a difference, is that the idea?

BATESON: Yes. You can receive news only of those differences which can be made into events in time.

RIEBER: Then the temporal dimension is important when you talk about the mind–body problem because it helps you understand the term "difference."

BATESON: That's true.

RIEBER: But I'll go one step further and say that you also need the term "space" as well, because when you perceive the difference it all takes place in space.

BATESON: But difference is not in space and time.

RIEBER: Where is it then, all in your mind?

BATESON: Precisely. It is all in your mind. It is a mental operation, the perception of the difference. The behaviorists believe that the mind is flat, because they do not believe that perceptual categories are in the mind of organisms.

RIEBER: In other words, they reduce mind to a flat abstraction which they call behavior.

BATESON: It does not belong to the individual. It's not the individual's.

RIEBER: I'm not sure that all behaviorists would agree with that. Nevertheless, you might say that that position does lead them away from the whole individual, or any gestalt for that matter.

BATESON: Precisely. It leads them away from any whole, because the whole is a sum of its parts. In other words, in behaviorism, you don't have two arms, you have an arm and an arm. To have two arms you have to have a *class*.

RIEBER: What then is meant by the "problem" when one refers to the mind–body problem?

BATESON: We have invented or borrowed from Descartes an idea about a separation between something which is of one nature, mind, and something of another nature, body. From there on, I cannot make any sense of anything. But perhaps we were wrong to begin with – there ain't no thing called "mind" or a thing called "body." It's an idea that they made up. Why they made it up I have no idea.

RIEBER: There's an organism.

BATESON: There's an organism. Right!

RIEBER: The organism has a thing called mind and body.

BATESON: No. Well, if you call it mind and body, yes.

RIEBER: But the organism has to have different levels of existence. Does it not?

BATESON: Yes. The "difference" is different from "state."

RIEBER: And these levels of existence somehow got translated into terms like "body" and "mind."

BATESON: I think actually, the step from mind to body is the step from state to difference.

RIEBER: From state to difference?

BATESON: Yes.

RIEBER: "State" means a condition which is dead.

BATESON: But life can exist only in terms of difference. As long as you have difference, that is, the possibility of moving your states, by rubbing them on differences, then you have "mind." You see, it's like a frog in a saucepan of cold water. If its temperature is raised so slowly that at no moment is there a sufficient doc/dt to activate his neurons, he does not jump. There is no time marker to tell him *when* to jump. He gets boiled. He just wasn't that much alive. I hate to tell you what this reflects upon our society.

RIEBER: How does this problem relate to contemporary psychosocial distress?

BATESON: The problem is we think we can maintain a state which we call deterrence by increasing the pace at which we make atom bombs. It's very strange and has something directly to do with the mind–body fallacy. They think about the body and mind in terms of one controlling the other. Thus, the phrase "mind over matter."

"Mind over matter" or "matter over mind"; whichever you say controls the other, the one that you say is not in control will take over.

RIEBER: Then in reality, neither is in control.

BATESON: Precisely, the word "control" is a fake anyway. It's one of those abstractions that are not represented by anything in the real world.

RIEBER: Now, perhaps we're approaching the heart of the matter. The more you look at it, the more it looks like it's all a hoax.

BATESON: A tour de force that didn't quite make it. And then whenever a materialistic phrasing doesn't quite make it, they invent a spiritualistic phrasing that's supposed to make it. And then you get a split between the mind and the body.

RIEBER: Today, on the other hand, we have the epiphenomenalistic position that sees the mind as a by-product of the brain.

BATESON: Yes, there are several "epiphenomenal" approaches around. The first one is spiritualism. Uri Geller is a good example of this. And the other is the one you referred to, namely, the mind being a "by-product" of the brain. They're both off base in different ways. You see, the brain is only an idea of the mind. One is as good a statement as the other. And the mind is only a function of the brain.

RIEBER: They appear to be perfect examples of either end of the hoax that we were talking about a moment ago. And that traps you and forces you to choose between the devil and the deep blue sea.

BATESON: Yes. It's just like asking, is your allergy mental or physical?

RIEBER: How, then, should the question be phrased so that it is actually answerable?

BATESON: But it isn't the question that's the problem. By making it a question, you make the division of mind and body. If you want to ask the question about the relationship between word and print, that's an interesting question that we're talking about. But once you split mind and body, you can't talk about anything sensibly.

RIEBER: OK then, let's not split mind and body and carry on from there and ask the question of how we study the unity of mind and body, that is, body within mind. Is the scientific method sufficient?

BATESON: Well, the scientific method as devised to study "bits of matter" is not a very good method for studying mental processes. Because you don't have any mental process until matter reaches certain degrees of organization, at which point you get mental processes. The characteristics of that organization, we can now lay down. Now, first, it is not one chunk. That is, to have that organization, you've got to have multiple parts. The parts themselves are not capable of that organization. That is, you may have a brain that's made of protein, but the carbon atoms in the protein don't think. Second, thinking is a matter of first derivatives of some sort. If you want to talk the language of material matter, you have to jump to derivatives – to dx/dt. In other words, the process depends upon the differences. This is the essence of what Gustav Fechner was talking about with his "just noticeable difference." That is to say, what perception depends upon is essentially difference – contrast or ratio – not state. And it took a hundred years from Fechner to the 1940s to discover the Fechner law on the efferent side of the central nervous system. This was the discovery of Norbert Weiner, namely, that the tension of an isometric muscle is a function of the log of frequency of the stimuli reaching it. This is the same as Fechner's law and still depends upon the difference. This is the second criterion of the aggregate of matter that can show mental process. The third criterion is that in order for the organism to respond to difference, it must have energy stored up ahead of the presentation of the difference. There is no energy in the difference. In other words, there is only negative entropy in the difference. Therefore, you've got to have energy on your side of the counter if you're going to do anything about the difference. For example, if you kick a dog, the dog responds with *his* energy, not with energy from your kick. It goes right through the whole psychology and makes energy an irrelevant consideration. Because the cause does not energize the effect, the cause being a "stimulus." Many stimuli don't exist. For example, a letter which you do *not* get can trigger your responses.

A fourth criterion is that mental process occurs when the trains of causation are circular or more complex. In other words, the lineal system can't make a steady state.

And finally, there are the conceptual levels of abstraction. For example, the name is different from the thing it stands for. And there can be a difference between two differences. And you can combine differences into systems of differences and so on and so forth. The moment you've got all those criteria, you've got mental process.

RIEBER: Is that what you call body and mind relating?

BATESON: Yes, that's the solution to what used to be called the mind–body problem. Mind is no more separate from body than velocity is separate from matter. Or than acceleration is separate from velocity.

RIEBER: Now that we have come this far, what do you think the goal of scientific inquiry should be? Are we making science in our own image?

BATESON: Yes, except that our own image is so inaccurate, that's the problem. You see, I'm a Platonist; you know, in the final analysis I think we should make science in our own image. And our own image should be in the image of science.

RIEBER: But you better get the image right.

BATESON: Ah, that's the trick isn't it? You see, you can always wreck anything. If you have a stomach ache, I can tell you, "It's only mental." And if you fall in love, I can tell you, "It's only physical." Either way, it would really do you no good.

RIEBER: And there are some who think that the whole business is just a delusionary system.

BATESON: Well, I believe it is much healthier on the whole to believe that the physical universe is an illusion and that the mind is real, than to believe that the mind is an illusion and the physical universe is real. But of course, on the whole neither is correct. But believing that the mind is real is one step better than believing that the physical universe is real.

RIEBER: When human beings engage in what we might call the meeting of minds, it seems that the major means of experiencing the phenomenon of differences is via language or communication.

BATESON: Yes, human beings talk.

RIEBER: Yes, they sure do; but they rarely really communicate, do they?

BATESON: I don't know; there was always a problem with two muddleheaded little old ladies. One was a good bridge player, and she managed to teach the other one to be a good bridge player. But no one knew how it happened, because they were both muddleheaded little old ladies.

RIEBER: Maybe the explanation lies in the possibility that one of the muddleheaded little old ladies had the same delusionary system as the other, and that enabled them to communicate and become good bridge players.

BATESON: Precisely, they shared delusionary systems and understood each other very well, but to everybody else, they looked like muddleheaded little old ladies.

BATESON: In order to illustrate a related point here, I conducted the following experiment with my students. I asked them to describe a drawing (Figure 12.3). Here's the object; what's your description of it?

RIEBER: Looks to me like Bateson's foot.

BATESON: That's one species of description, yes. Some called it a "boot." Any other description?

RIEBER: It seems to have no heel and a flat top over the toes and a point at the very end.

BATESON: About 10 percent go at it that way and describe it as a boot and then, if pushed, will point out the differences of peculiarity of the boot. The toe is bigger than the heel, etc., etc. But then, there are people who say, look, it's a hexagon and a rectangle, but there is sort of a gap and they're not quite complete. But in reality, there isn't any hexagon or rectangle; in fact, there isn't any boot there either.

RIEBER: It's just a bunch of lies, then, I guess. And if it's a boot, it is a boot only because I made it a boot.

BATESON: Yes, because you made it so. But then, there are other people, very ingenious people, who see that there is a line implicitly drawn; that imaginary line completes the hexagon, and that gives them all sorts of internal relations. That enables them to tell the various sizes of the two things, and so forth. These people are the real scientists. This is a demonstration in Maya, the world of illusion in Hinduism. In the final analysis, you make parts in order to make language, in order to understand things so that you can tell what they're like. But while you're making those parts, you should also be knowing that you're making them and that they are not actually real.

RIEBER: In what sense do you mean that they are not actually real?

BATESON: They're not like that object, they're on a higher level of abstraction that can't be experienced.

RIEBER: What's the purpose of studying differences, as you call it, anyway? What's the ultimate goal?

BATESON: Why study things? Well, partly because they're elegant and partly if you get things wrong it's very dangerous. Study it so

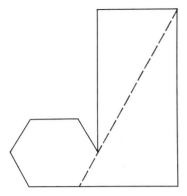

Figure 12.3.

that you can know it and therefore not go at it in the wrong way. Why do it? Well, I guess because it's bloody dangerous if you don't.

RIEBER: Fine – that's a good note to end on.

Author Index

Subject Index

adaptive value, 6
  adaptation, 11, 122
  consciousness, 25
aggression, 55, 57, 78, 80, 215, 228
alcoholics, 10
anti-intellectualism, 44, 45
anxiety, 200–2, 264, 272, 293
apes, 76, 77
associationism, 91, 105, 110, 121
attention and arousal, 226
autism, 8, 92, 147, 148, 150, 151, 152,
    156, 164, 168

behaviorism, 33, 34, 36, 327
blood pressure, 254, 262, 263, 267, 268,
    269, 270, 271, 273
body–mind relationship, 247
brain
  abnormalities, 52, 147, 164, 165
  central nervous system fault, 151
  as hormonal runway, 95–100
  mapping, 93, 95, 105

cerebral palsy, 147
child abuse, 68, 86
child language
  rehearsal of, 131
  delay and deviance, 147, 148, 149, 150,
    152
  protocols of deviance, 159–61
cholesterol, 248, 262, 263
communication
  aphasic, 282
  intersubjective, 107
  and kinesics, 280–98
  listener–speaker interaction, 107
  mother–child dyad, 105–20
  movement integrated with verbal mes-
    sage, 296
  nonverbal, 26, 102, 104, 107, 108
  object and body focused movement in,
    297
  production of language, 101

rhythmic movement in, 9, 17, 18, 19
rhythmic structure of, 102
competition, 71
consciousness, 118
  group, 74
continuum along poles, 15
  of dualistic traits, 39
  mutually dependent poles, 15
coronary prone behavior
  objective measure of, 27, 252
criminal justice system, 84, 303
crowding, 77
culture
  American, 85
  cultural heroes, 69, 70
  differences between members,
    238
  occidental vs. oriental, 324
  variations, 39
  world, 83, 88
cybernetics, 215, 228

decision making, 139–42
dependence, 207, 221, 223, 224
depression, 54, 284, 286, 291
differential association, 63
dissociative behavior, 55, 63, 65, 68
  in children, 68
  and dissociation from politics, 45
  in Nazi doctors, 75
  processes, 17, 18, 67
  and use of accomplice, 69
domination, 219, 220, 224, 225
double bind, 7, 8, 9, 107, 110, 113, 116,
    304, 306, 317
dualism, 40, 324

echolalia, 154
emotions, 253, 254
environmental interaction, 5, 16, 19, 94
  infants and, 103–5
  neurotransmitters and, 106
  patterns, 5, 7

341